MW01038957

DAVE LITFIN'S
EXPERT
HANDICAPPING

Winning Insights into Betting Thoroughbreds

•

REVISED EDITION

•

by Dave Litfin

DRF Press
NEW YORK

Published by
Daily Racing Form Press
100 Broadway, 7th Floor
New York, NY 10005

ISBN: 978-1-932910-84-1
Library of Congress Control Number: 2007930621

Cover and jacket designed by Chris Donofry
Text design by Neuwirth and Associates

Printed in the United States of America

All entries, results, charts and related information provided by

EQUIBASE
C O M P A N Y

821 Corporate Drive • Lexington, KY 40503-2794 Toll Free (800) 333-2211 or
(859) 224-2860; Fax (859) 224-2811 • Internet: www.equibase.com

The Thoroughbred Industry's Official Database for Racing Information

Contents

For Robin, the best winner I ever picked.
And for Walter and Audrae, who gave her to me.

Acknowledgments

"No book on handicapping can be written in isolation, nor can it represent solely its author's original thoughts on the subject."
—from *Handicapping by Example,*
by William L. Quirin, Ph.D.

IN THE SPIRIT OF the above, my sincere thanks to Bill Quirin, and the slew of authors whose works provided guidance and nourishment: Tom Ainslie, Andrew Beyer, Tom Brohamer, Charles Carroll, Joe Colville, Mark Cramer, Steven Crist, Steve Davidowitz, Steve Fierro, Dick Francis, Huey Mahl, Barry Meadow, Dick Mitchell, William Murray, James Quinn, Dr. Howard Sartin, and William L. Scott, to name a few.

Len Ragozin and Len Friedman of The Sheets, and Jerry Brown of Thoro-Graph, deserve a standing ovation for bringing form-cycle analysis to the mainstream. The game's most innovative minds are happy to share their insights with anyone interested enough to seek them out.

Thanks as well to Duane Burke of *Daily Racing Form*'s Information Technology department, who provided data on post-time favorites; Lee Tomlinson, who provided detailed background about his pedigree ratings; and Eric Wing of the National Thoroughbred Racing Association, who supplied payoff histories for the NTRA pick three and pick four.

Finally, thanks to Steven Crist and Dean Keppler of DRF Press for publishing this revised edition; and thanks to Robin Foster for patiently and expertly editing the manuscript, not to mention listening to Elliott Smith's No Name #6 countless times. It feels good to be a small part of the DRF Press collection—I'm in some pretty select company.

Introduction

"**An expert is a person who has made all the mistakes that can be made in a very narrow field.**"

—Niels Bohr

Then (1995):

There never was a better place and time to be 12 years old than New York City in 1970. Besides rooting for the Mets, Jets, and Knicks, I was feverishly testing my brand-new Kel-co Class Calculator on the races at Aqueduct. To my delight, the magical slide rule showed a profit for a month's worth of results.

The world would soon be mine.

On Saturdays I took the "A" train to the races (in those days a seventh-grader could ride the subway alone). Once in a while I forgot about seventh grade altogether and headed for the track on a weekday, hoping to parlay my lunch money into a new baseball glove or a coveted back issue of *Superman*. Once in a while I even got lucky and made a score. I'll never forget boxing Ferly and Lucie Honey in an exacta (shortly after exactas had come into existence) and listening to my pocket transistor radio in Spanish class as Harvey Pack came on with his *Pack at the Track* report:

"The winner, OTB letter G, Ferly. Thirty-nine dollars, sixteen-eighty, and nine-twenty. Second . . ."

I held my breath: *Please be J, please be J, please be . . .*

" . . . J, Lucie Honey. Six-forty, four-twenty. The G-J exacta returns two hundred sixty-three dollars and eighty cents."

YES! ONE TIME! YES!

I don't remember much from Spanish 101, but that payoff remains a vivid memory to this day. Not $263.20 . . . not $263.40 . . . but $263.80. I can still visualize the way that glorious G-J exacta looked in black Magic Marker on the result board of the 72nd Street OTB, as I bounded in to collect what seemed like all the money in the world.

Inevitably, I gave back that $263.80 . . . and then some. A pattern developed where I'd arrive at the track with a thick roll of $1 bills and leave with barely enough for a pretzel and a subway token home. My Kel-co Class Calculator had hit the skids, and a frightening realization had slapped me in the face:

Life wasn't going to be so simple after all.

. . . and Now (2007):

Looking back to when *Dave Litfin's Expert Handicapping* was first published in 1995, I probably should have voiced my reservations about the title, but I was too thrilled and delighted it was being published to bite the hand that fed me.

Expert sounds kind of presumptuous, doesn't it? Other than cutting school regularly, and performing basic calculations with horses' fractional times in *The Morning Telegraph,* and later in *Daily Racing Form,* how exactly did one go about the business of becoming an expert horseplayer?

Truth be told, by the end of the 1970s, at the ripe old age of 21, I was already well on my way to becoming an expert—at least compared to most of the other horseplayers in that cigar-smoke-filled OTB between Broadway and West End Avenue. After spending my formative years utterly enthralled by the likes of Secretariat, Ruffian, Affirmed and Alydar, Forego, and Spectacular Bid, I knew just enough to be dangerous. When Christmas rolled around and I needed fast cash, a session or two of intensive handicapping usually produced the desired results; back in the day, logical winners paid astounding prices.

Unlike my older but unwiser competition, who were set in their misguided ways, I had no bad habits to unlearn; and it was my supreme good fortune to come of age just as the handicapping information revolution dawned. I had a working knowledge of all 77 selected systems in *Ainslie's Complete Guide to Thoroughbred Racing*, the book that ushered in a new era of erudite handicapping literature by Andrew Beyer, Steve Davidowitz, James Quinn, and William L. Quirin, and the others that followed.

"The skills of the expert handicapper are, in fact, closely comparable to those of the good bridge, poker or chess player," wrote Ainslie in his landmark tome that started it all. "In any such competition, the player who depends on instinct, trial-and-error, inexpert advice, superstition or reckless guesses is at a disadvantage. He cannot hope to hold his own against persons who have acquired an understanding of the game as a whole."

After Ainslie, I read Beyer's *Picking Winners* backward, forward, and upside down until I was proficient at making speed figures; I memorized Quirin's impact values from *Winning at the Races* and learned to be prejudiced in favor of horses with early speed on dirt; I knew the offspring of sires like Stage Door Johnny and Little Current were virtual automatic bets when they switched to turf; I kept files of winning past performances arranged by trainer, as Davidowitz had advised in *Betting Thoroughbreds,* so I knew sharp Allen Jerkens-trained sprinters stretching out were money in the bank, and I had the skinny on dozens of other trainers in growing stacks of marble composition notebooks.

As Ainslie had instructed, I was acquiring an understanding of the game as a whole.

Slowly but surely, others with a similar passion were doing the same thing. Horseplayers can read, contrary to popular belief, and John Q. Punter was steadily sharpening his skills. Once the Beyer Speed Figures were published, first in *The Racing Times* and then in *Daily Racing Form* in the early 1990s, a lot of bad horseplayers became average horseplayers, and a lot of average horseplayers became break-even or winning players.

"Suddenly you couldn't get overlays on figure horses. You had to find other ways to win—you had to make a betting line or bet Pick Threes," said Bob the Brain in Ted McClelland's wonderful novel *Horseplayers* (Chicago Review Press, 2005).

The crowd—what was left of it—had become quite sophisticated by the time *Expert Handicapping* was originally published in 1995. But it's positively amazing to think how much things have changed since then. This book was first written on a word processor with no Internet capability, and printed on a dot-matrix printer that was only slightly faster than a monk transcribing the pages by hand. Funny, but it seemed like space-age technology at the time, and I couldn't fathom why I would ever need one of those newfangled computers my daughters were begging me to get.

Twelve years later, I can't imagine life without one. Computers have radically changed the way many handicappers approach the game. I still remember countless nights waiting for the delivery truck to drop off the bundle of *Form*s at the newsstand on 79th Street and Broadway; sometimes the truck was delayed, for whatever reason, and the *Form*s didn't show up until 10 o'clock—the night before the races. Nowadays, I just point, click, and print out the past performances (48 or 96 hours in advance), from the comfort of my den, usually in my bathrobe.

Those downloaded past performances have undergone an extreme makeover since Steven Crist spearheaded a deal to buy the *Form* in 1998. One of the key aspects of this revised edition of *Expert Handicapping* is a review and outline of the changes and additions that have occurred, both in print and on-line.

Along with their past performances, Thoroughbreds have also evolved (some would say devolved) to a significant extent. The way they are handled, especially stakes horses, has changed quite dramatically since this book's initial run. A sign of the times: Shortly before these words were written, the opening-day card at Belmont's spring meet, May 2, 2007, featured no fewer than four winners making their first start of the year, including Godolphin Stable's Utopia, off a 14-month absence in the Grade 3 Westchester Handicap.

No horse personifies the current state of the Thoroughbred more than Badge of Silver:

Badge of Silver			
Own: Ramsey Kenneth L. and Sarah K			

(Past performance chart — Badge of Silver, Dk. b or b. h. 6 (Mar). Sire: Silver Deputy (Deputy Minister) $30,000. Dam: Silveroo (Silver Hawk). Br: Liberation FM, Oratis TBS, Trackside FM (Ky). Tr: Frankel Robert J (0 0 0 0 .00) 2006:(585 139 .24). Life 16 7 4 1 $1,047,882 113 D.Fst 13 6 3 0 $690,892 113.)

In five seasons of racing, the immensely talented but creakingly brittle Badge of Silver made the grand total of 16 starts—just over three per year—while forced to miss numerous stakes engagements due to a variety of injuries and infirmities that would fill veterinary textbooks. By my unofficial count, those included surgery to have screws inserted into a hairline cannon-bone fracture; surgery to remove a keratoma (a fancy word for *wart*) on a foot; multiple foot abscesses; and a myectomy for a displaced soft palate. In between medical emergencies, however, Badge of Silver was fast and tough as nails on the racetrack—so much so that owner Ken Ramsey transferred him to Bobby Frankel as a 4-year-old in hopes of winning a Grade 1 stakes in New York. Ramsey said at the time, "I've been talking to a lot of breeders, and this horse is worth a lot of money if he can win a Grade 1."

Alas, Badge of Silver missed the 2004 running of the Grade 1 Carter Handicap due to an abscess in a front foot; and he missed the same race a year later due to an abscess in a hind foot. Frankel somehow managed to patch up the bionic horse in time to make the 2006 Breeders' Cup Mile off a 10-month layoff, and he ran well enough to finish third, beaten for second in a photo. Three weeks later, he ran back to his very best figures in the Cigar Mile, but had the misfortune to hook Discreet Cat's sizzling mile in 1:32.46, and settled for second.

Badge of Silver never got that elusive Grade 1 win, but still went to Airdrie Stud for the 2007 breeding season, where he stood for a $15,000 stud fee. As easy as it is to admire Badge of Silver as a racehorse, one can only wince to think of the maladies his progeny may inherit and in turn pass on to their offspring: The image comes to mind of a shopping cart with three good wheels and one that just spins around.

"He's got to make a great stallion, as courageous a horse as he is," was Frankel's hopeful take on the subject.

We'll delve into lightly raced horses more deeply in this revision, because dealing with them has become an integral part of the game.

Along with the Thoroughbred's increased fragility and growing dependence on medication, legal and otherwise, there has been a lot of negativity in general racing news in the new millennium, particularly as it pertains to New York's well-documented trials and tribulations. As this was written in May 2007, the New York Racing Association was a lame duck existing in desultory austerity, and there was no end in sight to the political wrangling that will eventually shape the circuit's future course.

But for all the gloom and doom and forecasts of racing's imminent demise, business is still pretty darned good. Evidently, despite all the slings and arrows of outrageous fortune, a lot of people still feel Thoroughbred racing is the greatest game played outdoors.

Count me among them. As this was written, Curlin had just come again with a relentless surge to nail Street Sense through a pulsating stretch run in the Preakness Stakes. This running of the Triple Crown's second jewel marked the anniversary of my first bet: $10 to place on No Le Hace in the 1972 running. Thirty-five years later, here I sit in the press box, mass-producing winners for a living, about 30 percent of the time, and making most of the mistakes that can be made in this very narrow field the other 70 percent. I have outlasted my beloved 72nd Street OTB, which recently fell to the wrecking ball in the name of urban development.

I like to think there's at least some level of expertise in what I do. Of course, we all know there is no absolute "right" way to play the races, but in this updated *Expert Handicapping*, I have attempted to spell out how I go about playing the races today, because it is vastly different from how I went about things even a few years ago. Barry Meadow put it best in his column, "The Skeptical Handicapper," in the May 2007 edition of *American Turf Monthly* headlined: "Who's An Expert? And Who Cares?"

He wrote: "A recent book, *Expert Political Judgment: How Good Is It? How Can We Know?* reported the results of a 20-year study involving more than 82,000 predictions made by 284 economists, political scientists, think-tankers and others who made their living commenting on trends or offering advice and judgment on various problems. The summary: Experts offered no special predictive insight about anything."

I knew I should've said something about the title.

*

CHAPTER 1

Condition Analysis and Speed Figures

You've got the wrong equation
Your figures fail so you make more up
All smiles and celebration
If only you could just change your luck
This time we can't lose
This time we can't lose

—Elliott Smith, "No Name #6"

WHEN I WENT TO Aqueduct or Belmont Park during my formative years, I would often skip over a few of the four basic food
groups at lunchtime in order to save a couple of extra bucks for
the daily double. Meanwhile, handicappers armed with a good set
of speed figures were dining on champagne and caviar. In those
days, speed figures weren't common knowledge, as they are now,
and class was the factor that most bettors paid attention to.
Claiming prices and purse values were widely regarded as the
proper tools for gauging horses' intrinsic abilities, but speed handicappers operated from a much different and more scientific per-
spective, and evaluated horses' moves up and down the class
hierarchy much more precisely. By developing "par times" for each
class—the normal final running times usually associated with
each type of horse—a handful of speed handicappers could meas-

ure the speed and resiliency of the racetrack on a given day, and make adjustments to the raw final times based on how much faster or slower than normal the times for the day were.

Speed handicapping seems elementary nowadays, but back then very few bettors had heard of this approach. For the enlightened few speed handicappers who were around, cashing in on high-priced winners was like shooting fish in a barrel; they knew, based on their adjusted final-time figures, exactly at what level of competition virtually any horse could be expected to perform well. Often, it had little or nothing to do with a horse's supposed "class." It was a tremendous edge, the likes of which will never be seen at a racetrack again.

When Andrew Beyer's *Picking Winners* brought speed handicapping into the mainstream in 1975, figures became "the Way, the Truth and the Light" for thousands upon thousands of players. But in *Beyer on Speed,* published in 1993, Beyer wrote: "The increasing sophistication of the American bettors was making the use of figures less and less profitable."

Such is the nature of parimutuel wagering. Top-figure horses that went off at 4–1 in the good old days now routinely go off at half that price, or less, thanks to the popularity of speed figures. Accepting short odds on these propositions no longer constitutes a wagering advantage. Even when a horse runs a clearly superior figure to today's rivals, there is no guarantee he will reproduce an effort of the same quality; horses run the same figures back-to-back only about one-third of the time.

Thankfully, two edges are available:

1. Most bettors are lazy, and have gotten into the habit of using speed figures as a crutch to avoid a thoughtful analysis of form cycles. A Thoroughbred's current form is constantly in a state of improvement or decline. These days it is not enough merely to have an idea of how fast a horse

ran in its most recent races; we must have some means of projecting whether today's performance will be better or worse than the ones that preceded it. The two most important questions are (a) how fast is the horse, and (b) what is he likely to do today?

2. There are figure patterns that portend short-term and long-term improvement and decline in form. Handicappers familiar with these patterns are in a position to bet on overlays (horses going off at odds greater than their true chances of winning) and steer clear of underlays (horses offered at odds less than their actual winning chances).

Long before *Picking Winners* went to print, Len Ragozin was making a living at the track with speed figures refined from a basic approach devised by his father, Harry Ragozin, back in the late 1940s. Today, Len Ragozin's figures—The Sheets—exert some influence on the tote board, and some stables use them, as well as rival Thoro-Graph, as a basis for buying and selling horses. Ragozin recalls how it all got started:

"This didn't start out as a business. It was just figures for me and my father to bet and claim horses. Len Friedman, who is my partner now, came to me and said, 'I have confidence in what you're doing, but when it comes to betting, you don't have time to do it right. How about this? You stay home and do the figures, and I'll go out to the track and bet.'

"So here's this guy with extra-wide size-13 feet who can't get shoes that fit, so he's out there in sneakers that have holes in them looking like a bum, and he's up at the hundred-dollar window with these funny-looking cards. So naturally people said, 'What are those? Can we get in on this?' That's how I got clients."

When Jerry Brown, a Ragozin associate, struck out on his own in 1982 to launch the competing figure service Thoro-Graph, even more people were armed with stacks of five-by-eight-inch sheets detailing the career speed-figure histories of every horse in every race.

Sheet-style figures differ from Beyer Speed Figures in a number of ways:

- A horse's sheet contains its entire history, beginning with figures earned as a 2-year-old (if any), which are placed in the left-most of four vertical columns. Figures for 3-year-olds are in the column just left of center. The figures for 4-year-olds are just right of center; 5-year-old figures are in the right-most column. Each column begins with January at the bottom and ends with December at the top. A horse's most recent race, therefore, is always at the top of the column farthest to the right.

- Sheet-style figures include adjustments for ground loss on turns. Horses that run wide are credited for having run farther.

- Sheet-style figures also include adjustments for wind (velocity and direction), and for the amount of weight carried—the theory being that these are things that can be accurately measured.

- The Sheets and Thoro-Graph employ their own clockers, who time races from the starting gate so as to include the run-up to the timing pole—the point where official timing of a race begins. Run-up distances vary, usually depending on the proximity of a turn to the start of the race.

- On sheets, the lower the number, the faster the race. Theoretically, a champion runs a 0 (zero) on its best day, though negative numbers are becoming more common.

Ghostzapper's Horse of the Year campaign in 2004 consisted of four races, for which he recorded figures ranging from -1 to -3 that ranked him as one of the fastest horses ever; his Beyer Speed Figure of 128 in the 2004 Iselin Handicap is the highest since the figures have been published in *The Racing Times* and *Daily Racing Form*. More typically, Grade 1 races nowadays are run in the neighborhood of -1 to 1; Grade 2 races go anywhere from 2 to 5; Grade 3 races go from 4 to 7; good allowance runners and high-priced claimers generally run in the range of 7 to 11. Maiden claimers in New York run in the mid to upper 20s. Turf figures for the corresponding class levels tend to run several points slower.

Plus and minus signs to the right of a figure on The Sheets indicate a quarter of a point slower or faster, respectively. A figure of 8+ is read as 8¼; a figure of 8- is read as 7¾. A quotation mark following the number indicates half a point: 8" is read as 8½. Thoro-Graph uses superscript figures to indicate quarter and half points: 8 with a superscript 1 is read as 8¼; 8 with a superscript 2 is read as 8½; 8 with a superscript 3 is read as 8¾.

The figures are arranged graphically, with the faster figures shifted to the left and the slower ones to the right. This makes patterns easier to spot, as Ragozin explains:

"If you're trying to analyze how horses come into and out of form, you will get to a point where you say, 'Hey, I've seen that kind of pattern before.' Even though you may have seen it before in a very high-class horse, and you're now looking at a very low-class horse, so that the numbers are entirely different, the way a healthy horse runs in and out on The Sheets is the same. The combination of accurate ratings and graphical presentation not only makes it possible to make meaningful judgments, they make it a lot of fun."

Even if you never use sheet-style figures, the form-cycle principles brought to light by Ragozin, Friedman, and Brown are universal.

"With a little practice, you'll be able to identify form cycles," notes Jerry Brown in Thoro-Graph's on-line tutorial. "Some run consistent patterns, varying from a simple good race/bad race pattern, bad race after an exceptionally good effort (the 'bounce'), or more complex 'circling' patterns where a horse gradually loses its form then slowly comes around toward its original level."

The Beyer figures are based on the more traditional "higher number is better" scale. The highest Beyer figures will be in the 120s, and these rarified figures are recorded by horses with championship potential. A figure of 110–115 wins most Grade 1 stakes races for older males. A figure of 100 wins lesser-quality stakes and allowance races on the major circuits. A figure of 90 wins an average $25,000 claiming race. A figure of 80 wins an average $10,000 claimer. Bottom-level $2,500 claimers at minor tracks can win with figures in the range of 55 to 60.

Explosive Horses

Three-year-olds that have recently run a figure equal to or slightly superior to their best 2-year-old figures are strong candidates to improve in the near future, especially if the slight forward move occurred soon after a return from a layoff.

If we think of Thoroughbreds in human terms, a 2-year-old is equivalent to a teenager, still growing and learning how to go about things; as the horse matures and grows stronger, it is logical to expect better performances as part of its normal, healthy course of development. By the same token, maturing horses that are unable to run as fast as they did in the earliest stages of their careers are exhibiting a negative sign of development.

Once a 3-year-old runs the key figure—a figure equal to or slightly better than its best performance as a 2-year-old—it may feel the effects of that exertion and require a short period of time to recover before making the forward move. This period of time is approximately five weeks, but this is only a general average and stated merely as a guideline. Some horses will throw in an "off" race if entered back quickly and then make the move in the second start following the key figure; others may return two or three weeks after the key figure and improve again right away.

The central point is this: Once a 3-year-old equals or slightly exceeds its best 2-year-old figure, handicappers can expect it to improve again sometime in the near future. Often, these horses are entered in races in which others have already run higher figures, and they go off at generous odds.

Lightly raced 4-year-olds that have recently equaled or slightly surpassed their top 3-year-old figures can be similarly evaluated, particularly if they were unraced or had only one or two starts at 2. In either case, once the breakthrough figure is delivered, handicappers should be prejudiced in favor of these horses in their upcoming starts.

The first time this really sank into my consciousness was at Saratoga in August of 1992. The sixth race on August 19 appeared inscrutable, but Bob Beinish, who was leading instructional seminars for The Sheets at the time, offered this opinion: "Everything is in place for Lochrima to run the best race of his life today," he said.

This was a bold statement, considering that every other experienced horse in the field had already run a Beyer figure as good, or better, than Lochrima's best race:

6 FURLONGS. (1.08) MAIDEN SPECIAL WEIGHT. Purse $24,000. 3-year-olds and upward foaled in New York state and approved by the New York state–bred registry. Weight: 3-year-olds 117 lbs. Older 122 lbs.

Super Sibling Ch. g. 6, by Fratello Ed—Superb Holme, by Superbity Lifetime 52 0 5 6 $57,450 1992 7 M 0 2 $4,770

SANTIAGO A (8 0 1 0 .00) Br.—Dehuke Dominick J (NY) 1991 26 M 3 2 $20,820

Own.—Roe Loraine M Tr.—Roe Lorraine M (1 0 0 0 .00) 122 Turf 3 0 0 0 Wet 6 0 2 1 $8,820

27Jly92- 7Pha fst 6f :222 :461 1:124 3+Md Sp Wt 50 9 10 63¾ 33½ 32½ 34½ Dentici A Lb 122 36.80 72-17 True Justice1223 Rudy'sBoy1151½SuperSibling122 Wide 10

26Jun92- 6Pha fst 7f :221 :452 1:244 3+Md Sp Wt 58 4 8 76¾ 66 55½ 56 Dentici A Lb 122 39.00 77-20 BlstOflc114nkTruJustic1221½MjorMcGrth122 No threat 11

15Jun92- 6Pha fst 6f :222 :462 1:121 3+Md Sp Wt 39 5 6 87¾ 99 710 712¾ Dentici A b 122 25.40 67-19 CmpltThPss1148MjrMcGrth122nkPrsdntsHp114 Outrun 9

5Apr92- 2Aqu fst 6f :232 :48 1:133 3+Md 30000 47 4 11 119½ 99 57½ 49 Martinez R R5 b 115 24.90 64-25 Clrwy1135¾SntPhilp1112VctorosBnnr111 Brk slow, wide 11

20Jan92- 2Aqu fst 170 ⊡:492 1:152 1:472 Md 30000 54 5 1 11 2hd 22 65½ Dentici A b 118 13.20 62-32 Sir Ciao118½ Dr.Bartolo1221½SpaDancer118 Speed, tired 8

13Jan92- 3Aqu fst 6f ⊡:23 :471 1:131 Md 30000 48 2 9 811 89½ 78 49¾ Dentici A b 118 22.10 67-27 Kuetch1224SeaportTown122½SpaDncer118 Broke slowly 9

4Jan92- 2Aqu sly 6f ⊡:234 :482 1:133 Md 30000 49 9 3 51¾ 53¼ 55 38¼ Dentici A b 118 20.10 67-24 AftertheDeluge1224¼SpDncer1184SuperSibling118 Wide 9

20Dec91- 9Aqu fst 6f ⊡:23 :472 1:13 3+ⓈMd Sp Wt 45 9 7 95¾105½ 811 810¾ Dentici A b 122 19.90 67-21 Convert1201½ Idasjack1201½ After theDeluge120 Outrun 12

15Dec91- 1Aqu fst 6f ⊡:23 :47 1:131 3+Md 30000 42 2 5 42 34 46½ 49½ Dentici A b 118 6.00 68-19 GunnryOfficr1166VlidMn116½AdmthK.116 Saved ground 7

28Nov91- 5Aqu fst 6f :223 :462 1:13 3+ⓈMd Sp Wt 48 1 6 65¼ 47 36½ 35 Dentici A b 122 10.60 71-19 Frln'sFr1133¼Al'sIcCstl1221½SprSblng122 Brk slw, wide 6

Gallant Pip Dk. b. or br. c. 3(May), by Star Gallant—Pipparee, by Rock Talk Lifetime 0 0 0 0 1991 0 M 0 0

DAVIS R G (70 9 10 7 .13) Br.—Irving Paparo (N.Y.)

Own.—Irving Papano Tr.—Schettino Dominick (2 0 0 1 .00) 117

LATEST WORKOUTS Aug 11 Sar 5f fst 1:003 H Aug 5 Sar 4f gd :50 Bg Jly 26 Sar 4f fst :483 H Jly 20 Bel 3f fst :354 Bg

Winlocs Getzaround B. c. 3(Jun), by Cormorant—Midwest Lake, by Dawn Flight Lifetime 0 0 0 0 1991 0 M 0 0

PEZUA J M (49 3 3 2 .06) Br.—Raymond A. Roncari (N.Y.)

Own.—Scrips R Farm Tr.—Miceli Michael (5 0 0 0 .00) 117

LATEST WORKOUTS Aug 13 Bel tr.t 4f fst :513 B Aug 7 Bel 5f fst 1:042 Bg Jly 26 Bel 5f fst 1:04 B Jly 15 Bel 3f fst :37 B

Look's Like Bob Ch. g. 3(Apr), by Hello Gorgeous—Tax Exempt, by Val de l'Orne Lifetime 10 0 2 2 $17,770 1992 10 M 2 2 $17,770

DAY P (82 11 15 12 .13) Br.—CBF Corporation (NY) 1991 0 M 0 0

Own.—Bartow Robert C Tr.—Dunham Bob G (3 0 0 1 .00) 117 Turf 1 0 0 0 Wet 3 0 1 0 $5,810

30Jly92- 9Sar fst 6f :222 :46 1:11 3+ⓈMd Sp Wt 47 10 3 77½ 44 36½ 512¼ Nelson D b 116 18.80 77-06 AppreciateIt1169Bordgry116nkConcur116 Flattened out 12

19Jly92- 5Bel fst 1⅛ :47 1:131 1:512 3+ⓈMd Sp Wt 23 4 2 25 3nk 58 728½ Rojas R I b 116 4.30 43-28 NiceShot1168½Concur116noWho'sBelivbl122 Bumped st 9

26Jun92- 9Bel fst 1$\frac{1}{16}$:463 1:12 1:433 3+ⓈMd Sp Wt 56 2 5 43 42 36 39¾ Rojas R I b 114 3.80 74-11 BlzonSong1143½NcShot1146½Look'sLkBb114 No threat 10

7Jun92- 1Bel gd 1⅛ :464 1:112 1:514 3+ⓈMd Sp Wt 65 4 3 32 2hd 2hd 21¾ Rojas R I b 114 5.40 68-22 GrnGitor1141¾Look'sLikBob114nkC.C.Shrp115 Held 2nd 8

29May92- 9Bel fm 1$\frac{1}{16}$ Ⓣ:451 1:10 1:42 3+ⓈMd Sp Wt 38 2 12 75 83 915 924½ Rojas R I b 115 9.40 62-14 Lonnegan1151¾Trilingul1172½SinktheShip115 Wide turn 12

18May92- 4Bel gd 1$\frac{1}{16}$:47 1:114 1:434 3+ⓈMd Sp Wt 64 1 4 32 3nk 2hd 33½ Rojas R I b 115 11.80 79-13 DuelZone12423¾TeddyC.115¾Look'sLikBob115 Bid, wknd 9

9May92- 1Bel my 1 :461 1:11 1:371 3+Md 35000 48 2 3 3nk 42½ 57½ 510¾ Rojas R I b 115 2.90 73-14 BrothrBrkfld115¾Dn'tThwrtM1156Clb120 Dueled inside 6

20Apr92- 9Aqu my 1⅛ :48 1:131 1:54 3+ⓈMd Sp Wt 62 7 1 11 13 2½ 23 Rojas R I b 115 21.50 63-25 Ptrot'sThndr1153Look'sLkBob1152½DlZn124 Held place 11

29Mar92- 9Aqu fst 1 :471 1:132 1:41 3+ⓈMd Sp Wt 49 9 3 31½ 54 99 78¼ Madrid A Jr b 115 14.20 49-33 T.V.Lnding124¾StockinPly115¾Tlcompote115 Used early 11

20Mar92- 6Suf my 6f :221 :464 1:141 Md Sp Wt 25 4 6 78 810 810 99½ Lozano J M Bb 122 11.70 66-20 AngryRection1222JoeyStwrt1221¾UmbrtoRx122 Outrun 11

LATEST WORKOUTS Aug 9 Sar 4f gd :53 B ●Jly 8 Aqu ⊡ 5f fst 1:023 B

Newyork Appeal B. c. 3(Mar), by Proud Appeal—Cool Answer, by Victorian Era Lifetime 1 0 0 0 1992 1 M 0 0

ANTLEY C W (100 21 15 13 .21) Br.—Jet M Farm & McMahon Anne C (NY) 1991 0 M 0 0

Own.—Ran-Dom Stable Tr.—Sciacca Gary (18 3 4 2 .17) 117

72- 9Bel fst 6f :223 :462 1:12 3+ⓈMd Sp Wt 46 1 8 1hd 3½ 53½ 57 Bailey J D 116 *1.80 73-14 Drmnthdyy1221ChppsT1163¼Fbn'sChc122 Dueled inside 12

EST WORKOUTS Aug 7 Sar 4f fst :48 B Jly 13 Bel 3f fst :361 H Jly 8 Bel 5f fst 1:00 H Jly 2 Bel 5f fst 1:003 H

But Lochrima exhibited the quintessential explosive sheet pattern: He had run a 27½ in his second career start, and had slightly bettered that figure by running a 26¾ in his first start as a 3-year-old. Lochrima had regressed slightly to a 28½ when run back on about two weeks' rest in his second start of the year, but it had now been six weeks since the key figure of 26¾, and Beinish was expecting another forward move—and perhaps a more significant one:

Len Ragozin — "The Sheets"™

XX		LOCHRIMA	89
3 RACES 91	10 RACES 92	5 RACES 93	

■35A031 MALE 4YO 31DEC93

AWA014

.32
⓶⑦
35"

v 50AQ22
50A014
v 50AQ 5

W 35AQ23
Y MSAQ 9
Y MSAQ29
35BE19

v 35BE 2

.24"
28"
⟨27-⟩

v8 MSST19
s 35BE25
MSBE 8

Note that the pattern is also present in the Beyer figures of Lochrima's past performances: He ran a 46 second time out as a 2-year-old, and equaled that figure in his return as a 3-year-old.

Beinish's argument convinced me that Lochrima was a legitimate contender at 20–1. I bet him to win, along with a pair of saver exactas keying him underneath 6–5 favorite Newyork Appeal, and a first-time starter, Gallant Pip, who was taking substantial tote action.

The anticipated improvement was indeed forthcoming, as Lochrima improved to a 24½ on The Sheets, and a Beyer of 58. Unfortunately, Lochrima was carried extremely wide after forcing the early pace, came again once he had been straightened out for the stretch run, but wound up third, beaten by about a length. It makes for a great example but a painful memory:

SIXTH RACE
Saratoga
AUGUST 19, 1992

6 FURLONGS. (1.08) MAIDEN SPECIAL WEIGHT. Purse $24,000. 3-year-olds and upward foaled in New York state and approved by the New York state-bred registry. Weight: 3-year-olds 117 lbs. Older 122 lbs.

Value of race $24,000; value to winner $14,400; second $5,280; third $2,880; fourth $1,440. Mutuel pool $280,064. Exacta Pool $486,902.

Last Raced	Horse	M/Eqt.A.Wt	PP	St	¼	½	Str	Fin	Jockey	Odds $1
22Jly92 9Bel5	Newyork Appeal	3 117	7	2	42½	3hd	2½	1hd	Antley C W	1.20
	Gallant Pip	b 3 117	4	6	3½	1½	1½	2¾	Davis R G	3.20
25Jly92 9Bel8	Lochrima	b 3 117	2	1	21	42	41½	33½	Carr D	20.00
27Jly92 7Pha3	Super Sibling	b 6 122	3	7	5hd	51½	52	4½	Santiago A	13.60
	Winlocs Getzaround	b 3 117	5	5	61½	6½	61	5nk	Pezua J M	27.60
30Jly92 9Sar4	Pago's Whim	3 117	1	3	11	2½	3½	65	Smith M E	3.40
30Jly92 9Sar5	Look's Like Bob	b 3 117	6	4	7	7	7	7	Day P	5.30

OFF AT 3:46 Start good for all but SUPER SIBLING, Won driving. Time, :21³, :45², :58², 1:12¹ Track muddy.

$2 Mutuel Prices:

8-(I)-NEWYORK APPEAL	4.40	3.00	2.80
5-(F)-GALLANT PIP		4.20	3.60
3-(D)-LOCHRIMA			5.20

$2 EXACTA 8-5 PAID $17.20

B. c, (Mar), by Proud Appeal—Cool Answer, by Victorian Era. Trainer Sciacca Gary. Bred by Jet M Farm & McMahon Anne C (NY).

NEWYORK APPEAL, well placed for a half, angled between horses rallying into the stretch then finished determinedly to wear down GALLANT PIP in the final strides. GALLANT PIP never far back while saving ground, rallied along the rail to gain the lead at the top of the stretch, continued on the front into deep stretch but couldn't hold the winner safe. LOCHRIMA forced the early pace from outside, was carried six wide at the top of the stretch then finished willingly to gain a share. SUPER SIBLING, failed to seriously threaten after getting off toa slow start. WINLOCS GETZAROUND never reached contention while racing wide throughout. PAGO'S WHIM set the early pace along the inside then drifted wide while tiring on the turn. LOOK'S LIKE BOB was never a factor while racing wide.

Owners— 1, Ran-Dom Stable; 2, Irving Papano; 3, Santangelo George L; 4, Roe Loraine M; 5, Scrips R Farm; 6, New Kan Stables; 7, Bartow Robert C.

Trainers— 1, Sciacca Gary; 2, Schettino Dominick; 3, Pascuma James J Jr; 4, Roe Lorraine M; 5, Miceli Michael; 6, O'Brien Colum; 7, Dunham Bob G.

Scratched—Silver Crash; Mick (19Jly92 5Bel4).

It is noteworthy that Lochrima's improved effort was delivered over a muddy track, even though he had apparently disliked the slop at Aqueduct the previous autumn. This brings up two points: First, no two racetracks have the same consistency when wet; because a horse handles or doesn't handle a particular wet track doesn't necessarily mean it will run the same way over another. There are many horses that have, for example, run well on wet Saratoga tracks throughout their careers while failing to run as well on any other wet surfaces. Second, horses exhibiting an explosive pattern are indicating they are in excellent overall condition and sitting on a big race. Horses that are in good condition are likeliest to perform well, no matter the circumstances; horses that are not in good condition have a strong tendency to use adverse circumstances such as wet tracks as an excuse not to perform to their true capabilities.

A 3-year-old that equals or slightly surpasses its best 2-year-old figure may throw in an "off" race immediately afterward, as did Lochrima, but that is not always the case. If the horse has been given a few weeks off since running the key figure, it may very well deliver another forward move with no intervening race:

Russian Bride — Dk. b. or br. f. 3(Feb), by Saratoga Six—Aurania, by Judger
MIGLIORE R (97 16 12 13 .16) — Br.—Eaton Lee (Ky)
Own.—Kentucky Blue Stable — Tr.—Jolley Leroy (7 1 0 1 .14) — **116**

Lifetime 11 3 2 1 $89,736 — 1993 5 2 1 1 $70,936 — 1992 6 1 1 0 $18,800 — Wet 2 2 0 0 $27,600

29Apr93- 8CD	fst	7f	:22⁴	:46²	1:24¹	ⒻLa Troienne	70	3	10	94	105½	66¾	68½	Santos J A	b	113	5.40e	80-08	TrvrsCty116hdAdddAsst1131½Blld113	Sluggish brushed 10
10Apr93- 8Spt	fst	1 1/16	:47³	1:12³	1:45	ⒻN J Clb Oak	73	3	3	32½	32½	34	38½	Bourque C C	b	115	4.30	82-11	TruAffr12033¼Boots'nJck1224¾RssnBrd115	Bore out turn 7
21Mar93- 8Aqu	gd	1 1/16	⊡:48³	1:13²	1:44	ⒻComely	88	4	4	42½	2½	2½	22	Migliore R	b	113	10.50	83-25	PrivtLight1122RussinBrid1131½TruAffir118	Good effort 6
21Mar93-Grade II																				
17Feb93- 7Aqu	fst	6f	⊡:23	:46³	1:11²	ⒻAlw 27000	70	1	8	52	2hd	11	16¾	Bravo J	b	116	6.80	86-09	RussinBrd1166¾HghBrgr1161ThThTth116	Drifted, drvng 8
14Jan93- 6Aqu	my	6f	⊡:23	:46⁴	1:13¹	ⒻClm 50000	70	2	6	21	22	2hd	12½	Migliore R	b	116	2.90	77-19	RussinBrid1162½PromisdRlc1181½TrckCtyGrl111	Driving 8
14Jan93-Claimed from Kentucky Blue Stables, Jolley Leroy Trainer																				
26Dec92- 2Aqu	fst	6f	⊡:23¹	:47²	1:13²	ⒻClm 35000	62	11	1	31	32	23½	21½	Migliore R	b	116	5.00	74-20	PnmJne1021½RussinBrid1164TnksforLunch116	2nd best 11
18Dec92- 7Aqu	gd	6f	⊡:23¹	:47	1:12	ⒻAlw 27000	46	6	1	2½	33½	69½	615½	Davis R G	b	116	6.10	67-18	NiceCrne1166½Woodmn'sGirl1093½Incinrt116	Weakened 6
19Nov92- 7Aqu	fst	7f	:23	:46³	1:24²	ⒻAlw 27000	47	7	1	52	43	912	919½	Migliore R		116	3.10e	64-16	TouchOfLove1?13½InHrGlory1185Mgroux116	Wide,tired 9
3Oct92- 8Bel	fst	6f	:22²	:45²	1:10⁴	ⒻPrsnl Ensign	74	8	7	77	88	811	59	Krone J A		116	10.70	77-17	MssdthStorm1164½FmlyEntrprz118¾TyWn118	No factor 8
3Jly92- 8Bel	fst	5½f	:22	:45¹	1:04²	ⒻAstoria	58	7	8	53½	54	56½	58	Cruguet J		112	4.70	85-11	DstnctHbt1122½D'Accrdrss1193TryInThSk116	Four wide 8
3Jly92-Grade III																				

LATEST WORKOUTS May 29 Bel 4f fst :51² B — May 22 Bel 6f fst 1:13⁴ H — May 13 Bel T 5f fm 1:03 B (d) — Apr 20 Kee 4f fst :49² B

Russian Bride's Thoro-Graph sheet (see next page) indicated an explosive pattern when she was entered in the Comely Stakes for 3-year-old fillies at Aqueduct on March 21, 1993. She was unable to get back to her debut figure of 16 until her eighth start, when she recorded another 16 in winning a first-level allowance on February 17. Significantly, there had been several gaps in between her races at age 2, but the key figure—the second 16—had been earned during the midst of regular racing, as it was her fifth start in three months. The combination of more regularly spaced racing and the return to her previous top figure suggested that whatever had been holding Russian Bride back during her 2-year-old season was no longer a problem:

RUSSIAN BRIDE			'90 dk b/ f Saratoga Six - Aurania
	2-YEAR-OLD	**3-YEAR-OLD**	**4-YEAR-OLD**
DEC	AQU 18 AQU 22³ gd		
NOV	AQU 25		
OCT			
SEP	BEL 18		
AUG			
JUL	BEL 20²		
JUN	BEL (16my)	BEL −12	
MAY			CD −12yd
APR		CD 19³ SPT 16²	KEE −11²
MAR		AQU 11³ gd	HIA −12²
FEB		AQU (16)	
JAN		AQU 18my	

Nearly five weeks had elapsed when Russian Bride was stretched out to two turns in the Comely. Handicappers were faced with this decision: The filly needed to improve again to contend with 3–5 favorite True Affair and 3–1 second choice Private Light. Was she capable of doing so? If so, how should she be bet?

At 10–1, it was worthwhile to assume Russian Bride had been given enough time to recover from her breakthrough effort. A good strategy was a win bet, along with exacta savers underneath the first two choices. This type of "exacta as place bet," as described by noted contrarian handicapping author Mark Cramer, dovetails nicely with explosive-line horses, since handicappers are often looking for them to improve at a price against rivals with faster figures; the horse may improve enough to beat one of them, but may be defeated by another. The win bet is protected, and the chance for a solid return is still in play when the overlay runs big but winds up second best.

In this case Russian Bride improved to a new top of 11¾, but was outkicked in deep stretch by Private Light; the exacta was an exceptionally generous $90.80.

EIGHTH RACE 1¹⁄₁₆ MILES. (1.41) COMELY S. Grade II. Purse $100,000
Aqueduct
MARCH 21, 1993
Value of Race: $113,800 Winner $68,280; second $25,036; third $13,656; fourth $6,828. Mutuel Pool $17,707,203.00 Exacta Pool $367,636.00

Last Raced	Horse	M/Eqt. A. Wt	PP	St	¼	½	¾	Str	Fin	Jockey	Odds $1
6Mar93 7Aqu²	Private Light	3 112	2	3	6	5¹	5⁵	3¹¹	1²	Davis R G	3.00
17Feb93 7Aqu¹	Russian Bride	b 3 113	4	6	4½	4²	2ʰᵈ	2ʰᵈ	2¹½	Migliore R	10.50
6Mar93 7Aqu¹	True Affair	3 118	5	4	3²	3¹½	1½	1ʰᵈ	3¹⁹	Bravo J	0.60
6Mar93 7Aqu³	CosmicSpeedQueen	3 112	1	1	5¹	6	6	6	4²	Chavez J F	16.60
3Mar93 7Aqu¹	Saucy Charmer	3 112	3	5	2½	2ʰᵈ	4¹	4¹½	5¹½	Smith M E	4.20
4Mar93 5Aqu³	She's Landing	bf 3 114	6	2	1²½	1½	3½	5⁶	6	Antley C W	26.00

OFF AT 4:10 Start Good For All But. Won . Track good.

TIME :24, :48³, 1:13², 1:38, 1:44 (:24.10, :48.79, 1:13.45, 1:38.05, 1:44.19)

$2 Mutuel Prices:

2 – PRIVATE LIGHT	8.00	4.60	2.10
4 – RUSSIAN BRIDE		7.80	2.10
5 – TRUE AFFAIR			2.10

$2 EXACTA 2–4 PAID $90.80

B. f, (Mar), by Private Account – Illuminating , by Majestic Light . Trainer McGaughey III Claude R. Bred by Ogden Mills Phipps (Ky).

Owners– 1, Ogden Mills Phipps; 2, Kentucky Blue Stables; 3, Winbound Farms; 4, R Kay Stable; 5, Heatherwood Farm; 6, Asteriglo Stables

Trainers– 1, McGaughey III Claude R; 2, Jolley Leroy; 3, Contessa Gary C; 4, Araya Rene A; 5, Schosberg Richard; 6, Martin Gregory F

Two weeks after the Comely, a similar situation arose, this time in a stakes race for 3-year-old males, the Gotham. Examine the past performances of the eight entrants, paying particular attention to their Beyer Speed Figures:

9 1 MILE AQUEDUCT (START / FINISH)

1 MILE. **(1.32²) 41st Running THE GOTHAM (Grade II). Purse $200,000. 3-year-olds. By subscription of $400 each which should accompany the nomination; $1,600 to pass the entry box, $1,600 to start. The Purse to be divided 60% to the winner, 22% to second, 12% to third and 6% to fourth. Weight, 126 lbs. Non-winners of a race of $100,000 at a mile or over in 1993 allowed 3 lbs. Of two races of $100,000 at anytime, 5 lbs. Of a race of $50,000, 8 lbs. Of a race other than Maiden or Claiming at a mile or over, 12 lbs. Starters to be named at the closing time of entries. Trophies will be presented to the winning owner, trainer and jockey. Closed Wednesday, March 10 with 40 Nominations.**

Castelli Street

Dk. b. or br. c. 3(May), by Lee Castelli—Power Street, by Balance of Power
CASTILLO H JR (—)
Own.—Castelli Stables
Br.—Edwards Robert L (NJ)
Tr.—Anderson William D (2 0 0 0 .00)
114
Lifetime 6 2 2 1 $41,702 — 1993 1 1 0 0 $10,500 — 1992 5 1 2 1 $31,202 — Wet 1 0 1 0 $3,366

25Mar93- 6GS gd 6f :22 :45³ 1:11² ⓈAlw 17500 74 5 3 4⁴ 4½ 2hd 1½ Migliore R 116 *.40 85-19 CstelliStret1162½WoodnShips116½Bb'sHonor111 Driving 6
5Dec92- 9Med fst 1 :48 1:13⁴ 1:40¹ Duel Site 77 1 4 4¹ 3² 3³½ 3¾ Gryder A T 113 5.00 78-24 DprtnCld120hdBrtsBbbltr113¾CstllStrt113 Finished well 7
19Nov92- 7Med fst 6f :22³ :46¹ 1:10⁴ ⓈMd Sp Wt 63 6 2 2¹ 2¹ 1½ 1⁵½ Gryder A T 118 *.30 89-11 CstelliStreet1185½MedievlLord1185¾OddsLss118 Driving 9
30Oct92- 6Aqu fst 1 :47⁴ 1:13¹ 1:38² Md Sp Wt 75 1 5 3¹ 3nk 2²½ 2⁵¾ Gryder A T 118 4.70 64-31 ColonlAffr1185¾CstllStrt1183¾BullInthHthr118 Good try 9
21Oct92- 8Aqu fst 7f :23 :46² 1:24 Cowdin 70 5 5 7⁴ 7⁴¾ 8⁷½ 4⁹½ Gryder A T 122 34.80 75-18 Wallenda122½WildZone1227DarienDecon122 Saved grnd 10
21Oct92-Grade II
9Oct92- 7Med sly 6f :22 :45¹ 1:11² ⓈMd Sp Wt 58 11 1 6⁸ 5⁶½ 3²½ 2¹½ Castillo H Jr 118 5.50 84-11 Mnnett1181½CstelliStreet1185SvvySmmy118 Slow start 12
LATEST WORKOUTS ●Mar 20 GS 6f fst 1:13² H ●Mar 8 GS 5f fst 1:00² H ●Mar 2 GS 6f fst 1:14 H ●Feb 24 GS 5f fst 1:00 Hg

Rohwer

Ch. c. 3(Apr), by Vanlandingham—Babe's Joy, by King of the Sea
MADRID A JR (46 6 7 4 .13)
Own.—Garren Murray M
Br.—Loblolly-Betz-Guscotts-Needham (Ky)
Tr.—Garren Murray M (13 1 0 3 .08)
114
Lifetime 15 3 3 5 $134,451 — 1993 6 1 1 2 $56,203 — 1992 9 2 2 3 $78,248 — Wet 2 1 0 0 $16,020

7Mar93- 7Aqu fst 1⅟₁₆ ⊡:47¹ 1:10⁴ 1:42¹ Seattle Slew 77 4 4 4³ 4³ 3⁷½ 3¹⁰½ Chavez J F 117 2.40 84-10 Lord Beer117nk Ozan117¹⁰ Rohwer117 Lacked rally 5
20Feb93- 8Aqu fst 1⅟₁₆ ⊡:48³ 1:13¹ 1:45¹ Whirlaway 92 3 2 3¹½ 1½ 2hd 2³ Chavez J F 114 24.90 76-24 Prairie Bayou117³ Rohwer114¾ Slews Gold114 2nd best 5
3Feb93- 6Aqu fst 170 ⊡:49² 1:14¹ 1:43⁴ Alw 29000 85 5 1 1hd 1hd 1² 1⁴ Davis R G 117 *1.40 83-22 Rohwer117⁴MangoMan117⁴¾DmHndsome112 Mild drive 7
24Jan93- 8Aqu fst 170 ⊡:48 1:12² 1:42⁴ Count Fleet 77 4 1 1hd 4⁴ 4⁶½ 3⁸½ Davis R G 117 17.30 79-24 PririeByou1175½SlewsGold1175½Rohwr117 Dueled, wknd 6
9Jan93- 7Aqu fst 1⅟₁₆ ⊡:49 1:14² 1:45¹ Alw 29000 70 6 2 2½ 2hd 4⁶ 7⁹½ Chavez J F 117 5.80 69-20 SlewsGold117¹HannibalLecter117⁶SkyDr.117 Used early 8
2Jan93- 7Aqu fst 6f ⊡:22² :46² 1:11³ Alw 27000 61 11 10 9¹² 9⁹½ 9¹¹ 8¹¹ Bisono C V⁵ b 112 *2.30 74-18 Tough Heart119¹½ Birdie's Fly117⁴½ Miler119 Outrun 12
23Dec92- 7Aqu fst 1⅟₁₆ ⊡:46⁴ 1:11³ 1:45 Alw 29000 83 4 5 4⁴½ 4⁵ 3⁵½ 3⁵¾ Chavez J F 117 *1.10 77-22 Bert'sBubbletor117²SlwsGold117³¾Rohwr117 Mild rally 8
10Dec92- 7Aqu fst 170 ⊡:48¹ 1:13⁴ 1:44¹ Alw 29000 76 6 3 2² 2¹ 3³ 4⁷½ Carr D 117 *.80 76-21 GulphGorg119⁴½StllitSignl117³Brd'sFly117 Lacked rally 9
5Dec92- 8Aqu fst 1⅟₁₆ ⊡:47¹ 1:12¹ 1:44³ Nashua 88 2 2 5² 4²½ 3⁶½ 2⁶½ Chavez J F 114 35.70 78-22 Dalhart114⁶½ Rohwer114² Peace Baby114 Second best 11
5Dec92-Grade III
27Nov92- 8Aqu my 6f :22² :46 1:10³ Alw 27000 68 6 2 4²½ 6⁵ 5⁷ 4⁹ Chavez J F 117 *1.10 79-22 InsurdWinnr117³½Birdi'sFly117⁴VrgnRpds117 No threat 6
LATEST WORKOUTS Mar 31 Bel tr.t 3f fst :36 B ●Mar 27 Bel tr.t 5f fst :59¹ H Mar 23 Bel tr.t 5f fst 1:00² H Mar 5 Bel tr.t 4f my :50 B

Itaka

B. c. 3(Mar), by Jade Hunter—Americanrevelation, by Foolish Pleasure
SMITH M E (43 7 5 8 .16)
Own.—Brophy Stable
Br.—Brophy B Giles (NY)
Tr.—Johnson Philip G (1 0 0 0 .00)
114
Lifetime 8 1 1 3 $28,630 — 1993 3 0 0 1 $3,760 — 1992 5 1 1 2 $24,870 — Wet 1 0 0 0

28Feb93- 6GP fst 7f :23¹ :46² 1:23¹ Alw 22000 89 1 5 1¹ 1¹ 2² 3⁴ Fires E b 117 6.90 83-19 JackLivingston1202FightforLove1122Itak117 Weakened 7
21Jan93- 8GP fst 7f :22¹ :45¹ 1:23² Alw 21600 73 2 9 5¹½ 5²½ 3⁵ 4³½ Gonzalez M A b 112 5.30 82-15 FrvrWhrl1151½ChntngGshk1152LvngVcrsl114 Late rally 11
9Jan93-10Crc sly 1⅛ :48¹ 1:12³ 1:53⁴ Trop Pk Dby 66 5 4 4⁴ 6⁶½ 9²⁰ 8¹⁴½ Bailey J D 112 9.30 76-15 SummrSt1121½Ducd'Sligovil112½SilvrofSlvr122 Faltered 10
9Jan93-Grade III
15Dec92- 7Crc fst 1⅟₁₆ :48³ 1:13³ 1:48¹ Alw 16600 79 1 5 5²½ 3¹½ 2¹½ 3¹ Santos J A 115 1.70 85-13 Kassec110no Duc d'Sligovil115¹ Itaka115 Good effort 5
18Nov92- 6Aqu fst 7f :23 :46³ 1:24³ Alw 27000 80 3 9 6³ 7³½ 5⁴½ 3³ Davis R G 119 15.70 79-16 Apprentice119no Slew's Gold117³ Itaka119 Late gain 9
22Oct92- 3Aqu fst 6½f :23³ :48 1:18⁴ ⓈMd Sp Wt 86 5 7 4² 2hd 1½ 1¹½ Smith M E 118 *.60 84-18 Itk1181½KoluctooJmmyAl1183½BoldDor118 Brk slw, drv 7
7Oct92- 6Bel fst 6f :22³ :46² 1:10⁴ ⓈMd Sp Wt 63 10 13 3² 2¹ 2⁶ 2¹¹½ Smith M E 118 *1.30 74-16 RushChirmnBill1181¹½Itk1186½BoldDor118 Broke poorly 13
13Aug92- 4Sar fst 6f :22⁴ :46³ 1:11⁴ ⓈMd Sp Wt 53 4 13 6⁴½ 4² 6²½ 6⁶½ Cruguet J 118 2.90 78-13 LodBrthr118nkBlmGn1185½MgcMdc118 Broke slw, wide 13
LATEST WORKOUTS Mar 31 Bel tr.t 3f fst :36² B ●Mar 20 Crc 6f sly 1:13² H (d) Mar 16 Crc 3f fst :37¹ B ●Mar 12 Crc 6f fst 1:14 H

As Indicated

Ch. g. 3(May), by Czaravich—Our Nice Sue, by Our Michael
BISONO C V (47 5 6 7 .11)
Own.—Heatherwood Farm
Br.—Perkins Margot I (Ky)
Tr.—Schosberg Richard (9 4 1 0 .44)
114
Lifetime 4 3 0 0 $62,400 — 1993 3 2 0 0 $48,120 — 1992 1 1 0 0 $14,280 — Wet 1 1 0 0 $14,280

20Feb93- 6Aqu fst 6f ⊡:23³ :47¹ 1:11¹ Swift — 1 5 — — — — Bisono C V 120 *1.50 — — LyLk120½FghtngDddy114noFrmnthfr120 Wheeled,lst rdr 5
31Jan93- 7Aqu fst 6f ⊡:22³ :45³ 1:10⁴ Sly Fox 100 7 1 1² 1hd 1½ 1no Bisono C V 117 *1.70 89-16 AsIndicted117noLzyLuke117³Frmonthefrewy117 Driving 7
16Jan93- 7Aqu fst 6f ⊡:22⁴ :45⁴ 1:10² Alw 27000 85 6 2 2½ 2¹ 2½ 1¹½ Bisono C V⁵ 112 5.00 91-13 AsIndicted1121½Birdie'sFly1176½OnTheBridl117 Driving 8
25Nov92- 6Grd my 4½f :22⁴ :47³ :54 Md Sp Wt 71 2 3 1¹½ 1hd 1½ Sabourin R B 120 *1.45 82-35 AsIndictd120½SlutThSunris1154½StllrOccson115 Driving 6
LATEST WORKOUTS Mar 29 Bel tr.t 5f my 1:01 B Mar 23 Bel tr.t 5f fst :59³ H ●Mar 16 Bel tr.t 6f fst 1:14³ B Mar 8 Bel tr.t 4f fst :47² B

Ozan

B. c. 3(Feb), by Cox's Ridge—Kiva, by Tom Rolfe
SAMYN J L (18 3 3 2 .17)
Own.—Loblolly Stable
Br.—Alexander Helen & Four A Stable Syn (Ky)
Tr.—Bohannan Thomas (—)
118
Lifetime 8 2 3 1 $61,014 — 1993 4 1 2 0 $35,484 — 1992 4 1 1 1 $25,530 — Wet 2 1 0 1 $19,900

7Mar93- 7Aqu fst 1⅟₁₆ ⊡:47¹ 1:10⁴ 1:42¹ Seattle Slew 95 5 5 2¹ 2¹ 2¹½ 2nk Samyn J L 117 *1.30 94-10 Lord Beer117nk Ozan117¹⁰ Rohwer117 Second best 5
25Feb93- 6Aqu fst 1⅟₁₆ ⊡:47⁴ 1:12³ 1:45 Alw 29000 86 5 6 5⁴½ 3² 1½ 1³½ Samyn J L 117 3.70 80-20 Ozan1173½ Shower of Silver117hd Iron Gavel117 Driving 8
25Jan93- 7Aqu fst 170 ⊡:47³ 1:13 1:43³ Alw 29000 79 5 7 6⁸ 4³ 2⁵ 2⁸ Samyn J L 117 8.20 78-27 HannibalLecter117⁸Ozan¹17½MangoMn117 Up for place 9
9Jan93- 7Aqu fst 1⅟₁₆ ⊡:49 1:14² 1:45¹ Alw 29000 72 3 6 6²½ 6⁴½ 7⁶½ 6⁸½ Samyn J L 117 3.30 71-20 Slews Gold117¹ Hannibal Lecter117⁶SkyDr.117 No rally 8
20Dec92-10Lrl my 1⅛ :48⁴ 1:13⁴ 1:52⁴ Inner Harbor 78 4 5 5³½ 5³½ 4³ 3³½ Samyn J L 113 *1.50e 72-32 JorgeofMexico113noPrairieByou1223½Ozn113 Rank wide 9
5Dec92- 9Med fst 1 :48 1:13⁴ 1:40¹ Duel Site 63 7 6 7³½ 7⁵½ 5⁷ 5⁸½ Samyn J L 113 2.20 71-24 DprtngClod120hdBrt'sBbbltr113¾CstllStrt113 No factor 7
6Nov92- 9Aqu my 7f :23⁴ :47⁴ 1:25³ Md Sp Wt 64 5 5 4¹½ 3½ 3nk 1¹½ Samyn J L 118 3.60 77-18 Ozan1181½ Halostrada118hd Majesty's Darby118 Driving 9
26Oct92- 5Aqu fst 6f :22³ :46¹ 1:11 Md Sp Wt 79 3 2 5¹½ 4¹½ 3² 2² Samyn J L 118 22.60 84-14 Apprentice118² Ozan1181½ InFirstLight118 Up for place 5
LATEST WORKOUTS Apr 1 Bel tr.t 4f sly :52¹ B Mar 27 Bel tr.t 5f fst 1:01¹ H Mar 20 Bel tr.t 4f fst :47¹ H Feb 18 Bel tr.t 4f fst :48¹ H

Hickory Lake

Ch. g. 3(Mar), by Meadowlake—Belle Courante, by Cougar II
MIGLIORE R (42 9 7 4 .21)
Own.—New Showtime Stable
Br.—Windfields Farm (Ont-C)
Tr.—Klesaris Robert P (11 2 3 1 .18)
114
Lifetime 5 1 0 1 $20,080 — 1993 4 1 0 1 $19,380 — 1992 1 M 0 0 $700

8Mar93- 1Aqu fst 6f ⊡:22² :45² 1:09² Alw 27000 78 5 2 1½ 1hd 2³ 3⁶ Antley C W b 117 *1.30 90-11 KngRucks1172½Tkn'Nms117³½HckoryLk117 Speed, tired 7
25Feb93- 6Aqu fst 1⅟₁₆ ⊡:47⁴ 1:12³ 1:45 Alw 29000 80 7 1 1¹½ 1½ 2½ 4³½ Migliore R b 117 2.40 76-20 Ozan1173½ShowerofSilver117hdIronGavel117 Dueled, trd 8
28Jan93- 5Aqu fst 6f ⊡:23 :46⁴ 1:11⁴ Md Sp Wt 81 3 5 1¹½ 1¹ 1²½ 1⁴ Bravo J b 122 *.60 84-18 Hickory Lake122⁴JessC'sWhirl122⁴Pilfer122 Ridden out 7
7Jan93- 6Aqu fst 6f ⊡:22 :44³ 1:10¹ Md Sp Wt 70 9 7 5⁶½ 5⁴ 4⁴½ 5³½ McCauley W H 122 6.40 89-11 GoldenPro122nkPalcePiper1221½ClssicLunch122 Evenly 9
17Nov92- 1Med fst 6f :22³ :46¹ 1:11² Md Sp Wt 35 3 5 5¹½ 5²½ 3¹ 4⁷ Wilson R 118 *.30 79-11 Thswrthdys1184½PhnFntsy1182½NskrPrnc118 Four wide 8
LATEST WORKOUTS ●Mar 19 Bel tr.t 5f fst 1:00⁴ H Feb 18 Bel tr.t 4f fst :49¹ H Feb 12 Bel tr.t 5f fst 1:04³ B

Fighting Daddy
DAVIS R G (56 10 8 13 .18)
Own.—Kimran Stables

Ch. c. 3(May), by Fight Over—Daddyslittleangel, by Rare Performer
Br.—Gallagher Mrs James H (Fla)
Tr.—Toner James J (4 1 1 1 .25)

114

Lifetime 8 3 2 0 $57,748 | 1993 2 1 1 0 $34,548 | 1992 6 2 1 0 $23,200

20Feb93- 6Aqu	fst	6f	⊡:23^{3}	:47^{1}	1:11^{1}	Swift	93	3	3	4^{2}	4^{1½}	3½	2½	Davis R G	b	114	9.50	86–20	LzyLuk120½FightingDddy114^{no}Frmonthfrwy120	Gamely 5
27Jan93- 7Aqu	fst	6f	⊡:23^{4}	:47^{4}	1:12^{2}	Alw 27000	87	6	5	4^{1½}	2^{hd}	1½	1^{3½}	Davis R G	b	117	*1.40	81–25	Fighting Daddy117^{3½} Zoom By117^{hd}LostPan117	Driving 7
21Dec92- 4Aqu	fst	6f	⊡:22^{3}	:45^{3}	1:10^{4}	Clm 75000	82	6	1	4^{4}	4^{3}	2^{3}	2^{2½}	Davis R G	b	112	9.60	87–14	GldCndT114^{2½}FhtnDdd112^{2½}OnThBrdl116	Gained place 6
10Dec92- 7Aqu	fst	1^{70}	⊡:48^{1}	1:13^{4}	1:44^{1}	Alw 29000	63	1	1	1^{2}	1^{1}	5^{5}	7^{15½}	Migliore R	b	117	8.40	69–21	GulphGorg119^{4½}StllitSgnl117^{3}Brd'sFly117	Used in pace 9
15Nov92- 7Crc	fst	7f	:22	:45^{3}	1:26^{4}	Clm 50000	67	4	1	3^{2}	1^{1½}	1^{5}	1^{2}	Gonzalez M A	Lb	118	*1.50	81–13	FightingDddy118^{2}Dr.RossHop114½FlyBirdFly114	Driving 6
25Oct92- 3Crc	fst	6f	:22	:45^{4}	1:12^{4}	Md 40000	72	6	1	1^{2}	1^{5}	1^{5}	1^{4½}	Gonzalez M A	Lb	118	*1.90	87–17	FightingDddy118^{4½}SurelyModst118^{4}GrtEstt114	Driving 9
3Oct92- 6Crc	fst	7f	:22	:45^{2}	1:27	Md Sp Wt	47	10	1	1^{4}	1^{5}	2½	5^{8}	Gonzalez M A	b	118	14.10	72–15	BdFrGld118^{1½}LsGldnKht118^{1½}NrthrWtss118	Weakened 10
28Aug92- 6Crc	fst	6f	:22^{1}	:46^{2}	1:13^{2}	Md 35000	43	6	5	4^{6}	5^{11}	5^{10}	5^{8½}	Alferez J O		116	10.10	75–20	Crafty Chris111^{3} Desert Cowboy113^{2}Truthski113	Faded 11

LATEST WORKOUTS Mar 27 Bel tr.t 5f fst :59^{2} H Mar 19 Bel tr.t 6f fst 1:16^{2} H Mar 10 Bel tr.t 4f fst :47^{3} H Mar 3 Bel tr.t 6f fst 1:14^{4} H

Strolling Along
ANTLEY C W (56 8 17 9 .14)
Own.—Phipps Ogden

Dk. b. or br. c. 3(Apr), by Danzig—Cadillacing, by Alydar
Br.—Phipps Ogden (Ky)
Tr.—McGaughey Claude III (7 1 2 2 .14)

121

Lifetime 7 2 2 0 $157,140 | 1992 7 2 2 0 $157,140

31Oct92- 8GP	fst	1$\frac{1}{16}$	:46	1:10^{2}	1:43^{2}	Br Cp Juv	67	7	7	7^{2½}	7^{5}	9^{10}	8^{11¾}	Antley C W	b	122	20.40	83–03	GildedTime122¾It'sli'lknownfct122½RivrSpcil122	5 wide 13
31Oct92-Grade I																				
10Oct92- 7Bel	gd	1	:44^{3}	1:09	1:34^{4}	Champagne	62	9	4	4^{3½}	4^{2½}	5^{8}	5^{19½}	Antley C W		122	*2.30	76–04	SeHero122^{5½}ScrtOdds122^{5½}PrssCrd122	Lacked respnse 10
10Oct92-Grade I																				
19Sep92- 6Bel	fst	7f	:22^{1}	:45	1:23^{3}	Futurity	88	4	7	7^{5½}	3^{4}	1^{hd}	1^{2}	Antley C W		122	*1.50	86–11	StrolingAlong122^{2}FghtforLov122^{1}Cponostro122	Driving 9
19Sep92-Grade I																				
30Aug92- 8Sar	fst	6½f	:22^{2}	:45	1:15^{3}	Hopeful	89	1	3	3^{1½}	4^{2½}	3^{3}	2^{3¾}	Antley C W		122	5.10	93–08	GrtNvgtr122^{3¾}StrllngAlng122¾EnglndEpcts122	Fin. well 8
30Aug92-Grade I																				
30Jly92- 8Sar	fst	6f	:21^{3}	:44^{4}	1:10^{2}	Sar Spec'l	87	1	10	2^{1½}	2½	1^{1}	2no	Antley C W		117	1.80	92–06	TctclAdntg117^{no}StrllngAln117^{5½}MCl117	Brk sl; gamely 10
30Jly92-Grade II																				
13Jly92- 5Bel	fst	5½f	:22^{1}	:45^{2}	1:03	Md Sp Wt	94	7	3	2^{4}	2^{4}	2^{1½}	1^{2½}	Antley C W		118	10.30	100–10	StrollngAlong118^{2½}DvlshlyYors118^{8½}Dr.Alfs118	Driving 10
26Jun92- 3Bel	fst	5½f	:22^{2}	:45^{3}	1:04^{3}	Md Sp Wt	50	5	7	8^{6½}	8^{5}	6^{6½}	5^{5½}	Antley C W		118	*.80	86–07	KissinKrs118^{hd}GrmlnGry118^{no}InsurdWnnr118	Late gain 9

LATEST WORKOUTS ●Mar 27 Bel tr.t 6f fst 1:10^{4} H Mar 22 Bel tr.t 6f fst 1:16^{2} B Mar 17 Bel tr.t 5f gd 1:03^{3} B Mar 10 Bel tr.t 4f fst :46^{4} B

Three horses—Fighting Daddy, Ozan, and Itaka—were coming off career-best performances according to their Beyers. Fighting Daddy had just run three consecutive new tops, moving 10 points to an 82, 5 points to an 87, and 6 points to a 93. Ozan had just moved twice, from 79 to 86 to 95. Once horses have made two or three forward moves in succession, the likelihood of their making yet another forward move is diminished. Neither Fighting Daddy nor Ozan was likely to show improvement in the Gotham, and in fact they would probably run something less than their best.

Itaka had also run a new top in his most recent start, but with a notable difference: Although the jump appeared significant at first glance—an 89 off a 73 in his previous start—the new top is properly evaluated in light of his best previous effort, the 86 he recorded as a 2-year-old in his third start; the 3-point move from 86 to 89 was a small one, and represented Itaka's first move past his best 2-year-old figure. Moreover, it had been nearly five weeks since the move.

Itaka's past performances withstood scrutiny. Though still eligible for his first-level allowance condition, he had faced some of the best 3-year-olds in Florida. Among them was Duc d'Sligovil, who had since won a second-level allowance and a division of a split Fountain of Youth, and Fight for Love, the runner-up in Belmont's Grade 1 Futurity the previous autumn. Itaka's best race at 2 had taken place at Aqueduct with Mike Smith up, and he was returning to the Big A with a switch back to that rider. Bullet works at Calder since the key figure of 89 were icing on the cake.

As often happens with this kind of improving horse, Itaka did improve (running a Beyer of 100) at a big price, but As Indicated ran back to his figure of 100 two races back and held on determinedly for the win. Even so, one need only have keyed Itaka with the first three betting choices to cash the $105.60 exacta and/or the $387 trifecta.

NINTH RACE

Aqueduct

APRIL 3, 1993

1 MILE. (1.32²) 41st Running THE GOTHAM (Grade II). Purse $200,000. 3-year-olds. By subscription of $400 each which should accompany the nomination; $1,600 to pass the entry box, $1,600 to start. The Purse to be divided 60% to the winner, 22% to second, 12% to third and 6% to fourth. Weight, 126 lbs. Non-winners of a race of $100,000 at a mile or over in 1993 allowed 3 lbs. Of two races of $100,000 at anytime, 5 lbs. Of a race of $50,000, 8 lbs. Of a race other than Maiden or Claiming at a mile or over, 12 lbs. Starters to be named at the closing time of entries. Trophies will be presented to the winning owner, trainer and jockey. Closed Wednesday, March 10 with 40 Nominations.
Value of race $200,000; value to winner $120,000; second $44,000; third $24,000; fourth $12,000. Mutuel pool $297,504. Exacta Pool $453,176 Triple Pool $521,597

Last Raced	Horse	M/Eqt.A.Wt	PP St	¼	½	¾	Str	Fin	Jockey	Odds $1
20Feb93 6Aqu	As Indicated	3 114	4 4	1¹	1½	1hd	1hd	1nk	Bisono C V	3.80
28Feb93 6GP3	Itaka	b 3 114	3 8	7½	6¹½	3½	3½	2¹½	Smith M E	14.00
31Oct92 8GP8	Strolling Along	3 121	8 1	3¹	2¹½	2¹	2¹	3nk	Antley C W	1.20
7Mar93 7Aqu2	Ozan	b 3 118	5 6	5hd	4¹	4½	4½	4nk	Samyn J L	2.70
25Mar93 6GS1	Castelli Street	3 114	1 7	2½	5¹	5½	5⁶	5¹⁶	Castillo H Jr	24.70
20Feb93 6Aqu2	Fighting Daddy	b 3 114	7 2	4½	3hd	6²	6¹½	6¹½	Davis R G	10.00
7Mar93 7Aqu3	Rohwer	3 114	2 5	6hd	7hd	7¹	7¹	7nk	Madrid A Jr	18.40
8Mar93 1Aqu3	Hickory Lake	3 114	6 3	8	8	8	8	8	Migliore R	30.30

OFF AT 4:50 Start good, Won driving. Time, :23², :46¹, 1:10³, 1:36¹ Track good.

$2 Mutuel Prices:

5-(E)-AS INDICATED		9.60	6.20	4.20
4-(D)-ITAKA			10.00	6.60
9-(I)-STROLLING ALONG				3.40

$2 EXACTA 5-4 PAID $105.60 $2 TRIPLE 5-4-9 PAID $387.00

Ch. g, (May), by Czaravich—Our Nice Sue, by Our Michael. Trainer Schosberg Richard. Bred by Perkins Margot I (Ky).
AS INDICATED sprinted clear in the early stages, set the pace along the inside on the backstretch, dug in when challenged by STROLLING ALONG midway on the turn, battled heads apart inside that one into midstretch, shook loose nearing the sixteenth pole then was all out to hold off ITAKA in the final strides. ITAKA reserved for a half after breaking a step slowly, moved up rapidly while four wide on the turn then closed steadily in the middle of the track but could not get up. STROLLING ALONG, never far back, moved to engage AS INDICATED for the lead nearing the half mile pole, drew on even terms with the winner entering the stretch, battled gamely into deep stretch and weakened under pressure in the final sixteenth. OZAN settled in good position for five furlongs, races within striking distance while between horses on the turn, remained a factor into midstretch and finished evenly in the final eighth. CASTELLI STREET up close early, lagged behind a bit along the backstretch lodged a mild rally while saving ground on the turn but could not sustain his bid. FIGHTING DADDY raced in close contention between horses for five furlongs, steadied midway on the turn then gradually tired thereafter. ROHWER was never a factor. HICKORY LAKE trailed throughout. CASTELLI STREET and HICKORY LAKE wore mud caulks.

Owners— 1, Heatherwood Farm; 2, Brophy Stable; 3, Phipps Ogden; 4, Loblolly Stable; 5, Castelli Stables; 6, Kimran Stables; 7, Garren Murray M; 8, New Showtime Stable.

Trainers— 1, Schosberg Richard; 2, Johnson Philip G; 3, McGaughey Claude III; 4, Bohannan Thomas; 5, Anderson William D; 6, Toner James J; 7, Garren Murray M; 8, Klesaris Robert P.

Scratched—Silver Key (5Mar93 8GS1).

Four-year-olds that have recently come around to their best figures from the previous year can be handled in much the same way. Some will take a backward step after recording the key figure, while others fire again right away.

Clover City — B. g. 4, by Malinowski—Wegotluck, by Lyphard — **117**
CARR D (38 3 9 5 .08) — Br.—Sunnyview Farm (NY)
Own.—Stock Michael L — Tr.—Terrill William V (12 1 2 3 .08)

Lifetime	1992	5 0 2 0		$12,760
16 1 2 0	1991	11 1 0 0		$17,040
$29,800	Turf	6 1 2 0		$28,360

4Sep92- 7Bel	yl	1 1/16	[T]:482	1:123	1:441	3+[S]Alw 29000	83	4	4	32	41½	32	22¼	Carr D	b	117	*2.40	75-20	ShomrmSocty1172¼ClovrCty1171¼EbonyBl117	Willingly	10
28Aug92- 5Sar	fm	1⅛	(T):462	1:104	1:484	3+[S]Alw 29000	83	10	5	42	5¾	33	2½	Carr D	b	117	23.30	85-11	Green Gaitor112½ Clover City1173½ TeddyC.114	Fin well	12
15Aug92- 2Sar	gd	1⅛	(T):472	1:112	1:501	3+[S]Alw 29000	73	12	2	2½	2½	31½	64½	Carr D	b	117	50.70	75-14	Complinim1141½GrnGtor1121½DulZon117	Bid, weakened	12
25Jly92- 5Bel	fst	6f	:222	:452	1:094	3+[S]Alw 27000	52	8	7	76	64¾	69½	614¾	Carr D	b	117	57.70	76-15	FtforRoylty1176ShomrmScty1173¾EbnyBl117	No factor	8
11Jly92- 3Bel	fst	1 1/16	:472	1:113	1:42	3+[S]Alw 29000	31	9	3	42½	55¾	931	941¾	Carr D	b	117	50.00	50-18	BlzonSong11310¾RelCielo1119¾PrinceJubile111	Stopped	9
7Dec91- 3Aqu	fst	170	[•]:483	1:14	1:44	3+Clm 25000	—	2	3	32	119¼	—	—	Antley C W	b	115	7.80e	— —	Sothmpton-Ar1153¾PrdClrs1156¾PcExprss117	Pulled up	11
2Dec91- 4Aqu	gd	7f	:224	:464	1:25	Clm 30000	48	9	4	68	97	910	818¾	Velazquez J R	b	113	40.30	59-22	SunshinChrli1154NicAinit1172¼Kck'sforKcks117	Outrun	9
2Nov91- 4Aqu	fm	1	(T):474	1:123	1:374	3+Alw 29000	63	6	5	64½	95	87½	714½	Velazquez J R	b	120	28.90	72-11	Devil'sCry117¾Punchpsser1155MdivlClssic117	No threat	9
23Oct91- 2Aqu	fm	1 1/16	(T):484	1:14	1:461	3+[S]Md Sp Wt	73	5	3	3½	41	1hd	11½	Krone J A	b	119	4.00	81-15	CloverCity1191½It'sS.S.Mri119nkScoutSetter119	Driving	10
12Oct91- 9Bel	fst	7f	:223	:462	1:26	3+Md 30000	58	6	8	64	97¾	74	65	Krone J A	b	115	15.00	69-17	Elan Beau119nkOronoColor's1152TenEyck115	No threat	13

LATEST WORKOUTS Sep 15 Bel 4f fst :492 B — Aug 26 Bel tr.t 4f fst :49 B — Aug 11 Bel 5f gd 1:013 H — Aug 4 Bel 4f fst :49 B

After matching his previous Beyer top of 73 with a surprising show of improved early speed at 50–1, Clover City returned shortly thereafter with a pair of runner-up finishes on firm and yielding turf, beginning with a two-move running line at 23–1 that completed a $301.80 exacta behind Green Gaitor, a logical contender who was third choice at 5–1.

Forging Horses

At a mid-1980s seminar on form cycles, Len Friedman explained the difference between explosive and forging horses this way:

"To me, the ones that are really explosive have made one small move through their 2-year-old top. In other words, they've just made one move past their 2-year-old top—and not a big move: a point, a point and a half at the most. The difference between explosive and forging horses is this: The explosive ones I'm looking to play with just about any excuse at all sometime around four to eight weeks from when they hit that number. In a lot of cases, I'd be willing to play the horse directly off that number if it's had a month off and I was getting good odds. Forging horses are the ones 'looping around' to better numbers, but I would want to see some kind of intervening pattern on those horses which indicates to me the horse is still going forward in its development."

Simply stated, handicappers can evaluate older, more heavily raced horses that have recently come back around to their best figures as they might evaluate their younger counterparts, with an important new wrinkle: More caution should be exercised. Before playing this type of horse to improve again or run back to its top figure, handicappers should be looking for a bit more time between peak efforts, along with some evidence the horse is headed back in the right direction.

The fifth race at Saratoga on August 17, 1992, was a $25,000 claiming sprint run in the mud, and it drew 10 fillies and mares. The race appeared wide open, with Majestic Willowa a lukewarm 5–2 favorite, and six others anywhere from 4–1 to 8–1. Among them was Bug's Chubbs, who exhibited a forging line:

5 6 FURLONGS SARATOGA (START / FINISH)

6 FURLONGS. **(1.08) CLAIMING. Purse $18,000. Fillies and mares, 3-year-olds and upward. Weights, 3-year-olds, 117 lbs.; older, 122 lbs. Non-winners of two races since July 15 allowed 3 lbs. Of a race since then, 5 lbs. Claiming price $25,000; for each $2,500 to $20,000, 2 lbs. (Races when entered to be claimed for $18,000 or less not considered.0**

Makin' Honey — Ro. f. 4, by Drone—Red Sash, by Go Marching
CRUGUET J (45 4 5 5 .09) — $20,000 — Br.—Santangelo George L (NY)
Own.—Lumot Stable — Tr.—DiMauro Stephen (12 0 1 2 .00) — 113
Lifetime 17 2 2 0 $46,656 — 1992 10 0 0 0 $3,096 — 1991 7 2 2 0 $43,560 — Turf 4 0 0 0 $150 — Wet 3 1 0 0 $16,680

21Jly92-10FL	gd	1	:491	1:151	1:422	3+ⒻAlw 6900	39	5	6	65½	710	712	612¾	McCarthy M J	b	116	8.10	59-29	WndswptAl116nkStckyRd1191¾Qn'sShllng108	No threat	8
12Jly92- 8FL	fst	6f	:22	:452	1:12	3+ⒻAlw 6900	40	3	8	711	814	711	614	Nicol P A Jr	b	116	3.00	72-19	Pssplnzy114noFstCrr11511Ashley'sObsession116	Outrun	8
21Jun92-10FL	fst	6f	:224	:46	1:124	3+ⒻAlw 7000	51	6	6	64½	68	57	46½	Nicol P A Jr	b	116	3.80	75-20	RomnGirl119½WindsweptAli1192LstRflction116	No rally	9
29May92- 7Bel	fm	1	Ⓣ:454	1:101	1:35	ⒻClm 35000	54	9	6	63¾	97	94¾	915	Pezua J M	b	117	19.90	72-14	Jolie Britt122hd Oriane1172 Final Road117	Outrun	9
21May92- 5Bel	fst	7f	:231	:463	1:242	ⒻClm 25000	55	5	3	32	31	43	48½	Cruguet J		117	12.60	74-16	SblWy1173Crl'sCommnd1175Undrnsurd117	Lacked rally	5
11May92- 4Bel	my	6f	:221	:452	1:111	ⒻClm 25000	69	1	7	45	32	31	42½	Pezua J M		117	34.60	81-10	FondRomance1152SablWy115½FinlRod113	Lacked rally	7
9Apr92- 9Aqu	fst	7f	:223	:454	1:251	ⒻClm 25000	50	9	1	55	65½	65½	78¾	Cruguet J		117	24.00	71-18	OneThird1172LostinFlight117hdSprklingHnnh112	Faded	9
27Mar92- 4Aqu	my	1	:461	1:112	1:37	ⒻClm 25000	48	7	8	88½	87	88½	816½	McCauley W H		117	7.30	61-23	ThrthtChrms1173½WrldClssPr1153½BrttnErn117	Outrun	8
8Mar92- 5GP	fst	7f	:231	:463	1:234	ⒻClm 40000	47	2	6	74¾	75½	79¾	618½	Douglas R R		113	34.60	68-12	Butter Cream116½ StarYum1161½Solly'sFolly116	Outrun	7
9Feb92- 6GP	fm	*1⅛ Ⓣ			1:512 +	ⒻClm 50000	48	1	4	38	1018	1126	1127½	Cruguet J		116	49.90	– –	PleasantReef1141KlassyIndividul120noAreis116	Faltered	11

LATEST WORKOUTS ●Aug 14 Sar 4f fst :472 H — Aug 7 Sar 4f fst :50 B

Brave Grecian — Dk. b. or br. f. 4, by Brave Shot-GB—Greek Nixy, by Snow Knight
SMITH M E (82 17 15 12 .21) — $20,000 — Br.—Schickedanz Gustav (Ont-C)
Own.—Kimran Stable — Tr.—Toner James J (7 0 1 0 .00) — 113
Lifetime 21 3 1 3 $42,085 — 1992 11 2 0 1 $19,140 — 1991 9 1 1 2 $22,945 — Wet 4 2 0 0 $19,500

8Jly92- 3Bel	fst	6f	:22	:451	1:103	ⒻClm 12000	70	6	4	12½	12½	11½	33½	Davis R G	b	113	10.80	84-16	TnCrk113¾MlHghGlry1172½BrvGrcn113	Svd Gnd, wknd	8
17Jun92- 2Bel	fst	6f	:223	:454	1:112	ⒻClm 12000	62	4	1	1½	1hd	2½	44	Davis R G	b	113	4.40	79-16	NrthrnWlly1172½Plythbgbys106¾TnCrk113	Used in pace	8
28May92- 5Bel	fst	6f	:221	:452	1:104	ⒻClm 14000	63	2	3	21	2½	32½	55	Bailey J D		117	5.90	81-14	Plthbbs1101½BrdfrdB1133ChttsDrm113	Frcd pace tired	9
9May92- 9Bel	gd	6f	:214	:444	1:092	ⒻClm 17500	60	3	2	42½	72½	65½	510	Gryder A T		117	6.50	83-07	Crli'sCommnd1171½EvrlstingStr1175LuckyNck117	Tired	9
17Apr92- 2Aqu	sly	6f	:214	:45	1:103	ⒻClm 14000	72	1	5	11	1½	12	14¾	Gryder A T		117	2.70	88-13	BraveGrecian1174¾Hagster1171½LurenMellis109	Driving	7
10Apr92- 3Aqu	fst	7f	:223	:453	1:25	ⒻClm 17500	53	8	1	2hd	1hd	32	610	Velazquez J R	b	117	8.00	70-18	FinlRod1171½SolidAngel117¾IceSociety112	Dueled tired	8
27Mar92- 4Aqu	my	1	:461	1:112	1:37	ⒻClm 22500	61	2	3	2hd	22	54½	79½	BrocklbnkGV5	b	110	24.60	68-23	ThrtlCrs1173½WrldClssPr1153½BrttEr117	Saved ground	8
18Mar92- 1Aqu	fst	7f	:23	:472	1:254	ⒻClm 25000	59	3	6	76	86¾	74¾	55¾	BrocklbnkGV5	b	112	35.10	70-23	SocilDelim117nkMisteV117noSwtn'SssyGl117	Saved grd	8
5Feb92- 3Aqu	fst	6f	⊡:232	:472	1:121	ⒻClm 20000	53	5	2	2½	3½	58½	515½	Gryder A T	b	115	28.40	67-22	NoCst1124½MssRdmndLn113hoSwtn'SssyGl117	Used up	6
26Jan92- 3Aqu	fst	6f	⊡:232	:47	1:122	ⒻClm 25000	61	6	4	43½	85	89	89½	Gryder A T	b	119	8.40	72-22	MdstGl117noStn'SssyGl1172½ChfMstrss117	Brief speed	8

LATEST WORKOUTS Aug 11 Sar 5f fst :593 H — Aug 3 Sar 5f fst 1:002 H — Jly 26 Bel 5f fst 1:03 B — Jly 18 Bel tr.t 4f fst :51 B

Mile High Glory — Ch. m. 6, by On To Glory—Too Nice, by Nice Catch
MIGLIORE R (47 7 5 7 .15) — $20,000 — Br.—October House Farm (Fla)
Own.—Hauman Eugene E — Tr.—Hushion Michael E (10 2 3 2 .20) — 113
Lifetime 27 8 3 2 $78,500 | 1992 7 1 2 0 $15,320 | 1991 6 1 0 1 $10,470 | Wet 5 3 0 0 $26,700

27Jly92- 1Bel my 6f :22 :45 1:10 ⒻClm 20000 23 60 4 4 57 55 56 513¼ Migliore R b 113 2.60 77-11 CrlsCmmnd117¾FndRmnc115½SrtNCrft110 In tght brk 9
8Jly92- 3Bel fst 6f :22 :451 1:103 ⒻClm 14000 15 76 4 1 22½ 22½ 21½ 2¾ Migliore R b 117 *1.70 86-16 TownCrek113¾MilHighGlory1172½BrvGrcin113 Good try 8
6May92- 2Bel fst 6f :221 :451 1:094 ⒻClm 35000 66 5 3 31½ 41 64½ 710 Nelson D b 117 *2.20 81-09 MjstcTrc117¾EphtcStl1172Undrsrd114 Lacked response 8
13Apr92- 9Aqu gd 6f :222 :452 1:09 3+ⒻAlw 28000 91 3 1 11 11 1½ 23 Migliore R b 119 4.90 93-08 KombtKt1193MilHighGlory1193½StolnButy113 2nd best 8
2Mar92- 6Aqu fst 6f ⊡:231 :47 1:131 ⒻClm c-30000 55 8 2 3nk 3nk 66½ 811¼ Migliore R b 114 3.60 65-30 MssRdndLn115noUndrsrd115½ShsAShr117 Used in pace 8
22Feb92- 5Pha fst 6f :221 :452 1:113 ⒻClm 17000 78 3 1 1hd 1½ 14 13 Lloyd J S Lb 114 2.30 83-20 MlHghGlry1143R'sRndvs1141¼TlcKnsscrt116 Easy score 7
2Jan92- 5SA fst 6f :211 :44 1:094 ⒻClm 25000 41 8 5 2½ 42½ 710 816¼ McCarron C J LBb 115 *2.10 71-11 Tiaradancer1142½ Chalk Box1172 Chip's De Mere114 9
2Jan92-Wide, not urged late
10Nov91- 6BM fst 6f :221 :45 1:101 3+ⒻClm c-16000 82 7 3 1hd 12 15 14 Boulanger G LBb 116 *2.50 85-16 MlHhGlr1164ImLttlNppr118noDltnPrncss116 Ridden out 8
20Oct91- 1SA fst 6f :212 :442 1:112 3+ⒻClm c-10000 65 6 2 2½ 11½ 11 4nk Oldham D W LBb 115 3.70 79-16 Mbltt-Br115nkBntM116noSsOfRc-Ir115 Drifted out lane 11
1May91- 8LaD fst 6f :222 :46 1:113 3+ⒻClm 25000 58 1 9 98½ 89¾ 87¾ 78¾ Bourque K Lb 117 6.00 80-14 Wild Win1143 Twinkle City117½ FlakyLady117 Steadied 9
LATEST WORKOUTS Aug 8 Bel 4f fst :474 H ●Jly 19 Bel 4f fst :463 H

Treegees — Ch. f. 4, by Geiger Counter—Gable's Girl, by Screen King
KRONE J A (72 12 8 12 .17) — $22,500 — Br.—Howard & Ross (Ont-C)
Own.—Heatherwood Farm — Tr.—Schosberg Richard (12 4 3 1 .33) — 115
Lifetime 19 5 3 2 $60,006 | 1992 1 0 0 0 | 1991 18 5 3 2 $60,006 | Turf 1 0 0 0 | Wet 1 0 0 0

7Aug92- 2Sar fst 7f :222 :451 1:231 3+ⒻClm 25000 18 67 1 11 85½ 54½ 75½ 67½ Krone J A b 117 5.70 81-10 NorthernWilly113nkBoots1175AbovThSlt115 Wide, tired 12
14Nov91- 5Aqu fst 6f :22 :451 1:101 ⒻClm 25000 65 8 9 84¾ 67 47 36½ Santos J A b 116 4.90 84-10 MissThiti1163½SlickDelivery1162¾Treegees116 Late gain 11
30Oct91- 3Aqu fst 7f :231 :472 1:254 ⒻClm 32500 66 6 5 53 41½ 45 67¾ Cordero A Jr b 114 10.30 65-25 MjesticTrick1163MissRdmondLn1161½Shimiss116 Faded 8
5Oct91- 6WO gd 7f :224 :461 1:253 ⒻClm 25000 62 7 10 95½ 76½ 57½ 53¾ David D J b 114 2.55e 81-14 HulRucks1141¼KnKt111¼HrdwoodFlo114 Saved ground 10
25Sep91- 5WO fst 6½f :223 :462 1:194 ⒻClm 20000 66 2 8 52 31½ 3½ 14 David D J b 116 4.30 76-18 Treegees1164 Petagaom1141½ Maine Shore114 In hand 11
15Sep91- 7WO fst 7f :221 :443 1:243 ⒻClm 25000 74 5 3 54 53½ 42½ 32½ David D J b 114 3.15 87-10 Commmorss108hdLvlyRlty1142½Trgs114 Closed willingly 7
4Sep91- 3WO fst 6f :222 :454 1:121 ⒻClm 20000 73 4 2 52¾ 31½ 3nk 1hd David D J b 114 *1.70 84-20 Treegees114hdShmrockSue1152¾SuleDuNord114 Driving 6
15Aug91- 3WO fst 6½f :222 :453 1:182 ⒻClm 20000 74 5 6 53 2hd 11½ 1no David D J b 114 2.75 83-10 Treegees114noGldCompny1083½DncOnthSnd117 Driving 6
7Aug91- 1WO fst 6f :223 :454 1:123 ⒻClm 25000 68 3 8 63¾ 44½ 31½ 2¾ David D J b 114 3.35 81-15 MoonHlo114¾Treeges114nkDncOnthSnd117 Closed well 9
25Jly91- 3WO fst 6f :224 :46 1:112 ⒻClm 20000 67 2 8 64½ 66 56½ 23 David D J b 114 *1.85 85-16 RefinedndBold1143Treegees114nkStrLikeTr109 Wide str 8
LATEST WORKOUTS Aug 5 Sar 3f gd :362 H Jly 30 Sar 5f fst 1:011 H Jly 23 Bel 4f fst :481 H Jly 17 Bel 4f fst :484 H

Fond Romance — B. f. 4, by Fappiano—Indian Romance, by Raja Baba
SANTAGATA N (1 0 0 1 .00) — $25,000 — Br.—Farish W S & Hudson E J (Ky)
Own.—Williams Michael D — Tr.—Imperio Joseph (6 0 0 1 .00) — 117
Lifetime 25 4 5 3 $78,120 | 1992 16 3 3 2 $59,560 | 1991 8 1 2 1 $17,120 | Turf 1 0 0 0 | Wet 4 1 1 1 $17,400

10Aug92- 3Sar fst 1⅛ :472 1:12 1:501 3+ⒻClm 25000 47 1 4 53 42½ 610 620¾ Smith M E b 117 3.10 66-09 RdTp1176PrciousPriss1155½BrttnyErn113 Saved ground 10
27Jly92- 1Bel my 6f :22 :45 1:10 ⒻClm 22500 72 3 6 68 68 66 28¾ Santagata N b 115 11.00 81-11 CrlsCmmnd1178¾FndRnc115½SrtNCrft110 Pinched brk 9
13Jun92- 9Bel fst 7f :231 :464 1:251 ⒻClm 25000 44 9 9 83¾116¼1011 914¼ Bailey J D b 117 19.40 63-18 CompnyGrl117½SnnyBrb117nkNorthrnWily117 No factor 11
1Jun92- 3Bel sly 1116 :471 1:114 1:433 ⒻClm 35000 72 2 1 12 1½ 43 58½ Madrid A Jr b 115 7.10 75-25 FoolnSprc113noRbcc'sGl1176AbovThSlt115 Speed, tired 7
11May92- 4Bel my 6f :221 :452 1:111 ⒻClm 22500 75 3 1 2hd 1hd 1½ 12 Madrid A Jr b 115 8.60 84-10 Fond Romance1152 SabalWay115½FinalRoad113 Driving 7
7May92- 2Bel fm 1116 Ⓣ:461 1:094 1:414 ⒻClm 35000 57 4 9 89 78½ 912 1014¼ Madrid A Jr b 117 18.70 72-15 Asaracket1172¾ GreatPass1172¾NotAScratch117 Outrun 11
22Apr92- 6Aqu my 1⅛ :48 1:122 1:514 ⒻClm 32500 76 5 5 43 32½ 33 39 Madrid A Jr b 115 17.30 68-30 LdLr1176¾SphstctdSm1172½FndRmnc115 Flattened out 7
5Apr92- 4Aqu fst 7f :23 :472 1:263 ⒻClm 35000 61 5 4 63 62¾ 54½ 59 Madrid A Jr b 117 6.60 63-25 TnyGrsshppr117nkOrn1131½CmpnyGrl117 Saved ground 8
22Mar92- 6Aqu fst 1 :462 1:112 1:371 ⒻAlw 31000 70 3 4 42 41 64½ 56½ Madrid A Jr b 117 9.30 69-25 TripleSox117nkFlyingCross1174Avie'sDisy117 No threat 6
9Mar92- 9Aqu fst 1116 ⊡:48 1:123 1:462 ⒻAlw 31000 72 6 6 63½ 64½ 65½ 89½ Madrid A Jr b 119 7.70 66-20 Rbcc'sGl1122FlyngCross117nkFoolnSprc112 No menace 9
LATEST WORKOUTS Jly 20 Aqu ⊡ 3f fst :382 B

Company Girl — B. m. 5, by Cormorant—Talcum Blue, by Talc
BAILEY J D (73 12 14 7 .16) — $25,000 — Br.—Fishback J (NY)
Own.—Wickman Joseph — Tr.—Lake Robert P (5 0 0 2 .00) — 117
Lifetime 55 9 6 9 $266,226 | 1992 13 1 0 3 $25,320 | 1991 13 2 3 3 $49,680 | Turf 2 0 0 0 $1,740 | Wet 11 2 0 1 $36,300

Entered 15Aug92- 9 SAR
31Jly92- 5Sar sly 6f :221 :452 1:102 3+ⒻClm 32500 18 74 5 5 46½ 57 55 46½ Bailey J D b 115 15.80 86-13 Approprtly117hdJoy'sJoJo1172½HghwyQn117 No threat 6
16Jly92- 9Bel fst 7f :22 :453 1:24 ⒻClm c-25000 62 2 11 109¾109¼ 75¾ 56¾ Davis R G b 117 8.50 77-14 MjstcFrdm117¾CrlsCmmnd1173FlmngLbrl113 No threat 11
16Jly92-Claimed from Stronach Frank, Sedlacek Michael C Trainer
28Jun92- 1Bel fst 7f :23 :461 1:23 ⒻClm 30000 71 4 5 54½ 63½ 44½ 45¾ Davis R G b 113 5.30 83-12 HdsnDncr1133AllPr1171SphstctdSm117 Bobbled break 6
13Jun92- 9Bel fst 7f :231 :464 1:251 ⒻClm 25000 75 6 7 114¾ 94½ 52½ 1½ Davis R G b 117 7.70 78-18 CompnyGirl117½SunnyBrbi117nkNorthrnWlly117 Driving 11
17May92- 4Bel my 7f :231 :463 1:234 ⒻClm 32500 59 1 6 44 43 64½ 68½ Santos J A b 115 7.20 76-13 MjstcFrdm115hdEmphtcStl1173MjstcTrck117 No threat 6
2May92- 1Aqu fst 7f :231 :46 1:24 ⒻClm c-25000 72 5 4 52¾ 53 54 32½ Rojas R I b 117 4.70 82-07 LstnFlght117½FlyngCrss1172CmpnyGrl117 Rallied wide 7
2May92-Claimed from Sunshine Hill Farm, Ribaudo Robert Trainer
25Apr92- 5Aqu fst 7f :224 :462 1:241 ⒻClm 35000 69 3 8 84½ 86½ 78¾ 76½ Smith M E b 117 4.60 77-15 Avie's Daisy117hd No Cost119½ SoontoSin113 Wide trip 9
5Apr92- 4Aqu fst 7f :23 :472 1:263 ⒻClm 35000 77 2 8 74½ 72¾ 42 31½ Smith M E b 117 3.50 70-25 TnyGrsshoppr117nkOrn1131½CompnyGrl117 Rallied wide 8
2Mar92- 6Aqu fst 6f ⊡:231 :47 1:131 ⒻClm c-35000 73 6 6 73¾ 64¾ 55½ 44¼ Antley C W 117 5.60 73-30 MssRdmndLn115noUndrnsrd115¾Sh'sAShr117 Late gain 8
6Feb92- 1Aqu fst 6f ⊡:232 :464 1:112 ⒻClm 45000 80 5 4 53½ 42½ 45½ 43¾ Antley C W 114 2.20 82-22 WldWrnng113hdEmphtcStyl117noSunnySr115 No threat 5
LATEST WORKOUTS ●Jly 8 Aqu ⊡ 5f fst 1:023 B Jun 23 Aqu 4f fst :481 H

Above The Salt — Ch. f. 4, by Master Derby—Salt In My Stew, by Dr Blum
DAVIS R G (62 8 10 5 .13) — $22,500 — Br.—Happy Hill Farm Inc (Ky)
Own.—Davis Barbara J — Tr.—Moschera Gasper S (16 5 2 3 .31) — 115
Lifetime 33 11 4 5 $152,200 | 1992 7 4 0 2 $54,000 | 1991 23 6 3 2 $82,680 | Wet 5 1 0 1 $10,440

7Aug92- 2Sar fst 7f :222 :451 1:231 3+ⒻClm 22500 16 72 3 7 75½ 87½ 53½ 35½ McCauley W H 115 — — 84-10 NorthrnWilly113nkBoots1175AbovThSlt115 Lacked rally 12
7Aug92-Raced for purse money only
22Jun92- 1Bel fst 1116 :474 1:12 1:432 ⒻClm 20000 82 4 2 22 2hd 11½ 1nk McCauley W H 117 1.50 85-15 AbovThSlt117nkThrlyghtChrms1171½Entrust110 Driving 6
1Jun92- 3Bel sly 1116 :471 1:114 1:433 ⒻClm 30000 77 6 2 22 3½ 31½ 36 Smith M E 115 *2.00 78-25 FoolnSpruc113noRbcc'sGl1176AbovThSlt115 Wide, tired 7
22May92- 4Bel fst 1116 :47 1:112 1:433 ⒻClm 30000 82 3 1 2hd 11½ 12 12½ Smith M E 113 3.60 84-16 AbovThSlt1132½SophistctdSm1081¾Clsky117 Drew clear 7
9May92- 2Bel my 1 :46 1:102 1:354 ⒻClm 45000 60 8 3 2½ 2½ 43½ 512¼ Pezua J M 113 *2.30 79-14 Strshrl115noAWnkAndANd1135¾Av'sDs113 Dueled, tired 8
9May92-Originally scheduled on turf
25Apr92- 7Aqu fst 7f :224 :462 1:24 3+ⒻAlw 27000 85 1 5 2½ 1½ 14 16 Pezua J M 119 3.20 85-15 Above TheSalt1196Viperous1103½R.E.Darla110 Drew off 6
11Apr92- 2Aqu sly 6f :22 :453 1:113 ⒻClm 14000 75 2 8 57¾ 36 21½ 1no Smith M E 117 3.10 83-14 AbovThSlt117noWigglsLw1172BrdfordBy110 Drifted drv 8
26Dec91- 2Aqu fst 6f ⊡:234 :481 1:133 ⒻClm c-25000 82 4 8 42 31 11 1½ Cordero A Jr 116 5.30e 75-24 AbThSlt116½SnnSr1163½MssRdmndLn116 Rail trp, drvg 10
14Dec91- 2Aqu my 6f ⊡:22 :454 1:113 ⒻClm 30000 71 1 6 2hd 31 67½ 65 Garcia L I5 107 7.30 80-13 MjsticTrick1161TinyGrsshoppr114½IvD116 Used in pace 8
6Dec91- 2Aqu fst 6f ⊡:222 :461 1:113 ⒻClm 17500 87 12 2 12 11½ 16 15½ Cordero A Jr 116 *1.90 85-19 AbovThSlt1165½RthrBSocil116nkKllrBuzz112 Ridden out 12
LATEST WORKOUTS Jly 27 Bel 4f my :524 B (d) Jly 19 Bel 3f fst :363 H

Magestic Willowa — Ch. m. 5, by Magesterial—Willowa, by Son Ange

WHITLEY K (1 0 0 0 .00) — $25,000 — Br.—Davis Jonathan H F (NY)

Own.—Perdue Edward C — Tr.—Perdue Edward C (3 0 1 0 .00) — 117

Lifetime 25 9 6 0 $84,975 — 1992 5 0 2 0 $3,300 — 1991 7 4 1 0 $33,180 — Wet 4 2 1 0 $16,170

1Aug92-10FL	my	1⅛	:491	1:15	1:513	3+ⒻⓈMonroe	58	5	1	3nk	33	25	59	Whitley K	b	115	3.90	50-40	HvnKnwsWhy1153¾AlbmAnn1171Llc'sStr115	Weakened	7
21Jly92-11FL	gd	6f	:221	:462	1:134	3+ⒻClm 30000	66	5	1	65½	44½	26	21½	Davila J R Jr	b	115	*.50e	75-28	MjstcAnr1131½MstcWll1153¾LttlAbrAn112	Rallied wide	6
31May92-9FL	sly	6f	:222	:462	1:111	3+ⒻHandicap	47	5	6	43½	23½	28	217½	Gutierrez J A	b	116	3.10	72-20	Tby'sTgr12017½MgstcWll1163½LttlAmbrAnn114	2nd best	6
9Jan92-5Aqu	fst	6f	⊡:224	:462	1:121	ⒻClm 35000	63	2	5	55	55	511	58½	Pezua J M	b	119	12.80	73-16	Ctchmnot1171½PhntomHill117noCompnyGirl117	Outrun	6
3Jan92-1Aqu	fst	6f	⊡:231	:463	1:111	ⒻClm 50000	46	6	6	74¾	79½	714	718	Madrid A Jr	b	117	11.70	69-20	EmphaticStyle1135¾Calisty113nkWildWrning113	Outrun	7
18Dec91-4Aqu	fst	6f	⊡:223	:464	1:13	3+ⒻClm 35000	81	6	1	64	64¾	43½	1½	Chavez J F	b	119	8.20	78-25	MgstcWllw119½SxNrrws117½MdstGl117	Up final strides	6
17Nov91-7FL	gd	6f	:231	:48	1:144	3+ⒻAlw 7300	63	2	6	41½	1½	12½	13	Nicol P A Jr	b	122	*.70	72-30	MgstcWllw1223MyLdySmnn1172MkmHppy116	Drew off	6
1Nov91-1Aqu	fst	1	:472	1:124	1:38	3+ⒻClm 45000	71	1	5	54	52¾	54½	512	Chavez J F	b	113	9.30	60-28	Embrcng1134¾DustyDonn1131¾CompnyGrl113	No threat	6
20Oct91-9FL	fst	6f	:22	:452	1:112	3+ⒻAlw 7500	77	4	1	34	31	11	14½	Grabowski J A	b	119	3.20	89-15	MgesticWillow1194½CrftyKtie119hdSssyBb113	Drew off	7
24Aug91-1Sar	fst	6½f	:231	:464	1:19	3+ⒻClm 25000	79	1	4	21½	43	32	1nk	Chavez J F	b	117	6.70	80-14	MstcWll117nkMjstcFrd1141½PrdFrnd117	Lggd in, drvg	8

LATEST WORKOUTS Aug 11 FL 5f fst 1:04 B — Jly 29 FL 4f fst :501 B — Jly 12 FL 5f fst 1:03 H — Jun 28 FL 5f fst 1:013 H

Rather Be Social — Dk. b. or br. f. 4, by Raised Socially—Rather Be Dancing, by Caro—Ir

MADRID A JR (24 4 4 2 .17) — $20,000 — Br.—Pollack Andrea Singer (Ky)

Own.—De Hass Stable — Tr.—Tilak Ileen I (—) — 113

Lifetime 48 3 8 7 $75,200 — 1992 16 1 1 2 $15,460 — 1991 25 2 7 4 $56,860 — Turf 3 0 0 0 — Wet 4 0 0 2 $4,500

26Jly92-7Bel	fst	7f	:224	:454	1:233	3+ⒻAlw 27000	57	7	5	86	87½	67	611½	Pezua J M	b	117	46.80	74-16	HudsonDncr1171½SblWy1171¾MySistrJulit113	No factor	8
19Jly92-3Bel	fst	7f	:224	:461	1:244	ⒻClm 12000	68	1	5	11	13½	16	16½	Pezua J M	b	113	1.90	80-13	RthrBScl1136½TrAlBrr1132ATmThtWs113	Kept to drive	7
3Jly92-4Bel	fm	1⅛	Ⓣ:472	1:112	1:423	ⒻClm 35000	58	6	10	1015	98	107½	1012¼	Madrid A Jr	b	117	25.50	71-15	LfOnthFrm1192¼LvndLgnd1171¾GrtR117	Took up break	10
27Jun92-9Bel	fst	7f	:23	:46	1:241	ⒻClm 12000	52	11	1	62¾	52½	33	37½	Velazquez J R	b	113	12.50	75-12	SpringHnnh1173Plthbbs1064½RthrBScl113	Lacked rally	11
17Jun92-2Bel	fst	6f	:223	:454	1:112	ⒻClm 13000	59	2	8	88	86½	65	55¼	Maple E		115	16.70	78-16	NrthrnWlly1172½Plythbgbys106¾TnCrk113	Chckd early	8
17May92-9Bel	my	7f	:223	:453	1:243	ⒻClm 12000	61	4	10	63½	88¾	32½	33¼	Velazquez J R		113	15.40	78-13	IToo1171½RoylSummit1172RthrBSocil113	Rallied inside	11
9May92-9Bel	gd	6f	:214	:444	1:092	ⒻClm 15500	60	5	6	77	83¾	76½	610	Velazquez J R	b	113	26.10	83-07	Crl'sCmmnd1171½EvrlstngStr1175LckNck117	Wide trip	9
20Apr92-3Aqu	my	6f	:213	:444	1:104	ⒻClm 15500	63	5	5	79	79	65	46½	Velasquez J	b	113	40.50	80-15	Ice Society117¾ Killer Buzz1175½EpicVilla117	Wide trip	7
8Apr92-2Aqu	fst	7f	:232	:474	1:264	ⒻClm 12000	43	7	6	73¾	84	97½	911½	Carr D	b	113	28.50	60-20	KllrBuzz117½NoholmsScrtry117¾TownCrk115	Chckd trn	11
4Apr92-2Aqu	fst	1	:472	1:131	1:393	ⒻClm 13000	48	7	1	1½	32	53¼	76¼	Verge M E	b	115	13.40	58-21	RocktBttl113nkPkboBby1191½GrbrGirl117	Dueled, tired	9

LATEST WORKOUTS Aug 13 Bel tr.t 4f fst :493 B

Bug's Chubbs — Ch. m. 5, by D'Accord—Lightning Bug, by Cornish Prince

MOJICA R JR (6 0 0 0 .00) — $22,500 — Br.—Free F William (NY)

Own.—Watral Michael — Tr.—Brida Dennis J (9 2 1 0 .22) — 115

Lifetime 30 6 3 1 $107,220 — 1992 7 0 0 0 $3,780 — 1991 14 5 2 1 $76,440 — Turf 5 0 0 0 $3,780 — Wet 2 0 0 1 $4,560

27Jly92-4Bel	yl	1	Ⓣ:463	1:113	1:374	ⒻClm 35000	72	5	3	2½	2hd	31½	53¾	Rodriguez RR7	b	1104	10.70	69-29	Slsflower1171LifOnthFrm1192½GrtRviw117	Dueled tired	9
27Jly92-Dead heat																					
28Jun92-8Bel	fm	1⅛	Ⓣ:461	1:092	1:41	3+ⒻⓈMntVrnon	63	6	1	11	11	65½	713¾	Pezua J M	b	113	41.40	77-11	Tlc'sCvntry113nkAsrckt113nkIrshActrss122	Speed, tired	9
28Jun92-Run in Divisions																					
15Jun92-8Bel	fm	6f	Ⓣ:22	:442	1:08	3+ⒻHandicap	81	5	2	2½	2½	32½	44	Pezua J M	b	109	18.40	98 —	Dr.Vlvt113noChchBmb1093½TBDzlng109	Frcd pace tired	6
29May92-7Bel	fm	1	Ⓣ:454	1:101	1:35	ⒻClm 35000	72	7	1	11½	11½	2½	45½	Rodriguez R R	b	117	14.00	82-14	Jolie Britt122hd Oriane1172 Final Road117	Tired	9
20May92-9Bel	fst	7f	:224	:46	1:243	ⒻClm 16500	65	5	3	2½	2hd	31½	56½	Pezua J M	b	115	4.30	75-13	SprlnHnnh1171½DlThrt1172SclDlm117	Frc'd pace, tired	9
26Apr92-4Aqu	yl	1⅛	Ⓣ:50	1:15	1:542	ⒻClm 45000	59	6	3	65	76	77	612½	Goossens L		114	15.40	59-25	IvoryTody1171½MmorBy1151HerCountss113	Done early	7
18Mar92-1Aqu	fst	7f	:23	:472	1:254	ⒻClm 22500	55	4	5	54½	76½	86½	67¾	Goossens L		115	10.90	68-23	SocilDelim117nkMisteeV117noSwtn'SssyGl117	No factor	8
10Jun91-1Bel	fst	7f	:233	:471	1:241	ⒻClm c-17500	21	1	5	3½	63	914	927½	Chavez J F	b	117	*2.10	56-15	SuperbSympathy1172½ⒹAnnd1174¾Kirky'sGirl117	Tired	9
31May91-3Bel	fst	6f	:221	:452	1:101	ⒻClm 17500	83	1	6	54½	53	22	2nk	Chavez J F	b	119	*.80e	89-03	DmdSoll117nkBug'sChubbs1195¾Crfty'sWsh111	Fin fast	7
24May91-3Bel	fst	1⅛	:47	1:123	1:522	ⒻClm 22500	33	3	1	11	1hd	613	628½	Chavez J F	b	115	3.70	38-31	WonnthSn1132Foxcroft119hdLostnFlght117	Speed tired	7

LATEST WORKOUTS Aug 13 Bel tr.t 4f fst :49 B — Aug 6 Bel 4f fst :50 B — Jly 21 Bel 3f fst :382 B

What made Bug's Chubbs so interesting was her series of races since returning as a 5-year-old. She had forged along to match her lifetime top of 15 (note the similar pattern of improvement on the Beyer scale of figures as she worked up to the 81), and then developed a nice intervening pattern—a 22 followed by a 20½ on The Sheets, and a corresponding 63 Beyer followed by a 72. Apparently, the peak figure hadn't knocked her for a loop as it had the year before: She had felt the effects of that race in her last two starts, but she had not fallen apart, especially in light of her most recent race, which involved a hard pace duel going a mile on yielding turf:

Condition Analysis and Speed Figures

XX				BUG'S CHUBBS	F&
9 RACES 90		14 RACES 91		11 RACES 92	

^22+   25AQ30

                                                        v 14AQ 5

g.21   25AQ24
24"   AWAQ11

                                                        17AQ21

                                                        v 35Sr27
                                                        vw 25Sr17

                                        ^=20"   35BE27

                                        =22   Y AWBE28
                                        =15"   V AWBE15
                    32 &db 17BE10
            15+   17BE31   Y 35BE29
                33-   25BE24   =19+   17BE20
            20+   vw 17BE13   23"
            27   Y 25AQ 4
25-   s[AWAQ22   19"   vw&RL 14AQ25   .=23"   50AQ26
32   AWAQ 9   ^20+   vs 25AQ14
               20-   25AQ 4
               G20- Yws AWAQ28
18-   AWAQ18   25-   ] 25AQ18
               23   AWAQ11
23-   AWAQ28   '18   w&JM 25AQ 3
               26   AWAQ15
17+   wMSAQ 7 .22"   Ys AWAQ 7
               18   vw AWAQ27
'31   B MSAQ22

Now, Bug's Chubbs was dropping in claiming price, switching from a double-bug to a journeyman rider, and had the look of a horse that had been legged up in pace duels on turf at longer distances. Two months had elapsed since her return to top form June 15, and if she ran a figure approaching that level again, she was a solid threat. Further, she was ideally situated in the outside post. In one-turn races the outside is a terrific spot for a pace-pressing horse, because the rider has some options: If no one wants the lead, he can angle over and seize the initiative; if the pace is hotly contested, he can opt to stalk the duel from close range without having to hustle up to avoid being shuffled back.

FIFTH RACE
Saratoga
AUGUST 17, 1992

6 FURLONGS. (1.08) CLAIMING. Purse $18,000. Fillies and mares, 3–year–olds and upward. Weights, 3–year–olds, 117 lbs.; older, 122 lbs. Non–winners of two races since July 15 allowed 3 lbs. Of a race since then, 5 lbs. Claiming price $25,000; for each $2,500 to $20,000, 2 lbs. (Races when entered to be claimed for $18,000 or less not considered.)

Value of race $18,000; value to winner $10,800; second $3,960; third $2,160; fourth $1,080. Mutuel pool $315,548. Exacta Pool $587,966

Last Raced	Horse	M/Eqt.A.Wt	PP	St	¼	½	Str	Fin	Jockey	Cl'g Pr	Odds $1
27Jly92 4Bel5	Bug's Chubbs	b 5 115	9	2	43	2½	11½	1½	Mojica R Jr	22500	6.20
31Jly92 5Sar4	Company Girl	b 5 117	6	8	82	8½	6hd	22½	Bailey J D	25000	5.60
26Jly92 7Bel6	Rather Be Social	b 4 113	8	1	74	4½	3½	31½	Madrid A Jr	20000	32.70
1Aug92 10FL5	Magestic Willowa	b 5 117	7	3	6hd	71	72	4hd	Whitley K	25000	2.50
10Aug92 3Sar6	Fond Romance	b 4 117	5	5	5½	61	5½	55	Santagata N	25000	6.20
21Jly92 10FL6	Makin' Honey	b 4 113	1	9	9	9	8½	6½	Cruguet J	20000	28.90
8Jly92 3Bel3	Brave Grecian	b 4 113	2	7	1½	1hd	21½	74	Smith M E	20000	6.20
27Jly92 1Bel5	Mile High Glory	b 6 113	3	6	31	5hd	9	82	Migliore R	20000	4.10
7Aug92 2Sar6	Treegees	b 4 115	4	4	2½	33	41	9	Velazquez J R	22500	8.70

OFF AT 3:18 Start good Won driving Time, :21⁴, :45², :57⁴, 1:10⁴ Track muddy.

$2 Mutuel Prices:

10–(J)–BUG'S CHUBBS	14.40	6.80	6.40
6–(F)–COMPANY GIRL		6.60	4.60
9–(I)–RATHER BE SOCIAL			7.00

$2 EXACTA 10–6 PAID $113.40

Ch. m, by D'Accord—Lightning Bug, by Cornish Prince. Trainer Brida Dennis J. Bred by Free F William (NY).

BUG'S CHUBBS stalked the leaders from outside for a half, surged to the front in upper stretch, opened a clear lead in midstretch then was all out to hold off COMPANY GIRL in the closing strides. COMPANY GIRL, outrun for a half, circled five wide entering the stretch then finding her best stride unleashed a strong late run but could not get up. RATHER BE SOCIAL, reserved early worked her way forward from outside on the turn then rallied mildly to gain a share. MAJESTIC WILLOWA unhurried for a half, failed to threaten while improving her position through the lane. FOND ROMANCE was never a serious threat. MAKIN' HONEY never reached contention. BRAVE GRECIAN set the pace along the inside to the top of the stretch and gradually tired thereafter. MILE HIGH GLORY showed only brief speed. TREEGEES was used up forcing the early pace. MILE HIGH GLORY wore mud caulks. ABOVE THE SALT WAS ORDERED SCRATCHED AT THE GATE BY THE STEWARDS ON THE ADVICE OF THE TRACK VETERINARIAN. ALL MONIES WAGERED ON ABOVE THE SALT IN THE PICK THREE, EXACTA AND MUTUEL POOLS WERE REFUNDED

The Grade 2 Ladies Handicap at Aqueduct on November 27, 1993, offered a fabulous betting opportunity for those with an awareness of forging horses.

The 6–5 favorite and highweight was Turnback the Alarm, and as a four-time Grade 1 winner meeting eight rivals that had combined for the grand total of one graded stakes win, that seemed perfectly reasonable. My first inclination was to concede the race to the favorite and try to find another horse to use in exactas underneath. It became apparent that most of them were evenly matched in terms of Beyer figures that ranged from the upper 80s to low 90s. Fadetta had run a 97 in the Rare Perfume, but she had never been beyond a mile, and had drawn the far outside post—never a good place to be in a two-turn route at Aqueduct. At 5–2 she was a contender, but an unappetizing betting prospect.

One thing that struck me was that it was late in the autumn, and most of these fillies had been through long campaigns. Bold as Silver had raced 15 times without a break; Avie's Daisy was making her 18th start of the year; Silky Feather, Star Guest, Miss Pocket Court, and In Her Glory had also been to the well many times.

Groovy Feeling was the freshest horse in the field, having returned from a June-to-October layoff three starts ago:

Aqueduct

7 ***1¼ MILES.*** (1:591) 123rd Running of THE LADIES HANDICAP. (Grade II) Purse $200,000. Fillies and mares, 3-year-olds and upward. By subscription of $400 each which should accompany the nomination; $1,600 to pass the entry box; $1,600 to start. The purse to be divided 60% to the winner, 22% to second, 12% to third and 6% to fourth. Weights Monday, November 22. Starters to be named at the closing time of entries. Trophies will be presented to the winning owner, trainer and jockey. Closed Wednesday, November 10, with 18 nominations.

1¼ MILES — START — FINISH

1 Groovy Feeling

Own: Donaldson Robert P
MCCAULEY W H (51 7 16 4 .14)

Ro. f. 4
Sire: Groovy (Norcliffe)
Dam: Millie and Me (Wise Exchange)
Br: Clay Catesby W (Ky)
Tr: Ferriola Peter (43 8 10 4 .19)

111

Lifetime Record: 23 7 4 1 $153,487										
1993	11	2	3	1	$79,962	Turf	2	1	0	0 $18,840
1992	12	5	1	0	$73,525	Wet	2	0	0	0 $1,155
Aqu	3	2	0	0	$65,607	Dist	0	0	0	0

13Nov93-6Lrl	yl	1	Ⓣ	:241 :49 1:144 1:402	3↑ ⒻAlw 28000N$Y	80	9	4	53¾	84½	74½	52¾	Verge M E	L 122	5.20	65-32	Ellin B.117¾ Grab The Green1171½ Nashly117nk	No threat	9
28Oct93-9Med	gd	1 1/16	Ⓣ	:231 :472 1:121 1:451	3↑ ⒻAlw 30000N$mY	80	5	3	41¾	61¾	33½	1no	Verge M E	L 115 f	4.10	73-27	Groovy Feeling115no Charlotte Augusta117¾ Lovely Bid1123¾	Driving	7
11Oct93-6Lrl	fst	7f		:233 :47 1:112 1:241	3↑ ⒻAlw 25000R	92	1	1	76	79	34	21½	Prado E S	L 117	10.70	87-18	Mixed Appeal1191½ Groovy Feeling1171½ Lip Sing1225½	Closed	7
20Jun93-8Pha	fst	1		:231 :463 1:114 1:383	3↑ ⒻAlw 25000N$Y	73	1	5	52½	64½	44	46½	Colton R E	L 116	*1.50	79-15	After The Glitter1194½ Meetmenow111½ Quinyan1161½	No rally	7
30May93-7Mth	fst	1 1/16		:23 :47 1:12 1:451	3↑ ⒻAlw 30000N$mY	82	1	3	33	33½	35	36½	Bravo J	L 117	3.70	72-24	Fall Semester1175½ Fran's Folly1171 Groovy Feeling1171¾	Tired late	9
1May93-11Spt	fst	1⅛		:472 1:113 1:364 1:491	3↑ ⒻSixty Sls H-G3	76	8	7	64	54	810	811½	Baird E T	L 114 b	22.50	83-11	Pleasant Baby1121¾ Miss Jealski113nk Steff Graf1151½	Wide, tired	9
17Apr93-8GS	fst	1 1/16		:232 :464 1:114 1:444	3↑ ⒻBetsy Ross HG3	80	1	4	63	52½	58½	56½	Black A S	L 116 f	1.70	84-15	Femma1194¾ Arlenes Money114½ Fall Semester118no	Even effort	10
25Mar93-8Aqu	fst	1⅛	⊡	:473 1:124 1:383 1:512	ⒻAlw 47000N$mY	92	2	2	21½	21	11½	12½	Smith M E	122 f	2.70	86-21	Groovy Feeling1222½ Maxamount1152½ Lady Lear1151	Driving	5
11Mar93-8Lrl	fst	1 1/16		:233 :47 1:114 1:44	ⒻAlw 25000N$Y	91	3	4	43	42½	32½	2hd	Wilson R	L 119	*1.90	90-26	Gallant Stinger114hd Groovy Feeling1196½ Dress Optional1147	Closed	6
20Feb93-9Lrl	fst	1⅛		:484 1:13 1:38 1:504	3↑ ⒻSquan Song H50k	89	7	4	42½	75¾	46	22	Wilson R	L 114	3.20	82-23	Gammy's Alden1122 Groovy Feeling114nk Dress Optional113½	Wide turns	7

WORKOUTS: ●Nov 8 Pha 5f fst 1:002 B 1/20 ●Oct 23 Pha 6f fst 1:141 H 1/4 Oct 4 Pha 4f fst :482 B 3/8 Sep 27 Pha 6f my 1:143 B 1/1

2 Bold as Silver

Own: Amherst Stable
LEON F (75 5 8 15 .07)

Gr. f. 3 (Mar)
Sire: Nasty and Bold (Naskra)
Dam: Silver Judy (Silver Series)
Br: Amherst Stable (Fla)
Tr: Johnson Philip G (25 5 3 2 .20)

110

Lifetime Record: 15 3 3 2 $85,320										
1993	15	3	3	2	$85,320	Turf	4	0	0	0 $3,420
1992	0	M	0	0		Wet	2	1	1	0 $22,660
Aqu	2	1	1	0	$28,880	Dist	0	0	0	0

17Nov93-7Aqu	fst	1⅛	⊗	:502 1:152 1:404 1:533	3↑ ⒻAlw 32000N2X	86	3	3	31	1½	12½	15	Leon F5	110	*.60	68-26	Bold As Silver1105 Chambolle115½ Home By Ten1172	Ridden out	6
24Oct93-5Aqu	fst	1⅛		:501 1:144 1:40 1:523	3↑ ⒻAlw 44000N$mY	89	3	2	1½	1½	2½	2¾	Leon F5	109	8.90	72-30	In Her Glory114¾ Bold As Silver1099 Winning The Day1165½	Gamely	5
9Oct93-2Bel	fst	7f		:234 :473 1:122 1:251	3↑ ⒻAlw 28000N1X	83	6	3	42½	31	1hd	1nk	Leon F5	109	3.10	77-23	Bold As Silver109nk Regal Solution114¾ Shady Willow1176	Wide, driving	6
23Sep93-5Bel	my	7f		:223 :462 1:121 1:252	3↑ ⒻAlw 28000N1X	79	3	6	75¾	63	3nk	2¾	Chavez J F	113	5.70	75-26	Pleasant Courtney108¾ Bold As Silver1131½ Stormbow1134¾	Rallied inside	8
8Sep93-6Bel	fst	1 1/16		:232 :462 1:104 1:433	3↑ ⒻAlw 30000N1X	70	6	8	83¾	62	42	32¾	Chavez J F	113	5.70	81-12	Nine Keys1132½ My Girl Rodes113nk Bold As Silver1131½	Late gain	8
22Aug93-8Sar	fm	1 3/16	Ⓣ	:473 1:114 1:361 1:542	3↑ ⒻAlw 28500N1X	69	2	1	1½	1½	73½	810	Chavez J F	112	17.50	86-13	Northern Emerald1123 Running On E1141½ Russian Tango1121½	Used up	10
9Aug93-6Sar	fst	6f		:22 :45 :571 1:10	3↑ ⒻAlw 26500N1X	74	5	9	98½	77½	53	54½	Santos J A	112	12.40	87-08	Strawberry'sLass1121½ ReglSolution1122 LdyAshford114¾	Saved ground	10
24Jly93-6Bel	fst	1		:24 :472 1:114 1:371	3↑ ⒻAlw 28500N1X	80	3	3	31	41½	31½	23½	Chavez J F	111	2.70	78-16	Sakiyah1133½ Bold As Silver111hd Fleeting Ways1115	Up for place	5
11Jly93-5Bel	fst	1 1/16		:242 :481 1:13 1:433	3↑ ⒻAlw 28500N1X	73	1	2	31½	32	33	31	Pezua J M	111	9.20	83-16	Imah114nk Splendid Launch111¾ Bold As Silver1114	Willingly	7
28Jun93-4Bel	fm	1¼	Ⓣ	:492 1:14 1:381 2:021	ⒻClm 75000	75	1	5	55	64	64	64¾	Samyn J L	111	5.60	74-16	Wonder Wave1112½ Doc's Josephine111nk This Ain'tKansas1131½	No factor	7

WORKOUTS: Nov 14 Bel tr.t 4f fst :482 H 2/16 Nov 10 Bel tr.t 4f fst :484 B 5/31 Nov 3 Bel tr.t 4f fst :50 B 25/55 Oct 4 Bel tr.t 3f fst :354 H 2/14 Sep 3 Bel tr.t 3f fst :361 B 3/7

3 Avie's Daisy

Own: Paraneck Stable
CRUGUET J (50 8 4 7 .16)

Ch. m. 5
Sire: Lord Avie (Lord Gaylord)
Dam: My Little Molly (Golden Eagle II)
Br: Jilerlane Stables (Md)
Tr: Wilson Ronald (12 1 3 0 .08)

113

Lifetime Record : 58 9 11 9 $300,440

1993	17	3	4	1	$127,510	Turf	4	0	0	0	
1992	20	3	4	6	$107,320	Wet	9	3	2	2	$83,860
Aqu	33	8	9	5	$235,940	Dist	0	0	0	0	

20Nov93- 9Med fst 1 1/16 :232 :464 1:113 1:45 3+ ⒻCastle Forbe40k 81 2 8 79¾ 77 63¼ 53½ Cruguet J 122 b 7.70 80-20 After The Glitter1191 Cozzene's Wish1171 Femma113nk Some gain 9
30Oct93- 7Aqu my 1 ⊗ :232 :471 1:134 1:411 3+ ⒻAlw 44000N$mY 86 6 6 46½ 33 3½ 13 McCauley W H 117 fb 5.50 58-33 Avie's Daisy1173 Poolesta117½ Bless Our Home1174½ Wide, driving 7
24Oct93- 6Aqu fst 7f :231 :46 1:102 1:23 3+ ⒻAlw 40000N$Y 89 6 7 76½ 75½ 52¾ 44½ Migliore R 117 b 6.70 85-10 Noble's Honey1173½ MissCloverAppeal117no EndlessDesire119¾ No threat 7
7Oct93- 8Bel fst 1 1/16 :243 :481 1:122 1:434 3+ ⒻAlw 44000N$mY 86 1 4 43½ 42½ 42½ 44½ Migliore R 117 b 7.30 78-22 Testy Trestle1192 Chinese Empress1172½ RegalVictress117nk Lacked rally 6
1Oct93- 8Bel fst 1 1/16 :222 :451 1:10 1:442 3+ ⒻHandicap48k 81 2 4 411 48 37 24½ Migliore R 114 b 9.10 71-25 Vivano1228½ Avie's Daisy114¾ Concorde's Gold1204 Late gain 4
4Sep93- 9Tim fst 1 1/16 :231 :473 1:134 1:48 3+ ⒻAlma North H40k 64 2 6 64½ 57 59 411 Douglas F G 113 b 5.00 60-33 ⒹJazzy One119hd Darinka1134 Starlight Surprise1117 No threat 7
Placed third through disqualification.
23Aug93- 6Sar fm 1 1/16 Ⓣ :25 :501 1:141 1:44 3+ ⒻAlw 46000N$Ym 59 4 6 75½ 78½ 79 814 Leon F5 112 b 45.30 65-16 Irish Actress1171½ Park Dream117nk Her Favorite117nk Outrun 8
12Jly93- 8Bel fst 1 1/16 :24 :473 1:113 1:421 3+ ⒻAlw 46000N$Y 79 5 5 54 52½ 52½ 46¾ Migliore R 116 fb 7.00 84-10 ⒹLizeality116no Queen Of Triumph116¾ Nanner1206 No threat 6
3Jly93- 6Bel sf 1⅜ Ⓣ :484 1:14 1:394 2:052 3+ ⒻAlw 46000N$Y 18 5 7 56 710 729 738 Pezua J M 119 fb 23.20 25-33 Royal Pageant11712 Low Tolerance119½ Ginny Dare1222½ Outrun 7
5Jun93- 3Bel fst 1 :224 :451 1:094 1:363 3+ ⒻAlw 46000N$mY 81 2 7 77½ 55 54½ 54½ Migliore R 119 b 9.40 76-15 Shared Interest1173½ Spinning Round1172 S. S. Sparkle1221½ No threat 7

4 Silky Feather

Own: Powell Stanton P
MIGLIORE R (117 15 13 22 .13)

Dk. b or br f. 3 (Apr)
Sire: Personal Flag (Private Account)
Dam: Fleur de Soie (Graustark)
Br: E. C. Johnston Jr. (NY)
Tr: Violette Richard Jr (10 3 1 2 .30)

113

Lifetime Record : 16 3 3 5 $222,776

1993	12	3	2	4	$217,800	Turf	1	0	0	1	$4,080
1992	4	M	1	1	$4,976	Wet	1	0	1	0	$7,480
Aqu	1	0	1	0	$7,480	Dist	2	0	0	2	$54,000

27Oct93- 6Aqu wf 1⅛ ⊗ :502 1:161 1:414 1:542 3+ ⒻAlw 34000N3X 90 2 3 23 22 21 2¾ Migliore R 114 *.60 63-39 MissPocketCourt117¾ SilkyFether11421 HurryUpMry1141½ Pinched break 4
8Oct93- 6Bel fm 1¼ Ⓣ :474 1:12 1:364 2:014 3+ ⒻAlw 34000N3X 80 5 2 12 1½ 2½ 34 Bailey J D 114 b 2.30 77-18 Belle Nuit114¾ Said Privately1163½ Silky Feather1148½ Bid, weakened 6
4Sep93- 8Bel fst 1⅛ :442 1:09 1:342 1:471 ⒻGazelle H-G1 89 8 6 718 610 45½ 27½ Migliore R 117 b 10.30 85-11 Dispute1207½ Silky Feather117hd In Her Glory112no Rallied inside 8
14Aug93- 9Sar fst 1¼ :464 1:112 1:371 2:032 ⒻAlabama-G1 93 7 5 59 41½ 41½ 33½ Migliore R 121 b 30.90 84-20 SkyBeauty1211½ FuturePretense1211¾ SilkyFether1211½ Drifted, weakened 8
11Jly93- 8Bel fst 1¼ :47 1:103 1:353 2:012 ⒻC C A Oaks-G1 92 3 3 33½ 32 43 32½ Migliore R 121 b 20.60 81-16 Sky Beauty121½ Future Pretense1212 Silky Feather1213 Lacked rally 5
6Jun93- 9Bel fst 1⅛ :464 1:11 1:361 1:493 ⒻMthr Gse-G1 88 2 4 42½ 44 35 38½ Migliore R 121 b 25.40 72-21 Sky Beauty1215 Dispute1213½ Silky Feather1215 No factor 4
8May93- 8Bel fst 1 :224 :453 1:10 1:352 ⒻAcorn-G1 82 5 6 65 54 56½ 413½ Migliore R 121 b 29.90 77-17 Sky Beauty1215½ Educated Risk1212½ In Her Glory1215¾ No threat 6
28Mar93- 9FG fst 1 1/16 :224 :461 1:11 1:434 ⒻF G Oaks-G3 87 2 5 511 56 32 12½ Perrodin E J L 113 b 39.80 95-09 Silky Feather1132¾ She's A Little Shy1212 Sum Runner1215 Driving 7
13Mar93- 6OP fst 1 1/16 :232 :482 1:142 1:47 ⒻAlw 23000N2L 74 1 3 31½ 21½ 1½ 11½ Borel C H L 115 b 7.60 66-23 Silky Feather1151½ Dancing Mahmoud112nk Lady Tasso115nk Driving 8
17Feb93- 6OP fst 1 1/16 :232 :471 1:121 1:443 ⒻAlw 22000N2L 66 6 2 31½ 48 510 512¾ Day P L 120 b 4.00 65-17 Mari's Key112¾ Highest Rank1153 Zilla Peel1126 Tired 6
WORKOUTS: Nov 21 Bel 1 fst 1:381 H 1/3 Nov 16 Bel 5f fst 1:012 B 11/19 Oct 23 Bel 5f fst :594 H 5/58 Sep 30 Bel 6f fst 1:133 H 3/9 ●Aug 29 Sar 5f fst :593 H 1/15

5 Star Guest

Own: Powhatan
DAVIS R G (175 35 29 27 .20)

B. f. 3 (Apr)
Sire: Assert (Be My Guest)
Dam: Violet (Chieftain)
Br: Raymond R. Guest (Ky)
Tr: Whiteley David A (10 2 1 2 .20)

111

Lifetime Record : 16 4 3 6 $105,579

1993	14	4	2	6	$101,479	Turf	6	1	2	3	$39,014
1992	2	M	1	0	$4,100	Wet	3	1	0	1	$24,480
Aqu	2	1	0	0	$20,640	Dist	0	0	0	0	

12Nov93- 6Aqu yl 1⅛ Ⓣ :484 1:143 1:404 1:532 3+ ⒻAlw 34000N3X 91 4 6 75 43 1hd 1¾ Migliore R 117 7.80 76-26 Star Guest117¾ Blazing Kadie1152 Dana's Wedding1155 Wide, driving 10
5Nov93- 6Aqu sly 1⅛ ⊗ :484 1:132 1:392 1:523 3+ ⒻAlw 32000N2X 88 2 2 22½ 21 1hd 1¾ Migliore R 115 2.70 73-30 Star Guest115¾ Cannon Opera11510 Home By Ten1174 Driving 9
14Oct93- 2Bel fst 1 :223 :453 1:101 1:353 3+ ⒻAlw 32000N2X 90 5 5 52½ 31½ 22 24 Antley C W 114 13.50 86-22 Link River1194 Star Guest1144¾ Saratoga Bid1144 Second best 6
26Sep93- 9Bel sly 1 ⊗ :224 :461 1:112 1:382 3+ ⒻAlw 32000N2X 54 6 6 55 44½ 39 311½ Perret C 113 *2.10 65-22 Tiffany Hall1128 R. E. Darla1173½ Star Guest1132 Wide trip 6
10Jly93- 7Bel fm 1¼ Ⓣ :502 1:152 1:393 2:031 3+ ⒻAlw 30500N2X 77 1 5 76 51½ 45 32½ Smith M E 113 *1.60 72-19 Hurry Up Marya1141½ Tiffany Hall117¾ Star Guest1132 Lacked room 7
26Jun93- 7Bel fst 1 1/16 :232 :471 1:122 1:443 3+ ⒻAlw 30500N2X 75 2 4 43½ 32 35½ 311½ Smith M E 112 2.30 68-29 Gravette110¾ Standard Equipment11410 Star Guest1126 No rally 6
5Jun93- 4Bel fm 1 1/16 Ⓣ :233 :464 1:101 1:411 ⒻTanya50k 82 7 7 77½ 63¾ 63½ 31 Desormeaux K J 116 3.90 89-13 Missymooiloveyou116nk Shannie'sDncer121¾ StrGuest1161¾ Belated rally 7
22May93- 3Bel fst 1⅛ :47 1:12 1:372 1:50 ⒻAlw 30500N2X 79 7 6 67½ 64 53½ 58¾ Bailey J D 121 5.60 72-15 TestyTrestle1164½ StndrdEquipment116no DefensSpnding116¾ Four wide 8
10May93- 6Bel fst 1 1/16 :23 :461 1:111 1:443 ⒻAlw 28500N1X 77 7 7 73½ 3½ 12½ 15 Bailey J D 116 *2.10 79-19 Star Guest1165 Life's Walk1162½ Lovely Lyric116no Drew off 7
21Mar93- 6GP fst 1 1/16 :24 :482 1:134 1:473 ⒻAlw 26500N1X 58 3 6 74½ 34 45 45½ Vasquez J 115 *.90 66-20 Future Starlet114½ Miss Kitty Fox1134 Nicely Wild1121 Faded 8
WORKOUTS: Nov 21 Bel 4f fst :483 H 6/16 Nov 4 Bel 3f fst :374 B 17/19 Oct 11 Bel 4f fst :51 B 29/29 Oct 5 Bel 4f fst :492 B 29/50 Sep 25 Bel 4f fst :491 B 30/83 Sep 20 Bel 4f gd :494 B 21/51

6 Turnback The Alarm

Own: Valley View Farm
CARR D (59 2 5 4 .04)

Ro. f. 4
Sire: Darn That Alarm (Jig Time)
Dam: Boomie's Girl E (Figonero)
Br: Burke Walter J (Fla)
Tr: Terrill William V (34 1 2 5 .03)

121

Lifetime Record : 21 8 5 4 $916,504

1993	7	3	0	2	$350,820	Turf	0	0	0	0	
1992	5	3	1	1	$336,496	Wet	3	1	0	1	$63,000
Aqu	5	1	3	0	$121,456	Dist	1	1	0	0	$150,000

6Nov93- 3Aqu sly 1⅛ :471 1:124 1:381 1:51 3+ Stuyvsnt H-G3 96 6 2 2hd 2hd 42½ 44½ Davis R G 118 2.70 76-20 Michelle Can Pass115nk Key Contender1151½ Primitive Hall1132½ Tired 8
16Oct93- 5Bel fst 1⅛ :452 1:091 1:34 1:471 3+ ⒻBeldame-G1 101 2 2 21½ 31 42½ 43¾ Antley C W 123 1.50 89-12 Dispute1191¾ Shared Interest123nk Vivano1231¾ Lacked response 6
19Sep93- 8Bel my 1 1/16 :232 :464 1:103 1:414 3+ ⒻRuffian H-G1 97 4 2 21 21 33 35½ Antley C W 123 2.50 87-16 Shared Interest1142½ Dispute1153 Turnback The Alarm1232½ Drifted, tired 5
5Sep93- 8Bel fst 1 :233 :462 1:104 1:36 3+ ⒻGo For Wand-G1 96 2 1 11 1½ 11 11½ Antley C W 123 1.20 88-14 Turnback The Alarm1231½ Nanner116hd November Snow1161 Driving 4
12Jun93- 8Bel fst 1⅛ :461 1:102 1:351 1:48 3+ ⒻHempstead H-G1 100 3 2 22 1½ 11½ 11½ Antley C W 119 *1.40 89-12 TurnbckThAlrm1191½ Dpution117no You'dBSurprisd11214 Drifted, driving 6
22May93- 8Bel fst 1 1/16 :223 :452 1:101 1:43 3+ ⒻShuvee H-G1 93 1 3 2½ 1½ 1hd 1¾ Antley C W 117 *1.70 87-15 TurnbackTheAlarm117¾ SharedInterest1132 Vivno112nk Drifted, driving 9
8May93- 1Bel fst 6f :221 :452 :571 1:10 3+ ⒻAlw 40000N$Y 92 3 3 2½ 31 31½ 31¾ Antley C W 119 *.40 88-17 Makin Faces1211 Lady Sage119¾ Turnback The Alarm1192½ Lacked rally 5
11Jly92- 8Bel fst 1¼ :50 1:133 1:38 2:032 ⒻC C A Oaks-G1 92 6 3 32 1hd 1½ 11½ Antley C W 121 *1.40 74-18 Turnback The Alarm1211½ Easy Now121 Pleasant Stage121 Driving 6
7Jun92- 8Bel fst 1⅛ :452 1:093 1:352 1:484 ⒻMothr Goose-G1 95 1 5 53½ 41 1hd 12½ Antley C W 121 7.20 85-22 TurnbackTheAlrm1212½ EsyNow1211½ QueenofTriumph121 Wide driving 7
23May92- 8Bel fst 1 :224 :453 1:10 1:35 ⒻAcorn-G1 91 1 1 1½ 11 2hd 33½ Antley C W 121 b 3.40 91-07 ProspectorsDelite1212 PlsntStg1211½ TurnbckThAlrm121 Speed, wknd 12
WORKOUTS: Nov 20 Bel tr.t 6f fst 1:131 B 1/2 ●Nov 13 Bel 5f fst :584 H 1/24 Nov 1 Aqu 5f my 1:024 B (d) 1/1 ●Oct 25 Bel 5f fst :592 H 1/22 ●Oct 12 Bel 4f fst :481 H 1/28 ●Oct 7 Bel 5f fst :594 H 1/26

7 Miss Pocket Court

Own: Nauman Eugene E
BRAVO J (31 7 7 3 .23)

B. f. 4
Sire: Court Trial (In Reality)
Dam: Pocket Power (Full Pocket)
Br: Mangurian Mr-Mrs H T Jr (Fla)
Tr: Hushion Michael E (28 9 4 2 .32)

110

Lifetime Record : 46 9 7 11 $146,414

1993	15	5	1	4	$89,230	Turf	12	2	0	4	$37,500
1992	20	3	4	5	$43,685	Wet	5	1	1	1	$23,710
Aqu	1	1	0	0	$20,400	Dist	1	1	0	0	$12,000

Entered 25Nov93- 7 AQU
27Oct93- 6Aqu wf 1⅛ ⊗ :502 1:161 1:414 1:542 3+ ⒻAlw 34000N3X 91 4 1 13 12 11 1¾ Lovato F Jr 117 f 1.40 64-39 Miss Pocket Court117¾ Silky Feather11421 Hurry Up Marya1141½ Driving 4
10Oct93- 4Bel fst 1 1/16 :23 :461 1:111 1:442 3+ ⒻClm c-50000 85 2 3 3nk 1hd 11 21 Alvarado F T 117 2.70 79-25 Fran's Folly1151 Miss Pocket Court1172½ Huckster Rose1135½ Gamely 6
Claimed from Miron Stephen E, Debonis Robert Trainer
12Sep93- 1Bel fst 1¼ ⊗ :49 1:132 1:39 2:033 3+ ⒻClm 35000 91 3 1 11 11½ 16 116 Alvarado F T 117 *1.60 73-17 Miss Pocket Court11716 Pushia1173 Won Scent1173 Mild drive 6
3Sep93- 9Bel fst 1 :233 :462 1:111 1:361 3+ ⒻClm 35000 79 2 10 64½ 52½ 34 38½ Alvarado F T 117 6.70 79-15 Butter Cream1178 Pontificate113nk Miss Pocket Court1174½ Mild rally 11
14Aug93- 4Sar fm 1⅛ Ⓣ :472 1:112 1:36 1:48 3+ ⒻClm 47500 72 10 9 86 96½ 93 85½ Alvarado F T 115 28.70 84-14 Home By Ten1131½ Fashion Miss119nk Turkolady117hd No factor 11
26Jly93- 2Bel fm 1¼ Ⓣ :493 1:134 1:38 2:02 ⒻClm c-35000 76 4 2 2hd 2hd 21 34½ Smith M E 117 *1.50 76-12 Bold Ryna1173½ Ivory Today1171 Miss Pocket Court1172 Forced pace 10
Claimed from West Point Stable, Reid Mark J Trainer
1Jly93- 6Bel fm 1¼ Ⓣ :501 1:141 1:374 2:024 ⒻClm 50000 79 5 4 33½ 33 33½ 42½ Smith M E 117 3.00 74-16 High Talent117½ Stephen's Joy113nk Insurprise1151½ Lacked rally 9
10Jun93- 2Bel gd 1⅜ Ⓣ :471 1:132 1:382 2:15 ⒻClm c-35000 84 8 7 65 42 1hd 1hd Smith M E 117 3.40 76-19 Miss Pocket Court117hd Stephen's Joy1175½ Sweet N' Saxy1175 Driving 9
Claimed from Miron Stephen E, Debonis Robert Trainer
21May93- 2Bel fm 1¼ Ⓣ :484 1:132 1:373 2:022 ⒻClm 35000 82 10 11 97½ 41½ 2½ 32 Smith M E 117 3.00 76-20 Turkolady1171½ Stephen's Joy119hd Miss Pocket Court1174 Bid, hung 12
1May93- 6Hia fm 1⅛ Ⓣ 1:483 3+ ⒻAlw 17000N3X 78 4 6 614 512 45½ 42½ Douglas R R L 120 2.90 93-02 Pleasant Reef117hd Bounding Boldly1202 Hopeful Angel117no Late rally 10
WORKOUTS: Nov 22 Bel tr.t 1 fst 1:442 B 1/2 Nov 12 Bel 5f fst 1:012 H 8/20 Nov 5 Bel tr.t 4f gd :49 B 10/32 Oct 23 Bel 7f fst 1:33 B 4/5 Sep 25 Bel tr.t 4f fst :48 B 3/61

8 In Her Glory

Dk. b or br f. 3 (Apr)
Sire: Miswaki (Mr. Prospector)
Dam: Forever Waving (Hoist the Flag)
Br: Foxfield (Ky)
Tr: Schulhofer Flint S (27 3 3 8 .11)

Own: Dash Stable
BAILEY J D (53) 11 10 6 .21)

111

	Lifetime Record:	14 5 1 3	$149,484
1983	12 4 0 3	$129,144	Turf 1 0 0 0
1982	2 1 1 0	$20,340	Wet 0 0 0 0
Aqu	4 3 1 0	$75,480	Dist 0 0 0 0

(past performance lines for In Her Glory)

WORKOUTS: Nov 19 Bel 5f fst :59 B 8/24 Nov 13 Bel 4f fst :47 H 3/27 Nov 2 Bel 4f fst :48 B 5/20 Oct 16 Bel 4f fst :47 B 8/29 Oct 10 Bel 5f fst 1:00¹ H 1/12

9 Fadetta

Dk. b or br f. 3 (Mar)
Sire: Fappiano (Mr. Prospector)
Dam: Glorious Natalie (Reflected Glory)
Br: Brereton C. Jones & Halo Farms (Ky)
Tr: Mott William J (27 7 3 5 .26)

Own: Mohammed Al Maktoum
PERRET C (27 5 1 4 .19)

111

	Lifetime Record:	5 3 2 0	$81,610
1983	4 2 2 0	$66,010	Turf 0 0 0 0
1982	1 1 0 0	$15,600	Wet 0 0 0 0
Aqu	1 1 0 0	$15,600	Dist 0 0 0 0

(past performance lines for Fadetta)

WORKOUTS: Nov 23 Bel tr.t 5f fst 1:02 B 2/15 Nov 16 Bel 7f fst 1:26⁴ B 1/1 Nov 10 Bel 5f fst 1:01¹ B 13/34 Nov 4 Bel 7f fst 1:31³ B 3/3 Oct 29 Bel 5f fst 1:04³ B 22/26 Oct 23 Bel 4f fst :50² B 64/86

Groovy Feeling had run a Beyer of 92 in her comeback race, a figure that matched her best races from earlier in the year. Thoro-Graph showed a similar pattern: the 9½ matched her best races back in March.

That she had returned to match her best figures was a positive sign, and so was the intervening pattern in a pair of grass races at the Meadowlands and at Laurel: She had "bounced" from the exertions of her comeback race, but the second grass race had been as good as the first one, especially in view of the fact that she displayed a two-move running line, racing within four lengths of the lead after a half-mile, dropping more than eight lengths off the lead after six furlongs, then gaining in position and in lengths at the stretch call and again to the finish, all while carrying 122 pounds—five more pounds than the top three finishers.

GROOVY FEELING			'89 ro m Groovy - Millie And Me
2-YEAR-OLD	**3-YEAR-OLD**	**4-YEAR-OLD**	**5-YEAR-OLD**
DEC	AQU 12	AQU 9^2my	
NOV		AQU 9^2 / LRL -12^1yl	
OCT	PHA 14^3 / PHA 21wf / MED 14^2	MED -13^3gd / LRL (9^2)	
SEP	PHA 17^1		
AUG	MTH 14 / MTH 16pd / MTH 28^1wf		
JUL			
JUN	MTH 20^3ry	PHA 15^3	
MAY	MTH 21 / PHA 17^3 / PHA 17^L	MTH 11^1	
APR		SPT 14^2 / GS 14^3	
MAR		AQU (9^2) / LRL (9^2)	AQU 8^2gd
FEB		LRL 10^2	AQU 7^2
JAN		AQU 12	AQU 8^3 / AQU 9

It had now been nearly seven weeks since Groovy Feeling's good return figure, and there was a reasonable chance she was ready for another forward move. There was little question Turnback the Alarm was the fastest and classiest entrant, but Groovy Feeling's conditioning edge over a slew of battle-worn rivals pointed her out as a live longshot at 12–1.

SEVENTH RACE
Aqueduct
NOVEMBER 27, 1993

1¼ MILES. (1.59^{1}) 123rd Running of THE LADIES HANDICAP. Purse $200,000. Fillies and mares, 3-year-olds and upward. By subscription of $400 each which should accompany the nomination; $1,600 to pass the entry box; $1,600 to start. The purse to be divided 60% to the winner, 22% to second, 12% to third and 6% to fourth. Weights Monday, November 22. Starters to be named at the closing time of entries. Trophies will be presented to the winning owner, trainer and jockey. Closed Wednesday, November 10, with 18 nominations.

Value of Race: $200,000 Winner $120,000; second $44,000; third $24,000; fourth $12,000. Mutuel Pool $287,374.00 Exacta Pool $464,110.00 Triple Pool $303,873.00

Last Raced	Horse	M/Eqt.	A.	Wt	PP	¼	½	¾	1	Str	Fin	Jockey	Odds $1
13Nov93 ^{6}Lrl^{5}	Groovy Feeling		4	111	1	$1^{1\frac{1}{2}}$	1^{1}	$1^{1\frac{1}{2}}$	1^{1}	1^{3}	1^{3}	McCauley W H	12.00
6Nov93 ^{3}Aqu^{4}	Turnback The Alarm		4	121	6	$3^{\frac{1}{2}}$	$3^{\frac{1}{2}}$	$3^{1\frac{1}{2}}$	$2^{1\frac{1}{2}}$	2^{1}	$2^{\frac{1}{2}}$	Carr D	1.20
20Nov93 ^{9}Med^{5}	Avie's Daisy	b	5	113	3	$6^{1\frac{1}{2}}$	5^{hd}	6^{9}	4^{hd}	$3^{\frac{1}{2}}$	$3^{1\frac{1}{2}}$	Cruguet J	28.40
24Oct93 ^{5}Aqu^{1}	In Her Glory		3	112	8	4^{3}	4^{2}	4^{hd}	6^{2}	$5^{1\frac{1}{2}}$	4^{1}	Bailey J D	8.30
10Oct93 ^{7}Bel^{2}	Fadetta		3	112	9	9	9	$8^{1\frac{1}{2}}$	$7^{3\frac{1}{2}}$	$6^{\frac{1}{2}}$	5^{hd}	Perret C	2.50
17Nov93 ^{7}Aqu^{1}	Bold as Silver		3	110	2	5^{hd}	6^{4}	5^{hd}	3^{hd}	4^{1}	6^{6}	Leon F	36.10
27Oct93 ^{6}Aqu^{1}	Miss Pocket Court	f	4	110	7	2^{1}	2^{1}	2^{hd}	5^{1}	7^{9}	$7^{10\frac{1}{2}}$	Bravo J	21.70
12Nov93 ^{6}Aqu^{1}	Star Guest		3	111	5	$7^{\frac{1}{2}}$	$8^{3\frac{1}{2}}$	7^{2}	8^{16}	8	8	Davis R G	20.00
27Oct93 ^{6}Aqu^{2}	Silky Feather		3	113	4	$8^{3\frac{1}{2}}$	$7^{\frac{1}{2}}$	9	9	—	—	Migliore R	5.70

Silky Feather: Eased

OFF AT 3:25 Start Good. Won driving. Time, :24, :49, 1:13^{3}, 1:39^{1}, 2:05^{4} Track fast.

$2 Mutuel Prices:			
1-(A)-GROOVY FEELING	26.00	8.20	8.00
6-(F)-TURNBACK THE ALARM		3.40	3.20
3-(C)-AVIE'S DAISY			8.20

$2 EXACTA 1-6 PAID $116.40 $2 TRIPLE 1-6-3 PAID $1,298.00

Ro. f, by Groovy–Millie and Me, by Wise Exchange. Trainer Ferriola Peter. Bred by Clay Catesby W (Ky).

GROOVY FEELING sprinted clear in the early stages, raced uncontested on the lead to the turn, then edged away under steady right hand encouragement. TURNBACK THE ALARM settled just behind the early leaders while saving ground, angled out while launching her bid on the turn, drifted out in midstretch, then outfinished AVIE'S DAISY for the place. AVIE'S DAISY reserved for six furlongs, split horses while advancing on the turn, then rallied mildly to gain a share. IN HER GLORY raced within striking distance from outside to the turn and lacked a strong closing response. FADETTA far back early, closed the gap a bit on the turn, then lacked a further response. BOLD AS SILVER made a run along the rail to reach contention on the turn and flattened out. MISS POCKET COURT forced the pace to reach contention on the turn, flattened out. STAR GUEST never reached contention. SILKY FEATHER steadied at the start, was never close and was eased in the stretch. MISS POCKET COURT wore mud caulks.

The Recovery Line

Statistical studies have identified horses making their third start back from a layoff as likely candidates for improvement. But by now the increasingly sophisticated handicapping community is well aware of this fact, and as a result such horses seldom catch anyone by surprise. It is not foreordained, however, that horses must return to top form the third time back; returnees with attractive patterns sometimes improve deeper into their form cycle. Handicappers with the means to anticipate the likeliest ones may be in a good position after the crowd has abandoned ship.

Explosive and forging principles can be applied effectively to horses that have had a few starts since returning from a layoff. The pattern is slightly different, but the basic premise is similar: First time back, the horse runs a figure several lengths slower than its previous best; this initial exertion knocks it off form for a few races, but the horse then signals impending improvement by "circling" or "looping" back around to equal or slightly surpass the initial comeback figure.

Permit had developed such a pattern—a "recovery line," as termed by Len Friedman—when entered in Aqueduct's fifth race on November 18, 1992:

5 **6½ FURLONGS.** (1.15) ALLOWANCE. Purse $28,000. 3-year-olds and upward which have never won two races other than Maiden, Claiming or Starter. Weight: 3-year-olds 120 lbs. Older 122 lbs. Non-winners of a race other than Maiden or Claiming since November 1 allowed 3 lbs. Of such a race since October 15, 5 lbs.

Hope Us — B. g. 4, by Tridessus—Hope At Last, by Cutlass

Uncas Chief — B. c. 3(Mar), by Ogygian—Lido Isle, by Far North

Crafty Coventry — Ch. c. 3(May), by Crafty Prospector—Kate Coventry, by Viceregal

[28]

Rockford — Ch. c. 3(Feb), by Bucksplasher—Dedicated to B F, by Master Derby
Br.—Turesdale B A & Pamela (Fla)
Tr.—Toner James J (9 1 1 1 .11)
DAVIS R G (96 17 9 11 .18)
Own.—Kimram Stable
115
Lifetime 27 5 4 2 $83,116 | 1992 16 3 2 1 $57,658 | 1991 11 2 2 1 $25,458 | Wet 9 4 1 1 $49,131

2Nov92- 5Aqu fst 6f :223 :452 1:101 Clm 45000 90 3 1 1½ 1½ 11½ 12½ Davis R G b 113 5.00 90-18 Rockford1132½CaseStudy117½OceanSplsh117 Drfted drv 7
11Oct92- 2Bel gd 6f :221 :451 1:103 Clm 50000 80 1 1 1½ 1hd 2½ 42¾ Bailey J D b 117 14.20 84-18 PerlssPrformr117nkYros1171½GotchLst117 Dueled, tired 8
27Sep92- 2Bel my 6f :22 :444 1:092 Clm 70000 39 3 2 2hd 44 611 620½ Bailey J D b 113 *1.10 72-14 Hwk'sFlm1142½GtchLst1131¾LrdWllstn113 Dueled, tired 6
11Sep92- 1Bel sly 6f :22 :444 1:101 Clm 70000 87 1 1 2hd 1½ 12 21½ Davis R G b 113 3.30 88-10 BnAl'sRllh1171½Rockford1133RoscommnPrd113 Gamely 6
11Sep92-Originally scheduled on turf
30Aug92- 4Sar fst 6f :221 :45 1:09 3↑ Alw 28000 58 4 4 72¾ 53 66 615¾ Bailey J D b 112 15.70 83-08 BorderCat1129CseStudy1121TheGretM.B.112 No factor 7
25Jun92- 1Bel my 6f :22 :45 1:10 Clm 50000 88 5 2 1½ 11½ 13½ 13 Bailey J D b 117 3.40 90-09 Rockford1173RomanChorus117nkPayforPlay117 Driving 7
13Jun92- 3Bel fst 6f :221 :453 1:103 Clm 70000 73 3 2 2½ 2hd 53½ 69½ Bailey J D b 113 6.10 78-18 IrshDmn113½PrlssPrfrmr1133RmnChrs115 Dueled, tired 6
1Jun92- 6Bel sly 6f :22 :444 1:093 3↑ Alw 28000 48 4 5 43½ 56 59 519½ McMahon H I7 b 105 *1.00 73-13 Tlc'sBd1174LIrLIt1175½RchrdOfEnglnd112 Broke slow 5
1Jun92-Awarded fourth purse money
10May92- 5Bel sly 6f :221 :444 1:092 Clm 50000 98 7 2 1hd 1½ 12 13 Bailey J D b 117 5.40 93-12 Rockford1173AlienShore1134HighestLevl106 Drew clear 8
27Apr92- 5Aqu fst 6f :213 :441 1:101 Clm 70000 63 4 7 31 44½ 59 613 Santos J A b 114 6.70 77-14 UnrelMot1137½LitheFntsy1131½WinningForce115 Faded 7
LATEST WORKOUTS Nov 12 Bel tr.t 4f fst :501 B ●Oct 29 Bel 3f fst :342 H ●Oct 23 Bel tr.t 5f fst 1:014 H Oct 7 Bel tr.t 4f fst :49 B

Midnight Sunny — Ch. g. 4, by Sunny North—Glorious Evening, by Jig Time
Br.—Big C Farms (Fla)
Tr.—Marti Carlos (2 0 0 0 .00)
CORPES M A (5 0 0 0 .00)
Own.—Fabjac Stables
117
Lifetime 28 6 8 3 $86,997 | 1992 5 2 2 0 $22,420 | 1991 11 2 3 3 $40,720 | Turf 1 0 0 0 | Wet 4 2 2 0 $24,230

6Nov92- 2Aqu my 7f :23 :461 1:253 3↑ Clm c-14000 76 6 1 2½ 1hd 1hd 1hd Velazquez J R b 117 *1.30 77-18 MdnghtSnny117hdMrThnElt113¾TwrOfTrsrs119 Driving 7
6Nov92-Claimed from Andy Mart Stable, Figueroa Carlos R Jr Trainer
12Oct92- 1Bel my 6f :22 :45 1:084 3↑ Clm 25000 81 3 2 21 2hd 23 27½ Velazquez J R b 117 4.00 88-09 Wrgod1157½MidnightSunny117nkAncntSuc110 2nd best 6
21Sep92- 9Bel fst 6f :221 :452 1:11 3↑ Clm 14000 87 3 9 21 1hd 1½ 13 Velazquez J R b 117 *2.40 85-18 MidnightSunny1173NobleOffic119hdWlkonir119 Driving 9
2Sep92- 2Bel fst 6f :22 :451 1:102 3↑ Clm 14000 81 4 2 31½ 1½ 1½ 2½ Velazquez J R b 117 3.10 87-15 NobleOffice113½MidnightSunny117¾Wlkonir117 Gamely 10
10Jly92- 1Bel fst 6f :222 :45 1:094 Clm c-35000 73 2 1 32 44 78½ 710½ Santos J A b 117 10.80 80-11 Reappeal1172¾ Talc's Bid1171 Two Eagles117 Tired 7
10Jly92-Claimed from Maynard Robert, Kimmel John C Trainer
23Nov91- 5Aqu gd 6f :22 :451 1:101 3↑ Alw 28000 88 1 7 1½ 1hd 1hd 41½ Santos J A b 115 15.70 88-14 SllsCrr115noCrrsPlsr1151½RdHtRd115 Dueled weakened 8
31Oct91- 8Aqu fst 6f :223 :461 1:104 3↑ Alw 28000 74 4 2 42 42 66 68¾ Velazquez J R b 114 11.00 78-19 ShiningBid114¾RedHotRed1141¾MichelMunyk114 Tired 8
7Oct91- 7Bel fst 6f :222 :451 1:10 3↑ Alw 28000 87 1 1 2½ 1hd 31 32¾ Santos J A b 114 6.90 87-11 SngsAccnt114¾ShllsChrmr1142MdnhtSnn114 Weakened 7
16Aug91- 5Sar fst 7f :222 :443 1:222 Clm 72500 86 5 3 3½ 33½ 31 34¾ Santos J A b 115 *2.10 88-11 DvddDcd1174Pnn'sBck113¾MdnghtSnn115 Lacked rally 7
7Aug91- 1Sar fst 6f :222 :453 1:094 Clm 50000 97 3 4 1½ 11 11½ 12 Santos J A b 117 6.30 95-09 MidnightSunny1172FortyHells1133Chels'sPt113 Driving 7
LATEST WORKOUTS Oct 27 Aqu 3f fst :363 H

Permit — B. c. 3(Apr), by Imperial Fling—Logiealmond, by Master Derby
Br.—Shields Joseph V Jr (Fla)
Tr.—Galluscio Dominic G (11 0 2 2 .00)
ROMERO R P (71 6 10 8 .08)
Own.—Shields Joseph V Jr
115
Lifetime 18 3 5 1 $73,976 | 1992 15 3 3 0 $66,576 | 1991 3 M 2 1 $7,400 | Wet 4 0 0 0 $4,836

8Nov92- 1Aqu fst 1 :47 1:113 1:37 Clm 50000 79 8 1 1hd 1½ 1½ 2¾ Romero R P 117 9.40 76-24 Danzig's Dance117¾ Permit117no WildDante106 Gamely 9
25Oct92- 9Aqu fst 7f :23 :464 1:25 3↑ Alw 28000 75 10 1 2½ 1½ 3½ 95½ Krone J A b 114 8.30 75-19 RomnChors114hdAncntSc117½BoldlyDn116 Dueled, tired 11
10Oct92- 1Bel my 6f :22 :442 1:082 Gulch 72 6 5 56 58 58½ 412½ Migliore R b 115 24.40 86 — Detox1153¾ Belong to Me1225½ BorderCat119 No threat 6
27Sep92- 2Bel my 6f :22 :444 1:092 Clm 75000 79 6 3 54 34 35½ 45 Migliore R b 117 5.70 88-14 Hwk'sFlm1142½GotchLst1131¾LordWllstn113 Lk'd rally 6
19Aug92- 9Sar my 7f :221 :443 1:233 3↑ Alw 28000 59 6 3 2hd 2½ 94½ 811¾ Migliore R b 113 10.00 75-17 Keratoid112nkBorderCat112½Prioritizer112 Steadied str 10
19Aug92-Placed seventh through disqualification
7Aug92- 9Sar fst 6f :214 :443 1:10 3↑ Alw 28000 72 10 4 62 41¾ 42 86½ Migliore R b 113 5.30 88-10 RnsGrsn1121½RchrdOfEnlnd112hdMnR112 Flattened out 11
6Jun92- 2Bel my 1⅛ :451 1:092 1:413 3↑ Affirmed 91 2 1 13 12 22½ 68 Pezua J M b 109 22.50 86-08 MchllCnPss1195Isn'tThtSpcl115hdFrllW115 Speed, tired 8
21May92- 4Bel fst 7f :222 :453 1:223 Clm 70000 95 3 4 23 1hd 12½ 12¾ Migliore R b 113 14.40 91-16 Permit1132¾ Polonium1132½ Roman Chorus113 Driving 7
29Mar92- 1Aqu fst 6½f :224 :462 1:164 Alw 28000 61 3 2 2hd 3½ 49½ 415¾ Migliore R b 117 2.80 78-17 BlongtoM1178¾RomnChors1172TrDtch117 Dueled inside 4
21Mar92- 8Aqu gd 7f :22 :443 1:213 Bay Shore 68 5 2 32 31 812 916¾ Rojas R I b 114 60.30 80-11 ThreePet1143½Goldwter117noBstDcortd114 Bobbled brk 10
21Mar92-Grade II
LATEST WORKOUTS Nov 6 Bel 3f sly :363 B Nov 2 Bel tr.t 4f fst :49 B Oct 20 Bel 4f fst :50 B Oct 7 Bel 4f fst :503 B

Real Cielo — Ch. c. 3(Mar), by Conquistador Cielo—Lady Calpurnia, by Proudest Roman
Br.—Stephens Lucille E (NY)
Tr.—Stephens Woodford C (3 0 0 0 .00)
BAILEY J D (70 14 15 15 .20)
Own.—Stephens Lucille E
115
Lifetime 20 3 6 0 $93,920 | 1992 15 2 6 0 $79,240 | 1991 5 1 0 0 $14,680 | Turf 2 0 0 0 $180 | Wet 4 1 1 0 $25,240

6Nov92- 1Aqu my 6f :221 :452 1:10 3↑ Alw 28000 53 1 4 55 55 54½ 415½ Migliore R 115 2.20 75-18 Prepornt1153½StrtFight1152CrriedIntersl120 No threat 5
25Oct92- 9Aqu fst 7f :23 :464 1:25 3↑ Alw 28000 82 1 11 64½ 52½ 52 41¾ Perret C 114 *2.60 78-19 RomnChors114hdAncntSc117½BldlyDn116 Broke slowly 11
15Oct92- 8Bel fst 6f :223 :453 1:101 3↑ Alw 28000 82 6 5 53 5¾ 2hd 21 Maple E 114 2.90 88-15 DcisionMkr1171RlCilo114noBnAl'sRullh114 Up for place 7
8Oct92- 7Bel fst 1 :46 1:11 1:363 3↑ Alw 31000 88 6 6 52¾ 41½ 21 22½ Maple E 114 5.30 85-13 PrivtTrsurr1142½RlCilo1141¼SprklingSky114 Rlld inside 8
27Sep92- 8Bel sly 7f :223 :46 1:242 3↑ [S]Hudson H 73 3 9 86½ 62½ 72¾ 76¾ Maple E 111 3.80 76-14 ArgylLk113nkWhAlng110noMjsty'sTm114 Steadied early 9
10Sep92- 8Bel sly 7f :224 :454 1:224 3↑ Alw 28000 87 1 6 65½ 33 23 22¾ Maple E 113 *1.50 87-17 CseStudy1132¾RlCilo1131¼RomnChorus113 Up for place 7
27Aug92- 3Sar gd 7f :23 :454 1:23 Clm 75000 91 6 2 64¾ 33 1hd 13 Maple E 112 5.70 90-12 RelCielo1123RomnChorus112hdHwk'sFlme113 Wide drv 6
10Aug92- 1Sar fst 1 :454 1:102 1:362 Clm 70000 86 3 4 43 41½ 32 4nk Antley C W 115 10.50 — — BordrCt117nkRomnChrs113hdWdnWgn117 Carried wide 6
1Aug92- 1Sar my 1 :453 1:104 1:381 3↑ [S]Alw 29000 76 2 3 22½ 21 2½ 1¾ Maple E 112 *.60 — — RelCielo112¾Drminthdywy1173InnrTruth117 Hard drive 8
25Jly92- 3Bel fst 6f :224 :462 1:103 3↑ [S]Alw 27000 74 7 7 52½ 3½ 52½ 41¾ Maple E 111 *.70 85-15 Jinglic1111TmmyTwo106¾MorThnElt117 Checked, wide 7
LATEST WORKOUTS Nov 14 Bel 4f fst :493 B Nov 4 Bel 4f sly :503 B Oct 23 Bel 4f fst :482 B Oct 13 Bel 4f fst :483 B

On the Beyers, it appeared as though it would take a figure in the range of 90 to win this race. Hope Us, the 8–5 favorite, had run a 94 recently; Rockford had run a 90 last out; Uncas Chief, Midnight Sunny, and Real Cielo regularly ran in the mid-80s.

Permit had run figures of 95 and 91 in May and June before going to the shelf for two months. Those figures were good enough to contend at 6–1, but what were his chances of running back to that level? Pretty good, judging from his pattern on the Beyers and Thoro-Graph: Permit recorded a 79 Beyer off a five-week break, regressed to 72 and 75, and then rebounded to the telltale 79 on November 8. Permit's Thoro-Graph history revealed a nearly identical cycle— a 13½, which was 3½ points off his career best, followed by a pair of 16s, and the key "recovery" figure of 13¼ last out:

PERMIT			'89 b h Imperial Fling - Logiealmond
2-YEAR-OLD	**3-YEAR-OLD**	**4-YEAR-OLD**	**5-YEAR-OLD**
AQU 21	AQU 8sy		
AQU 20¹gd AQU 25¹	AQU 10		
	AQU 13 AQU (13¹)		
	AQU 16¹ BEL 16¹my		
	BEL (13²my)		
	SAR 21gd SAR 16¹		
		SAR 9 BEL −11¹	
	BEL 13sy	BEL −12²	
	BEL 10	BEL 11² AQU 7	
		AQU 8	
	AQU 21¹ AQU 19¹gd		
	AQU 21 AQU 13	AQU 11² AQU 12 AQU 8	
	AQU 16² AQU 17 AQU 16²	AQU 8	

Condition Analysis and Speed Figures

Off this line, Permit ran another 13, good enough to win the race at $14.80, and then went on to a productive winter campaign, winning several more times while rising in class, and working his way to three consecutive 8s and ultimately a 7 in late April.

FIFTH RACE
Aqueduct
NOVEMBER 18, 1992

6 ½ FURLONGS. (1.15) ALLOWANCE. Purse $28,000. 3-year-olds and upward which have never won two races other than Maiden, Claiming or Starter. Weight: 3-year-olds 120 lbs. Older 122 lbs. Non-winners of a race other than Maiden or Claiming since November 1 allowed 3 lbs. Of such a race since October 15, 5 lbs.

Value of race $28,000; value to winner $16,800; second $6,160; third $3,360; fourth $1,680. Mutuel pool $172,403. Exacta Pool $348,582.

Last Raced	Horse	M/Eqt.A.Wt	PP	St	¼	½	Str	Fin	Jockey	Odds $1
8Nov92 ¹Aqu²	Permit	3 115	6	1	3 1½	2 1½	2 2½	1 1	Romero R P	6.40
2Nov92 ⁵Aqu¹	Rockford	b 3 115	4	6	1½	1½	1 hd	2 1¾	Davis R G	4.30
6Nov92 ¹Aqu⁴	Real Cielo	3 115	7	3	5½	4 1	3½	3¾	Bailey J D	2.70
23Oct92 ⁸Aqu⁸	Crafty Coventry	3 115	3	4	7	6½	4 2	4 1½	Migliore R	5.00
8Nov92 ⁷Aqu⁴	Hope Us	4 117	1	5	6½	7	5 hd	5 2½	Madrid A Jr	1.60
6Nov92 ²Aqu¹	Midnight Sunny	b 4 117	5	2	4½	5½	6 6	6 15	Corpes M A	26.80
19Aug92 ⁹Sar¹⁰	Uncas Chief	b 3 115	2	7	2 1	3½	7	7	Smith M E	22.20

OFF AT 2:17 Start good for all but UNCAS CHIEF and ROCKFORD. Won driving. Time, :23⁴, :47¹, 1:11³, 1:18¹ Track fast.

$2 Mutuel Prices:

6-(F)-PERMIT	14.80	7.40	4.20
4-(D)-ROCKFORD		6.00	3.80
7-(G)-REAL CIELO			2.80

$2 EXACTA 6-4 PAID $67.80

A month later, another recovery-line opportunity came in the form of World Contender.

WORLD CONTENDER		'88 dk b/ g World Appeal - Gallent Taj		
	3-YEAR-OLD	**4-YEAR-OLD**	**5-YEAR-OLD**	**6-YEAR-OLD**
DEC		AQU 11²gd / AQU (14)	PHA 24³ / MED 17	
NOV	HIA 15²	AQU 17my / AQU 21² / AQU (14²)	MED 11³ / MED 11	
OCT	CRC −15²ry / CRC (11²) / CRC 16²	AQU 19¹	MED 15 / MED 13²	
SEP	CRC 15³ / CRC 18		BEL 25¹ / BEL 36²gd / BEL 21³	PHA 10gd / PHA 11 / PHA 16¹
AUG	CRC 18²ry / CRC 23¹ / CRC 18²			ATL 20²
JUL	ATL 23¹			
JUN	ATL −23¹ / MTH −25¹			PHA −22 / PHA 13³ / PHA 16 / PHA 18
MAY	DEL 26²		BEL 15	PHA 13²my / DEL ◆
APR			AQU 12¹ / AQU 15 / AQU 11²	PHA 13
MAR			AQU 15	PHA 21ry / PHA 17 / GS 21¹
FEB			AQU 14² / AQU 15 / AQU 14	GS 15²
JAN			AQU 15¹ / AQU 16 / AQU 18²	GS 11²sy

World Contender ran an 11½ in October of his 3-year-old season, and after two more starts was sidelined for nearly a year. He ran a 14½ second time back, circled back around to a 14 three starts later (winning for a $12,000 tag on December 9), and then improved to an 11½, scoring a repeat victory off a double-jump up the claiming ladder at 7–1.

The Bounce

One of the main tenets of form-cycle analysis holds that comparing a horse to itself is as important as comparing it with the rest of the field. When a 3-year-old with an explosive pattern, like Itaka in the Gotham, is going off at a big price, I will not hesitate to bet it right off a career-best figure, provided the breakthrough move was a small one and the horse hasn't been entered back on unusually short rest. Conversely, there should be no hesitation in taking a position against horses that have just run a number that is likely to set them back. Although even the most casual handicappers are by now aware of the "bounce" phenomenon, most still rate a horse solely on its most recent race with little regard to the havoc a sudden overexertion might wreak.

Horses that have just run a figure many lengths superior to anything they've previously run are eligible to be muscle-sore and physically drained from the effort; if they run back too soon, they often show these ill effects with a subpar performance, and this is known as "bouncing" off a big figure. Statistically, sprinters are more susceptible to a bounce than routers; fillies are likelier to bounce than males; cheap horses are likelier to bounce than classier horses; and dirt horses are likelier to bounce than turf horses. Other factors to consider include the expertise of the trainer, how much of an improvement the figure was in relation to the horse's previous top, how much time has elapsed since the big figure, and how the horse has handled similar situations in the past.

As a filly claiming sprinter coming back on short rest, For the Queen had a few strikes against her when she stopped badly at 5-2 on July 23, 1993. Just 11 days earlier, she had returned from a layoff of nearly 11 months, and turned in the best sprint figure of her career:

1 For the Queen
PP - 1
Own: Joques Farm
SANTOS J A (47 7 5 6 .15)

B. m. 5
Sire: Believe the Queen (Believe It)
Dam: Danzitup (Danzig)
Br: duPont Mrs Richard C (Md)
Tr: Moschera Gasper S (7 1 2 1 .14)

117

Lifetime Record:	10	3	1	0	$35,130							
1993	2	0	1	0	$3,850	Turf	0	0	0	0	
1992	3	1	0	0	$11,990	Wet	1	0	0	0	$180
Sar	0	0	0	0		Dist	0	0	0	0	

Entered 6Aug93- 2 SAR

23Jly93- 9Bel	fst	7f	:231 :463 1:113 1:25	ⒻClm c-22500	54	1	3	11	1hd	5¾	511¼	Rojas R I	115	*2.60	67-17	Jackie P.1191¼ All Too Well1122 Fortune Wand1152¼	Used in pace	9
Claimed from Bohemia Stable, Jerkens H Allen Trainer																		
12Jly93- 2Bel	fst	6f	:223 :452 :572 1:094	ⒻClm 25000	77	7	7	32	21	21	22¼	Rojas R I	117	3.50	88-10	BiddyMullign1172¼ ForTheQueen1172 GettingAroundtoit117no	Held place	7
21Aug92- 6Lrl	fst	6f	:224 :461 :582 1:102 3↑	ⒻAlw 20800	44	7	4	5¾	44	68	615¾	Chavez S N	117	2.90e	73-16	Rollicking Dolly1125¾ Salute theGirl1132¾ StarlightSurprise114	Fell back	7
6Jun92-10Mth	my	6f	:213 :443 :572 1:11 3↑	ⒻAlw 18000	51	5	2	23	42¾	55¼	510	Wilson R	116	1.70	76-12	Sister Mac116¾ No White116nk Special Vice116	Outrun	6
5Jan92- 9Lrl	fst	1 1/16	:233 :473 1:122 1:442	ⒻAlw 19000	85	3	1	1½	13	15	17	Saumell L	114	*1.70	91-17	For the Queen1147 Alanna1142 Herman's Match119	Driving	6
6Dec91- 6Lrl	fst	6f	:221 :454 :583 1:111 3↑	Alw 16500	76	7	4	43	3¼	1¼	12	Wilson R	115	4.50	85-21	For the Queen1152 Desert Victress1152 Chrisappeal120	Driving	7
16Nov91- 8Lrl	fst	6f	:22 :454 :59 1:12	ⒻAlw 16500	48	3	7	717	720	714	47	Wilson R	115	7.40	74-16	WinnstyPrincess1155 PerfectEscpe1151¼ HerAssets117	Stumbled badly	7
1Nov91- 8Lrl	fst	6½f	:223 :454 1:11 1:173	ⒻClm 25000	55	5	3	42¼	43¼	6½	810	Wilson R	114	6.50	79-19	Ameri Allen1144 Graceful Lil114¾ Saucy Bird114	Gave way	9
10May91- 8Pim	fst	6f	:23 :462 :59 1:114	ⒻAlw 16500	67	1	3	2hd	1hd	2hd	55	Wilson R	113	2.90	81-15	Gold Rusher1142¼ Graceful Lil112¾ Cafe West114	Weakened	6
19Mar91- 4Pim	fst	6f	:233 :48 1:01 1:133 3↑	ⒻMd 50000	65	4	4	42	6¼	5¾	1hd	Wilson R	114	3.40	77-22	For the Queen114hd Maid of Glory109nk Creole114	Driving	8

WORKOUTS: Jly 10 Bel tr.t 4f fst :49 B 5/28 Jly 7 Bel 5f fst 1:002 H 6/33 Jun 30 Bel 6f fst 1:144 B 5/7 Jun 16 Bel tr.t 5f fst 1:053 B 4/4 Jun 11 Bel tr.t 4f fst :482 H 3/18

For the Queen was not exactly the Lou Gehrig of racing. Despite being a 5-year-old, she had made it to the races only 10 times—a profile of a horse unable to withstand the rigors of normal training. When she produced "an effort" after a long period of inactivity, handicappers were correct in expecting it to take a toll.

When young horses do too much too soon, it can set them back significantly. There is no better example than the 2004 running of the Fountain of Youth Stakes, otherwise known as the St. Valentine's Day massacre, in which Read the Footnotes prevailed by a neck over Second of June after a protracted stretch drive with a Beyer of 113, an uncommonly high figure for 3-year-olds so early in the season.

Read the Footnotes
Own: Klaravich Stables Inc

B. h. 6 (Apr)
Sire: Smoke Glacken (Two Punch) $25,000
Dam: Baydon Belle (Al Nasr*Fr)
Br: Lawrence Goichman (NY)
Tr: Violette R A Jr

Life	8	5	0	0	$450,660	113	D.Fst	7	5	0	0	$450,660	113
							Wet(378)	1	0	0	0	$0	86
2004	3	1	0	0	$210,000	113	Synth	0	0	0	0	$0	-
2003	5	4	0	0	$240,660	105	Turf(238)	0	0	0	0	$0	-

1May04-10CD	sly	1¼	:463 1:114 1:371 2:04	KyDerby-G1	86	12	64¼	42	34	45½	714¾	Albarado R J	L126	22.50	64-21	SmartyJones1262¾ LionHeart1263¼ Imperilism1262	Stdied 1st turn,wkened	18
13Mar04- 9GP	fst	1⅛	:47 1:112 1:373 1:511	FlaDerby-G1	86	3	33	34½	2hd	2½	44	Bailey J D	L122	*1.00	79-15	Friends Lake122¾ Value Plus122¾ The Cliff's Edge1222¼	Rail trip, gave way	10
14Feb04-11GP	fst	1 1/16	:234 :473 1:111 1:423	FntnOYth-G2	113	8	32½	31	21	2½	1nk	Bailey J D	L122	2.10	96-14	RdthFootnots122nk ScondofJun1207½ SilvrWgon1205½	Long drive, just up	8
29Nov03- 8Aqu	fst	1⅛	:481 1:121 1:373 1:503	Remsen-G2	105	9	21	2½	1hd	16	13¾	Bailey J D	L122	*2.00	83-19	RdthFootnots1223¾ MstrDvid11610¾ WstVirgn116¾	When roused, kept busy	11
2Nov03- 8Aqu	fst	1	:232 :461 1:102 1:362	Nashua-G3	92	1	1½	1½	1hd	12	12¼	Bailey J D	L118	2.90	83-20	RedthFootnots1182¼ Pddington1206¾ WhoIsChrisG1163¼	Pace inside, clear	9
4Oct03- 7Bel	fst	1 1/16	:234 :481 1:133 1:44	Champagn-G1	68	6	2hd	2½	32½	512	615	Santos J A	L122	4.10	65-26	Birdstone1222¼ ChpelRoyl1226¾ DshbordDrummr1222	Pressed inside, tired	7
7Sep03- 6Bel	fst	7f	:223 :453 1:103 1:232	Alw 47000N1x	89	2	4	42	42¼	2½	12¼	Bailey J D	116	*.45	83-20	Read the Footnotes1162¼ Adage119nk Artie Schiller1194½	Rallied 4 wide	6
17Aug03- 2Sar	fst	5f	:22 :451 :572	ⓈMd Sp Wt 41k	93	4	6	1hd	1½	15½	19¼	Velazquez J R	119	*1.05	102-08	RedtheFootnotes1199¼ RodneyBy1197¼ Sptso119¾	Drew away when roused	8

Second of June
Own: Cesare Barbara

Dk. b or b. h. 6 (Jun)
Sire: Louis Quatorze (Sovereign Dancer) $10,000
Dam: Whow (Spectacular Bid)
Br: Lambholm & E. Feicher (Fla)
Tr: Cesare William J

Life	14	4	6	2	$528,800	113	D.Fst	14	4	6	2	$528,800	113
							Wet(354)	0	0	0	0	$0	-
2006	3	0	2	1	$143,400	106	Synth	0	0	0	0	$0	-
2005	3	0	1	1	$155,000	108	Turf(236)	0	0	0	0	$0	-

2Sep06- 9Sar	fst	1⅛	:471 1:114 1:371 1:503	3↑ Woodward-G1	106	7	1hd	1hd	1½	2hd	2½	Gomez G K	L126 f	21.40	83-22	Premium Tap126½ SecondofJune126¾ SunKing1263¼	Fought it out gamely	10
29Jly06- 8AP	fst	1 3/16	:46 1:092 1:532	3↑ WashPkH-G2	93	5	36½	38½	33½	35	37¼	Albarado R J	L116 f	4.60	97-11	Suave1185 Perfect Drift1192¼ Second of June1163¼	No winning bid	7
16Jun06-10CD	fst	1	:23 :461 1:104 1:351	3↑ OC 100k/c-N	94	4	31½	3½	2hd	2hd	2no	Albarado R J	L120 f	2.80	94-10	Suve120no SecondofJun1204¼ TpDncingMuk1205¾	Ex brushes wire,missed	5
9Apr05- 9OP	fst	1⅛	:492 1:131 1:371 1:492	4↑ OaklawnH-G2	108	1	21½	21½	22	22½	2nk	Valenzuela P A	L117 f	6.80	91-17	GrndRewrd112nk ScondofJun1171¼ Eddington1175¾	Chased,drifted,missed	5
12Mar05- 9FG	fst	1⅛	:452 1:10 1:353 1:483	4↑ NwOrlnsH-G2	100	6	44¼	44	31½	22	36	Coa E M	L115 f	11.80	94-08	BdgeofSilver1181 Limehouse1155 ScondofJun115¾	Loomed 3w,weakened	9
29Jan05-10GP	fst	1⅛	:462 1:103 1:354 1:49	4↑ ⓇSMClassic1000k	94	5	94½	105¾	94¾	66½	68	Velasquez C	L120 f	4.80	- -	MusquTojors122nk Zkocty1201¼ ClsscEndvor122½	Steadied leaving bkstr	12
27Dec04- 6Crc	fst	1 1/16	:244 :492 1:134 1:46	3↑ OC 62k/N4x-N	100	1	21½	21	2½	2hd	2nk	Velasquez C	L114 f	*.70	82-21	SmoothLovr117nk ScondofJn1141 Consrvton1175	Bobbled st,brushed str	5
14Feb04-11GP	fst	1 1/16	:234 :473 1:111 1:423	FntnOYth-G2	113	7	21½	2½	11	1½	2nk	Velasquez C	L120 f	*1.50	96-14	RedtheFootnots122nk ScondofJun1207½ SilvrWgon1205½	Off rail, gamely	8
17Jan04-10GP	fst	1 1/16	:24 :481 1:122 1:43	HolyBull-G3	111	5	4¾	2½	2hd	11½	12¾	Velasquez C	L122 f	2.80	94-24	SecondofJune1222¾ SilverWagon12010 FriendsLake122½	3 wide, drew clear	9
13Dec03- 9Crc	fst	1 1/16	:234 :483 1:133 1:453	WhatAPlesr100k	97	3	31	21½	21	13	15	Velasquez C	L115 f	2.20	84-25	SecondofJune1155 TwicesBd111hd SilverWgon1171¾	3 wide move, drew off	9
3Nov03- 9Crc	fst	1	:234 :473 1:13 1:394	Alw 24000N1x	86	6	42½	32	2hd	12½	14¾	Cruz M R	L117 f	*.80	82-24	SecondofJune1174¾ Mr.WillieJoe117¾ MoonWarrior1208	3 wide, drew away	7
20Sep03-10Crc	fst	170	:24 :483 1:141 1:45	FoolshPlsr100k	87	3	53	43	42	21½	2¾	Cruz M R	L116	9.00	99-21	Stolen Time116¾ Second of June1163¾ Imperialism1142¾	Gaining slowly	10

Read the Footnotes returned a month later in the Florida Derby, and bounced badly as the even-money favorite. He then went into the Kentucky Derby off a seven-week layoff, hardly ideal, and backed up through the stretch. He came out of the Derby with knee chips, attempted a comeback in the fall, and was retired in December due to ongoing problems.

A few hours after his gut-wrenching run in the Fountain of Youth, his second huge figure in a row, Second of June was diagnosed with a condylar fracture of a cannon bone, and underwent surgery the next day. In terms of longevity he fared better than Read the Footnotes, but though he finished in the money in six of seven subsequent starts, he never won again and never got back to his best figures.

When horses ship to the United States from Europe and run big first time out, a regression typically follows; nevertheless, the horses are often bet heavily:

George Augustus was racing competitively in Germany in late summer of 1993, shipped over for the Turf Classic, and rallied mildly for third with a Beyer of 106. On the strength of that performance he was installed at 7–5 in the Laurel Turf Cup two weeks later, and bounced a dozen points to finish a nonthreatening third.

Brazany
Own: Paulson Madeleine

B. c. 3 (Mar)
Sire: Strawberry Road (Whiskey Road)
Dam: Waffle's Lake (Kings Lake)
Br: Allen E Paulson (Ky)
Tr: Mott William I (—)

122

Lifetime Record:	9	1	1	3	$84,659						
1993	6	1	0	2	$71,031	Turf	9	1	1	3	$84,659
1992	3	M	1	1	$13,628	Wet	0	0	0	0	
Bel	0	0	0	0		Dist	0	0	0	0	

16Oct93-3Bel sf	1½ ⓣ :501 1:162 2:064 2:323	Lawrence ReaG3	89	5 52½ 52 73½ 75	Smith M E	113	*2.30	54-29	Strolling Along114½ Scattered Steps113¹ Noble Sheba114½	No late bid	12
29Aug93-8AP sf	1¼ ⓣ :481 1:134 1:404 2:083	Secretariat-G1	103	13 109½ 611 56½ 31½	Desormeaux K J	114	18.70	53-40	Awad120¹½ Explosive Red123no Brazany114¹½	Late bid	14
6Jun93♦ San Siro(Ity) Tr: Francois Boutin	gd *1 ⓣRH 1:391 3+	Stk 120000 Premio Emilio Turati-G2		42¾	St-Martin E	119	8.70	— —	Culture Vulture126nk Prospective Ruler129¹ Ventiquattrofogli119²½	5th into stretch 3f out, lacked rally	9
25Apr93♦ Longchamp(Fr)	sf *1 5/16 ⓣRH 2:182	Stk 80200 Prix Greffulhe-G2		57¾	Asmussen C	128	7.50	— —	Hunting Hawk128¹½ Bigstone128¹½ Talloires128¾	Chased in 5th, no rally, never a factor	6
16Mar93♦ Saint-Cloud(Fr)	gd *1 5/16 ⓣLH 2:201	Stk 37100 Prix Maurice Caillault(Listed)		32	Asmussen C	123	*1.50	— —	Fantastic Dream123½ Sawasdee127¹½ Brazany123¹½	Led to final 16th, outfinished	5
3Mar93♦ Evry(Fr)	sf *1 ⓣLH 1:47	Maiden 30100 Prix de l'Ile aux Paveurs		12½	St-Martin E	128	3.50	— —	Brazany128²½ Demidoff123¹½ St Edmond128nk	Settled towards rear, wide rally 2f out, led final furlong, driving	13
8Dec92♦ Saint-Cloud(Fr)	hy *1 ⓣLH 1:57	Maiden 31600 Prix Prompt		22½	Head F	128	5.00	— —	Regency128²½ Brazany128¹½ Extra Point128⁶	4th halfway, 6th 2f out, rallied into 2nd, never catching winner	15
11Nov92♦ Saint-Cloud(Fr)	hy *1¼ ⓣLH 2:311	Maiden 31500 Prix Maurepas (Div 1)		31½	Head F	128	5.70	— —	Epaphos128nk Cimarron Creek128¹ Brazany128²	Unhurried in 7th, rallied 1f out, bid for lead 100y out, outfinished	12
26Aug92♦ Deauville(Fr)	hy *1 ⓣRH 1:561	Mdn (FT)35000 Prix de Bonneville		515½	Head F	128	3.20	— —	Appliance124²½ Irish Prospector128² River Erne124³	Close up in 4th, led briefly halfway, weakened 3f out	7

WORKOUTS: Oct 12 Bel ⓣ 5f fm 1:022 B (d) 1/2 Oct 7 Bel ⓣ 7f fm 1:334 B (d) 5/5 Aug 27 AP ⓣ 5f fm 1:07 B 1/1

At Belmont a week earlier, Brazany had been favored in the Lawrence Realization off his U.S. debut—a fast-closing third in the Grade 1 Secretariat Stakes. His 103 Beyer for the Secretariat was superior to anything his rivals in the "Larry Real" had ever run, but it was Strolling Along, the second-fastest horse on figures, who won at 9–2, as Brazany nosedived 14 points.

Stagecraft–GB
Own.—Darley Stud Management

B. h. 6, by Sadler's Wells—Bella Colora, by Bellypha-Ir
Br.—Meon Valley Stud (GB)
Tr.—Mott William I (35 11 7 4 .31)

115

Lifetime				1993	2	1	0	1	$62,640
16	5	3	6	1992	3	0	1	1	$21,580
$414,916				Turf	16	5	3	6	$414,916

13Feb93-10GP fm	1⅛ ⓣ:472 1:104 1:474 +	3+ Can Turf	103	10 3 34 33½ 32 1nk	Bailey J D		112	3.90	93-12	Stagecraft-GB112nk Roman Envoy121½ Carterista114		10
13Feb93-Altered course upper stretch. Fully extended												
30Jan93- 8GP fm	*1⅛ ⓣ 1:534 +	Alw 29000	95	4 10 106½ 62½ 32 3nk	Bailey J D		122	*1.10	77-23	ImALIDI112nk PdgnsPrms114hd Stgcrft-GB122	Late rally	10
15Nov92- 8CD yl	1⅛ ⓣ:483 1:122 1:491	3+ River City H	102	1 4 32 42 31½ 3½	Day P	LB	114	3.70	89-10	Cozzn'sPrnc117no LotsPol118½ Stgcrft-GB114	Hung late	8
19Oct92- 8Bel gd	1⅜ ⓣ:47 1:371 2:143	3+ Tidal H	89	7 5 42½ 31½ 53 77½	Bailey J D	b	122	*.80	70-23	Rssr114²½ HnrRjn111³ TmfrLghtnng110	Lacked response	11
19Oct92-Grade II												
7Oct92- 7Bel fm	1 1/16 ⓣ:473 1:11 1:404	3+ Alw 47000	101	5 5 42 42 22½ 2½	Bailey J D	b	115	*.80	93-13	Thakib115½ Stgecrft-GB115¾ WildCtrct115	Rallied wide	6
19Oct91♦2Newmarket(Eng) gd	1¼ 2:014	ⓣ DubaiChampionStks(Gr1)		75¾	Cauthen S		129	12.00	— —	Tel Quel 124½ Cruachan 124½ In The Groove126	Evenly	12
5Oct91♦3Longchamp(Fra) yl	*1 3/16 2:04	ⓣ Prix Dollar(Gr1)		3¾	Cauthen S		130	*.90	— —	Wiorno121¾ Muroto128hd Stagecraft130	Prom, no gain	7
14Sep91♦3Leopardst'n(Ire) gd	1¼ 2:064	ⓣ IrishChampionStk(Gr1)		36	Cauthen S		132	5.00	— —	SvDncr123⁴ EnvrnmntFrnd123² Stgcrft132	Bid, no gain	7
20Aug91♦3York(Eng) gd	*1¼ 2:16	ⓣ JuddmonteInternat'l(Gr1)		35½	Cauthen S		132	*.80	— —	Trmon132² QustForFm132³½ Stgcrft132	Rated, mild bid	6
6Jly91♦4Sandown(Eng) gd	1¼ 2:073	ⓣ Coral-EclipseStks(Gr1)		2hd	Cauthen S		133	*2.00	— —	EnrnmntFrnd122hd Stcrft133⁷ Snlmr133	Led str, missed	7

LATEST WORKOUTS Mar 3 GP ⓣ 4f fm :50 B (d) Feb 25 GP 5f fst 1:033 B Feb 10 GP ⓣ 4f fm :532 B (d) Jan 27 GP 5f gd 1:03 B

Stagecraft returned from a 50-week layoff with a sharp race in a classified allowance in his U.S. debut, but bounced 12 points at 4–5 in the Tidal Handicap next out.

When today's conditions are similar to those that previously have produced a bounce, play devil's advocate if the horse is a short price and assume history will repeat itself:

12 Fairy Garden PP - 2
Own: Payson Virginia Kraft
PINCAY L JR (90 11 15 15 .12)

B. m. 5
Sire: Lyphard (Northern Dancer)
Dam: Possible Mate (King's Bishop)
Br: Evans Edward P (Va)
Tr: Attfield Roger L (—)

L 123

Lifetime Record:	28	9	2	2	$462,809						
1993	7	4	0	0	$286,622	Turf	27	9	2	2	$462,809
1992	11	4	0	1	$128,646	Wet	0	0	0	0	
SA Ⓣ	0	0	0	0		Dist Ⓣ	2	1	0	0	$120,000

11Sep93-8Bel	sf	1¼ [T]	$:49^2$	$1:14^2$	$1:39^1$	$2:03^4$	3↑ ⒻFlowr Bwl H-G1	82	5	4	4^4	$3^{2½}$	$5^{5½}$	$5^{7½}$	Smith M E	120 f	3.60	64-24	FarOutBeast111½ Dahlia'sDremer110½ LdyBlessington118¾	Lacked rally	10
27Aug93-8Sar	fm	1⅝ Ⓣ	$:49^3$	$1:38^4$	$2:02^2$	$2:39^3$	3↑ Seneca H-G3	103	4	6	6^3	$5^{3½}$	3^1	$1^{2½}$	Smith M E	114 f	3.80	97-12	Fairy Garden114²½ Summer Ensign115no Dr. Kiernan120²	Going away	9
31Jly93-8WO	fm	1⅛ Ⓣ	$:44^3$	$1:08^4$	$1:33^4$	$1:46^2$	3↑ ⒻWO Bd BC H-G2C	80	3	6	8^{12}	8^{13}	$8^{8½}$	7^7	Seymour D J	L 120 f	2.15	90-13	MyrtleIrene115¹ ProminentFether114no DnceForDonn113no	Showed little	8
14Jly93-7Atl	fm	1⅜ Ⓣ	$:49^3$	$1:13^4$	$1:38^4$	$1:57^4$	3↑ ⒻMatchmaker-G2	91	6	7	4^4	3^2	$2^½$	1^{nk}	Smith M E	L 120 f	*1.00	71-21	FairyGrden120nk SrtogSource118hd Logn'sMist118³	Betw horses, driving	8
22Apr93-8Kee	fm	1⅛ Ⓣ	$:49^1$	$1:13^3$	$1:38^1$	$1:50^3$	ⒻBewitch-G3	89	7	6	5^5	6^4	$6^{4½}$	4^2	Ramos W S	L 122 f	2.80	82-16	Miss Lenora112nk Hero's Love117½ Radiant Ring119¼		8
Wide,backstretch, no late threat																					
31Mar93-10GP	fm	1½ Ⓣ	$:46^3$	$1:11^1$	$2:01^3$	$2:25^3$	3↑ ⒻOrchid H-G2	104	8	7	$5^{4½}$	$4^{4½}$	$1^{1½}$	1^5	Ramos W S	L 115	6.20	92-12	Fairy Garden115⁵ Rougeur115no Trampoli115¹¾	Ridden out	14
10Mar93-9GP	fm	1⅜ Ⓣ	$:49^3$	$1:15^3$	$1:39^2$	$2:14^3$	3↑ ⒻVery One H50k	99	8	6	$6^{5½}$	4^2	1^1	1^1	Ramos W S	L 113	6.90	96-07	Fairy Garden113¹ Trampoli115³¾ Tango Charlie114²		11
Ducked out twice from left handed whip driving																					
1Nov92-7GP	fm	1½ Ⓣ	$:49^2$	$1:14^4$	$2:03^1$	$2:26^2$	+ 3↑ ⒻGaily Gly 250k	89	11	5	$8^{4½}$	$8^{3½}$	$8^{3¾}$	$8^{3½}$	Krone J A	L 113	*3.80	85 —	Rougeur112¹½ Good To Dance-Ir113¹½ Indian Chris-Br113	Steadied str	13
4Oct92-8Bel	fm	1⅜ [T]	$:49^1$	$1:13^4$	1:38	$2:13^3$	3↑ ⒻAthenia H-G3	97	2	3	4^2	$4^{1½}$	$3^{1½}$	1^{hd}	Krone J A	112	6.00	83-17	Fairy Garden112hd Passagere du Soir-GB117½ Seewillo113	Driving	5
12Sep92-8Bel	yl	1¼ [T]	$:47^4$	1:12	$1:36^2$	2:01	3↑ ⒻFlwr Bowl H-G1	90	8	5	$5^{6½}$	$5^{3½}$	6^5	$6^{6¾}$	Gryder A T	112	21.00	78-20	Christiecat116¹½ Ratings114⁴½ Plenty Of Grace115	Lacked rally	9

WORKOUTS: Nov 3 WO tr.t 5f fst 1:03 B 7/17 Oct 20 WO 5f fst $1:02^3$ B 13/23 Oct 14 WO Ⓣ 5f fm :58 H (d) 1/2 ●Oct 7 WO tr.t [T] 7f fm $1:26^4$ H (d) 1/8 Sep 30 WO tr.tⓉ 6f gd $1:15^3$ B (d)2/5 Sep 22 WO tr.tⓉ 4f fm $:48^3$ B (

Fairy Garden bounced from a 104 to an 89 in the April 22 Bewitch, when shortened in distance and picking up weight from her previous start. She finally got back to that level by running a figure of 103 months later, and promptly bounced 21 points when again shortened in distance and saddled with extra weight.

Pair-Ups

A common pattern occurs when horses run the same figure, or virtually the same figure, in back-to-back starts that represent peak efforts. This can be a positive or negative development, largely dependent on the type of horse, and how the first of the paired figures is evaluated. In the case of Second of June, the 111 Beyer he ran in the Holy Bull was a significant 14-point improvement over his previous best, and might've had handicappers looking for a bounce in the Fountain of Youth; when he instead produced a 113 after a knockdown drag-out brawl, the combined effects of those two efforts were nearly catastrophic.

Riboletta (Brz)
Own: Jones Aaron U. and Marie D

B. m. 5 (Jul)
Sire: Rei Normand (Exclusive Native)
Dam: Joy Valley*Brz (Ghadeer*Fr)
Br: Haras Santa Ana do Rio Grande (Brz)
Tr: Inda Eduardo(0 0 0 0 .00) 2000:(0 0 .00)

Life	28	13	3	3	$1,555,103	115	D.Fst	10 6 0 1 $1,200,183 115
2000	11	7	0	2	$1,384,860	115	Wet(280)	6 4 1 0 $216,514 100
							Synth	0 0 0 0 $0 -
1999	6	1	0	1	$82,226	98	Turf(342)	12 3 2 2 $138,406 98
Cd	1	0	0	0	$0	93	Dst(315)	4 3 0 0 $810,000 115

4Nov00-3CD	fst	1⅛	:461 1:102 1:344 1:473	3+ⒻBCDistaf-G1	93	8	54	45	52	78½	78¾	McCarron C J	L123	*.40	89 -	Spain1201½ *Surfside*1201½ *Heritage of Gold*123¾	4 wide, lacked rally	9
14Oct00-8Bel	fst	1⅛	:46 1:091 1:331 1:46	3+ⒻBeldame-G1	115	1	24½	25	22	12	12	McCarron C J	L123	*.50	101- 09	Riboletta1232 BeautifulPlesure12314½ Penttonic1232¼	Not fully extended	5
16Sep00-9Bel	fst	1 1/16	:234 :47 1:104 1:401	3+ⒻRuffianH-G1	115	3	2hd	1hd	1hd	15½	17½	McCarron C J	L125	*1.05	96- 14	*Riboltt*1257½ GourmtGirl1141¾ *CountryHidwy*114no	When asked, ridden out	7
12Aug00-7Dmr	fst	1 1/16	:232 :47 1:11 1:42	3+ⒻCLHrschH-G2	107	6	23	2½	2hd	11½	11½	McCarron C J	LB125	*.40	93- 12	*Riboletta*1251½ Bordelaise115½ Gourmet Girl1152	Bid,led,clear,driving	6
25Jun00-6Hol	fst	1⅛	:474 1:113 1:354 1:482	3+ⒻVanityH-G1	111	3	21	2½	1hd	15	15½	McCarron C J	LB123	*.60	87- 20	*Riboletta*1235½ *SpekingofTime*1082½ ExcellntMting120½	Bid btwn,ridden out	6
28May00-9Hol	fst	1 1/16	:23 :454 1:102 1:42	3+ⒻMladyBCH-G1	110	1	2hd	1hd	11	12½	13¼	McCarron C J	LB120	*1.00	90- 10	*Ribolett*1203¼ Bordelise1171½ ExcellentMeting121no	Rail,strong hand ride	6
7May00-4Hol	fst	1 1/16	:233 :464 1:111 1:421	3+ⒻHawthrnH-G2	105	5	3½	31	1½	13	17	McCarron C J	LB117	3.20	89- 15	*Ribolett*1177 ExcellentMting122nk SpkingofTim1118	3wd,drew clear,drvng	5
9Apr00-8GG	fm	1 Ⓣ	:24 :471 1:103 1:344	3+ⒻMissAmrcaH100k	69	5	31½	31½	46	47	313	Alvarado F T	LB118	3.40	84- 03	Penny Marie115no Dianehill11413 *Riboletta*1182	Stalked 3w, empty	5
5Mar00-8SA	sly	1⅛	:47 1:112 1:37 1:502	4+ⒻSMrgrtaH-G1	100	1	1hd	2hd	1½	12½	13	Nakatani C S	LB115	5.80	83- 20	Riboletta1153 Bordelaise1144 Snowberg114½	Rail,clear,held gamely	5
13Feb00-8SA	wf	1 1/16	:232 :471 1:11 1:423	4+ⒻSntMriaH-G1	97	6	63	73¾	62¾	42¾	44½	Blanc B	LB114	25.40	85- 13	Manistique125½ Snowberg1141½ Gourmet Girl1162½	Angled in,no late bid	8

WORKS: Oct29 CD 5f fst 1:003 B *6/38* ●Oct23 CD 3f fst :35 H *1/12* Oct6 SA 5f fst 1:00 H *9/39*
TRAINER: +180Days(1 .00 $0.00) Dirt(4 .25 $1.30) Routes(27 .11 $0.48) Stakes(13 .23 $1.00)

In the 2000 Breeders' Cup Distaff, Riboletta was a mare to be approached with great caution at 2–5, after pairing up enervating 115 Beyers in the Ruffian and Beldame at Belmont Park. Five-year-old mares with 27 races under their belt cannot reasonably be expected to run figures of that magnitude in three consecutive, closely spaced starts, even if, like Riboletta, they have won six Grade 1 or Grade 2 stakes in a row and stand at the head of their division. Riboletta finally cracked in the Distaff.

Older horses like Riboletta can be expected to react negatively off paired top figures, especially pairs of high figures earned in demanding efforts.

Examine two more negative pair-ups that produced vulnerable favorites:

Bonnie Shopper
Own: Jewel–E Stables
LUTTRELL M G (13 2 2 4 .15) $50,000

B. m. 5
Sire: Shelter Half (Tentam)
Dam: Farrage (Oxford Accent)
Br: Joe–Dan Farm (NJ)
Tr: Friedman Mitchell (2 0 1 0 .00)

1125

Lifetime Record:	29	9	5	10	$139,878					
1994	4	3	0	0	$41,460	Turf	0 0 0 0			
1993	12	2	1	6	$41,822	Wet	1 1 0 0	$14,220		
Bel Ⓣ	0	0	0	0		Dist Ⓣ	0 0 0 0			

9Apr94-5Aqu	fst	1	:224 :452 1:10 1:37	ⒻClm 80000	76	4	3	2½	1½	3nk	42½	Luttrell M G5	109 b	*1.00	80 - 14	Seattle Vice112½ Bold As Silver118nk Fleeting Ways1181¾	Led, tired	6
12Mar94-6Aqu	fst	170 ⊡	:233 :47 1:11 1:41	ⒻClm 70000	101	3	1	1½	12½	17	17½	Luttrell M G5	108 b	2.20	93 - 20	Bonnie Shopper1087½ Seattle Vice1132¾ S. S. Sparkle1135	Mild drive	6
2Feb94-4Aqu	fst	170 ⊡	:243 :493 1:134 1:414	ⒻClm 32500	101	1	1	11½	16	114	120½	Luttrell M G5	110 b	4.20	89 - 31	Bonnie Shopper11020 Galloping Proudly1172½ Chambolle117hd	Ridden out	6
23Jan94-1Aqu	fst	1 1/16 ⊡	:233 :484 1:142 1:483	ⒻClm 22500	71	1	1	11	11½	12½	1¾	Luttrell M G5	110 b	3.00	62 - 31	BonnieShopper110¾ SchwayBabySwy1175½ GllopingProudly117no	Driving	11
29Dec93-5Aqu	fst	1 1/16 ⊡	:234 :491 1:152 1:483	3+ ⒻClm 22500	70	5	2	1hd	11½	11	32	Rojas C	115 fb	5.00	60 - 33	Streaming1172 Noble Girl115no Bonnie Shopper1151	Bid, tired	8
25Nov93-8Med	fst	6f	:221 :451 :574 1:102	3+ ⒻⓈGirl Power H32k	66	5	8	32½	33	44½	67¾	Rojas C	L 115 fb	*1.60e	81 - 16	Sister Dell1171½ Merri Tales1201¾ Lena's Angel1142	Tired	10
13Nov93-2Med	fst	170	:23 :462 1:11 1:42	3+ ⒻClm 22000	83	5	3	31½	11½	13	13	Rojas C	L 115 fb	2.70	86 - 14	Bonnie Shopper1153 Landing Mate1194 Dun Roamin Lady1133¾	Driving	8
21Oct93-9Med	sly	6f	:221 :454 :581 1:111	3+ ⓈAlw 23700N3X	82	6	8	51¾	31	11	11	Rojas C	L 113 fb	8.20e	85 - 16	Bonnie Shopper1131 Ox1141½ Kind One115nk	Driving	9
13Oct93-3Med	fst	170	:223 :463 1:12 1:422	3+ ⒻClm 25000	82	2	2	31½	21	1½	2no	Rojas C	L 116 fb	*1.30e	84 - 15	Miss Cover Girl114no Bonnie Shopper1163¾ Quinyan1144¾	Gamely	7
28Sep93-7Med	fst	6f	:22 :444 :57 1:094	3+ ⒻClm 20000	75	1	6	52½	65½	54½	32½	Castillo R E	116 b	6.80	89 - 11	PennyForJessie119½ Stlictricity1192 BonniShoppr1164½	Saved ground	8

WORKOUTS: May 5 Bel Ⓣ 4f fm :49 H (d) *3/8* Apr 3 Bel tr.t 4f fst :50 B *20/26* Mar 9 Bel tr.t 3f fst :362 H *3/18* Mar 1 Bel tr.t 3f fst :39 B *10/10* Feb 23 Bel tr.t 3f fst :371 B *2/10* Feb 15 Bel tr.t 4f fst :524 B *29/34*

Bonnie Shopper's established top Beyer was in the low 80s prior to her back-to-back 101s. The comment lines "Ridden out" and "Mild drive" implied she won with something in reserve, but appearances can be deceiving after exceptionally fast races back to back. Subjected to a faster, pressured pace when cut back to a one-turn mile on April 9, 1994, Bonnie Shopper had nothing left in the tank through the stretch, and faded to fourth at even money.

Jericho Blaise
Own: Koziarz Ted
SANTAGATA N (52 5 11 6 .10)

B. c. 3 (Apr)
Sire: Exuberant (What a Pleasure)
Dam: Arts and Clever (Arts and Letters)
Br: Rustlewood Farm Inc (Fla)
Tr: Koziarz Ted (1 0 0 0 .00)

110

Lifetime Record:	11	3	2	2	$57,385			
1994	3 2 0 0	$33,000	Turf	0	0	0	0	
1993	8 1 2 2	$24,385	Wet	2	0	1	0	$3,200
Bel	0 0 0 0		Dist	6	1	0	2	$21,545

16Apr94- 8Aqu	sly	6f		$:21^3$	$:44^1$	$:56^2$	$1:09^1$	Best Turn-G3	53	7	1	$5^{1½}$	$4^{4½}$	6^{10}	$7^{19¾}$	Santagata N	115	*1.70	77-09	Rizzi117^5 Mr. Shawklit117^{2½} Memories Of Linda115^1	Gave way	7
1Apr94- 7Aqu	fst	6½f		$:22^1$	$:45^1$	$1:09^4$	$1:16^2$	Alw 29000N2X	101	1	1	$1^{2½}$	1^2	1^7	1^7	Santagata N	117	2.20	99-16	Jericho Blaise117^7 Gold Tower117^{½} Memories Of Linda117^{6½}	Ridden out	5
21Feb94- 7Aqu	fst	6f	⊡	$:22^3$	$:45^4$	:58	$1:10^4$	Alw 26000N1X	101	4	1	$2^{½}$	1^1	1^4	1^7	Santagata N	117	8.60	89-20	Jericho Blaise117^7 Storm Street117^{¾} Jacksome117^{2½}	Kept to task	6
2Dec93- 7Med	fst	6f		$:22^1$	:45	$:57^3$	1:10	Alw 23500N1X	71	8	3	$3^{½}$	2^1	$2^{1½}$	$3^{3½}$	Thomas D B	L 117	10.10	87-15	MedowFlight117^{hd} Lynn'sNotebook117^{3½} JerichoBlis117^{5½}	Finished evenly	8
24Nov93- 9Med	fst	1		:23	:47	1:13	$1:39^1$	Princeton40k	61	6	5	$5^{4½}$	$4^{½}$	4^1	$4^{4¾}$	Velasquez J	L 114	7.00	71-25	Personal Merit115^7 Natural Fact117^{1½} SladyRoberto113^{nk}	Finished evenly	9
3Nov93- 1Med	fst	1		$:23^3$	$:47^1$	$1:12^1$	$1:38^4$	Md Sp Wt	72	8	3	$1^{1½}$	1^5	1^5	$1^{3¾}$	Bravo J	L 118	3.20	82-17	Jericho Blaise118^{3¾} Barge In118^2 Pleasant Dancer118^2	Driving	9
21Oct93- 6Med	sly	1		$:23^1$	$:46^3$	$1:12^1$	1:39	Md Sp Wt	63	7	2	$3^{½}$	$2^{1½}$	2^4	$2^{6¾}$	Bravo J	L 118	*1.50	74-19	Dinner Affair113^{6¾} Jericho Blaise118^{4¾} SashaSashaSasha118^{1½}	Best of rest	7
9Oct93- 5Med	fst	6f		$:22^2$	$:46^2$	$:59^2$	$1:13^1$	Md Sp Wt	55	1	8	$7^{4½}$	$6^{4½}$	$5^{2½}$	$4^{1½}$	Nelson D	L 118	2.50	74-25	Powerful Patch118^{1½} Settle Quick118^{hd} Drop Em118^{no}	Finished well	9
5Sep93- 1Mth	fst	6f		:22	$:45^2$	$:57^4$	1:10	Md Sp Wt	45	6	4	$6^{3¾}$	$5^{4½}$	5^9	4^{10}	Castillo H Jr	118	9.90	71-15	Slip Mahoney118^{3¾} Storm Street118^{5¾} Solly's Honor118^{4½}	No rally	8
25Aug93- 7Mth	fst	6f		$:21^2$	:45	$:57^3$	1:11	Md Sp Wt	62	4	5	4^2	$5^{1¾}$	$3^{5½}$	3^9	Castillo H Jr	118	5.40	75-19	Hold My Tongue118^3 Palance118^6 Jericho Blaise118^{3¾}	Mild rally	8

WORKOUTS: ●May 14 Mth 5f fst $:59^4$ H 1/15 May 4 Bel 4f fst $:48^2$ B 10/56 Apr 12 Bel tr.t 3f fst :35 H 2/17 Mar 27 Bel tr.t 4f fst $:48^3$ B 4/18 Mar 23 Bel tr.t 4f fst $:48^1$ B 9/34 Mar 7 Bel tr.t 4f fst :47 H 3/58

Jericho Blaise received an 11-week freshening after a juvenile campaign when he consistently ran figures in the 60s and low 70s. Upon returning, he advanced through two allowance conditions with 101s, winning each time by seven lengths. The comment line for the second win was "Ridden out," again implying the horse won with something left. But two races in succession 30 points above a previously established top do not usually leave anything in a horse's reserves, no matter how visually impressive the efforts appeared. Thrown into the Grade 3 Best Turn two weeks later, he finished last at 17–10.

With lightly raced horses, and nonclaiming horses with solid forging patterns, paired figures are usually a positive sign—provided they haven't been too much of an improvement over the previous top figure. These types can be expected to move ahead in the near future, sometimes after throwing in an "off" race right after the pair.

At different points in horses' careers, short-term patterns such as pairs can mean different things, as Thoro-Graph's Jerry Brown explains:

"Pairs of new tops by 2-year-olds are a positive sign; paired tops from 3-year-olds early in the season may suggest a bounce before another good race; paired tops by older horses may be too much of an 'extension' and knock them off form."

Hansel, Pine Bluff, Devil His Due, and Strike the Gold all reacted similarly to paired tops. The bounce off the pair was the prelude to a significantly faster top next time out—what Brown has coined the "Spring 3-Year-Old Pattern":

STRIKE THE GOLD			'88 ch h Alydar - Majestic Gold
3-YEAR-OLD	**4-YEAR-OLD**	**5-YEAR-OLD**	**6-YEAR-OLD**
DEC			
NOV			
CD 4²	GP 7²		
OCT BEL 5¹	BEL 2²gd		
SEP BEL 4²w	BEL 2²		
SAR 7	SAR 7¹		
AUG	MTH 6		
SAR 5¹			
JUL	BEL 3		
JUN BEL 4¹	BEL 2my	BEL 2	
MAY PIM 10		PIM 6³	
CD 6	PIM 4¹		
APR KEE 7gd		AQU 3³	
	AQU 7³		
MAR GP 10¹	GP 6²		
FEB GP 10¹	GP 5		
JAN GP 16²	GP 8³		
	GP 8²		

Condition Analysis and Speed Figures

PINE BLUFF						'89 b h Danzig - Rowdy Angel	
		2-YEAR-OLD	3-YEAR-OLD		4-YEAR-OLD		5-YEAR-OLD
DEC	AQU	6^2					
NOV	AQU	11					
	CD	15^3					
OCT	BEL	14^2					
SEP	BEL	14^2wf					
AUG	SAR	14^2					
JUL							
JUN	BEL	21wf	BEL 3^2gd				
MAY			PIM 3^2				
			CD 9^1				
APR			OP 6^2				
MAR			OP 6^2				
			OP 9				
FEB							
JAN							

[41]

DEVIL HIS DUE

'89 dk b/h Devil's Bag - Plenty O'Toole

	2-YEAR-OLD	3-YEAR-OLD	4-YEAR-OLD	5-YEAR-OLD
DEC				
NOV			SA 5^1	
OCT		AQU 9^1 / BEL 7_{gd}	BEL 7	
SEP		BEL 8^2 / BEL 9	BEL $6^2{}_{sy}$	BEL 2^2
AUG		SAR 6	SAR 2^3	SAR 0
JUL		SAR 8^2 / BEL $8^1{}_{my}$	MTH 2^3 / BEL 2^3	BEL 3
JUN			BEL 4	BEL 0
MAY		BEL 18^1 / CD 14	PIM 3^2	BEL 4 / PIM 2^2
APR		AQU $8^2{}_{gd}$ / AQU 8^2	AQU 3^3	OP 4
MAR		GP 12^3 / GP 11	GP 4^1	
FEB		GP 11^2	GP 7^1	GP 7
JAN		GP 13^1		GP 4

HANSEL			'88 b h Woodman - Count On Bonnie
	3-YEAR-OLD	4-YEAR-OLD	6-YEAR-OLD	6-YEAR-OLD

	3-YEAR-OLD
DEC	
NOV	
OCT	
SEP	
AUG SAR	4
JUL MTH	11gd
JUN BEL	5¹
MAY PIM	2¹
CD	10²
APR KEE	6³
TP	6³
MAR GP	11¹
FEB GP	17
JAN	

Hansel and Pine Bluff paired tops in their final two preps for the Kentucky Derby, bounced in the Derby, and then ran new tops to win the Preakness.

Devil His Due shows the pattern—a pair of 11s, a regression to 12¾, followed by an 8½ in the Gotham, in which he dead-heated for the win at 10–1. Strike the Gold shows the pattern "in spirit," with a 7 in the Blue Grass, a 6 to win the Derby, a bounce to a 10 in the Preakness, and a new top of 4¼ when edged by Hansel in the Belmont.

Lightly Raced Horses

In the new millennium it is crucial to evaluate lightly raced horses, because horses make fewer starts than they did back in the day; a growing number of them are here today and gone tomorrow. Consider that:

- In 1985, horses started an average of 8.28 times per year; by 2005, the average had dipped to 6.45 starts.
- In 1976, the average starter in the Kentucky Derby had already made 11.5 starts; by 1985 that average was down to 8.9 starts; and by 1994 it was down to 6.6 starts.
- From 2000 through 2007, eight Kentucky Derby winners had *combined* for 22 starts as 2-year-olds—an average of just 2.8 juvenile starts each.
- When Bernardini won the 2006 Preakness, he was making just the fourth start of his life, and just his second since a maiden win 11 weeks earlier!

Maiden and first-level allowance races filled with second-time starters and third-time starters offer excellent betting opportunities, because many bettors accept what they see at face value. In reality, these volatile races contain horses prone to extreme and sudden fluctuations of form, depending on what kind of figures they initially ran.

Any horse can lose its first race. Even Secretariat got into all kinds of trouble first time out, and wound up finishing fourth. The majority of horses that are not subjected to an overly taxing effort first out will improve with a race under their belt; there's just no substitute for experience, and often the improvement will be dramatic, especially when the horse is well-bred and well-connected.

Pine Bluff   B. c. 2(May), by Danzig—Rowdy Angel, by Halo

Own.—Loblolly Stable
Br.—Loblolly Stable (Ky)
Tr.—Bohannan Thomas

Lifetime 1991 2 1 0 0 $14,400
2 1 0 0
$14,400

16Aug91- 6Sar fst 7f :22¹ :45¹ 1:23⁴   Md Sp Wt   5 8 42½ 42½ 2½ 11½   Perret C   118   3.00   86-11 Pine Bluff118¹½ Harry the Hat118² Noactor118⁷   Wide drv 10

13Jun91- 4Bel fst 5f :21² :44 :56¹   Md Sp Wt   7 8 54 5⁴ 43½ 510¾   Smith M E   118   4.30   95-05 Lure118⁵ In a Walk118²¾ Money Run118³   Brk slowly 8

LATEST WORKOUTS   ●Sep 1 Bel 4f fst :46 H   Aug 27 Bel 5f fst 1:02² B   Aug 12 Sar tr.t 4f fst :50 H   Aug 7 Sar tr.t 5f fst 1:05³ B

Totemic   Ch. f. 2(Feb), by Vanlandingham—Strong Totem, by Fappiano

Own.—Loblolly Stable
Br.—Loblolly Stable (Ky)
Tr.—Bohannan Thomas

Lifetime 1991 2 1 0 0 $14,400
2 1 0 0
$14,400

31Aug91- 3Bel gd 7f :22² :45¹ 1:23¹   ⒿMd Sp Wt   3 5 41½ 41½ 1hd 12   Krone J A   117   6.40   86-11 Totemic117² Fateful Beauty117²½ Sleek Stephie117²½   Driving 7

10Jly91- 6Bel fst 5½f :22¹ :46¹ 1:06¹   ⒿMd Sp Wt   6 9 84½ 83½ 86½ 77½   Smith M E   117   21.90   76-17 BlssOurHom117½FuturQston117¹½PrttyMlody117¹½   No factor 9

LATEST WORKOUTS   Aug 23 Bel 5f fst 1:01¹ Bg   Aug 18 Bel tr.t 4f fst :48⁴ B   Aug 13 Bel tr.t 4f fst :48² H

Zimmerman   Dk. b. or br. c. 2(Feb), by Cox's Ridge—Prove Us Royal, by Prove It

SMITH M E (58 8 10 6 .12)
Own.—Loblolly Stable
Br.—Anthony John Ed & Conrad Marian L (Ky)
Tr.—Bohannan Thomas (6 1 1 2 .17)

Lifetime 1992 2 1 0 0 $14,400
2 1 0 0
$14,400

122

26Aug92- 9Sar fst 6f :22¹ :45³ 1:10²   Md Sp Wt   8 3 4 5 55¼ 42½ 2hd 1¹   Smith M E   118   5.20   92-07 Zimmerman118⁷RglnRod118½Environment118   Drew off 8

6Jly92- 3Bel gd 6f :22² :45⁴ 1:11   Md Sp Wt   4 1 5 5 3¾ 43½ 68 711½   Perret C   118   5.50   73-12 StelliteSignl118½Wllnd118⁴¾ShdsofSilvr118   Tired badly 9

LATEST WORKOUTS   Sep 14 Bel 3f fst :35⁴ H   ●Sep 8 Bel tr.t 4f fst :48 H   ●Aug 25 Bel tr.t 4f fst :47² H   Aug 19 Bel tr.t 4f my :48³ H

Trainers have different philosophies about handling their young horses. Tom Bohannan developed the likes of 1992 Preakness winner Pine Bluff, but even that supremely gifted colt showed relatively little in his first start.

"Mine have a tendency to run much better the second time they start," Bohannan explained. "I try not to put too much pressure on them. I don't expect anything out of the horse the first time they run. I just hope they finish well."

Pine Bluff, Totemic, and Zimmerman didn't do anything more than Bohannan was expecting of them in their debuts, finishing no better than fifth, and no closer than 7½ lengths to the winner; but each received several weeks off afterward, and showed considerably more polish when returned to win second time out.

Pine Bluff and Totemic (also a stakes winner at 3) were stretching out to seven furlongs, after getting their first taste of competition in shorter sprints. Very often, the way young horses run in one or two sprints gives little indication of their true potential; they can show a lot more once they've gotten their feet wet and are at last well-meant.

The second start often marks the biggest single-race improvement of a horse's career, and many of them win as overlays, particularly those that flashed a hint of ability first out—a show of early speed, or a middle move on the turn before flattening out, or simply an even effort to finish in the middle of the pack.

Generally, the faster a horse runs first time out, the less likely it is to improve in its second start. The past performances of the 426 Triple Crown nominees for 2006, published prior to Round 1 of the Kentucky Derby Futures Wager, provided a wealth of information regarding this point. Based on the horses with the requisite data—their first two starts came in North America and received a Beyer figure—they were divided into three categories: second-time starters that improved by 5 or more points; second-time starters who essentially ran the same race again, differing by 4 points or less either way; and second-time starters who regressed by more than 5 points. Three subsets were used: those who earned a Beyer figure no higher than 70 first out; those who earned a Beyer of 80 or higher; and those who earned a Beyer of 90 or higher. The results:

Debut Beyer 70 or Lower: The 177 horses who met this requirement were strong candidates to improve.
Improved by at least 5 points: 123 (69 percent)
Stayed the same: 31 (18 percent)
Regressed by more than 5 points: 23 (13 percent)

Debut Beyer 80 or Higher: The 36 horses that reached this level first out were far less likely to improve, and far more likely to regress than those who ran lower figures.
Improved by at least 5 points: 4 (11 percent)
Stayed the same: 11 (31 percent)
Regressed by more than 5 points: 21 (58 percent)

Debut Beyer 90 or Higher: Only 14 horses reached this rarified level first out, and nearly two-thirds were negatively impacted next time.
Improved by at least 5 points: 1 (7 percent)
Stayed the same: 4 (29 percent)
Regressed by more than five points: 9 (64 percent)

Among the five horses that Beyered 90 or better first out and did not regress, one was Latent Heat, an eventual Grade 1 winner, who paired 97s. The average decline among the nine who bounced was 25 points, and most were well-backed at the betting windows.

Horses such as Latent Heat are the exception to the rule. Horses that run a figure of 90 or higher first out should be avoided at short odds in their follow-up starts until and unless they demonstrate the fast race wasn't too much, too soon; at the very least, they should not be relied upon to anchor multirace exotic plays.

Often, second-timers like Thru n' Thru and Jamacian Kev bounce badly:

10 Thru n' Thru
Own: Watson and Weltman Performances LLC a
Purple Red, Red 'Mp' On Yellow Ball, Yellow
ESPINOZA V (—) 2007: (461 88 .19)
Ch. f. 3 (Apr) BARMAR06 $130,000
Sire: Stormy Atlantic (Storm Cat) $30,000
Dam: Thruthelookinglass (Alydar)
Br: Mr & Mrs G J Stautberg (Ky)
Tr: Baffert Bob(—) 2007:(169 33 .20)
L 118
Life 2 1 0 0 $33,000 94 | D.Fst 2 1 0 0 $33,000 94
2006 2 1 0 0 $33,000 94 | Wet(369) 0 0 0 0 $0 -
2005 0 M 0 0 $0 - | Synth 0 0 0 0 $0 -
CD 0 0 0 0 $0 - | Turf(320) 0 0 0 0 $0 -
Dst(363) 1 0 0 0 $6,000 48

1Jly06-9Hol fst 6f :212 :443 :5721:104 ⒻLandaluce100k 48 6 1 1½ 1½ 2½ 510¾ Arroyo N Jr LB116 b 2.00 72-11 Pinata116nk HollyTorqueTngo1165¾ SwissRose1162½ Steadied 1/8,wkened 8
Placed 4th through disqualification
15Jun06-6Hol fst 5f :212 :45 :574 ⒻMd Sp Wt 46k 94 7 2 1½ 1½ 1hd 11 Espinoza V • LB120 b 4.00 92-13 ThrunThru1201 CocoBelle1156½ *SuperFreaky*1202½ Dueled,clear,held game 9
WORKS: Apr29 SA 6f fst 1:113 H 2/3 ●Apr23 Hol ◈6f fst 1:114 Hg 1/30 Apr17 SA 4f fst :48 H 3/12 Apr11 SA 6f fst 1:13 H 2/9 Apr4 SA 6f fst 1:121 H 3/8 Mar26 SA 4f fst :481 H 8/28
TRAINER: +180Days(31 .29 $3.21) Dirt(478 .24 $1.73) Sprint(327 .23 $1.65) Alw(133 .25 $2.02) J/T 2006-07 CD(3 .00 $0.00) J/T 2006-07(161 .30 $1.80)

Jamacian Kev
Own: Paraneck Stable
Black, Cherry Ball, Black 'P,' Cherry
VELASQUEZ C (15 2 2 5 .13) 2007: (579 89 .15)
Dk. b or br c. 3 (Feb) FTKOCT05 $100,000
Sire: Tale of the Cat (Storm Cat) $37,500
Dam: Miss Moonwaki (Miswaki)
Br: WinStar Farm LLC (Ky)
Tr: DeMola Joseph(—) 2007:(36 5 .14)
L 118
Life 2 1 0 0 $34,050 94 | D.Fst 2 1 0 0 $34,050 94
2007 2 1 0 0 $34,050 94 | Wet(377) 0 0 0 0 $0 -
2006 0 M 0 0 $0 - | Synth 0 0 0 0 $0 -
Bel 0 0 0 0 $0 - | Turf(286) 0 0 0 0 $0 -
Dst(390) 0 0 0 0 $0 -

21Apr07-3Aqu fst 7f :233 :47 1:111 1:232 OC 100k/n1x-N 71 3 4 41½ 41½ 42½ 47¼ Garcia Alan L122 *1.35 77-12 NotfrMny1181¼ ⒹRckwyTd1182¾ MstrWhtScks1182¾ Bumped after start 4
7Apr07-3Aqu fst 6½f :23 :46 1:093 1:16 3+Md Sp Wt 53k 94 1 5 2½ 2hd 1½ 12 Garcia Alan L118 16.70 97-09 Jamacian Kev1182 Hedge Fund1231¾ *Truman's Gold*1181¾ Vied inside, clear 6
WORKS: ●May3 Aqu 5f fst 1:003 H 1/11 Apr19 Aqu 4f fst :48 H 3/22 Mar28 Aqu⊡ 5f fst 1:012 H 5/10 Mar21 Aqu⊡ 5f fst 1:02 Bg 3/18 Mar10 Aqu⊡ 5f fst 1:024 B 10/16 Mar4 Aqu⊡ 4f fst :484 H 8/18
TRAINER: Dirt(60 .12 $1.72) Sprint(29 .07 $1.50) Alw(13 .00 $0.00) J/T 2006-07 BEL(1 .00 $0.00) J/T 2006-07(2 .00 $0.00)

Horses who are overextended second time out are also candidates to bounce. As with first-time starters who overextend themselves first out, they should be regarded with caution until they come back around and produce another big figure:

Superfly
Own: LaPenta Robert V
Maroon, Gold Epaulets, Maroon Cap
JARA F (13 1 0 1 .08) 2006: (599 59 .10)
Dk. b or br c. 3 (Mar) KEESEP04 $210,000
Sire: Fusaichi Pegasus (Mr. Prospector) $125,000
Dam: Marozia (Storm Bird)
Br: Barnett Enterprises (Ky)
Tr: Zito Nicholas P(3 0 0 0 .00) 2006:(311 53 .17)
L 117
Life 10 1 2 3 $173,210 97 | D.Fst 8 1 1 2 $116,280 97
2006 5 0 1 1 $27,390 86 | Wet(334) 2 0 1 1 $56,930 83
2005 5 1 1 2 $145,820 97 | Turf(254) 0 0 0 0 $0 -
Bel 2 0 0 1 $97,700 89 | Dst(355) 2 1 0 1 $84,620 80

26Aug06-7Sar fst 7f :223 :452 1:10 1:232 3+OC 75k/n1x-N 86 5 5 62¼ 63¼ 61 52 Leparoux J R5 L112 3.70 85-11 SimonPure117[illegible]nk OnBordAgin1171½ Bumped backstretch 9
15Apr06-9OP fst 1⅛ :462 1:104 1:373 1:511 ArkDerby-G2 54 11 2½ 42 32½ 1120 1127 Martinez W L122 b 37.50 55-22 LwyerRon1222¾ Steppnwolfr1181½ PrivtVow1227¼ With early pace, faded 13
25Mar06-10TP fst 1⅛ ◈ :471 1:114 1:38 1:51 LanesEnd-G2 78 3 42 52¼ 41½ 32½ 55¾ Rose J L121 4.20 87-09 With a City1211¼ Seaside Retreat1211½ Malameeze1213 Drifted out 3/16 pl 12
4Mar06-3GP fst 1⅛ :472 1:111 1:354 1:481 Alw 33000n1x 80 3 21½ 2hd 1hd 33½ 39¼ Prado E S L118 *.80 92-02 Sunriver118½ High Blues1188¾ Superfly11810 Slim lead, tired 5
4Feb06-5GP slyS 7f :22 :442 1:09 1:221 Alw 33000n1x 83 1 5 21 1hd 22 23 Prado E S L118 *.70 94-04 Go Bucky Go1223 Superfly118½ Tactoro1184 Inside bid, no match 7
29Oct05-4Bel fst 1 1/16 :23 :453 1:103 1:413 BCJuvnle-G1 89 1 137½ 105½ 83¼ 56 58½ Coa E M L122 48.50 83-11 StevieWonderboy1221¼ *HnnyHughs*1222 FirstSmuri1225½ 3 wide run, tired 14
8Oct05-9Bel slyS 1 :213 :433 1:083 1:361 Champagn-G1 80 3 32 43 511 513 312½ Coa E M L122 11.50 67-23 FirstSamuri1222¾ HennyHughes1229¾ Superfly122¾ Chased inside, no bid 6
17Sep05-8Del fst 1 :233 :472 1:122 1:38 WhrlingAsh57k 78 1 1½ 11 1hd 1½ 11½ Dominguez R A L115 *.50 90-17 Superfly1151½ Kid Lemonade1207¾ Vegas Play1173½ Came o,straightend 5
27Aug05-6Sar fst 6f :222 :454 :572 1:093 Md Sp Wt 45k 97 4 2 22 2½ 23 23½ Stevens G L L118 *2.05e 88-13 *Discreet Cat*1183½ *Superfly*11811 Ivanovsky118nk Tried winner 1/4 pole 9
6Aug05-5Sar fst 6½f :22 :451 1:111 1:182 Md Sp Wt 45k 76 9 4 42¾ 3½ 2hd 3¾ Dominguez R A L118 27.00 81-11 Grand Survival118½ *Cab*118nk Superfly1182¼ Chased outside, gamely 11
WORKS: ●Sep10 Sar tr.t 5f fst 1:01 B 1/13 ●Aug12 Sar tr.t 4f fst :48 B 1/10 Aug5 Sar tr.t 4f fst :49 B 3/17 ●Jly29 Sar tr.t 3f gd :35 H 1/6 Jly22 Sar tr.t 3f fst :37 B 2/11 Jly15 Sar tr.t 3f fst :394 B 6/8
TRAINER: 2Off45-180(100 .15 $1.11) Sprint/Route(110 .19 $1.52) Dirt(709 .19 $1.69) Routes(465 .19 $1.57) Alw(217 .25 $2.08) J/T 2005-06 BEL(1 .00 $0.00) J/T 2005-06(5 .20 $2.56)

Superfly freaked with a 97 Beyer second time out, but had the terrible misfortune to hook Discreet Cat in the fastest juvenile maiden race of 2005. Three weeks later, he broke his maiden in a minor stakes at 1–2, even while bouncing 19 points. As he went deeper into his 3-year-old campaign without getting back to his 97 as a 2-year-old, it became more and more of a negative sign, and there were several opportunities to bet against him.

When debut efforts have been hard-fought, second-time starters are vulnerable regardless of how fast the figure was:

Whistlin' challenged for the lead on the turn and battled head and head all the way to the wire when nipped first out at Saratoga on August 5, 2006. He was pounded down to just under 6–5 for his next start, which by today's standards came on very short rest just 13 days later, and threw in a real clunker to fade completely out of the trifecta picture.

However, when Whistlin' returned four weeks later to break his maiden stylishly, and with a figure exceeding his debut, it was a positive sign and a springboard to a series of even faster races.

•

CHAPTER 2

Beyond Figures

"Handicapping information is of little use unless it is synthesized and analyzed by the creative mind."

—Mark Cramer, author, handicapper,
and renowned contrarian

The Expanded Past Performances

BACK IN THE DAY, handicappers seriously motivated to make profits accumulated stacks upon stacks of yellowed *Daily Racing Form*s that served as a key reference library. Situations regularly arose where horses returned to previous winning circumstances that no longer appeared in their current block of 10 past performances; there was a wide chasm between players in the know and those who were completely in the dark.

But the modern handicapper has everything handed to him on a silver platter, thanks to *Daily Racing Form*'s vastly expanded past performances, which go back 12 races at most major tracks, and contain a long laundry list of informative features, so that there is no longer any reason to turn one's handicapping work area into a fire hazard.

And if there is any ambiguity about what is shown in a horse's current block of past performances, *Daily Racing Form*'s Formulator 4.1 software allows users to scour its entire career:

Unswept
Own: Eagle View Farm

Dk. b or b. g. 7 (Jan)
Sire: End Sweep (Forty Niner) $34,500
Dam: Dress (Topsider)
Br: Dr. Jerry Bilinski, Martin Zaretsky & Marc Roberts (NY)
Tr: Russo Frank J(5 0 1 1 .00) 2007:(24 2 .08)

	Life	48	9	7	7	$334,013	100	D.Fst	38	7	5	5	$265,569	92
	2007	2	0	0	2	$4,400	78	Wet(361)	6	2	2	2	$65,132	100
	2006	15	1	1	2	$56,361	100	Synth	0	0	0	0	$0	-
								Turf(273)	4	0	0	0	$3,312	85
	Aqu⊡	17	7	2	4	$210,004	100	Dst(363)	34	8	4	5	$260,426	100

[Past performance chart data]

WORKS: Mar21 Bel tr.t 3f fst :38² B 1/27
TRAINER: 31-60Days(18 .11 $5.67) Sprint(58 .07 $0.71) Stakes(1 .00 $0.00)

This is actually an encore appearance for Unswept, a likable old winter warrior who originally appeared in Dean Keppler's *Trainer Angles,* published by DRF Press in 2006, as an example of what to look for in terms of spacing between races: Unswept seemed to flourish with a month or so between starts.

What was also true about Unswept is that he was twice the racehorse on Aqueduct's inner-dirt track that he was on any other surface: As of spring 2007, he had compiled a record of 7-2-4 from 17 starts on the Big A's inner track, and was a mere 2-5-3 from 31 starts on any other footing.

Unswept's proficiency on the inner track was not lost on Gary Contessa, who trained him for his first 18 races before losing him via the claim box on November 10, 2004.

Contessa watched Unswept win all three of his starts on the inner track soon afterward during the first months of 2005, and reclaimed the gelding when he returned from a three-month freshening on September 5 of that year. Unswept had another productive winter on the inner track, winning two of five starts, and narrowly missing a third score in an allowance race with a $47,000 purse.

Contessa lost Unswept again on June 11, 2006, this time to connections that apparently (and erroneously) felt he would be successful on turf. Contessa waited patiently for the summer to come to an end, as Unswept was put in all the wrong spots, and reclaimed the gelding yet again on August 30, 2006, with the idea of freshening him up for another go-round on his favorite track.

By this time, however, Unswept had a lot of mileage on the equine odometer, and when he returned on December 1, 2006, he could only manage a third-place finish. Ostensibly, a third-place finish is not so terrible. But there was an important development here, and until and unless Unswept provides evidence to the contrary, he should be avoided at the betting windows.

Why? Consider that the Beyer figure of 53 was the lowest figure he had ever recorded on dirt—and it came on Aqueduct's inner track, the surface he had relished during four previous winter campaigns. Moreover, his peak figure of 100 had been delivered the last time he had raced over a sealed inner track (the superscript "s" is a recent addition to the track conditions). Under the circumstances, that was just an alarmingly subpar performance that stamped Unswept as a bet-against.

Unswept improved a bit next out on December 30, but his figure of 71 was still far below his previous level on the inner track, and he remained a horse to avoid when he made his first start as a 7-year-old. Frank Russo reclaimed him for $20,000 nevertheless, and he was sidelined for nearly 11 weeks. He remained a horse to steer clear of when he resurfaced for a mere $7,500 in April 2007.

Tomlinson Ratings

Less than 15 years ago, the upper-right corner of horses' past performances contained the lifetime record, the record for the last two years, and the record on turf and wet tracks. That was it. The expanded career box now also contains the record at today's track, the record on fast dirt, the record on synthetic tracks, the record at the distance, and Tomlinson Ratings for wet tracks, turf, and today's distance.

The Tomlinson Ratings are especially useful when a horse is encountering unfamiliar footing for the first time. They are the brainchild of Lee Tomlinson, who recalled how it all got started:

"After having one too many losing days at the track whenever the condition was listed as sloppy or muddy, I realized that past performances on a fast track were often useless.

"At that time, the *Daily Racing Form* did not show the wet-track record for each runner. Rather, they just used a symbol, placed just after the horse's name, to indicate whether the horse was 'fair,' 'good,' or 'superior' on off tracks. All well and good for horses that had already demonstrated their ability to handle the mud or the slop, but what if a horse had never run on either of those surfaces?

"In the fall of 1985, I locked myself in a room for about three days, accompanied by 500 to 600 copies of old *Racing Form*s I had on hand, and began to go through every set of past performances and result charts I found . . . It soon became clear that pedigree could, indeed, be a factor. Certain names, like Relaunch, In Reality, Valid Appeal, and Shimatoree began to appear more often than others. I then prepared for my own use two typewritten pages of 'off' track sires, rating them from 1 (above average) to 5 (outstanding). I then did the same research for turf sires. After a month or two of successfully testing my numbers, a friend suggested I sell them. And so 'Mudders & Turfers' was born. Manually prepared ratings were soon computerized, and access to a huge database led to more scientific and accurate ratings. A few years later, the same research was used to compile distance ratings, and with that came another publication, 'Sprinters & Stayers.'"

The Tomlinson Ratings are based on the actual performances of all progeny of every sire, grandsire, and broodmare sire. The ratings range from 0 to 480 (a perfect score).

Beyond the guidelines found in *Daily Racing Form* (a rating of 320 or better merits further consideration on wet tracks; a rating of 280 or better merits further consideration on turf; a distance rating of 320 is considered average), Tomlinson offers these guidelines for maximizing the use of the ratings:

Situation: A young horse, after having run in nothing but sprint races on the dirt, is entered in a one-mile race on the turf. Thus, we have a horse trying two new things.

Suggestion: Combine the two Tomlinson ratings. For example, the horse's turf rating (let's say 320) would be added to its distance rating (let's say 370), giving a combined rating of 690. And while 690 is very good, it should be compared to the combined ratings of others in the same race, especially those that haven't already proven to be turf failures.

A combined turf + distance rating of 630 or more merits further consideration.

A combined wet + distance rating of 680 or more merits further consideration.

Situation: A European import is making its first start in the United States, and the race is on dirt. All of the horse's races abroad were on turf, and it was somewhat successful despite the fact that its turf pedigree was nothing special. In light of that, perhaps the horse might run better on dirt than on turf. This is similar to the case of Cigar, sired by Palace Music, a below-average turf sire. Cigar raced 11 times on the grass before his connections realized the horse might be better suited for the dirt. Indeed, in his second lifetime start, Cigar won a six-furlong dirt sprint at Hollywood Park in 1:09⅖, and with the benefit of hindsight it's astounding that he was subsequently transferred to the turf for 11 straight starts from May 1993 to October 1994.

Suggestion: Check the Tomlinson Rating for any horse trying a surface it has never been on before. The higher the rating, the more you should consider its chances.

Situation/Suggestion: A young horse is making its second lifetime start. In its debut it was well-bet but did not run very well. However, the track was sloppy that day and now the horse is running on a fast track. If the Tomlinson wet rating is low (less than 350), you might want to give the horse another chance to demonstrate its ability on a surface that should be more to its liking.

Situation/Suggestion: The flip side of the previous example would be the case of a young horse coming off a great performance on a sloppy or muddy track. However, today's race is on a fast track. If the Tomlinson rating is 350 or higher, you might surmise that the off track last time out enhanced the horse's performance, which might tend to reduce one's expectations in light of the surface change it faces today.

Situation/Suggestion: A field of 3-year-olds is scheduled to go 1¼ miles for the first time. While several entrants have gone 1⅛ miles, none has ever crossed the threshold of today's final furlong and raced at a longer distance. The Tomlinson distance rating might provide a clue as to which runner has the endurance to excel at the longer distance.

Then and Now

To see how radically past performances have changed, here is a 2-year-old maiden race at Keeneland from April 22, 1993, that served as an example race in the original version of *Expert Handicapping*:

4 ½ FURLONGS. (.51) MAIDEN. SPECIAL WEIGHT. Purse $15,600 (includes $2,600 from KTDF). Fillies. 2-year-olds. Weight, 117 lbs. (Preference to fillies catalogued in 1993 Keeneland 2-year Sale.)

Cahaba Dancer
Dk. b. or br. f. 2(Apr), by Marshua's Dancer—Country Chic, by Cox's Ridge
Lifetime 0 0 0 0 / 1993 0 M 0 0
MELANCON L (12 2 1 1 .17)
Br.—Dawahare A F (Ky)
Own.—Dawahare A F & Ellis William
Tr.—McPeek Kenneth G (10 2 0 2 .20)
117
LATEST WORKOUTS   Apr 20 Kee 3f fst :38³ Bg   Apr 15 CD 4f sly :50 Bg   ●Apr 4 CD 3f fst :36¹ B

Bob's Claim
Dk. b. or br. f. 2(Feb), by Claim—How's That, by Lord Avie
Lifetime 0 0 0 0 / 1993 0 M 0 0
ARGUELLO F A JR (1 0 0 0 .00)
Br.—Lake Charles III (Ky)
Own.—Dike Charles E
Tr.—Montano Angel (6 0 0 1 .00)
117
LATEST WORKOUTS   Apr 16 Kee 4f gd :50² Bg   Mar 31 Kee 3f fst :37 Bg

Crafty and Evil
Ch. f. 2(Mar), by Crafty Prospector—Evil Elaine, by Medieval Man
Lifetime 0 0 0 0 / 1993 0 M 0 0
STEINER J J (9 1 0 4 .11)
Br.—Wood M L Mr-Mrs (Ky)
Own.—Siegel Jan-Mace & Samantha
Tr.—Mayberry Brian A (10 0 0 3 .00)
117
LATEST WORKOUTS   Apr 18 Kee 3f fst :37¹ B   Mar 28 Kee 3f fst :37³ B

Autumn In Dixie
B. f. 2, by Dixieland Band—Autumn Olive, by Gallant Lad
Lifetime 0 0 0 0 / 1993 0 M 0 0
SELLERS S J (68 19 9 7 .28)
Br.—Cheney Mark Mr-Mrs W (Ky)
Own.—Cheney Terrell
Tr.—Wilkinson Jack R III (—)
117
LATEST WORKOUTS   Apr 18 Kee 4f fst :48² B   Apr 10 Kee 3f my :36³ B

Normandy Belle
B. f. 2, by FK To Fight—French Flick, by Silent Screen
Lifetime 0 0 0 0 / 1993 0 M 0 0
PERRET C (38 9 10 5 .23)
Br.—Firman Pamela Mrs H (Ky)
Own.—Humphrey G Watts Jr
Tr.—Pierce Joseph H Jr (4 1 0 1 .25)
117

Odie West
Ch. f. 2(Apr), by Westheimer—Miss Odie, by Cannonade
Lifetime 2 0 2 0 / 1993 2 M 2 0 $6,240
OUZTS P W (15 0 2 0 .00)
Br.—O'Neal Dr & Mrs Dave (Ky)
Own.—Lunsford Clyde
Tr.—Short Thomas (6 0 2 0 .00)
117
$6,240   Wet 1 0 1 0 $3,120
14Apr93– 1Kee sly 4½f   :22²   :46²   :52³   ⓕMd Sp Wt   46 3 5   56¼ 45½ 2¹¼ Ouzts P W   117   7.30   94-08 AshlsSprft117¹⅛OdWst117ʰᵏChttCd117 Bid, fully extend 10
6Apr93– 3Kee fst 4½f   :22⁴   :47¹   :53⁴   ⓕMd Sp Wt   25 4 4   45 43¼ 2¼ Ouzts P W   117   19.60   89-07 CityJoyc117¹⅛OdiWst117ⁿᵉSpphrBds117 Swung out late 6
LATEST WORKOUTS   Apr 1 KHC 4f fst :50³ Hg

Flip The Cannon
Dk. b. or br. f. 2, by Cannon Dancer—Tribute Of Gold, by Full Out
Lifetime 0 0 0 0 / 1993 0 M 0 0
NEAGLE W J (10 1 0 3 .10)
Br.—Demeritte Larry (Ky)
Own.—Demeritte Beryl
Tr.—Demeritte Larry (1 0 1 0 .00)
117

New Fe
B. f. 2(Apr), by King Merraw—Fefe La Canard, by Qui Native
Lifetime 0 0 0 0 / 1993 0 M 0 0
STACY A T (15 1 2 3 .07)
Br.—King Warren L (Ky)
Own.—War-Bec Farm
Tr.—King Warren L (2 0 1 0 .00)
117
LATEST WORKOUTS   Apr 20 Kee 3f fst :36 Bg   Apr 14 Kee 4f fst :48² Hg   Apr 11 Kee 3f fst :36² B   Apr 4 Kee 3f fst :38 B

The bare-bones data made it difficult to develop any kind of a meaningful opinion, which is why, in the mid-1990s, the recommendation was made in this book's original version to consult peripheral sources such as *Maiden Stats,* the annual phone-book-sized publication from Bloodstock Research Information Services:

	SIRE INFO						DAM INFO									SIBLING INFO		YRLG SALES INFO	
Horse	wnr/str	2yo wnr/str	Mxd 1st	Turf wnd	wl/sts	wl/sts	1stT $pi	prf $pi	fls	wnr/str	2yo sw wnr/str	Mxd and	wl/sts	Turf wnr/str	Dosage Index	Top Sibling	/Raisd	Price/Sire avg Bnk/sld	Stud Fee
CRAFTY AND EVIL	163/192	60/115	23 6.4	72/ 304	71 :387	5	2.67	:w 0.23	2	0/ 1	0 0/ 1	0.0	0/ 1	0/ 1	4.45			100,0/15 44k 1/28	15k
CRAFT BALLI	67/144	18/ 90	1 6.6	9/ 251	4/	47 9	0.31	5p	3						2.60				
CRAFTY KORBIX	246/323	73/198	8 7.3	20/259	27 487	7	0.97	w 3.08	9	5/ 6	0 2/ 4	7.3	31/ 16	2/ 2	5.67	Treasured	/5409k		

Crafty and Evil's listing suggested she was to be taken seriously: Her sire, Crafty Prospector, was shown as winning with 23 percent of his first-time starters. Among the 28 Crafty Prospector yearlings sold in 1992, Crafty and Evil's $100,000 purchase price was the highest, indicating there was something about this filly's pedigree, conformation, and/or overall demeanor that a buyer had paid a premium for. She won and paid $21.

Fast-forward 14 Aprils to 2007, and the past performances for another field of 2-year-olds had evolved to look like this in *Daily Racing Form:*

2 **Keeneland** *4½ Furlongs* **Md Sp Wt 50k** Purse $50,000 (include $6,000 KTDF - KY TB Devt Fund) For Maidens, Two Year Olds. Weight, 118 lbs.

Coupled – Billie Bob and One Hot Wish

2 Digital
White   Own: Elkhorn Oaks Inc
Emerald, White Inverted Chevron, Emerald
MENA M (2 0 0 0 .00) 2007: (373 70 .19)
B. c. 2 (Mar)
Sire: Zavata (Phone Trick) $7,500
Dam: Crafty Personality (Crafty Prospector)
Br: Elkhorn Oaks Inc (Ky)
Tr: Jackson James R(3 0 0 0 .00) 2007:(51 6 .12)
118

Life	0 M 0 0	$0	–	D.Fst	0 0 0 0	$0	–
2007	0 M 0 0	$0	–	Wet(363*)	0 0 0 0	$0	–
2006	0 M 0 0	$0	–	Synth	0 0 0 0	$0	–
Kee	0 0 0 0	$0	–	Turf(211)	0 0 0 0	$0	–
				Dst(358*)	0 0 0 0	$0	–

WORKS: Apr9 Kee ⊗ 3f fst :37³ B 9/10   Apr4 Kee ⊗ 3f fst :37¹ Bg 6/20   Mar30 Kee ⊗ 3f fst :38¹ B 20/22
TRAINER: 1stStart(17 .06 $1.14) 1stLasix(3 .00 $0.00) 2YO(54 .04 $0.45) Synth(140 .11 $1.06) Sprint(197 .17 $1.41) MdnSpWt(35 .00 $0.00)

3 Caviarbythecreek
Blue   Own: Ditola & Dare to Dream Stable LLC Tri
Black, White Horse Head, White Diamonds
GUIDRY M (4 0 0 1 .00) 2007: (218 28 .13)
Dk. b or br f. 2 (Mar)   BARJAN06 $2,200
Sire: Storm Creek (Storm Cat) $5,000
Dam: Copper Caviar (End Sweep)
Br: Kelly Brintle & Suzanna Brintle (Cal)
Tr: Rivelli Larry(—) 2007:(41 8 .20)
115

Life	0 M 0 0	$0	–	D.Fst	0 0 0 0	$0	–
2007	0 M 0 0	$0	–	Wet(315)	0 0 0 0	$0	–
2006	0 M 0 0	$0	–	Synth	0 0 0 0	$0	–
Kee	0 0 0 0	$0	–	Turf(307)	0 0 0 0	$0	–
				Dst(317)	0 0 0 0	$0	–

WORKS: Mar19 GP 3f fst :35⁴ Bg 2/5
TRAINER: 1stStart(11 .18 $1.16) 1stLasix(2 .00 $0.00) 2YO(14 .14 $0.51) Sprint(182 .22 $1.34) MdnSpWt(24 .12 $0.69)   J/T 2006-07 KEE (1 .00 $0.00) J/T 2006-07(4 .00 $0.00)

4 Ready in the Morn
Yellow   Own: Ralph Stroope
Silver, Gold Beehive, Black Cap
NAKATANI C S (—) 2007: (204 31 .15)
Ch. c. 2 (Jan)
Sire: More Than Ready (Southern Halo) $40,000
Dam: Morning Spice (Personal Hope)
Br: Ralph Stroope (Ky)
Tr: Werner Ronny(—) 2007:(87 11 .13)
118

Life	0 M 0 0	$0	–	D.Fst	0 0 0 0	$0	–
2007	0 M 0 0	$0	–	Wet(365)	0 0 0 0	$0	–
2006	0 M 0 0	$0	–	Synth	0 0 0 0	$0	–
Kee	0 0 0 0	$0	–	Turf(319)	0 0 0 0	$0	–
				Dst(357)	0 0 0 0	$0	–

WORKS: ●Apr5 Kee ⊗ 4f fst :47¹ Hg 1/32   ●Mar8 LS 3f fst :35⁴ Bg 1/13
TRAINER: 1stStart(50 .06 $0.50) 2YO(48 .19 $2.49) Synth(22 .09 $0.57) Sprint(238 .21 $1.87) MdnSpWt(105 .14 $1.73)

1 Billie Bob

Own: Robert C Tanklage and Wesley A Ward
Red   Black, Gold 'W', Gold Band On Sleeves
BEJARANO R (14 3 2 1 .21) 2007: (466 68 .15)

Dk. b or br f. 2 (Feb)
Sire: Bring the Heat (In Excess*Ire) $2,000
Dam: Purgatory (Devil's Bag)
Br: Wesley Ward (Cal)
Tr: Ward Wesley A(3 1 0 1 .33) 2007:(64 21 .33)

🅛 115

							D.Fst	0 0 0 0	$0	–
Life	0 M 0 0	$0	–				Wet(371)	0 0 0 0	$0	–
2007	0 M 0 0	$0	–				Synth	0 0 0 0	$0	–
2006	0 M 0 0	$0	–				Turf(312*)	0 0 0 0	$0	–
Kee	0 0 0 0	$0	–				Dst(371*)	0 0 0 0	$0	–

WORKS: ●Apr7 Kee ◈3f fst :34³ Hg 1/15 Apr1 Kee ◈3f fst :38 B 3/5 Mar21 GP 3f fst :37 Bg 2/6
TRAINER: 1stStart(39 .31 $1.75) 1stLasix(10 .20 $0.78) 2YO(53 .30 $1.52) Synth(7 .14 $1.09) Sprint(242 .24 $1.90) MdnSpWt(25 .40 $3.16)

J/T 2006-07 KEE(2 .50 $3.80) J/T 2006-07(3 .33 $2.53)

5 High Bridled

Own: Gary S Logsdon Donnie Kelly and Jamie
Green   Black, White Diamond and Stars, White
ALBARADO R J (15 0 4 2 .00) 2007: (364 65 .23)

Ch. c. 2 (Mar)   KEESEP06 $60,000
Sire: Unbridled's Song (Unbridled) $200,000
Dam: Highbury (Seattle Slew)
Br: Swordlestown Stud (Ky)
Tr: Sanders Jamie(5 0 0 0 .00) 2007:(66 1 .02)

🅛 118

							D.Fst	0 0 0 0	$0	–
Life	0 M 0 0	$0	–				Wet(400)	0 0 0 0	$0	–
2007	0 M 0 0	$0	–				Synth	0 0 0 0	$0	–
2006	0 M 0 0	$0	–				Turf(320)	0 0 0 0	$0	–
Kee	0 0 0 0	$0	–				Dst(381)	0 0 0 0	$0	–

WORKS: ●Apr2 Kee ◈4f fst :46² Hg 1/34 Mar25 Kee ◈3f fst :36² B 1/3 Mar21 VHT 3f gd :38² B 3/8
TRAINER: 1stStart(25 .04 $2.01) 1stLasix(4 .00 $0.00) 2YO(93 .08 $2.57) Synth(54 .04 $0.41) Sprint(124 .06 $1.03) MdnSpWt(64 .05 $2.39)

J/T 2006-07 KEE (6 .33 $9.67) J/T 2006-07(38 .13 $2.26)

6 Must Acquit

Own: Heiligbrodt Racing Stable
Black   White, Burnt Orange Star, Orange Band On
GOMEZ G K (16 5 2 1 .31) 2007: (334 84 .25)

B. c. 2 (Jan)
Sire: Successful Appeal (Valid Appeal) $40,000
Dam: Gloria (Honour and Glory)
Br: Heiligbrodt Racing Stable (La)
Tr: Asmussen Steven M(4 1 1 0 .25) 2007:(554 118 .21)

🅛 118

							D.Fst	0 0 0 0	$0	–
Life	0 M 0 0	$0	–				Wet(426)	0 0 0 0	$0	–
2007	0 M 0 0	$0	–				Synth	0 0 0 0	$0	–
2006	0 M 0 0	$0	–				Turf(324)	0 0 0 0	$0	–
Kee	0 0 0 0	$0	–				Dst(420)	0 0 0 0	$0	–

WORKS: Apr3 Kee ◈4f fst :49 B 24/35 Mar27 Kee ◈4f fst :50 Bg 24/35 Mar18 Hou 4f fst :49¹ Bg 16/77 Mar3 Hou 3f fst :38² Bg 31/48 Feb25 Hou 3f fst :37² B 11/61
TRAINER: 1stStart(110 .20 $1.69) 1stLasix(13 .31 $1.75) 2YO(124 .27 $1.82) Synth(6 .17 $1.10) Sprint(1005 .20 $1.50) MdnSpWt(267 .23 $1.52)

J/T 2006-07 KEE (2 .50 $3.30) J/T 2006-07(18 .50 $2.72)

1a One Hot Wish

Own: Robert C Tanklage and Wesley A Ward
Red   Black, Gold 'W', Gold Band On Sleeves
BEJARANO R (14 3 2 1 .21) 2007: (466 68 .15)

Ch. f. 2 (May)
Sire: Bring the Heat (In Excess*Ire) $2,000
Dam: Wish for a Jeanne (Roar)
Br: Wesley A Ward (Cal)
Tr: Ward Wesley A(3 1 0 1 .33) 2007:(64 21 .33)

🅛 115

							D.Fst	0 0 0 0	$0	–
Life	0 M 0 0	$0	–				Wet(379)	0 0 0 0	$0	–
2007	0 M 0 0	$0	–				Synth	0 0 0 0	$0	–
2006	0 M 0 0	$0	–				Turf(326*)	0 0 0 0	$0	–
Kee	0 0 0 0	$0	–				Dst(385*)	0 0 0 0	$0	–

WORKS: Apr7 Kee ◈4f fst :47³ Hg 16/74 Apr1 Kee ◈3f fst :38¹ B 4/5 Mar21 GP 3f fst :37 Bg 2/6
TRAINER: 1stStart(39 .31 $1.75) 1stLasix(10 .20 $0.78) 2YO(53 .30 $1.52) Synth(7 .14 $1.09) Sprint(242 .24 $1.90) MdnSpWt(25 .40 $3.16)

J/T 2006-07 KEE(2 .50 $3.80) J/T 2006-07(3 .33 $2.53)

7 Lantana Mob

Own: Vinery Stables LLC
Orange   Green, White Yoke, Green Stripes On
BRIDGMOHAN S X (13 0 4 2 .00) 2007: (207 23 .11)

B. c. 2 (Feb)
Sire: Posse (Silver Deputy) $12,500
Dam: Lantana (Copelan)
Br: Thomas/Burleson/Visagie (Ky)
Tr: Asmussen Steven M(4 1 1 0 .25) 2007:(554 118 .21)

🅛 118

							D.Fst	0 0 0 0	$0	–
Life	0 M 0 0	$0	–				Wet(359)	0 0 0 0	$0	–
2007	0 M 0 0	$0	–				Synth	0 0 0 0	$0	–
2006	0 M 0 0	$0	–				Turf(230)	0 0 0 0	$0	–
Kee	0 0 0 0	$0	–				Dst(369)	0 0 0 0	$0	–

WORKS: Apr3 Kee ◈4f fst :48² Bg 17/35 Mar25 Hou 4f fst :49² Bg 24/61 Mar18 Hou 4f fst :49³ Bg 29/77 Mar11 Hou 4f fst :52¹ Bg 37/43 Mar4 Hou 3f fst :39 B 28/36 Feb25 Hou 3f fst :38¹ B 27/61
TRAINER: 1stStart(110 .20 $1.69) 1stLasix(13 .31 $1.75) 2YO(124 .27 $1.82) Synth(6 .17 $1.10) Sprint(1005 .20 $1.50) MdnSpWt(267 .23 $1.52)

J/T 2006-07 KEE(21 .24 $1.36) J/T 2006-07(171 .18 $1.40)

Aside from the fact that Keeneland races are now run on Poly-track (more about that later), consider some of the important differences from then to now:

- Workouts are ranked.
- Meet *and* year-to-date records are shown for trainer and jockey.
- Expanded pedigree info includes grandsire, auction price, where sold, and when.
- Trainer Form shows up to six relevant stat categories at the bottom of the horse's record.
- Jockey/Trainer combination is shown at the race meet and overall since the start of the previous year.
- Medication (Lasix) indicated.
- Tomlinson Ratings are listed for wet, turf, and distance.
- Previous starts (if any) on synthetic (all-weather) surfaces.

Obviously, the word was out on One Hot Wish, as might have been surmised based on trainer Wesley Ward's (also the breeder and co-owner) high win percentage with first-time starters. She whipped the boys by more than a dozen lengths in world-record time.

SECOND RACE 4½ FURLONGS. (.484) MAIDEN SPECIAL WEIGHT. Purse $50,000 (includes $6,000 KTDF – Kentucky TB Devt Fund) FOR MAIDENS, TWO YEAR OLDS. Weight, 118 lbs.

Keeneland

APRIL 12, 2007

Value of Race: $45,800 Winner $27,280; second $10,000; third $5,000; fourth $2,200; fifth $1,320. Mutuel Pool $219,820.00 Exacta Pool $153,160.00 Trifecta Pool $99,199.00 Superfecta Pool $40,147.00

Last Raced	Horse	M/Eqt.	A.	Wt	PP	St	¼	Str	Fin	Jockey	Odds $1
	One Hot Wish	L b	2	115	5	1	1^2	1^4	$11^{12\frac{1}{4}}$	Bejarano R	1.30
	Lantana Mob	L	2	118	6	3	3^5	$2^{1\frac{1}{2}}$	$22\frac{1}{2}$	Bridgmohan S X	11.00
	High Bridled	L	2	118	3	4	4^2	4^1	$31\frac{1}{2}$	Albarado R J	5.60
	Must Acquit	L	2	118	4	2	2^{hd}	3^4	4^2	Gomez G K	2.80
	Ready in the Morn	L	2	118	2	5	$53\frac{1}{2}$	5^8	$519\frac{3}{4}$	Nakatani C S	3.30
	Digital	L	2	118	1	6	6	6	6	Mena M	30.90

OFF AT 1:45 Start Good. Won driving. Track fast.

TIME :21², :43, :48⁴ (:21.45, :43.05, :48.87)

(New Track Record)

$2 Mutuel Prices:

1A– ONE HOT WISH	4.60	3.40	3.20
7 – LANTANA MOB		6.60	4.00
5 – HIGH BRIDLED			3.20

$2 EXACTA 1–7 PAID $38.40 $2 TRIFECTA 1–7–5 PAID $159.00
$2 SUPERFECTA 1–7–5–6 PAID $366.20

Ch. f, (May), by Bring the Heat – Wish for a Jeanne , by Roar . Trainer Ward Wesley A. Bred by Wesley A Ward (Cal).

ONE HOT WISH broke in front, quickly opened a clear advantage from the three path, then widened in the stretch under energetic hand urging as much the best in world record time. LANTANA MOB tracked the winner four or five wide and couldn't menace ONE HOT WISH while superior to the others. HIGH BRIDLED drifted in at the break bumping READY IN THE MORN, raced five wide and couldn't threaten while improving position. MUST ACQUIT chased the winner four wide until the stretch and weakened. READY IN THE MORN hopped at the start, was bumped by HIGH BRIDLED and forced in slightly on DIGITAL, then failed to menace. DIGITAL, bumped at the start, always was outrun.

Owners– 1, Tanklage Robert C and Ward Wesley; 2, Vinery Stables; 3, Sanders Jamie Logsdon Gary S and Kelly Donnie; 4, Heiligbrodt Racing Stable; 5, Stroope Ralph; 6, Elkhorn Oaks Inc

Trainers– 1, Ward Wesley A; 2, Asmussen Steven M; 3, Sanders Jamie; 4, Asmussen Steven M; 5, Werner Ronny; 6, Jackson James R

Scratched– Billie Bob , Caviarbythecreek

$2 Daily Double (3–1) Paid $232.60 ; Daily Double Pool $87,751.

Among the plethora of new data for 2-year-olds, an exceptionally strong predictive factor involves those juveniles who were sold at in-training sales earlier in the year. Lots of fashionably bred yearlings sell for sky-high prices based primarily on bloodlines, conformation, overall physicality, and that intangible "look of eagles" or "presence" in the auction ring, but those who sell nicely as 2-year-olds have put in timed workouts—usually one furlong, sometimes longer—so that a much clearer picture of actual ability emerges.

Ironically enough, the day after the prestigious 2006 Fasig-Tipton yearling sales in Saratoga, a trio of maiden races were dominated by 2-year-olds that had been purchased in training just months earlier:

```
3  Panty Raid                          Dk. b or br. f. 2  (Mar)  KEEAPR06 $275,000           Life  0 M 0 0    $0  –    D.Fst    0 0 0 0    $0  –
   Own: Glencrest Farm                 Sire: Include (Broad Brush) $12,500                   2006  0 M 0 0    $0  –    Wet(390*) 0 0 0 0   $0  –
Blue  Canary Yellow And Green Hoops, Green Cap   Dam: Adventurous Di (Private Account)       2005  0 M 0 0    $0  –    Turf(292*) 0 0 0 0  $0  –
   VELAZQUEZ J R (61 8 7 9 .13) 2006: (535 137 .26)   Br: Heaven Trees Farm (Ky)   118        2005  0 M 0 0    $0  –    Turf(292*) 0 0 0 0  $0  –
                                       Tr: Pletcher Todd A(37 7 2 7 .19) 2006:(727 203 .28)  Sar   0 0 0 0    $0  –    Dst(355)  0 0 0 0   $0  –
WORKS: Aug6 Sar 4f fst :504 B 35/47  Jly31 Sar 5f fst 1:012 H 19/67  Jly24 Sar 5f fst 1:003 B 7/32  Jly15 Sar tr.t 4f fst :503 Bg 27/55  Jly7 Sar tr.t 5f fst 1:03 B 2/18  Jun30 Sar tr.t 5f fst 1:05 B 26/33
      Jun20 Sar tr.t 5f fst 1:06 B 16/16  Jun13 Sar tr.t 4f fst :512 B 48/58  Jun7 Sar tr.t 4f fst :51 B 21/46  May31 Sar tr.t 4f fst :52 B 5/7  May23 Sar tr.t 4f fst :381 B 16/37
TRAINER: 1stStart(240 .23  $1.76)  1stLasix(27 .26  $1.35)  2YO(331 .30  $2.11)  Dirt(1187 .29  $1.89)  Sprint(653 .25  $1.67)  MdnSpWt(528 .27  $1.77)       J/T 2005-06 SAR(109 .23  $1.79)  J/T 2005-06(696 .29  $1.94)
```

Race 2 contained a blue-blooded homebred by A.P. Indy and a Touch Gold filly that had been purchased as a yearling for $340,000. But the runaway winner, by nearly eight lengths, was Panty Raid, who had sold in April for $275,000—exactly 22 times her sire Include's stud fee; she must have been ultra-impressive in her training. She paid $10.

```
6  Admiral Bird                        Dk. b or br c. 2  (Feb)  KEEAPR06 $250,000            Life  0 M 0 0    $0  –    D.Fst    0 0 0 0    $0  –
   Own: Dogwood Stable                 Sire: Royal Academy (Nijinsky II) $15,000             2006  0 M 0 0    $0  –    Wet(371)  0 0 0 0   $0  –
Black  Green, Yellow Dots And Collar, Yellow   Dam: Sea Puffin (Mt. Livermore)    118        2005  0 M 0 0    $0  –    Turf(350) 0 0 0 0   $0  –
   GOMEZ G K (62 11 9 13 .18) 2006: (729 137 .19)   Br: Berkshire Stud (NY)                  Sar ⊕ 0 0 0 0   $0  –    Dst⊕(340) 0 0 0 0   $0  –
                                       Tr: Clement Christophe(10 3 2 2 .30) 2006:(243 47 .19)
WORKS: Aug3 Sar tr.t①4f fm :48 B(d) 4/17  Jly24 Bel 4f fst :48 B 8/47  Jly9 Bel 4f fst :481 B 14/53  Jly2 Bel 4f fst :493 Bg 16/25  ●Jun25 Sar tr.t 3f fst :37 B 1/11  Jun13 Sar tr.t 3f fst :382 Bg 24/43
TRAINER: 1stStart(84 .12  $2.09)  1stTurf(67 .16  $1.88)  2YO(32 .19  $2.50)  Debut>=1Mile(45 .13  $1.61)  Turf(440 .22  $1.62)  Routes(483 .20  $1.46)       J/T 2005-06 SAR(3 .67  $5.17)  J/T 2005-06(14 .21  $1.84)
```

Race 4 was a juvenile turf route at 1 1/16 miles, and the only entrant purchased at a 2-year-old sale was Admiral Bird—especially noteworthy because the majority of horses owned by Dogwood Stable are homebreds. The son of Royal Academy overcame a slow pace to win by a head, and paid $5.

```
6  Five Star Daydream                  B. f. 2  (May)  FTFFEB06 $250,000                     Life  1 M 1 0   $8,600  89   D.Fst    1 0 1 0   $8,600  89
   Own: Armstrong Stewart L            Sire: Five Star Day (Carson City) $15,000             2006  1 M 1 0   $8,600  89   Wet(362)  0 0 0 0   $0  –
Black  Black, Sky Blue Triangular Panel And Cap   Dam: September Charmer (Septieme Ciel)     2005  0 M 0 0    $0  –    Turf(253*) 0 0 0 0   $0  –
   PRADO E S (75 11 8 14 .15) 2006: (830 156 .19)   Br: W Keenan Rand Jr (Ky)   L 118        2005  0 M 0 0    $0  –    Turf(253*) 0 0 0 0   $0  –
                                       Tr: McGaughey III Claude R(10 1 2 1 .10) 2006:(108 14 .13)  Sar  0 0 0 0   $0  –    Dst(397)  1 0 1 0   $8,600  89
14Jly06-4Bel fst 5f  :22  .444  .57  ③Md Sp Wt 43k       89 6 8  52  42  34½  24  Prado E S      L118    6.30   95 – 12  MgiclRide118¼ FiveStrDydrem118²¼ ThisJustIn118ⁿᵏ  Game finish outside 8
WORKS: Aug4 Sar tr.t 4f sly :524 B 2/2  Jly28 Sar tr.t 3f fst :372 B 3/9  Jly16 Bel 4f fst :474 B 6/53  Jun29 Bel 4f fst :483 Hg 13/41  Jun23 Bel 4f fst :50 B 34/52  Jun17 Bel 4f fst :50 Bg 21/41
TRAINER: 2ndStart(28 .04  $0.09)  2YO(28 .04  $0.41)  Dirt(219 .20  $1.79)  Sprint(83 .11  $0.71)  MdnSpWt(97 .16  $1.72)       J/T 2005-06 SAR(17 .06  $0.48)  J/T 2005-06(89 .19  $1.45)
```

```
4  Imperial Reign                      B. f. 2  (Apr)  OBSMAR06 $1,000,000                   Life  0 M 0 0    $0  –    D.Fst    0 0 0 0    $0  –
   Own: Darley Stable                  Sire: Indian Charlie (In Excess*Ire) $25,000          2006  0 M 0 0    $0  –    Wet(385)  0 0 0 0   $0  –
Yellow  Maroon, White Sleeves, Maroon Cap, White   Dam: V Sign (Robellino)    118            2005  0 M 0 0    $0  –    Turf(324) 0 0 0 0   $0  –
   GOMEZ G K (62 11 9 13 .18) 2006: (729 137 .19)   Br: Antrim Oaks (Fla)                    2005  0 M 0 0    $0  –    Turf(324) 0 0 0 0   $0  –
                                       Tr: Harty Eoin(6 0 0 2 .00) 2006:(103 18 .17)         Sar   0 0 0 0    $0  –    Dst(390)  0 0 0 0   $0  –
WORKS: Aug6 Sar 4f fst :502 B 32/47  Jly31 Sar 4f fst :472 H 2/110  ●Jly10 Bel 3f fst :362 Bg 1/10  ●Jly5 Bel tr.t 5f fst 1:002 B 1/16  Jun29 Bel 5f fst 1:01 H 10/27  Jun18 Bel 3f fst :361 Hg 3/18
      Jun11 Bel 4f fst :481 B 9/68  May27 Bel 4f fst :48 B 6/21  May21 Bel 3f fst :362 H 4/24
TRAINER: 1stStart(50 .14  $1.49)  1stLasix(11 .09  $0.31)  2YO(20 .20  $1.69)  Dirt(196 .22  $1.88)  Sprint(149 .17  $1.45)  MdnSpWt(147 .16  $1.17)       J/T 2005-06 SAR(1 .00  $0.00)  J/T 2005-06(26 .15  $1.20)
```

Three of the nine fillies in Race 6 were 2-year-old sales graduates, including winner Five Star Daydream and runner-up Imperial Reign. The latter returned to win at odds-on later at the meet, as a universal single for many pick-six players diving into a large two-day carryover pool.

According to Data Track International's "BreezeFigs" (available on-line at drf.com), nearly 4,000 horses are sold at eight major 2-year-old sales each year, and all of them have at least one timed workout. They are separated into three "Sales Class Edge" levels that reflect the overall quality of the stock:

Class Edge **High:**
OBSFEB—Ocala Breeders' sale at Calder in early February
FTFFEB—Fasig-Tipton sale at Calder in late February
BAR—Barretts Select sale at Fairplex Park in early March
KEEAPR—Keeneland sale in Lexington in early April

Class Edge **Good:**
OBSMAR—Ocala Breeders' sale in Ocala in mid-March
EASMAY—Fasig-Tipton sale in Maryland in mid-May

Class Edge **Moderate:**
OBSAPR—Ocala Breeders' sale in Ocala in mid-April
OBSJUN—Ocala Breeders' sale in Ocala in mid-June

BreezeFigs suggests horses coming out of the OBSFEB, FTFFEB, and OBSMAR sales should be strongly considered in New York-bred maiden races. At the 2006 Saratoga meet, the following 2-year-old New York-bred maiden winners came out of one of those sales: Graeme Central ($6); Baltimore Drive ($8.40); Crosstown Traffic ($9.50); Quick and Easy ($6.90); Precious Too ($10.60); and Don't Mind Me ($39.80).

Also, Whatdreamsrmadeof ($5, OBSJUN) and Market Psychology ($4.90, EASMAY) came out of other sales to win New York-bred maiden races at the 2006 Saratoga meet.

Handicappers can look at all manner of data in maiden races full of first-time starters, but sometimes what's there has to be synthesized and analyzed creatively, as Mark Cramer said. Assuming at least a passing familiarity with New York racing, examine the following field of 12 juvenile maiden fillies going 5½ furlongs on the final Friday of the Saratoga meet, along with their post-time odds. Can you spot an exceptionally "live" newcomer?

Saratoga 5½ Furlongs (1:03¹) ⑤ **Md Sp Wt 47k** Purse $47,000 (UP TO $8,930 NYSBFOA)
For Maidens, Fillies Two Years Old. Weight, 118 lbs.

1 Dancing Cherokee 7-1
Own: Starview Stable
Dark Green, Red Stars And Collar, Red
CASTELLANO J J (135 21 16 18 .16) 2006: (750 129 .17)

2 For a Prayer SCR
Own: Hobeau Farm
Orange, Light Blue Blocks On Sleeves
SUTHERLAND C (20 0 0 2 .00) 2006: (253 20 .08)

3 Chocolate Chip 31-1
Own: Schaffel Lewis
White And Black Blocks, Red Sleeves
JARA F (147 11 19 14 .07) 2006: (549 53 .10)

4 Lauren's Heather 58-1
Own: Eldridge Sr Brendan A
Colors Unavailable
HILL C (99 2 8 8 .02) 2006: (712 49 .07)

5 Perfect Forest 7-2
Own: Evans Edward P
Green, Black Diamond Hoop, Black
VELAZQUEZ J R (161 25 23 26 .16) 2006: (638 154 .24)

6 Bold Assurance 17-1
Own: Manhattan Racing Stable
Red, Black Diamond, Two Black Hoops
GOMEZ G K (149 32 21 25 .21) 2006: (825 158 .19)

7 Striking Tomisue 7-2
Own: Menard John R Hilbert Tomisue
Yellow, Royal Blue Epaulets, Yellow Cap
LEPAROUX J R (164 24 21 17 .15) 2006: (1227 302 .25)

[61]

8 Gentle Grace 70-1
Own: Wigmore Stephen
Pink Blue, Light Blue Diamonds, Blue Cap
SANTOS J A (62 5 10 6 .08) 2006: (485 70 .14)
Ch. f. 2 (Mar) FTKNOV04 $35,000
Sire: Woodman (Mr. Prospector) $20,000
Dam: Gentle Minister (Deputy Minister)
Br: Judy Primiano & Pete Primiano (Ky)
Tr: Ubillo Rodrigo A(9 0 0 0 .00) 2006:(37 3 .08)
118
Life 0 M 0 0 $0 - | D.Fst 0 0 0 0 $0 -
2006 0 M 0 0 $0 - | Wet(335) 0 0 0 0 $0 -
2005 0 M 0 0 $0 - | Turf(284) 0 0 0 0 $0 -
Sar 0 0 0 0 $0 - | Dst(300) 0 0 0 0 $0 -
WORKS: Aug25 Sar 5f fst 1:012 Hg 9/21 Aug12 Sar 4f fst :491 Bg 12/48 Jly31 Sar 4f fst :51 B 91/112 Jly22 Sar 4f fst :513 B 16/21 Jly14 Sar tr.t(T) 3f gd :381 B(d) 2/2 Jly7 Sar tr.t(T) 3f fm :374 B(d) 3/4
TRAINER: 1stStart(7 .00 $0.00) 2YO(3 .00 $0.00) Dirt(42 .05 $0.46) Sprint(22 .00 $0.00) MdnSpWt(41 .07 $0.87) J/T 2005-06 SAR(2 .00 $0.00) J/T 2005-06(20 .15 $1.78)

9 Tres Dream 19-1
Own: Robertson Philip Robertson Brenda
Turqse White, Red Emblem And Bowtie, Black
BRIDGMOHAN S X (54 3 7 5 .06) 2006: (694 88 .13)
B. f. 2 (Feb) KEESEP05 $30,000
Sire: Chester House (Mr. Prospector) $20,000
Dam: Dreamy Maiden (Meadowlake)
Br: ClassicStar (Ky)
Tr: Blasi Scott(36 7 7 4 .19) 2006:(320 56 .18)
L 118
Life 0 M 0 0 $0 - | D.Fst 0 0 0 0 $0 -
2006 0 M 0 0 $0 - | Wet(372) 0 0 0 0 $0 -
2005 0 M 0 0 $0 - | Turf(336) 0 0 0 0 $0 -
Sar 0 0 0 0 $0 - | Dst(361) 0 0 0 0 $0 -
WORKS: Aug28 Sar 4f fst :473 H 4/24 Aug21 Sar tr.t 5f fst 1:01 B 2/6 Aug14 Sar 4f fst :49 Bg 21/66
TRAINER: 1stStart(28 .04 $0.42) 1stLasix(4 .25 $3.10) 2YO(99 .17 $2.25) Dirt(237 .19 $1.73) Sprint(208 .18 $2.07) MdnSpWt(61 .13 $2.81) J/T 2005-06 SAR(23 .13 $0.92) J/T 2005-06(55 .15 $0.88)

10 Lilly Carson 7-2
Own: Spence James C
Purple Yellow, Brown Ball, Yellow 'Jcs,' Brown
VELASQUEZ C (180 26 26 27 .14) 2006: (1111 181 .16)
Ch. f. 2 (Feb)
Sire: Carson City (Mr. Prospector) $35,000
Dam: Golden Lilly (Deputy Minister)
Br: James C Spence (Ky)
Tr: Nicks Ralph E(13 0 1 1 .00) 2006:(126 14 .11)
L 118
Life 0 M 0 0 $0 - | D.Fst 0 0 0 0 $0 -
2006 0 M 0 0 $0 - | Wet(420) 0 0 0 0 $0 -
2005 0 M 0 0 $0 - | Turf(258) 0 0 0 0 $0 -
Sar 0 0 0 0 $0 - | Dst(399) 0 0 0 0 $0 -
WORKS: Aug27 Sar 3f fst :363 B 5/21 Aug21 Sar 5f fst 1:012 Bg 13/40 Aug14 Sar 4f fst :501 B 53/65 ●Aug7 Sar 4f gd :474 Hg 1/24 Jly31 Sar 4f fst :483 B 35/112 Jly23 Sar 3f my :382 B 2/2 Jly15 CD 3f gd :382 B 14/21
TRAINER: 1stStart(31 .06 $0.59) 1stLasix(3 .00 $0.00) 2YO(53 .17 $3.83) Dirt(226 .16 $2.34) Sprint(123 .16 $2.77) MdnSpWt(50 .16 $2.15) J/T 2005-06 SAR(1 .00 $0.00) J/T 2005-06(7 .29 $4.40)

11 Queen Joanne 7-1
Own: Zayat Stables LLC
Gray Turquoise, Gold Ball Sash And 'Z,' Gold
PRADO E S (174 35 27 21 .20) 2006: (932 180 .19)
B. f. 2 (May) KEESEP05 $350,000
Sire: Mr. Greeley (Gone West) $35,000
Dam: Heat Lightning (Summer Squall)
Br: John Gunther Tony Holmes & Walter Zent (Ky)
Tr: Mott William I(62 10 10 9 .16) 2006:(414 88 .21)
118
Life 0 M 0 0 $0 - | D.Fst 0 0 0 0 $0 -
2006 0 M 0 0 $0 - | Wet(343) 0 0 0 0 $0 -
2005 0 M 0 0 $0 - | Turf(300) 0 0 0 0 $0 -
Sar 0 0 0 0 $0 - | Dst(337) 0 0 0 0 $0 -
WORKS: Aug21 Bel tr.t 4f fst :502 B 45/67 Aug14 Bel tr.t 4f fst :48 B 4/43 Aug7 Bel 4f fst :494 Bg 29/69 Jly15 Sar tr.t 4f fst :503 Bg 29/55 Jly9 Sar tr.t 3f fst :374 B 4/10 Jun30 Sar tr.t 3f fst :39 B 29/47 Jun21 Sar tr.t 3f fst :393 B 28/30
TRAINER: 1stStart(111 .13 $1.43) 2YO(133 .18 $1.73) Dirt(347 .19 $1.40) Sprint(227 .19 $1.45) MdnSpWt(336 .17 $1.88) J/T 2005-06 SAR(7 .14 $1.83) J/T 2005-06(60 .28 $1.74)

12 Frozen Prospect 21-1
Own: Donato John
Lime Yellow, White Ball, Yellow 'B,' White
DESORMEAUX K J (132 17 12 19 .13) 2006: (563 98 .17)
B. f. 2 (Mar) OBSAPR06 $150,000
Sire: Suave Prospect (Fortunate Prospect) $6,500
Dam: Almost Ice (It's Freezing)
Br: Farnsworth Farms (Fla)
Tr: Rice Linda(33 6 0 3 .18) 2006:(280 52 .19)
L 118
Life 0 M 0 0 $0 - | D.Fst 0 0 0 0 $0 -
2006 0 M 0 0 $0 - | Wet(369) 0 0 0 0 $0 -
2005 0 M 0 0 $0 - | Turf(211) 0 0 0 0 $0 -
Sar 0 0 0 0 $0 - | Dst(370) 0 0 0 0 $0 -
WORKS: Aug23 Sar 5f fst 1:003 H 3/21 Aug11 Sar 4f fst :481 B 2/27 Aug7 Sar tr.t(T) 4f fm :482 B 23/50 Jly31 Sar 4f fst :482 Hg 25/112 Jly21 Bel tr.t 4f fst :473 H 2/34 Jly12 Bel tr.t 4f fst :482 B 5/27 Jly3 Bel tr.t 4f fst :494 B 9/15
TRAINER: 1stStart(66 .09 $1.09) 1stLasix(5 .00 $0.00) 2YO(58 .19 $1.75) Dirt(461 .16 $1.36) Sprint(398 .21 $1.87) MdnSpWt(141 .17 $1.56) J/T 2005-06 SAR(2 .00 $0.00) J/T 2005-06(4 .00 $0.00)

Also Eligible:

13 Dance Band SCR
Own: Overbrook Farm
Brown White, Blue Ball, Green Circle, White
VELASQUEZ C (180 26 26 27 .14) 2006: (1111 181 .16)
Dk. b or br f. 2 (May)
Sire: Storm Cat (Storm Bird) $500,000
Dam: Ho Baby (Gilded Time)
Br: Overbrook Farm (Ky)
Tr: Lukas D Wayne(44 4 6 5 .09) 2006:(344 30 .09)
118
Life 3 M 0 1 $7,350 64 | D.Fst 3 0 0 1 $7,350 64
2006 3 M 0 1 $7,350 64 | Wet(415) 0 0 0 0 $0 -
2005 0 M 0 0 $0 - | Turf(343) 0 0 0 0 $0 -
Sar 1 0 0 0 $2,350 55 | Dst(437) 2 0 0 1 $7,350 57
3Aug06-2Sar fst 5f :213 :453 :594 (F)Md Sp Wt 47k 55 7 7 5¾ 4¾ 4¾ 4¾ Bejarano R 118 b 10.30 79- 17 CherokeeSheik1181¼ TleoftheQuen1181 SsidAffir1183¼ Bumped after start 7
15Jly06-6CD fst 5½f :221 :461 :582 1:05 (F)Md Sp Wt 48k 57 9 3 1hd 1hd 2½ 3¾ Toups R5 115 b 6.20 88- 14 Taletobetold115nk *Nola Star*1205 Dance Band115½ Duel,3-4w,weakened 12
16Jun06-8CD fst 4½f :222 :45 :51 (F)Md Sp Wt 42k 64 1 2 6¾ 6½ 6¼ Toups R5 114 b 17.40 92- 09 Chagall1191½ Seaside Affair1142 Gold Minx119¾ Inside,no rally 10
WORKS: Aug28 Sar tr.t 4f fst :514 B 17/19 Aug19 Sar tr.t 4f fst :522 B 26/27 Jly24 Sar tr.t 4f fst :504 B 13/20 Jly9 CD 4f fst :49 B 8/45 Jly1 CD 3f fst :38 B 6/15 Jun24 CD 4f sly :502 B 27/43
TRAINER: 2YO(217 .11 $0.88) Dirt(831 .12 $1.29) Sprint(544 .11 $1.08) MdnSpWt(379 .10 $1.06) J/T 2005-06 SAR(34 .18 $1.68) J/T 2005-06(60 .15 $1.44)

14 All Giving 9-1
Own: Concepts Unlimited Stable Smith Cathe
Maroon Light Gray, Dark Blue Hoop, Blue
DESORMEAUX K J (132 17 12 19 .13) 2006: (563 98 .17)
Dk. b or br f. 2 (Mar) EASMAY06 $75,000
Sire: Allen's Prospect (Mr. Prospector) $15,000
Dam: Slew the Dragoness (Slew City Slew)
Br: Baywood LLC (Md)
Tr: Bailes W Robert(11 1 0 3 .09) 2006:(137 17 .12)
L 118
Life 1 M 0 0 $1,410 58 | D.Fst 1 0 0 0 $1,410 58
2006 1 M 0 0 $1,410 58 | Wet(333) 0 0 0 0 $0 -
2005 0 M 0 0 $0 - | Turf(240) 0 0 0 0 $0 -
Sar 1 0 0 0 $1,410 58 | Dst(331) 1 0 0 0 $1,410 58
10Aug06-6Sar fst 5½f :22 :46 :584 1:053 (F)Md Sp Wt 47k 58 5 1 2hd 2hd 32 5¾ Desormeaux K J 118 b 26.00 83- 13 FiveStrDydrem118¾ ImperilReign1181¼ Shssinnr1133½ Vied outside, tired 9
WORKS: Aug23 Sar tr.t 4f fst :492 B 3/16 Aug7 Sar 3f gd :36 Bg 3/13 Jly31 Sar tr.t 5f fst 1:02 B 2/10 ●Jly22 Cnl 4f fst :481 Bg 1/22 Jly15 Cnl 4f fst :504 B 11/19 Jly9 Cnl 4f fst :483 B 2/11
TRAINER: 2ndStart(13 .08 $0.54) 1stLasix(6 .00 $0.00) 2YO(28 .11 $0.82) Dirt(280 .11 $0.98) Sprint(157 .08 $0.62) MdnSpWt(25 .16 $1.21) J/T 2005-06 SAR(7 .14 $1.66) J/T 2005-06(7 .14 $1.66)

15 Tale of the Queen SCR
Own: Marylou Whitney Stables
Khaki Eton Blue, Brown Hoop, Blue Sleeves
PRADO E S (174 35 27 21 .20) 2006: (932 180 .19)
Dk. b or br f. 2 (May)
Sire: Tale of the Cat (Storm Cat) $50,000
Dam: Queen Inca (Capote)
Br: Marylou Whitney Stables (Ky)
Tr: Abreu Reynaldo(12 0 2 0 .00) 2006:(67 6 .09)
L 118
Life 2 M 2 0 $18,800 68 | D.Fst 2 0 2 0 $18,800 68
2006 2 M 2 0 $18,800 68 | Wet(392) 0 0 0 0 $0 -
2005 0 M 0 0 $0 - | Turf(291) 0 0 0 0 $0 -
Sar 2 0 2 0 $18,800 68 | Dst(397) 1 0 1 0 $9,400 68
20Aug06-7Sar fst 7f :223 :451 1:104 1:242 (F)Md Sp Wt 47k 66 5 2 2hd 2hd 1hd 2no Velazquez J R L118 2.85 82- 09 DebbieGotEven113no TleoftheQueen118½ Allude1185¼ Dug in, yielded late 9
3Aug06-2Sar fst 5f :213 :453 :594 (F)Md Sp Wt 47k 68 3 3 712 6¾ 3½ 2¼ Desormeaux K J L118 23.80 84- 17 CherokeeSheik1181¼ TleoftheQueen1181 SsidAffir1183¼ Greenly, lugged in 7
WORKS: Jly28 Sar 5f fst 1:013 H 5/30 ●Jly14 Sar 5f wf 1:01 B 1/8 Jly8 Sar tr.t 5f fst 1:04 B 14/16 Jun30 Sar tr.t 4f fst :511 B 48/74 Jun12 Sar tr.t 5f fst 1:03 B 11/28
TRAINER: 2YO(21 .19 $2.82) Dirt(63 .16 $1.14) Sprint(58 .17 $1.89) MdnSpWt(50 .16 $1.32) J/T 2005-06(5 .00 $0.00)

Three fillies vied for favoritism at 7–2, two of which could have been expected to attract that much support, and perhaps even more: Perfect Forest was from leading trainer Todd Pletcher, and showed a recent bullet workout from the gate. Striking Tomisue was trained by Nick Zito, who made headlines earlier at the meet by saddling no fewer than six 2-year-olds to win their debuts; she had trained purposefully, and had apprentice sensation Julien Leparoux aboard.

Given their high-profile backgrounds, 7–2 was neutral or lukewarm support for those two. But sitting unobtrusively on the tote board at the same price was Lilly Carson, whose trainer, Ralph Nicks, is not exactly a household name in Saratoga Springs, New York. Moreover, casual fans who noted Nicks's 0-for-13 donut at the meet, and 2-for-31 record with first-time starters, surely were looking elsewhere. So, odds of 7–2 hinted that people behind the scenes were betting with both hands, especially considering this was a full field of 12.

FOURTH RACE

Saratoga

SEPTEMBER 1, 2006

5½ FURLONGS. (1.03¹) MAIDEN SPECIAL WEIGHT. Purse $47,000 (UP TO $8,930 NYSBFOA) FOR MAIDENS, FILLIES TWO YEARS OLD. Weight, 118 lbs.

Value of Race: $47,000 Winner $28,200; second $9,400; third $4,700; fourth $2,350; fifth $1,410; sixth $135; seventh $135; eighth $135; ninth $135; tenth $135; eleventh $135; twelfth $130. Mutuel Pool $539,411.00 Exacta Pool $470,356.00 Quinella Pool $47,186.00 Trifecta Pool $315,684.00

Last Raced	Horse	M/Eqt.	A.	Wt	PP	St	¼	⅜	Str	Fin	Jockey	Odds $1
	Lilly Carson	L	2	118	9	6	1½	1^{2}	$1^{2½}$	$1^{2¾}$	Velasquez C	3.50
	Tres Dream	L	2	118	8	7	4½	3½	2^{6}	$2^{5½}$	Bridgmohan S X	19.30
	Perfect Forest	L	2	118	4	4	7½	8^{2}	$6^{1½}$	3no	Velazquez J R	3.65
	Bold Assurance	L	2	118	5	1	5^{3}	5^{hd}	5^{1}	4¾	Gomez G K	17.00
	Chocolate Chip	L	2	118	2	11	11^{3}	9½	9^{1}	5¾	Jara F	31.50
	Striking Tomisue	L	2	113	6	10	$8^{1½}$	7½	7^{hd}	$6^{1½}$	Leparoux J R[5]	3.95
	Frozen Prospect	L	2	118	11	12	10½	$10^{2½}$	11^{6}	$7^{1½}$	Espinoza J L	21.10
	Gentle Grace		2	118	7	9	12	11^{1}	10½	$8^{1¼}$	Santos J A	70.00
	Queen Joanne		2	118	10	8	6^{3}	6^{3}	8½	9^{1}	Prado E S	7.60
10Aug06 ⁶Sar⁵	All Giving	L b	2	118	12	3	$2^{2½}$	$2^{1½}$	4^{hd}	$10^{1½}$	Desormeaux K J	9.60
	Dancing Cherokee	L	2	118	1	2	$3^{1½}$	$4^{5½}$	3^{hd}	$11^{6½}$	Castellano J J	7.20
	Lauren's Heather		2	118	3	5	9½	12	12	12	Hill C	58.25

OFF AT 4:38 Start Good. Won driving. Track fast.

TIME :22, $:45^{2}$, :58, $1:04^{4}$ (:22.05, :45.57, :58.12, 1:04.95)

$2 Mutuel Prices:

10 – LILLY CARSON	**9.00**	**6.00**	**4.40**
9 – TRES DREAM		**15.00**	**6.80**
5 – PERFECT FOREST			**4.30**

$2 EXACTA 10–9 PAID $167.50 $2 QUINELLA 9–10 PAID $135.50

$2 TRIFECTA 10–9–5 PAID $1,293.00

Ch. f, (Feb), by Carson City – Golden Lilly, by Deputy Minister. Trainer Nicks Ralph E. Bred by James C Spence (Ky).

LILLY CARSON dueled early along the rail, opened a clear advantage on the turn then drew clear while being kept to the task. TRES DREAM moved up along the backstretch, launched a rally three wide leaving the turn and finished willingly to clearly best the others. PERFECT FOREST raced well back to the top of the stretch and rallied belatedly along the inside to gain a share. BOLD ASSURANCE angled to the inside on the far turn, saved ground to the turn, angled out in upper stretch and finished evenly. CHOCOLATE CHIP stumbled and checked in tight at the start, circled five wide into the stretch, steadied while being bothered in upper stretch and closed mildly in the middle of the track. STRIKING TOMISUE checked at the start, raced four wide to the turn, angled out entering the stretch, steadied in traffic in upper stretch and lacked a strong closing response. FROZEN PROSPECT steadied in tight in the early stages, raced well back while five wide on the turn and passed only tiring horses. GENTLE GRACE never reached contention. QUEEN JOANNE chased three wide to the turn, drifted out in upper stretch and steadily tired thereafter. ALL GIVING pressed the early pace from outside, drifted wide at the quarter pole, ducked out causing crowding in upper stretch and gave way. DANCING CHEROKEE chased inside for a half and faltered. LAUREN'S HEATHER saved ground and tired.

Owners– 1, Spence James C; 2, Robertson Brenda and Philip; 3, Evans Edward P; 4, Manhattan Racing Stable; 5, Schaffel Lewis; 6, Hilbert Tomisue and Menard John R; 7, Donato John; 8, Wigmore Stephen; 9, Zayat Stables LLC; 10, Concepts Unlimited Stable and Smith Catherine J; 11, Starview Stable; 12, Eldridge Sr Brendan A

Trainers– 1, Nicks Ralph E; 2, Blasi Scott; 3, Pletcher Todd A; 4, Hennig Mark; 5, Clement Christophe; 6, Zito Nicholas P; 7, Rice Linda; 8, Ubillo Rodrigo A; 9, Mott William I; 10, Bailes W Robert; 11, Kimmel John C; 12, Sanders Jamie

Scratched– For a Prayer, Dance Band (03Aug06 ²Sar⁴), Tale of the Queen (20Aug06 ⁷Sar²)

$2 Pick Three (1–8–10) Paid $298.00; Pick Three Pool $102,117.

Lilly Carson shrugged off pace pressure on the turn and maintained a clear margin through the stretch, while Perfect Forest and Striking Tomisue never entered contention. In her first start against winners six weeks later, Lilly Carson set the pace to midstretch and held for third in the Grade 1 Frizette Stakes.

Along the same lines, here is a field of 3-year-old New York-bred maiden fillies that raced six furlongs toward the end of a long 2006–07 winter meet on Aqueduct's inner track, along with their post-time odds. One of the seven first-time starters is exceptionally live:

4 Aqueduct 6 Furlongs (1:07⁴) Ⓢ Ⓕ Md Sp Wt 41k Purse $41,000 For Maidens, Fillies Three Years Old Foaled In New York State And Approved By The New York State–bred Registry. Weight, 120 lbs.

Coupled – Too Much Zip and Chi Chi's Dream

1 Too Much Zip 8-5
Red Own: Team Penney Racing
Gold, Royal Blue Yoke And 'Tpr,' Blue
DOMINGUEZ R A (317 76 51 53 .24) 2006: (1417 385 .27)

2 Flash Lightning SCR
White Own: Audrey H Cooper
Hot Pink, White Cross Of Lorraine, White
VANHASSEL C (20 0 0 3 .00) 2006: (109 14 .13)

3 Automatic Appeal 13-1
Blue Own: Jeffrey L Nielsen
Red, Red Emblem, Red Seams On Sleeves
LOPEZ C C (327 59 47 33 .18) 2006: (713 134 .19)

4 Greg's Lassy 17-1
Yellow Own: West Point Stable Brooks Donald
Gold, Black Star, Black Sleeves, Gold
COA E M (419 82 79 60 .20) 2006: (1612 321 .20)

5 Nantasket 18-1
Green Own: Downey Walter
White And Camel Quarters, White Sleeves
BRIDGMOHAN S X (236 25 31 30 .11) 2006: (1068 134 .13)

1a Chi Chi's Dream 8-5
Red Own: Minnella Martin J
Royal Blue, Yellow Stars, Yellow
LUZZI M J (307 45 40 47 .15) 2006: (1304 176 .13)

[64]

6 So Smashley 6-1
Own: Wycoff Kirk
Black Orange, Lemon Yellow Ball Sash, Yellow
GARCIA ALAN (291 50 39 46 .17) 2006: (1108 154 .14)

B. f. 3 (Jan) EASMAY06 $39,000
Sire: Officer (Bertrando) $40,000
Dam: So Much Splendor (Coronado's Quest)
Br: JMJ Racing Stables (NY)
Tr: McLaughlin Kiaran P(79 19 17 8 .24) 2006:(406 80 .20)

(L) 120

Life	0	M	0	0	$0	-	D.Fst	0	0	0	0	$0	-
2007	0	M	0	0	$0	-	Wet(388)	0	0	0	0	$0	-
2006	0	M	0	0	$0	-	Turf(303*)	0	0	0	0	$0	-
Aqu ⊡	0	0	0	0	$0	-	Dst(414)	0	0	0	0	$0	-

WORKS: Feb28 Bel tr.t 4f fst :48 H *3/45* Feb21 Bel tr.t 4f fst :49^{2} B *9/21* Feb8 Bel tr.t 4f fst :50^{4} B *15/22* Jan28 Bel tr.t 3f fst :36^{2} B *7/46*
TRAINER: 1stStart(62 .18 $2.60) Dirt(391 .23 $2.45) Sprint(249 .23 $2.54) MdnSpWt(183 .27 $3.62) J/T 2006-07 AQU(29 .38 $4.22) J/T 2006-07(34 .35 $5.14)

7 Daring Dreamer 9-1
Own: Three Friends Stable
Orange Red And White Diagonal Quarters, Blue
PINO M G (5 2 1 0 .40) 2006: (927 197 .21)

B. f. 3 (Apr)
Sire: Royal Academy (Nijinsky II) $15,000
Dam: Cherokee Promise (Cherokee Run)
Br: Paper Clipper Farms Inc & Richard Hornstein (NY)
Tr: Tagg Barclay(8 0 0 1 .00) 2006:(209 47 .22)

(L) 120

Life	0	M	0	0	$0	-	D.Fst	0	0	0	0	$0	-
2007	0	M	0	0	$0	-	Wet(390)	0	0	0	0	$0	-
2006	0	M	0	0	$0	-	Turf(332)	0	0	0	0	$0	-
Aqu ⊡	0	0	0	0	$0	-	Dst(332)	0	0	0	0	$0	-

WORKS: ●Mar3 Fai tr.t ◇4f fst :47^{3} B *1/16* Feb23 Fai tr.t ◇4f fst :50 B *1/2* Feb8 Fai tr.t ◇5f fst 1:01 B *2/7* Jan31 Fai tr.t ◇4f fst :49^{1} B *4/8* ●Jan24 Fai tr.t ◇4f fst :47^{3} B *1/4* ●Jan18 Fai tr.t ◇4f fst :48^{2} B *1/6*
Jan12 Fai tr.t ◇3f fst :38^{4} B *2/2* Dec26 Fai tr.t ◇5f fst 1:02 B *3/3* ●Dec20 Fai 4f fst :47^{4} B(d)g *1/8* Dec15 Fai 4f fst :49^{4} B(d) *2/2* Dec9 Fai tr.t ◇4f fst :47^{1} B *2/11* Dec4 Fai 3f fst :37 B(d) *5/10*
TRAINER: 1stStart(24 .21 $2.58) Dirt(131 .24 $1.97) Sprint(98 .16 $1.30) MdnSpWt(66 .23 $2.43) J/T 2006-07(11 .36 $1.95)

8 Mighty Eros 2-1
Own: Sequel Racing
Pink Burgundy, Hunter Green Bowtie, Cream
ARROYO N JR (203 36 31 20 .18) 2006: (658 90 .14)

Dk. b or br f. 3 (Apr) OBSFEB06 $55,000
Sire: Freud (Storm Cat) $10,000
Dam: Mighty Emy (Mighty Adversary)
Br: Thomas/Lakin (NY)
Tr: Bush Thomas M(82 11 14 12 .13) 2006:(246 36 .15)

(L) 120

Life	0	M	0	0	$0	-	D.Fst	0	0	0	0	$0	-
2007	0	M	0	0	$0	-	Wet(348)	0	0	0	0	$0	-
2006	0	M	0	0	$0	-	Turf(274)	0	0	0	0	$0	-
Aqu ⊡	0	0	0	0	$0	-	Dst(372)	0	0	0	0	$0	-

WORKS: Mar1 Bel tr.t 5f fst 1:03^{1} B *21/32* Feb22 Bel tr.t 5f fst 1:03 Hg *7/20* Feb13 Bel tr.t 4f fst :49^{1} B *11/44* Feb9 Bel tr.t 4f fst :50^{3} B *31/53* Feb3 Bel tr.t 4f fst :50 B *43/76* Jan28 Bel tr.t 3f fst :37^{4} B *30/46*
Dec21 Crc 3f fst :38 Bg *8/10* Oct5 Crc 3f sly :39^{3} Bg *10/12*
TRAINER: 1stStart(34 .03 $0.30) Dirt(248 .15 $1.34) Sprint(155 .11 $1.10) MdnSpWt(99 .09 $0.61) J/T 2006-07 AQU(31 .23 $2.04) J/T 2006-07(36 .19 $1.75)

9 Money Oriented 34-1
Own: Tri Kappa Racing
Turqse Maroon, White Ball, Maroon 'Tkt,' White
ESPINOZA J L (83 5 9 11 .06) 2006: (569 31 .05)

B. f. 3 (Jan)
Sire: Good and Tough (Carson City) $3,000
Dam: Expensive Tap (Pleasant Tap)
Br: Thomas/Lakin (NY)
Tr: O'Brien Colum(7 0 0 1 .00) 2006:(68 2 .03)

L 120

Life	2	M	0	1	$4,510	36	D.Fst	2	0	0	1	$4,510	36
2007	2	M	0	1	$4,510	36	Wet(436)	0	0	0	0	$0	-
2006	0	M	0	0	$0	-	Turf(333)	0	0	0	0	$0	-
Aqu ⊡	2	0	0	1	$4,510	36	Dst(394)	2	0	0	1	$4,510	36

16Feb07-6Aqu fst 6f ⊡ :23 :46^{4} :59 1:11^{3} ⒻⓈMd Sp Wt 41k 36 2 5 5^{10} 4^{7½} 3^{13} 3^{16¼} Castellano A Jr L120 b 9.70 70- 17 SilvercupBby120^{4¾} TexsStrlt120^{11½} MonyOrintd120^{½} Steadied repeatedly 7
21Jan07-2Aqu fst 6f ⊡ :22^{4} :46^{4} :59^{1} 1:12^{1} ⒻⓈMd Sp Wt 41k 31 4 6 3^{1½} 3^{2½} 4^{9} 6^{16¼} Castellano A Jr L119 b 7.70 66- 17 SltWtrRgn119^{6¼} *TlkngTrsr*119^{7} PrcsonFootwrk119^{¾} Close up inside, tired 7
WORKS: Mar3 Bel tr.t 4f gd :48^{2} B *3/17* Feb7 Bel tr.t 3f fst :36^{1} B *2/6* Feb3 Bel tr.t 5f fst 1:03 B *17/28* ●Jan13 Bel tr.t 4f fst :47^{3} Hg *1/45* Jan6 Bel tr.t 4f gd :49 B *3/13* Dec30 Bel tr.t 5f fst 1:02^{2} B *4/16*
TRAINER: Dirt(46 .02 $1.28) Sprint(50 .02 $1.18) MdnSpWt(29 .03 $0.66) J/T 2006-07 AQU(8 .13 $7.38) J/T 2006-07(22 .05 $2.68)

10 Little Miss Popeye 12-1
Own: D and B Stable
Purple Gold And White Diamonds, White And Gold
MARTIN E M JR (257 31 29 43 .12) 2006: (863 82 .10)

B. f. 3 (Apr) NEWAUG05 $4,000
Sire: You and I (Kris S.) $5,000
Dam: Fancy 'n Fabulous (Somethingfabulous)
Br: Tea Party Stable Inc (NY)
Tr: Hertler John O(57 9 8 10 .16) 2006:(210 16 .08)

L 120

Life	3	M	0	1	$4,438	47	D.Fst	3	0	0	1	$4,438	47
2007	2	M	0	1	$4,274	47	Wet(338)	0	0	0	0	$0	-
2006	1	M	0	0	$164	27	Turf(256)	0	0	0	0	$0	-
Aqu ⊡	3	0	0	1	$4,438	47	Dst(334)	3	0	0	1	$4,438	47

25Feb07-4Aqu fst 6f ⊡ :22^{4} :47^{1} 1:00 1:13^{1} ⒻⓈMd Sp Wt 41k 47 1 2 2^{hd} 2^{½} 1^{½} 3^{nk} Martin E M Jr L120 14.40 78- 16 CliJen120^{no} GoldenMnn115^{nk} LittleMissPopeye120^{nk} Came again, caught 9
1Feb07-4Aqu fst 6f ⊡ :22^{3} :46^{3} :59^{3} 1:12^{4} ⒻⓈMd 50000 8 8 3 4^{1¾} 4^{1¾} 6^{11} 6^{18} Martin E M Jr L120 19.20 62- 15 PsychotcClrs120^{1½} WLvOrKds120^{2½} GldnMnn120^{4¾} Chased outside, tired 8
27Dec06-4Aqu fst 6f ⊡ :23^{2} :47^{2} 1:00 1:12^{4} ⒻⓈMd Sp Wt 41k 27 8 4 6^{2¼} 6^{4¼} 6^{7¼} 6^{8½} Martin E M Jr 120 24.00 66- 17 Abbyroar120^{1¼} Positive Charge120^{no} Freakazoid120^{2} Chased, tired 10
WORKS: Jan27 Bel tr.t 4f fst :49^{2} B *7/20* Jan18 Bel tr.t 4f fst :50^{3} B *24/32* Dec20 Bel tr.t 4f fst :51 B *30/35*
TRAINER: Dirt(179 .09 $2.17) Sprint(138 .11 $2.69) MdnSpWt(109 .10 $3.00) J/T 2006-07 AQU(17 .18 $0.92) J/T 2006-07(17 .18 $0.92)

11 Dash of Luck 56-1
Own: Kazamias Peter
Gray Red, White Diamond Hoop, Red Cap
HILL C (304 31 37 35 .10) 2006: (1147 82 .07)

B. f. 3 (Feb)
Sire: Devil His Due (Devil's Bag) $10,000
Dam: Dasharoo (Buckaroo)
Br: Kaz Hill Farm (NY)
Tr: Kazamias Peter(17 5 1 0 .29) 2006:(139 13 .09)

(L) 120

Life	0	M	0	0	$0	-	D.Fst	0	0	0	0	$0	-
2007	0	M	0	0	$0	-	Wet(358)	0	0	0	0	$0	-
2006	0	M	0	0	$0	-	Turf(245)	0	0	0	0	$0	-
Aqu ⊡	0	0	0	0	$0	-	Dst(331)	0	0	0	0	$0	-

WORKS: Feb28 Bel tr.t 5f fst 1:01^{1} Hg *5/24* Feb12 Bel tr.t 4f fst :48^{3} B *5/42* Feb10 Bel tr.t 4f fst :53^{2} B *70/70* Jan19 Bel tr.t 4f fst :54 B *41/44* ●Dec27 Pim 4f fst :50^{4} B *1/6* Nov18 Pim 4f fst :50^{1} Bg *11/23*
Oct25 Pim 4f fst :50^{4} B *2/12*
TRAINER: 1stStart(6 .00 $0.00) Dirt(140 .12 $2.13) Sprint(83 .10 $1.69) MdnSpWt(14 .00 $0.00) J/T 2006-07 AQU(3 .00 $0.00) J/T 2006-07(5 .00 $0.00)

Coming out of the high-class OBSFEB sale as a 2-year-old, Mighty Eros was being bet down to 2–1 second choice in a field of 10 betting interests. Given this situation, by far and away the most interesting stat of the race was trainer Tom Bush's current 1-for-34 record with first-time starters. Someone must have known something, because a 3 percent win rate is typically a big turnoff to the crowd under normal circumstances—and especially in a situation where (a) Automatic Appeal shows a couple of fast workouts and (b) So Smashley is well-bred, and shows a relatively fast work (ranked 3/45) for a live trainer winning at 24 percent for the whole winter, and with a profitable ROI with first-time starters.

RACE 4 Aqu–11Mar07 6 Furlongs (1.074), 3 yo Ⓕ Ⓢ Md Sp Wt

Value of Race: $41,000. 1st $24,600 ; 2nd $8,200 ; 3rd $4,100 ; 4th $2,050 ; 5th $1,230 ; 6th $137 ; 7th $137 ; 8th $137 ; 9th $137 ; 10th $137 ; 11th $135 . Mutuel Pools: $410,931 Ex $338,394, Quin $33,045, Tri $251,415, Pick–3 $66,085

Last Raced	Horse	M/Eq	A	Wt	PP	St	¼	½	Str	Fin	Odds$1
	Mighty Eros	L	3	120	8	2	2½	1½	1⁷	11¹¹¼	2.40
	Greg's Lassy	L	3	120	3	9	3²	33½	2hd	2¾	17.10
	Automatic Appeal	L f	3	120	2	4	1½	2¹	3⁵	31½	13.40
	So Smashley	L	3	120	6	8	8²	6⁵	54½	43¼	6.50
16Feb07 6Aqu3	Money Oriented	L b	3	120	9	7	7hd	4²	4hd	51¾	34.25
19Feb07 6Aqu5	Nantasket	L b	3	120	4	3	4hd	7½	62½	6¾	18.10
	Chi Chi's Dream	L	3	120	5	11	10hd	8½	8²	7¾	a- 1.75
25Feb07 4Aqu4	Too Much Zip	L	3	120	1	10	9³	9hd	7½	8⁴	a- 1.75
	Daring Dreamer	L	3	120	7	5	11	103½	9²	9⁴	9.10
	Dash of Luck	L	3	120	11	1	6¹	11	11	101¼	56.00
25Feb07 4Aqu3	Little Miss Popeye	L	3	120	10	6	5½	5hd	102½	11	12.20

a–Coupled: Chi Chi's Dream and Too Much Zip.

OFF 2:25 Start Good. Won driving. Track fast.
TIME :23, :471, :591, 1:114 (:23.11, :47.36, :59.31, 1:11.92)

8 – **MIGHTY EROS**	6.80	4.60	4.20
4 – **GREG'S LASSY**		15.40	11.40
3 – **AUTOMATIC APPEAL**			9.70

$2 Ex (8-4) 75.50 $2 Quin (4-8) 66.00 $2 Tri (8-4-3) 663.00
$2 Pick-3 (1-4-8) 433.00

Mighty Eros, bet to 2–1 in the face of her trainer's dismal current stats with first-timers, romped by the length of the stretch, and came back to win a division of the New York Stallion Stakes with similar authority.

Someone knew about her the day she was unveiled, and the tote board overruled the first-out stat on Bush—a trainer who is well above average, as any halfway serious follower of the New York racing scene knows.

Less than two weeks later, another Bush first-timer surfaced in the second race, March 22:

2

Aqueduct *5¹⁄₂ Furlongs* (1:03⁴) ⑤⑥**Md Sp Wt 41k** Purse $41,000 For Maidens, Fillies
Three Years Old Foaled In New York State And Approved By The New York State–bred Registry. Weight, 120 lbs.

START
5¹⁄₂ FURLONGS
INNER DIRT COURSE
FINISH

---

1 Kall Me K
Own: Seahorse Stable
Red Kelly Green, Yellow Cross Sashes, Green
ARROYO N JR (217 41 33 22 .19) 2006: (658 90 .14)

Ch. f. 3 (Apr)
Sire: Kelly Kip (Kipper Kelly) $4,000
Dam: Folly Go Rightly (Distinctive Pro)
Br: Dr Cary Shapoff (NY)
Tr: Grusmark Karl M(—) 2006:(283 57 .20)

L 120

	Life	2 M	1	0	$9,535	50	D.Fst	1	0	1	0	$9,400	50
	2006	2 M	1	0	$9,535	50	Wet(431)	1	0	0	0	$135	22
	2005	0 M	0	0	$0	–	Turf(246)	0	0	0	0	$0	–
	Aqu⊡	0	0	0	0	$0	–	Dst(399)	1	0	0	0	$135	22

28Aug06–8Sar fst 6f :23 :46² :58⁴1:11⁴ ⑤Md Sp Wt 47k 50 8 1 3¹ 3²¹₂ 2⁷ 29¹₂ Badamo J J L118 4.60 71–17 Whtdremsrmdeof118¹₂ KllMeK118⁶ ThnThrEys118⁴₂ 3 wide, second best 9
28Jly06–4Sar my 5¹₂f :22² :46⁴ 1:00 1:07 ⑤Md Sp Wt 47k 22 10 10 11¹⁸ 11¹² 8¹⁶ 8¹⁷₂ Bracaloni N D 118 13.80 66–21 DistinctPleasure118₁ Megan'sWorld118¹₃ IcyCity113¹₂ Wide, no response 12
WORKS: Mar20 Lrl 3f fst :37 B 4/5 Mar4 Lrl 4f fst :49¹ B 6/22 Feb25 Lrl 5f fst 1:05 B 7/8 Feb19 Lrl 4f fst 1:04 B 1/1 Feb11 Lrl 4f fst :52 B 16/17 ●Jan21 Lrl 3f fst :36⁴ B 1/6
TRAINER: +180Days(5 .20 $1.60) Dirt(310 .18 $1.69) Sprint(182 .13 $1.32) MdnSpWt(21 .19 $1.25)

---

2 What's the Scoop
Own: Caladon Farms Harter James
White Blue, Gray Ball, Blue 'C,' Gray Hoop On
SUTHERLAND C (104 10 11 12 .10) 2006: (402 31 .08)

B. f. 3 (May)
Sire: Good and Tough (Carson City) $3,000
Dam: Spend Doe (Spend a Buck)
Br: Donald A Nitchman (NY)
Tr: DeMola Richard(13 0 2 1 .00) 2006:(59 2 .03)

L 120

	Life	3 M	0	0	$528	34	D.Fst	3	0	0	0	$528	34
	2007	2 M	0	0	$410	32	Wet(419)	0	0	0	0	$0	–
	2006	1 M	0	0	$118	34	Turf(325)	0	0	0	0	$0	–
	Aqu⊡	3	0	0	0	$528	34	Dst(392)	1	0	0	0	$205	26

25Feb07–4Aqu fst 6f :23 2 6 1ʰᵈ 1¹₂ 2¹₂ 6⁸¹₂ Sutherland C L120 fb 34.75 71–16 Ahvee'sDestiny120⁴ LoveCove120₂ Vied outside, tired 9
28Jan07–4Aqu fst 5¹₂f :22³ :46³ :59²1:05² ⑤Md Sp Wt 41k 26 6 6 3⁴ 6⁴ 7⁹⁴₂ 9¹³ Sutherland C L119 f 72.75 79–08 Mrs.Gottlieb119³¹₂ It'sAllGood119⁴ Nantasket119ⁿᵏ Chased 3 wide, faded 9
31Dec06–9Aqu fst 6f :214 ⑤Md Sp Wt 41k 34 2 12 12¹⁶ 11¹⁶ 10¹¹ 9¹¹ Branch K⁷ L113 f 62.50 69–13 Ahvee'sDestiny120⁴ LoveCove120₂₁ ItsAllGood120¹ Bumped start, off slow 12
WORKS: Mar14 Aqu⊡ 3f fst :36⁴ B 3/9 ●Feb13 Aqu⊡ 3f fst :35¹ B 1/4 Jan26 Aqu⊡ 4f fst :50² B 5/10 Dec27 Aqu⊡ 3f fst :36³ B 5/7
TRAINER: Dirt(60 .03 $1.24) Sprint(56 .04 $1.32) MdnSpWt(21 .00 $0.00)   J/T 2006–07 AQU(2 .00 $0.00) J/T 2006–07(2 .00 $0.00)

---

3 Mia
Own: Ferrari Louis P
Blue Blue And Red Diamonds, Blue Sleeves, Red
MARTIN E M JR (283 33 31 49 .12) 2006: (863 82 .10)

Dk. b or br–f. 3 (Apr)
Sire: Vice Regent (Vice Regent) $10,000
Dam: Naive Misiya (Miswaki)
Br: Louis P Ferrari (NY)
Tr: Maker Michael J(15 1 2 3 .07) 2006:(210 51 .24)

L 120

	Life	2 M	0	0	$528	33	D.Fst	2	0	0	0	$528	33
	2007	1 M	0	0	$410	29	Wet(330)	0	0	0	0	$0	–
	2006	1 M	0	0	$118	33	Turf(263)	0	0	0	0	$0	–
	Aqu⊡	2	0	0	0	$528	33	Dst(338)	0	0	0	0	$0	–

7Feb07–2Aqu fst 6f :23 :47³ 1:01 1:14 ⑤⑥Md Sp Wt 41k 29 7 1 2⁴ 64¹₂ 68¹₂ Bridgmohan S X L120 b 13.10 66–24 AbsolutHvn120₁ SmokmlfHvm120₂ TxsStrlt120³¹₂ Chased outside, tired 7
31Dec06–9Aqu fst 6f :21⁴ :45¹ :58 1:113 ⑤Md Sp Wt 41k 33 7 10 10¹⁴ 9¹⁴ 9¹¹ 10¹¹¹₂ Garcia Alan L120 27.75 69–13 Ahvee's Destiny120⁴ Love Cove120₂ It's All Good120¹ No factor 12
WORKS: Mar13 Bel 4f fst :50² B 15/37 Feb28 Bel tr.t 4f fst :51 B 41/45 Feb21 Bel tr.t 5f fst 1:02⁴ B 3/15 Jan20 Bel tr.t 5f fst 1:04 B 13/18 Dec22 Bel tr.t 5f fst 1:02¹ B 6/29
TRAINER: 31-60Days(57 .05 $1.43) Dirt(257 .23 $2.19) Sprint(141 .20 $1.40) MdnSpWt(21 .33 $2.64)   J/T 2006–07 AQU(3 .33 $22.17) J/T 2006–07(4 .25 $16.62)

---

4 Ruth Drive
Own: Indy Stables
Yellow Emerald Green, Black Panel, White
DOMINGUEZ R A (347 83 55 58 .24) 2006: (1417 385 .27)

Ch. f. 3 (Mar) OBSMAR06 $50,000
Sire: Good and Tough (Carson City) $3,000
Dam: Pierpont Account (Private Account)
Br: Bill Terrill (NY)
Tr: Bush Thomas M(88 14 14 13 .16) 2006:(246 36 .15)

L 120

	Life	0 M	0	0	$0	–	D.Fst	0	0	0	0	$0	–
	2007	0 M	0	0	$0	–	Wet(451)	0	0	0	0	$0	–
	2006	0 M	0	0	$0	–	Turf(320)	0	0	0	0	$0	–
	Aqu⊡	0	0	0	0	$0	–	Dst(394)	0	0	0	0	$0	–

WORKS: - Mar11 Bel tr.t 5f fst 1:01¹ B 4/22 Mar4 Bel tr.t 4f fst :47² Bg 4/74 Feb16 Bel tr.t 4f fst :50² B 12/20 Feb8 Bel tr.t 3f fst :36² B 4/23 Jan28 Bel tr.t 3f fst :35³ H 2/46 Jan14 Bel tr.t 3f fst :37¹ B 3/13
TRAINER: 1stStart(36 .06 $0.49) 1stLasix(1 .00 $0.00) Dirt(255 .16 $1.38) Sprint(157 .11 $1.13) MdnSpWt(101 .11 $0.72)   J/T 2006–07 AQU(3 .67 $8.43) J/T 2006–07(5 .50 $7.54)

---

5 Golden Manna
Own: Tam Ping W
Green Lavender, Blue Hoop, Lavender Cap, Blue
HILL C (327 34 39 39 .10) 2006: (1147 82 .07)

Dk. b or br–f. 3 (Apr) NEWAUG05 $10,500
Sire: Wheelaway (Unbridled) $6,000
Dam: Treasure Flight (Meadow Flight)
Br: Cascade Farm LLC (NY)
Tr: Barker Edward R(31 3 3 4 .10) 2006:(59 7 .12)

L 120

	Life	6 M	1	2	$17,324	54	D.Fst	6	0	1	2	$17,324	54
	2007	3 M	1	2	$14,900	53	Wet(359*)	0	0	0	0	$0	–
	2006	3 M	0	0	$2,424	54	Turf(218*)	0	0	0	0	$0	–
	Aqu⊡	4	0	1	2	$15,110	53	Dst(324)	0	0	0	0	$0	–

25Feb07–4Aqu fst 6f :22⁴ :47¹ 1:00 1:13¹ ⑤⑥Md Sp Wt 41k 48 5 8 7¹³ 6⁸ 4² 2ⁿᵒ Ponce J⁵ L115 4.30 78–16 ClJJen120ⁿᵒ GoldenMnn120ᵏ LittleMissPopeye120ⁿᵏ Checked after start 9
Previously trained by McLaughlin Kiaran P 2006: (406 80 74 44 0.20)
1Feb07–4Aqu fst 6f :22³ :46³ :59²1:124 ⑤⑥Md Sp 50000 42 7 1 3¹¹₂ 3ⁿᵏ 2³¹₂ 3⁴ Fragoso P L120 5.00 76–15 PsychotcColors120¹₁ WLovOrKds120²₁ GldnMnn120⁴₂ 3 wide move, tired 8
7Jan07–3Aqu fst 6f :22⁴ :46³ 1:00 1:13¹ ⑤⑥Md Sp Wt 41k 53 6 2 2¹ 2¹ 2³¹₂ 2⁸ Fragoso P L119 11.20 79–14 ClynthClods119⁵₂ SmokmlfHvm119¹ GldnMnn119² Chased outside, tired 9
6Dec06–4Aqu fst 1 :24² :48³ 1:14 1:40 ⑤⑥Md Sp Wt 42k –0 8 5²¹₂ 5¹¹ 9¹⁹ 9²⁹ 9⁴²¹₂ Jara F L119 11.20 41–12 RosiesAttitude119²₂ PureBusiness119²₂ RglPlytim119³ Tired after a half 9
Previously trained by Harty Eoin 2006(as of 10/21): (143 26 26 18 0.18)
21Oct06–2Bel fst 7f :23 :46³ 1:11¹₂ 1:242 ⑤⑥Md Sp Wt 41k 2 5 9 87¹₂ 810 9²⁹ 7³²¹₂ Smith M E L120 20.80 46–15 Sagamoon120²¹₂ Guts Game120⁵₂ Regal Playtime120²₂ Had no rally 11
17Sep06–7Bel fst 6f :21 :44³ 1:11¹₂ ⑤⑥Md Sp Wt 41k 54 3 8 7⁵¹₂ 76¹₂ 6¹⁰ 4⁷₁ Smith M E L120 22.50 75–14 Second Marriage118²₂ Guts Game118₁ Alchera118₁ In tight start, bobble 9
WORKS: Mar13 Aqu⊡ 3f fst :37⁴ B 1/2 Feb22 Aqu⊡ 4f fst :50 B 7/8 Jan21 Bel tr.t 4f fst :50 B 12/20 Dec29 Bel tr.t 4f fst :49¹ B 11/42 Dec22 Bel tr.t 4f fst :49³ B 53/117
TRAINER: Dirt(76 .13 $3.65) Sprint(27 .07 $2.23) MdnSpWt(15 .07 $0.58)   J/T 2006–07 AQU(3 .00 $0.00) J/T 2006–07(3 .00 $0.00)

---

6 Caterina's Term's
Own: Vangelatos Peter
Black White And Blue Diamonds, White Sleeves
BRIDGMOHAN S X (246 27 32 32 .11) 2006: (1068 134 .13)

B. f. 3 (Mar)
Sire: Private Terms (Private Account) $3,000
Dam: Kuru Klata (Vice of I'Orne*Fr)
Br: Peter Vangelatos (NY)
Tr: Sciacca Gary(90 4 8 5 .04) 2006:(306 28 .09)

L 120

	Life	4 M	0	0	$1,194	26	D.Fst	3	0	0	0	$654	20
	2007	3 M	0	0	$1,030	26	Wet(343)	1	0	0	0	$540	26
	2006	1 M	0	0	$164	–	Turf(245)	0	0	0	0	$0	–
	Aqu⊡	4	0	0	0	$1,194	26	Dst(297)	0	0	0	0	$0	–

2Mar07–9Aqu gd 6f :22⁴ :46⁴ 1:00 1:13ᵇ 3+⑤⑥Md 35000 26 2 8 8¹⁰ 7¹⁷ 7¹³ 5¹²¹₂ Hill C L118 b 23.80 64–24 Zip of Fools118¹⁸ Leaveitinthering123⁴ Union Center123⁴₂ Had no rally 8
1Feb07–5Aqu fst 1¹₁₆ :24 :48¹ 1:14 1:48¹ ⑤⑥Md Sp Wt 42k –0 2 5⁴ 66¹₂ 8¹⁵ 831 7³⁹ McNeil B⁵ L115 b 118.75 30–22 Junkanoo Party120₁ Papa's Kara120⁵₁ Laura'sFury120⁶₂ Inside trip, tired 8
15Jan07–6Aqu fst 1 :23² :47² 1:12³1:39³ ⑤⑥Md Sp Wt 42k 20 4 8¹³ 8¹⁶ 8¹⁹ 8²³ 8²⁶¹₂ Ponce J⁷ L120 12.75 56–15 Flightofthepelican194⁴₂ SilvercupBaby119¹ WinlocsIrene119⁴₂ No response 8
27Dec06–4Aqu fst 6f :22³ :47² 1:00³1:14⁴ ⑤⑥Md Sp Wt 42k –0 1 9 10¹² 10¹³ 10¹⁷ 10²²¹₂ Luzzi M J L120 25.75 53–17 Abbyroar120¹ Positive Charge120ⁿᵒ Freakazoid120² Steadied start 10
WORKS: Mar15 Bel tr.t 4f fst :50 B 31/46 Feb25 Bel tr.t 5f fst 1:04 B 22/28 Feb18 Bel tr.t 4f fst :51¹ B 65/93
TRAINER: Dirt(264 .09 $1.71) Sprint(142 .07 $1.09) MdnSpWt(59 .08 $1.58)   J/T 2006–07 AQU(16 .13 $3.62) J/T 2006–07(23 .13 $3.01)

---

7 Duchess of Rokeby
Own: Whitbred Howard T Christine Brennan
Orange Beige, Ivory Braces, Ivory Sleeves, Two
SMITH M E (130 10 14 17 .08) 2006: (685 64 .09)

Ch. f. 3 (May)
Sire: City Zip (Carson City) $20,000
Dam: Palace Lady (His Majesty)
Br: Christine Brennan & H T Whitbred (NY)
Tr: Gyarmati Leah(59 7 7 7 .12) 2006:(211 21 .10)

120

	Life	0 M	0	0	$0	–	D.Fst	0	0	0	0	$0	–
	2007	0 M	0	0	$0	–	Wet(346)	0	0	0	0	$0	–
	2006	0 M	0	0	$0	–	Turf(335)	0	0	0	0	$0	–
	Aqu⊡	0	0	0	0	$0	–	Dst(331)	0	0	0	0	$0	–

WORKS: Mar10 Bel tr.t 5f fst 1:03¹ B 2/17 Mar4 Bel tr.t 5f fst 1:02⁴ B 14/36 Feb18 Bel tr.t 4f fst :48 Bg 6/93 Jan30 Bel tr.t 4f fst :51 B 13/19 Jan22 Bel tr.t 4f fst :51 B 22/36 Jan13 Bel tr.t 4f fst :51 B 37/45
TRAINER: 1stStart(8 .00 $0.00) Dirt(227 .11 $1.58) Sprint(131 .09 $1.50) MdnSpWt(77 .19 $2.83)   J/T 2006–07 AQU(15 .20 $2.72) J/T 2006–07(15 .20 $2.72)

---

8 Gypsy Gale
Own: Richlyn Farm
Pink Red, White Star, White Sleeves, Red
ESPINOZA J L (9 5 9 11 .05) 2006: (569 71 .05)

Dk. b or br–f. 3 (Jan) SARAUG05 $45,000
Sire: Pleasant Tap (Pleasant Colony) $15,000
Dam: Bright Tribute (Barrera)
Br: Mrs Gerald A Nielsen (NY)
Tr: Kelly Patrick J(—) 2006:(242 25 .10)

120

	Life	0 M	0	0	$0	–	D.Fst	0	0	0	0	$0	–
	2007	0 M	0	0	$0	–	Wet(345)	0	0	0	0	$0	–
	2006	0 M	0	0	$0	–	Turf(277)	0	0	0	0	$0	–
	Aqu⊡	0	0	0	0	$0	–	Dst(328)	0	0	0	0	$0	–

WORKS: Mar12 Bel tr.t 4f fst :50 B 52/70 Mar5 Bel tr.t 3f fst :36⁴ B 7/26 Feb25 Bel tr.t 4f fst :49⁴ H 31/33 Feb18 Bel tr.t 3f fst :38⁴ B 24/28 Jan28 Bel tr.t 4f fst :50¹ B 30/75 Jan24 Bel tr.t 4f fst :51 B 39/47
TRAINER: 1stStart(15 .07 $0.80) Dirt(129 .05 $1.41) Sprint(136 .09 $1.38) MdnSpWt(114 .09 $1.37)

Like stablemate Mighty Eros, Ruth Drive was a graduate of an OBS sale; she showed a recent half-mile breeze from the gate ranked 4/74 in preparation for her debut, and was facing what could charitably be described as an ordinary group. Given the performance of Mighty Eros, and the heavy tote action on Ruth Drive, Bush's current stats with first-time starters were nothing more than a red herring. She won for fun, and paid $4.10 as the first leg of the day's early pick four.

SECOND RACE
Aqueduct
MARCH 22, 2007

5½ FURLONGS. (1.03⁴) MAIDEN SPECIAL WEIGHT . Purse $41,000 INNER DIRT FOR MAIDENS, FILLIES THREE YEARS OLD FOALED IN NEW YORK STATE AND APPROVED BY THE NEW YORK STATE–BRED REGISTRY. Weight, 120 lbs.

Value of Race: $41,000 Winner $24,600; second $8,200; third $4,100; fourth $2,050; fifth $1,230; sixth $410; seventh $410. Mutuel Pool $185,423.00 Exacta Pool $181,111.00 Quinella Pool $17,973.00 Trifecta Pool $122,933.00

Last Raced	Horse	M/Eqt.	A.	Wt	PP	St	¼	⅜	Str	Fin	Jockey	Odds $1
	Ruth Drive	L f	3	120	4	2	1¹	1³	1⁶	1³½	Dominguez R A	1.05
25Feb07 ⁴Aqu²	Golden Manna	L	3	120	5	3	3³½	3⁵½	2½	2⁶	Hill C	3.70
28Aug06 ⁶Sar²	Kall Me K	L	3	120	1	1	4½	4¹	4¹½	3²¼	Arroyo N Jr	2.10
25Feb07 ⁴Aqu⁶	What's the Scoop	L bf	3	120	2	4	2³	2²½	3⁶	4¹½	Sutherland C	20.10
7Feb07 ²Aqu⁶	Mia	L b	3	120	3	5	5⁵½	5⁶	5⁵	5⁴½	Martin E M Jr	24.25
2Mar07 ⁹Aqu⁵	Caterina's Term's	L b	3	120	6	6	6⁷	6⁷	6⁶	6³¼	Bridgmohan S X	73.75
	Duchess of Rokeby	f	3	120	7	7	7	7	7	7	Smith M E	15.50

OFF AT 1:28 Start Good. Won driving. Track fast.
TIME :22², :46, :58³, 1:05¹ (:22.55, :46.12, :58.63, 1:05.39)

$2 Mutuel Prices:

4 – RUTH DRIVE	4.10	2.50	2.40
5 – GOLDEN MANNA		3.20	2.30
1 – KALL ME K			2.50

$2 EXACTA 4–5 PAID $13.60 $2 QUINELLA 4–5 PAID $8.20
$2 TRIFECTA 4–5–1 PAID $26.20

Ch. f, (Mar), by Good and Tough – Pierpont Account , by Private Account . Trainer Bush Thomas M. Bred by Bill Terrill (NY).

RUTH DRIVE showed good speed from the start, soon opened a clear lead, set the pace while in hand, drew away when asked and was ridden out to the finish. GOLDEN MANNA was unhurried early and rallied to get the place. KALL ME K posed no real threat. WHAT'S THE SCOOP stumbled after the start, was steadied on the backstretch and tired. MIA stumbled after the start and was outrun. CATERINA'S TERM'S tired. DUCHESS OF ROKEBY ducked out at the start and trailed throughout. A claim of foul against the winner by the rider of the fourth place finisher, alleging interference on the backstretch, was not allowed.

Owners– 1, Indy Stables; 2, Tam Ping W; 3, Seahorse Stable; 4, Caladon Farms Harter James; 5, Ferrari Louis P; 6, Vangelatos Peter; 7, Whitbred Howard T and Brennan Christine

Trainers– 1, Bush Thomas M; 2, Barker Edward R; 3, Grusmark Karl M; 4, DeMola Richard; 5, Maker Michael J; 6, Sciacca Gary; 7, Gyarmati Leah

Scratched– Gypsy Gale

$2 Daily Double (3–4) Paid $80.00 ; Daily Double Pool $200,353 .

The thing to remember is that "Trainer Form," which now appears at the bottom of the past performances, can be a very useful guideline—but it is not always the bottom line, so to speak.

As Charles Carroll, the author of the thought-provoking book *Handicapping Speed,* eloquently stated in an on-line article at icapper.com:

"What is often lost in these broad-based computer studies is the importance of the variability that makes up the day-to-day reality of the two main sets of information: racing data . . . and tote-board data . . . which are part and parcel of the 'variance' that makes betting 'scores' possible. There are many questions in horse racing where it would be nice to have a population of 15,000 races, but there are many more where smaller, more compact and focused populations identify patterning, which large populations completely obscure. Large populations of races for statistical studies are valuable for large, fundamental questions, but usually small profit. The variability that we move on as value bettors is more often short-term—sometimes instantaneous—and a lot more profitable."

Benjamin Disraeli put it a bit more succinctly when he said: "There are three kinds of lies: lies; damned lies; and statistics."

Trainers

With the development of *Daily Racing Form*'s Formulator 4.1 software, one of the record-keeping disciplines that I have jettisoned is the key-race method. Formulator 4.1 provides the charts of horses' three most recent races, and handicappers can look up the past performances of every horse in those races to get a gauge on the strength of the field; then you merely select "next race" to see if any have run back. Even without Formulator's help, it's easy to spot a key race now that next-out winners are italicized in the company lines of the past performances.

One of the record-keeping habits I have not given up, however, is clipping and saving the winning past performances on my circuit (New York) and filing them by trainer.

I toyed with the idea of giving up the practice, because Formulator 4.1 can massage trainer data six ways from Sunday (for the definitive treatment of that software, consult *Trainer Angles,* by Dean Keppler). But nothing beats the tactile sensation of a dog-eared loose-leaf notebook; and for public handicappers working on deadline, it is actually faster than a trip to cyberspace.

Besides, after reading the conclusion of *Handicapping 101* by my West Coast counterpart, Brad Free, I couldn't very well pull the plug:

"To prepare for my return, I imitated New York colleague Dave Litfin, a meticulous record-keeper. Litfin clipped past performances of each trainer and filed them under the trainer's name. Great, still more tedious paperwork. Before returning to California, I clipped and filed winners' past performances for the three previous race meets. The one-season experiment has grown to years of data—past performances of every Southern California winner, filed under trainer, since 1998. There is no better way to get familiar with the nuances of a trainer, or a class level. The time-consuming procedure offers keen insight to trainer idiosyncrasies that is unavailable anywhere else."

The best thing is that you don't have to have a master's degree in computer science, because the basic skills—cutting and pasting—are the ones you mastered in kindergarten.

The influence of trainers should never be underestimated, because they're the ones calling the shots. Competent trainers do whatever they can to nurture and encourage the best qualities of their horses, and they often go to great lengths to orchestrate a revival of circumstances that previously led to peak condition and performance. But as with any other field, trainers bring widely varied levels of expertise to their profession, and we shouldn't make the mistake of assuming universal competence.

Trainer patterns are nothing new, and reliable conditioners develop methods that produce results season after season. You don't have to be maniacal about things and keep tabs on everyone. Pick a handful of trainers who have impressed you for one reason or another on the circuit(s) you concentrate on, and perhaps another handful that are part of the national stakes scene. Underneath the past performances, simply note the date of the win, the class, the distance, the win price, and any miscellaneous data that seems noteworthy; it's not a bad idea to do the same for horses that finish second, or even a close third, at long odds.

I promise you will be amazed at the live horses at big prices that come running out of those marble composition or loose-leaf notebooks, even from the "designer" barns that receive extensive media coverage.

There's no higher-profile trainer than Bobby Frankel, for example, yet he continually fools the general betting public when he ships horses into seemingly ambitious spots where they seem to be biting off more than they can chew:

Peace Rules
Own: Gann Edmund A

Ch. c. 4 (Apr) OBSMAR02 $35,000
Sire: Jules (Forty Niner) $6,000
Dam: Hold to Fashion (Hold Your Peace)
Br: Newchance Farm (Fla)
Tr: Frankel Robert J(0 0 0 0 .00) 2004:(0 0 .00)

Life	19	9	2	2	$3,084,278	113	D.Fst	11	6	1	2	$2,788,700 113
2004	6	3	0	0	$1,024,288	113	Wet(356)	3	0	0	0	$91,888 98
							Synth	0	0	0	0	$0 -
2003	7	3	1	1	$1,850,000	109	Turf(214)	5	3	1	0	$203,690 102
Bel	1	1	0	0	$300,000	111	Dst(347)	0	0	0	0	$0 -

7Aug04-9Sar	fst	1⅛		:451 1:084 1:344 1:482	3↑WhitneyH-G1	100	8	31	31	34	63¾	68¼	Bailey J D	L121	*3.05	85-14	*RosesinMy*114no PerfctDrift1172¼ BowmnsBnd114no	Chased outside, tired	9
3Jly04-7Bel	fst	1¼		:461 1:091 1:334 1:592	3↑SuburbnH-G1	111	3	11	1½	1hd	2½	1nk	Bailey J D	L120	3.20	100 -	PeaceRules120nk Newfoundland114no FunnyCide117¾	Came again gamely	8
12Jun04-9CD	sly	1⅛		:473 1:122 1:372 1:502	3↑SFosterH-G1	96	2	11½	11½	11½	42	48¾	Bailey J D	L121	2.80	76-17	ColonilColony111no SouthrnImg1225 PrfctDrft1193¾	Pace,inside,faltered	6
3Apr04-11OP	fst	1⅛		:452 1:093 1:352 1:481	4↑OaklawnH-G2	112	3	21	2½	2hd	11½	12	Bailey J D	L120	*.80	97-09	Peace Rules1202 Ole Faunty116nk Saint Liam1142¼	Quick duel,stayd clear	6
29Feb04-9FG	fst	1⅛		:47 1:102 1:352 1:483	4↑NwOrlnsH-G2	113	5	12	12	11	1hd	1hd	Bailey J D	L119	3.60	101-05	*Peace Rules*119hd Saint Liam1142¾ *Funny Cide*1181¼	Headed, fought back	8
24Jan04-6SA	fst	1⅛		:453 1:092 1:342 1:473	4↑[R]SMClassic1000k	93	6	64½	54½	54	46½	48½	Bailey J D	LB120	*1.00	87-07	*SothrnImg*1203 ExcssSmmr1205 ThJdgSzWho122½	Bobbled bit strt,empty	12
25Oct03-4SA	fm	1	ⓣ	:221 :452 1:092 1:334	3↑BCMile-G1	71	1	11	1hd	2hd	125	1315½	Prado E S	LB122	*3.10	77-04	SxPrfctons119¾ TochofthBls126nk CntryCty1261¼	Speed,inside,gave way	13
23Aug03-11Sar	fst	1¼		:461 1:094 1:352 2:02	Travers-G1	105	3	2hd	2½	2hd	2½	24½	Bailey J D	L126	*2.30	92-03	*TenMostWnted*1264½ PeceRules12610 *StrongHop*126¾	Vied outside, gamely	6
3Aug03-11Mth	fst	1⅛		:47 1:104 1:36 1:491	HskIInvH-G1	109	1	11½	11½	11½	13	11¾	Prado E S	L121	2.30	95-08	Peace Rules1211¾ Sky Mesa1187¼ Funny Cide1231	Pace off rail,driving	7
17May03-12Pim	gd	1 3/16		:47 1:113 1:362 1:553	Preaknes-G1	98	7	2hd	11	1½	35	410½	Prado E S	L126	2.40	84-12	Funny Cide1269¾ Midway Road126¾ Scrimshaw126no	2wd,brushed,wknd	10
3May03-10CD	fst	1¼		:461 1:102 1:353 2:01	KyDerby-G1	106	4	2½	2hd	1½	2hd	31¾	Prado E S	L126	6.30	92-06	*Funny Cide*1261¾ *Empire Maker*126hd Peace Rules126hd	Pressed,led,gamely	16
12Apr03-9Kee	fst	1⅛		:47 1:111 1:374 1:513	BlueGras-G1	104	2	11½	11½	11	11	13½	Prado E S	L123	*.60	82-30	Peace Rules1233½ Brancusi1234½ Offlee Wild12310½	Rated on pace,driving	9
9Mar03-9FG	fst	1 1/16		:232 :463 1:103 1:423	LaDerby-G2	105	9	21	21½	2½	11	12¼	Prado E S	L122	9.40	97-17	*Peace Rules*1222¼ [D]Kafwain1221 Funny Cide122½	Bid, clear, driving	10
28Dec02-3SA	fm	1	ⓣ	:232 :461 1:102 1:352	HillRise76k	102	2	22	23	21	12½	1¾	Espinoza V	LB120	*.40e	85-18	*Peace Rules*120¾ Singletary1171¼ Bis Repetitas1166	Bid,cleared,held	5
30Nov02-6Hol	fm	1	ⓣ	:233 :464 1:104 1:352	Generous-G3	99	8	2hd	12	11	12	11¼	Espinoza V	LB118	2.60e	87-12	*PeaceRules*1181¼ *LismoreKnight*121½ *OuttHere*115½	Dueled,clear,held game	9
24Oct02-7SA	fm	1	ⓣ	:23 :464 1:11 1:343	[R]Pinjara52k	88	5	1½	12½	11½	11½	2hd	Valenzuela P A	LB116	*1.10e	89-15	Man Among Men116hd *Peace Rules*1168 Gohalo1161½	Inside,clear,caught	8
Previously trained by Contessa Gary C 2002(as of 9/25): (553 80 92 70 0.14)																			
25Sep02-6Bel	fm	1	ⓣ	:224 :461 1:103 1:344	Md Sp Wt 46k	87	1	12	12½	11½	13	14	Santos J A	119	9.20	86-14	Peace Rules1194 *Kon Tiki*1194½ AventuraPlace1192¼	Vigorous hand urging	10
24Aug02-4Sar	sly	6½f		:22 :452 1:114 1:182	Md Sp Wt 45k	81	9	4	42	41¾	41	54½	Arroyo N Jr	119	7.90	78-17	Atfirst Blush1191 *Outer Reef*1191 Ozzie Cat119½	Chased inside, no bid	11
31Jly02-6Sar	fst	5f		:221 :454 :582	Md Sp Wt 45k	70	1	1	45½	43½	43	32½	Arroyo N Jr	118	16.00	93-08	Mister Deux1182¼ Pick'em118nk Peace Rules118no	Game finish outside	8

WORKS: ●Aug27 Sar 5f fst :594 B *1/13* ●Aug20 Sar 4f fst :473 B *1/24* Jly31 Sar 5f fst 1:012 B *22/57* Jly25 Bel tr.t 5f gd 1:01 B *10/26* Jly17 Bel 4f fst :472 B *4/67* Jun27 Bel 4f fst :473 H *2/87*
TRAINER: +180Days(91 .24 $1.95) Dirt(305 .29 $1.98) Routes(529 .24 $1.70) Stakes(217 .18 $1.51)

Wild Spirit had regularly been bet to odds-on in her native Chile, but it's usually difficult for handicappers to get a handle on how South American form translates to the Northern Hemisphere. But Frankel evidently had quite a solid handle on Wild Spirit as he prepared her for her U.S. debut, because instead of looking around for a soft spot to get her going off a five-month layoff, he put her right into the Grade 2 Shuvee Handicap, one of New York's marquee events for fillies and mares. The fact that Wild Spirit was spotted so aggressively spoke volumes about Frankel's opinion of where she belonged, yet she got away at 10–1 in a short six-horse field.

Peace Rules was purchased for a reported $350,000 after a maiden turf win as a 2-year-old in the fall of 2002, shipped out to Southern California, and began earning back some of that amount in three grass stakes to close out the season. After a freshening of a little more than two months, Frankel shipped the newly turned 3-year-old to the Fair Grounds for the Louisiana Derby—on dirt. Primarily because Peace Rules looked like a "turf horse" at that point, he was dismissed at 9–1, yet he won decisively.

There were actually three keys here: (1) Frankel's aggressiveness—why bother shipping all the way to New Orleans to run a horse on the wrong surface if the horse "needed" a race? (2) He had a dirt pedigree, so it was possible he had been running well on the grass *in spite* of that. (3) He had lost the first two starts of his career sprinting on dirt, but as we know, the first couple of starts may be the least definitive for a horse, particularly since the Louisiana Derby was his first dirt start on Lasix.

About 11 months after he shipped Peace Rules from California to win the Louisiana Derby, Frankel sent Miss Coronado to Gulfstream Park to win the Grade 2 Davona Dale Stakes at better than 8–1—switching from turf to dirt and making her first start against winners! As with Wild Spirit and Peace Rules, the underlying message of Frankel's aggressive approach was confidence: Why go right from a maiden win to a Grade 2, why switch to dirt, and why ship across the country to do it? Once again, Frankel knew his horse better than the bettors.

Top trainers like Bobby Frankel handle stakes horses pretty much the same way season after season, but an equally lucrative area of trainer handicapping involves short-term patterns. This is especially true during the early stages of a race meeting, if and when it becomes clear a trainer has geared up for an assault right out of the box:

Victory Pool
Own: New Farm

Ch. m. 5 (Mar)
Sire: Victory Gallop (Cryptoclearance) $10,000
Dam: Taliesin (Talinum)
Br: L O R Stables, Ltd (Tex)
Tr: Perkins B W Jr(29 8 2 6 .28) 2006:(154 28 .18)

Life	18	5	6	3	$218,949	89	D.Fst	17	5	5	3	$210,549	89
2007	1	0	0	1	$7,059	89	Wet(358)	1	0	1	0	$8,400	74
							Synth	0	0	0	0	$0	-
2006	6	2	2	0	$94,200	88	Turf(257)	0	0	0	0	$0	-
Aqu ⊡	7	1	3	3	$91,709	89	Dst(335)	1	0	0	1	$4,100	54

13Jan07-8Aqu fst 1 1/16 ⊡ :24² :48 1:12³ 1:44¹ 3↑Ⓕ AfectntlyH70k 89 1 42½ 42½ 43 23½ 3¾ Coa E M L118 3.60 88-16 GretIntntions115nk Homrtt115nk VictoryPool1187¾ Saved ground, gamely 6
16Dec06-8Aqu fst 170 ⊡ :23⁴ :47¹ 1:13 1:43² 3↑ⒻⓇ GoldBeauty67k 87 7 56 45½ 32½ 2½ 11½ Coa E M L118 7.80 83-21 Victory Pool1181½ Dina1161 Samsincharge1236¼ Rallied 3 wide 7
10Sep06-6Mth fst 1 1/16 :23³ :47⁴ 1:12 1:44⁴ 3↑Ⓕ Alw 55000c 66 1 51¾ 62½ 63¼ 54¼ 46¼ Bravo J L119 *1.40 74-14 *PlsntChms*1211½ LdyBlzbub1193¼ BlssfulIgnornc1191½ Even finish outside 7
9Jly06-9Mth fst 170 :23² :47 1:11³ 1:43 3↑Ⓕ MthBeach65k 66 6 51¾ 42 43½ 49 411¼ Bravo J L120 3.80 68-22 EmeraldErrings122¾ Silmril118nk GipsyLimits11810½ Inside 1/4,lacked bid 7
6Jun06-7Del fst 1 1/16 :23³ :48² 1:13 1:45¹ 3↑Ⓕ OC 35k/N3x-N 88 3 11 1½ 11½ 13 11½ Dominguez R A L119 *.60 87-22 Victory Pool1191½ *Katie's Love*119½ LoveIsKind1194¾ Solid pace, prevailed 7
9Mar06-8Aqu fst 1 ⊡ :24¹ :47⁴ 1:12³ 1:38 4↑Ⓕ OC 75k/N3x-N 86 6 43½ 52¼ 2½ 2hd 22¾ Luzzi M J L118 8.80 90-18 No Sleep1232¾ *Victory Pool*1181¾ Game Card1134¼ Led between calls 6
22Jan06-8Aqu fst 1 ⊡ :24 :48¹ 1:12⁴ 1:38³ Ⓕ SmrColony61k 72 3 43 42½ 33 36½ 27 Dominguez R A L119 6.40 83-16 Pool Land1177 Victory Pool1192½ Amazing Buy1232½ Rallied for place 7

WORKS: Jan10 Bel tr.t 3f fst :36⁴ H *4/17* Dec10 Bel tr.t 4f fst :49² B *59/125* Nov10 Mth 5f fst 1:01² B *3/14* Oct30 Mth 4f fst :50 B *16/39* Oct24 Mth 4f fst :49⁴ B *6/20*
TRAINER: 2Off45-180(25 .20 $1.79) Route/Sprint(15 .00 $0.00) Sprint(151 .19 $1.92) Stakes(37 .22 $1.74)

Just Wild
Own: New Farm

Dk. b or b. c. 3 (Mar)
Sire: Forest Wildcat (Storm Cat) $35,000
Dam: Infomint (Key to the Mint)
Br: New Farm (Ky)
Tr: Perkins B W Jr(29 8 2 6 .28) 2006:(154 28 .18)

Life	2	1	0	0	$26,140	73	D.Fst	2	1	0	0	$26,140	73
2006	2	1	0	0	$26,140	73	Wet(352)	0	0	0	0	$0	-
							Synth	0	0	0	0	$0	-
2005	0	M	0	0	$0	-	Turf(293)	0	0	0	0	$0	-
Aqu ⊡	1	1	0	0	$25,800	73	Dst(360)	2	1	0	0	$26,140	73

30Dec06-2Aqu fst 6f ⊡ :22⁴ :45⁴ :58² 1:11² Md Sp Wt 43k 73 9 1 11 13 14 14 Lopez C C L120 b *2.55 82-16 Just Wild1204 Philomatt1203 Chaldean's Rocket115no Ridden out 10
27Oct06-5Med fst 6f :21⁴ :44³ :57 1:10³ Md Sp Wt 34k -0 3 2 32 69 816 824¾ Garcia Alan L119 3.10 62-09 AlarmingGlory119¾ MajorBob1192½ ReatsTiger114nk Chased inside, faded 8

WORKS: Jan12 Bel tr.t 4f fst :48² B *4/67* ●Dec17 Bel tr.t 4f fst :46² Bg *1/92* ●Dec9 Bel tr.t 4f fst :48 Bg *1/42* Nov11 Mth 4f fst :48³ B *2/42* ●Oct23 Mth 5f fst 1:01 Hg *1/15*
TRAINER: 31-60Days(53 .23 $2.64) Sprint(151 .19 $1.92) Stakes(37 .22 $1.74)

Wild Jam
Own: New Farm

B. g. 6 (Apr)
Sire: Forest Wildcat (Storm Cat) $35,000
Dam: Gold Plum (Cahill Road)
Br: New Farm (Ky)
Tr: Perkins B W Jr(29 8 2 6 .28) 2006:(154 28 .18)

Life	26	7	5	7	$283,021	100	D.Fst	21	7	5	5	$270,771	100
2007	1	1	0	0	$33,600	88	Wet(358)	4	0	0	2	$11,820	87
							Synth	0	0	0	0	$0	-
2006	8	1	2	3	$88,201	99	Turf(312)	1	0	0	0	$430	65
Aqu ⊡	7	3	1	3	$131,241	100	Dst(382)	19	4	5	4	$213,961	100

4Jan07-8Aqu fst 6f ⊡ :221 :45 :57 1:094 4↑OC 100k/c-N 88 2 7 5¹¼ 4³ 3²½ 1nk Luzzi M J L119 4.40 95- 10 WildJam119nk MrWhitestone117nk MddysLion1173 Gamely between foes 7
25Aug06-8Lrl fst 6f :221 :45 :5711:094 3↑OC 50k/N$Y-N 87 4 6 5⁶½ 6⁷½ 6⁴¾ 5²¼ Pino M G L120 4.00 91- 14 Acclimt120¾ YourBluffing120nk CrftySchmr122nk Sluggish,5wd,belatedly 6
8Jly06-6Mth fst 6f :22 :442 :5621:09 3↑MrProspctr65k 98 5 2 5⁴ 3² 2¹½ 2² Bravo J L122 4.70 93- 15 High Blitz1222 Wild Jam1224½ Razor118no Widest,2nd best 5
22Jun06-3Bel fst 6½f :224 :46 1:1031:171 4↑OC 100k/c-N 95 2 3 4³ 4⁴½ 4³ 3¹ Luzzi M J L122 6.00 85- 18 Spooky Mulder120nk Tani Maru118¾ Wild Jam1222½ Came wide, gamely 4
29May06-9Mth fst 6f :221 :45 :57 1:092 3↑WolfHill65k 91 2 5 5²½ 3²½ 3³½ 2⁷ Bravo J L121 2.00 86- 14 *High Blitz*1177 Wild Jam121no *Spooky Mulder*117¾ Light bump start,rail 5
23Apr06-8Pim gd 6f :224 :452 :5711:10 3↑Hoover75k 87 2 5 4³ 4⁵ 4⁸ 6⁵½ Rodriguez E D L120 *2.00 91- 09 *The Student*118¾ P.Kerney1201¾ GoldCluster118hd Angled 5-6wd 1/8,empty 7
11Mar06-8Aqu fst 6f ⊡ :22 :443 :5621:091 3↑ToboggnH-G3 96 6 3 5¹½ 3² 3⁵½ 3⁴ Coa E M L115 4.30 89- 13 Kazoo1164 *Bishop Court Hill*117no Wild Jam1152½ Good finish outside 6

WORKS: Dec28 Bel tr.t 4f fst :494 B *35/77* Dec21 Bel tr.t 5f fst 1:014 B *5/31* ●Dec14 Bel tr.t 4f fst :463 H *1/26* ●Dec8 Bel tr.t 4f fst :48 B *1/10*

TRAINER: Sprint(151 .19 $1.92) Stakes(37 .22 $1.74)

It's a Monster
Own: New Farm

Ch. g. 8 (Jun)
Sire: Meadow Monster (Meadowlake) $3,000
Dam: Satisfy (Known Fact)
Br: New Farm (Ky)
Tr: Perkins B W Jr(29 8 2 6 .28) 2006:(154 28 .18)

Life	23	10	4	3	$311,890	101	D.Fst	18	8	3	3	$235,490	101
2007	1	1	0	0	$22,800	78	Wet(378)	5	2	1	0	$76,400	101
							Synth	0	0	0	0	$0	-
2006	7	1	3	0	$44,490	86	Turf(269)	0	0	0	0	$0	-
Aqu ⊡	3	1	1	0	$30,400	82	Dst(356)	19	8	4	2	$269,890	101

5Jan07-3Aqu fst 6f ⊡ :222 :46 :5911:123 4↑Clm 30000(35-25) 78 1 4 5⁸½ 5⁴¾ 2½ 1¹¾ Garcia Alan L117 5.00 81- 24 *It's a Monster*1171¾ *Auto City*117hd Hostile Witness1201½ Broke open gate 7
21Sep06-7Mth fst 6f :224 :453 :5721:093 3↑Clm 35000(35-30) 74 5 1 3² 5³ 6²¾ 6⁵ Garcia Alan L119 7.40 87- 10 *Pushed*121hd Ojibway1193 Letters119nk Chased between, tired 6
30Aug06-5Mth sly^s 6f :222 :451 :5721:093 3↑Clm 35000(35-30) 86 3 4 4¹ 4²½ 5¹¾ 2²¼ Garcia Alan L119 6.20 89- 14 *Pushed*1192¼ ItsMonster119no KeepCrusing121nk Moved 4-w,got 2nd wire 7
13Aug06-7Mth fst 6f :223 :46 :5811:103 3↑Clm 25000(25-20) 86 4 3 6¹¾ 4¹¾ 2hd 1¾ Garcia Alan L119 9.60 87- 17 It's a Monster119¾ Vinemeister1191 Pine Cay1192¼ Angled to rail 1/8,drv 8
15Jly06-5Mth fst 6f :22 :444 :57 1:10 3↑Clm 30000(30-25) 64 2 5 4³ 3⁵ 3⁵ 6¹² Garcia Alan L119 4.70 78- 13 *Jose*1216½ Fourthirteen119nk Departing Now112¾ Broke out some,inside 7
20May06-7Mth fst 6f :223 :461 :5831:111 3↑Clm 35000(35-30) 77 7 5 6²¾ 5¹½ 3²½ 2⁵ Garcia Alan L119 5.50 79- 18 Desert Border1195 It's a Monster1191 Our Wildcat119nk Mild rally inside 7
18Mar06-1Aqu fst 6f ⊡ :224 :47 :5911:114 4↑Clm 25000(25-22.5) 82 4 1 6³ 4² 3½ 2no Morales P5 L115 6.50 80- 17 CatchMyCat120no ItsaMonster115nk BettheChlk1201 Game finish outside 8
5Feb06-6Aqu gd 6f ⊡ :232 :454 :5741:103 4↑Clm 17500(17.5-15.5) 71 6 3 7¹ 8⁷ 8³¾ 4¹ Morales P5 L115 f 9.90 85- 12 *LuckyGmbl*120nk *CongrssionlRun*120¾ DylnsDstiny120no Going well outside 8

WORKS: ●Dec16 Bel tr.t 4f fst :473 H *1/65* Nov4 Mth 4f fst :51 B *29/38* Oct17 Mth 4f fst :511 B *25/32*

TRAINER: 31-60Days(53 .23 $2.64) WonLastStart(36 .22 $1.79) Sprint(151 .19 $1.92) Stakes(37 .22 $1.74)

In the span of about three weeks during the early stages of Aqueduct's 2006–07 winter meet, Ben Perkins Jr. struck with four winners who had been laid off since the summer and fall.

Victory Pool, the lone router among the quartet, led the invasion by winning a restricted stakes off a 97-day absence; she was followed soon afterward by the sprinters Just Wild, Wild Jam, and It's a Monster.

After watching Just Wild and Wild Jam win off some sharp half-mile workouts just a few days apart, trainer handicappers had little doubt about readiness or intent when It's a Monster returned off a best-of-65 bullet work.

Sweetsinginanita
Own: Sisters in Racing Stables

Dk. b or b. f. 3 (May) KEENOV04 $13,000
Sire: Langfuhr (Danzig) $25,000
Dam: El Gato Loco (Crafty Prospector)
Br: John J. Greeley, III (Ky)
Tr: Gyarmati Leah(10 3 2 0 .30) 2007:(57 9 .16)

Life	1	1	0	0	$25,800	66	D.Fst	1	1	0	0	$25,800	66
2007	1	1	0	0	$25,800	66	Wet(391)	0	0	0	0	$0	-
							Synth	0	0	0	0	$0	-
2006	0	M	0	0	$0	-	Turf(255)	0	0	0	0	$0	-
Aqu	1	1	0	0	$25,800	66	Dst(357)	0	0	0	0	$0	-

18Apr07-4Aqu fst 6½f :231 :462 1:1111:174 ⒻMd Sp Wt 43k 66 1 8 8⁷¾ 6⁴½ 3²½ 1nk Martin E M Jr 120 f 53.00 88- 12 Sweetsinginanita120nk Prtid120no SocilQueen1203¼ Along in final strides 8

WORKS: Apr11 Bel tr.t 6f fst 1:182 B *2/3* Mar28 Bel tr.t 5f fst 1:012 Bg *13/32* Mar21 Bel tr.t 4f fst :502 Bg *60/97* Mar12 Bel tr.t 4f fst :484 B *11/72* Mar4 Bel tr.t 5f fst 1:022 B *14/36* Feb25 Bel tr.t 4f fst :502 B *50/68*

TRAINER: 2ndStart(9 .22 $2.81) WonLastStart(24 .08 $0.67) Dirt(245 .12 $2.17) Sprint(146 .11 $2.46) Stakes(7 .00 $0.00)

Smokin Sarah
Own: Cedar Bridge Stable

Gr/ro. f. 3 (Apr)
Sire: Smokin Mel (Phone Order) $2,500
Dam: Sarah's a Winner (Cormorant)
Br: Gene Stuchbury (NY)
Tr: Gyarmati Leah(10 3 2 0 .30) 2007:(57 9 .16)

Life	1	1	0	0	$24,600	72	D.Fst	1	1	0	0	$24,600	72
2007	1	1	0	0	$24,600	72	Wet(339*)	0	0	0	0	$0	-
							Synth	0	0	0	0	$0	-
2006	0	M	0	0	$0	-	Turf(251*)	0	0	0	0	$0	-
Aqu	1	1	0	0	$24,600	72	Dst(338)	1	1	0	0	$24,600	72

21Apr07-4Aqu fst 6f :23 :463 :5831:112 3↑ⒻⓈMd Sp Wt 41k 72 7 5 2hd 1½ 1²½ 1¾ Arroyo N Jr L118 f 7.80 85- 12 SmokinSarh118¾ GoldenMnn118½ SweetSlm1183¼ When ready, kept busy 8

WORKS: Apr18 Bel tr.t 3f fst :361 B *6/28* Apr11 Bel tr.t 5f fst 1:03 B *12/26* Mar29 Bel tr.t 4f fst :484 B *10/37* Mar23 Bel tr.t 4f fst :50 B *25/41* Mar12 Bel tr.t 4f fst :494 B *38/72* Mar4 Bel tr.t 3f fst :362 B *7/26*

TRAINER: 2ndStart(9 .22 $2.81) WonLastStart(24 .08 $0.67) Dirt(245 .12 $2.17) Sprint(146 .11 $2.46) Stakes(7 .00 $0.00)

Similarly, after Leah Gyarmati sent out the 3-year-old filly Sweetsinginanita to win her debut at 53–1 off a series of ordinary-looking workouts, handicappers had to respect Gyarmati's next 3-year-old filly newcomer, Smokin Sarah, when she was unveiled 72 hours later off a thoroughly benign work tab.

Sometimes the claimed-from line will yield a pattern. Rick Dutrow Jr. claimed Sis City from Steve Asmussen out of a nose win in a $50,000 maiden sprint at Saratoga, and stretched her out a few weeks later to win a small stakes by 16 lengths; she later won three consecutive Grade 1 or 2 stakes by a combined 30 lengths. The following summer at the Spa, Dutrow reached in and plucked Last Romance from Asmussen out of a runner-up finish in a sloppy $65,000 maiden sprint. She returned from a two-month break to graduate at six furlongs, before stretching out on Aqueduct's inner track to win a first-level allowance and an overnight stakes.

```
Tora                                     Dk. b or b. f. 3 (Jan)                                  Life 5 2 0 0 $57,470 84 | D.Fst     2 0 0 0  $7,200 67
Own: Goldfarb Sanford J                  Sire: El Corredor (Mr. Greeley) $30,000                 2007 2 1 0 0 $31,670 81 | Wet(323)  3 2 0 0 $50,270 84
                                         Dam: Everyone's Honour (Mt. Livermore)                                          | Synth     0 0 0 0      $0  -
                                         Br: Heiligbrodt Racing Stable (Ky)                      2006 3 1 0 0 $25,800 84 | Turf(285) 0 0 0 0      $0  -
                                         Tr: Dutrow R E Jr(1 1 0 0 1.00) 2007:(186 52 .28)       Cd   3 2 0 0 $51,070 84 | Dst(338)  1 1 0 0 $31,270 81

4May07-6CD slys 6f :212 :444 :573 1:11 ⒻAlw 50000n1x 81 7 2 3½ 32 3½ 1hd Prado E S L118 7.90 82-17 Tora118hd Gem Sleuth1181¾ Featherbed1181¼ 3-4w,gamely driving 12
13Apr07-5GP gd 6½f :221 :451 1:11 1:174 ⒻOC 62k/n1x-N 64 4 9 63¼ 85¼ 78¼ 68¾ Cruz M R L117 *1.50 74-20 DynamiteDiv1171¾ MddysHert119nk Adjusting1175¼ Off slowly, rough trip 10
16Aug06-8Sar fst 6½f :214 :45 1:114 1:19 ⒻAdrndkBC-G2 62 5 3 31 32½ 2½ 53¾ Prado E S L118 9.20 75-16 Octave1181¼ TrueAddiction118½ MagiclRide1181¾ Bobbled start, bumped 9
13Jly06-1CD slys 5½f :221 :461 :582 1:043 ⒻMd c-(80-75) 84 3 1 1½ 1½ 13¼ 112½ Bridgmohan S X L120f *.80 95-15 Tora12012½ Rapidian1201¼ Psychodrama1201¼ Drft in bmp start,drvg 8
  Claimed from Heiligbrodt Racing Stable for $80,000, Blasi Scott Trainer 2006(as of 7/13): (6 2 3 0 0.33) Previously trained by Asmussen Steven M 2006(as of 6/16): (987 210 170 140 0.21)
16Jun06-8CD fst 4½f :222 :45 :51 ⒻMd Sp Wt 42k 67 5 5 32 55 55¼ Bridgmohan S X L119f 15.10 92-09 Chagall1191¼ Seaside Affair1142 Gold Minx119¾ Between foes,empty 10
WORKS: Apr9 PmM 4f fst :48 H 1/3 Apr3 PmM 5f fst 1:011 H 6/8 ●Mar28 PmM 5f fst :593 H 1/16 Mar16 PmM 5f fst 1:004 H 3/19 Mar10 PmM 5f fst 1:012 H 6/23 Mar4 PmM 4f fst :481 H 8/40
TRAINER: 1-7Days(34 .18 $0.98) WonLastStart(188 .29 $2.03) Dirt(714 .25 $1.91) Sprint(480 .27 $2.07) Stakes(164 .16 $1.67)
```

While Asmussen was serving a suspension in the summer of 2006, Dutrow took Tora from his assistant, Scott Blasi, for the rather pricey sum of $80,000. She contested the pace to midstretch of the Grade 2 Adirondack Stakes shortly thereafter, but then went to the shelf. Trainer-pattern players had to wait until Kentucky Oaks Day the following spring to cash in at nearly 8–1.

Gary Contessa was New York's leading trainer in 2006, when he fell just short of Hall of Famer Frank "Pancho" Martin's record 156 winners in 1974. As good a year as 2006 was for Contessa, he was actually ahead of that pace through the first few months of 2007, one of the main reasons being his ability to move up new acquisitions swiftly and surely:

```
Waytotheleft                             B. m. 5 (Feb)                                           Life 26 6 3 4 $246,521 85 | D.Fst     19 4 1 4 $162,611 84
Own: Winning Move Stable                 Sire: Abaginone (Devil's Bag) $289                                                | Wet(316)   5 1 2 0  $49,510 85
                                         Dam: Waywayanda (Belong to Me)                          2007  5 3 0 1 $110,604 85 | Synth      0 0 0 0       $0  -
                                         Br: Questroyal Stables Inc. (NY)                        2006 10 0 2 1  $31,730 79 | Turf(272)  2 1 0 0  $34,400 76
                                         Tr: Contessa Gary C

18May07-4Pim fst 6f :233 :461 :58 1:104 3↑ⒻⓇWhimsical84k – 2 3 32 33 36½ 35½ Dominguez R A L122b *1.00 87-11 La Chica Rica118½ Homesteader1185 Waytotheleft1224½ 3wd trip, empty 4
13Apr07-8Aqu gd 7f :223 :461 1:112 1:251 4↑ⒻOC 75k/n3x-N 85 2 4 42 3nk 1½ 11½ Dominguez R A L123b 2.45 75-24 Waytotheleft1231½ Veneti1184 Towering Escape1183½ 3 wide move, clear 6
4Mar07-8Aqu fst 6f ⊡ :223 :451 :574 1:104 3↑ⒻⓈBroadwayH72k 84 7 2 73¾ 46 21 13¼ Dominguez R A L115b 22.30 90-14 Waytotheleft1153¼ GretLdyK116¾ SlewMotion115hd Large opening on rail10
11Feb07-5Aqu fst 6f ⊡ :223 :454 :582 1:11 4↑ⒻOC 75k/n1x-N 76 1 6 52½ 53¾ 21½ 14¾ Hill C L120b 7.00 89-13 Wytotheleft1204¾ OutofthLoop120¾ MissBvrly1203½ Steadied backstretch 7
28Jan07-5Aqu fst 5½f ⊡ :222 :451 :572 1:04 4↑ⒻⓈOC c-30k/n2x 54 5 6 73¾ 77 59 49½ Hill C L118b 3.90 89-08 R B's Token1184½ Lady Jove1184¼ Shea d'Lady123¾ Belatedly outside 7
  Claimed from Waring Henry T. for $30,000, Carroll Del W II Trainer 2006: (171 13 24 27 0.08)
31Dec06-3Aqu fst 6f ⊡ :222 :452 :572 1:10 3↑ⒻOC 75k/n1x-N 72 5 4 83¾ 64¼ 64¾ 55¼ Hill C L121b 28.50 83-13 ABitofPressure122no SummrPlc1204½ HrRoylNibs1211 Angled out, no rally 8
29Nov06-8Aqu fst 6f ⊡ :224 :454 :58 1:104 3↑ⒻOC 75k/n1x-N 72 3 5 3½ 2½ 2hd 21¼ Coa E M L120b 9.30 83-13 GretLdyK1201¼ Wytotheleft1203¾ MedowMirge1203¼ Chased, second best 7
10Nov06-5Aqu fst 6f :222 :463 :591 1:122 3↑ⒻClm 45000(45-35) 59 6 7 53¾ 63 44¾ 46¼ Castellano J J L119b 7.90 69-26 Nevaeh119½ ClassicExmple1192 TxConsidertions1194 Came wide, no rally 8
12Oct06-8Bel fst 6f :224 :46 :574 1:101 3↑ⒻⓈOC 30k/n2x 73 5 5 2½ 2hd 21 31¼ Castellano J J L120b 12.70 86-15 GirlinUniform1181 Neveh120nk Wytotheleft1201½ Pressed pace, weakened 9
17Sep06-10Bel fst 6f ⊗ :222 :453 :572 1:103 3↑ⒻAlw 54000n1x 64 3 4 61½ 73½ 77 78 Luzzi M J L119b 27.75 77-14 EndlssVirtu1171 BrushdByou1172¾ TigrOnthLoos1171 Inside, no response 9
27Aug06-10Sar gd 5½f ⊗ :221 :461 :591 1:061 3↑ⒻAlw 60000n1x 51 6 8 76¼ 83¼ 83¾ 79½ Morales P L119b 15.30 78-22 GoldnKnolls116½ StndbythPhon1164¾ MostButiful116¾ Wide, no response 8
12Mar06-8Aqu gd 6f ⊡ :221 :46 :582 1:114 3↑ⒻⓈBroadwayH70k 49 7 6 67¾ 68¼ 712 714¾ Luzzi M J L115b 21.40 65-23 Magnolia Jackson1201¼ Sweet Sweet1152 Fighting Speedy1132½ Tired7
WORKS: May12 Aqu 4f fst :473 H 2/8 May3 Aqu 5f fst 1:013 H 7/11 ●Apr26 Aqu 4f fst :472 H 1/7 Apr7 Aqu 5f fst 1:022 B 30/36 Mar27 Aqu⊡ 5f fst 1:014 B 5/9
```

```
Papi Chullo                              Gr/ro. h. 5 (Feb)                                       Life 18 4 4 0 $295,325 108 | D.Fst      17 4 4 0 $295,325 108
Own: Winning Move Stable Team Stallion Rac  Sire: Cowmmons (Jolie's Halo) $3,000                                            | Wet(362)    1 0 0 0       $0  80
                                         Dam: Leggy Super Model (Vigors)                         2007 3 1 0 0  $30,000 105  | Synth       0 0 0 0       $0   -
                                         Br: Philip Matthews & Karen Matthews (Fla)              2006 8 2 2 0 $178,765 108  | Turf(272*)  0 0 0 0       $0   -
                                         Tr: Contessa Gary C

4May07-3Bel fst 1 1/16 :233 :462 1:10 1:394 4↑OC 75k/n3x-N 105 2 2½ 31 31½ 16 17¼ Garcia Alan L118b 1.85 101-10 Papi Chullo1187¼ Tall Story1232 Tasteyville1187½ Clear trip on rail 4
  Previously trained by Green Jennie C 2007(as of 4/7): (16 2 2 2 0.13)
7Apr07-10OP fst 1⅛ :473 1:12 1:364 1:49 4↑OaklawnH-G2 60 4 54¼ 55½ 55¼ 713 729½ Coa E M L116b 18.90 66-15 LawyerRon1204 BrotherBobby116nk Bobomn1161½ Gave way, well beaten 7
  Previously trained by Teater Louise M 2006: ( - )
27Jan07-10GP fst 1⅛ :464 1:104 1:362 1:494 4↑ⓇSunMilClsc1000k 92 7 116 117 116½ 64½ 66¼ Smith M E L122 8.50 82-15 McCnnsMojve122¾ SummrBook122½ SilvrWgon122nk Couldn't sustain bid12
  Previously trained by Menghini Peter J 2006(as of 12/9): (7 1 1 0 0.14)
9Dec06-8Aqu fst 1 3/16 ⊡ :48 1:12 1:37 1:55 3↑QeensCoH-G3 100 1 32½ 42 33½ 26 26¼ Smith M E L116 5.60 96-13 MagnaGrdute1186¼ PpiChullo1169½ SmrtGrowth1152 Inside, second best 6
26Nov06-3Aqu fst 1⅛ :48 1:114 1:362 1:491 3↑OC 35k/n2x-N 95 5 46½ 56½ 32 1hd 11½ Coa E M L119 *.90 89-16 Papi Chullo1191½ Indian Hawke1173¾ DeputyIndy122nk 3 wide move, clear 6
  Previously trained by Vargas J Buenaventura 2006(as of 11/4): (62 6 5 7 0.10)
4Nov06-2CD fst 1 :231 :453 1:10 1:343 3↑AckAckH-G3 95 9 82¾ 74 62¾ 55 43¼ Velasquez C L116b 15.20 93-07 ItsNoJoke119nk IrenesMon1111½ LevlPlyingfild1131¾ Between,slight gain 12
30Sep06-8Haw wf 1¼ :473 1:113 1:373 2:034 3↑HawGldCH-G2 80 3 46½ 47½ 45½ 68 616 Albarado R J L117b 2.80 71-27 It's No Joke1181 A. P. Arrow1126 Kid Grindstone1154½ Off rail, gave way 7
2Sep06-9Sar fst 1⅛ :471 1:114 1:371 1:503 3↑Woodward-G1 99 2 41 41¾ 33 32½ 44¾ Coa E M L126b 40.25 79-22 Premium Tap126½ Second of June126¾ SunKing1263½ Saved ground, tired 10
20Aug06-7EmD fst 1 :224 :452 1:092 1:342 3↑LgaMileH-G3 101 10 32 21½ 2½ 2½ 2nk Albarado R J LB117b *2.00 93-21 Flmthrowntxn120nk PpChllo1175 SthrnAfrc1191¾ Stalked3w,bumped late 11
22Jly06-8Dmr fst 1 1/16 :224 :46 1:094 1:42 3↑SnDiegoH-G2 96 4 43 42 41½ 21½ 32¼ Arroyo N Jr LB112b 5.40 97-07 Giacomo117hd Prechintthebr1172½ ⒹPpiChullo1121¼ 4wd 1/4,came in 3/16 7
  Disqualified and placed 7th
2Jly06-7Hol fst 7½f :22 :442 1:084 1:272 3↑OC 62k/n2x-N 108 6 6 85¼ 86¼ 61½ 15 Gomez G K LB120b 10.80 98-09 Papi Chullo1205 County120½ Jack's Wild120¾ 4wd into lane,clear 11
  Previously trained by Gonzalez Salvador G 2005(as of 8/7): (13 5 3 0 0.38)
7Aug05-12Mth fst 1⅛ :473 1:113 1:363 1:494 HskllnvH-G1 88 3 52½ 53¾ 55 68¼ 612¼ Lopez D G L116 22.10 77-16 RomanRuler1191½ SunKing1192 PrkAvenueBll1181 No response final turn 7
WORKS: Apr29 Aqu 6f fst 1:162 B 2/2 Apr22 Aqu 5f fst 1:023 B 10/11 Apr4 OP 4f fst :491 B 5/12 Mar28 PBD 5f gd 1:021 B 1/1 Mar23 PBD 5f gd 1:001 B 3/4 ●Mar18 PBD 4f gd :48 B 1/7
```

Waytotheleft had been blanked from 10 starts in 2006, yet Contessa thought enough of the mare to claim her for $30,000. She ripped off three straight wins, including an upset of the Broadway Handicap at 22–1.

Papi Chullo, who was ambitiously spotted through much of his career, changed hands after being basically eased in the Grade 2 Oaklawn Handicap on April 7, 2007. In his first start for Contessa four weeks later, he won his third-level allowance condition at Belmont Park, running 1¹⁄₁₆ miles in 1:39.89, just .38 seconds off the track record.

Less than two weeks later, another Contessa reclamation project appeared:

Rumspringa had a forgettable winter in Florida, one that culminated with a pair of last-place finishes. The 5-year-old gelding was now returning to Belmont, where he had won with a career-best Beyer of 103 the previous year, but based on his recent form it required a real leap of faith to climb aboard at 6–1. In retrospect, the most important consideration was the transfer from a no-win trainer—whose 63 starters for the year had produced zero wins and only five in-the-money finishes—to the leading trainer in New York. Despite stumbling badly at the start, he came through inside the leaders turning for home and won going away.

It's all well and good to have the lowdown on a trainer's modus operandi; just make sure to keep in mind that sometimes things change. There is no better example than Nick Zito, whose 2-year-old first-time starters have evolved from throw-outs to potential stick-outs:

One might've guessed that Marylou Whitney's Birdstone was well-meant on August 2, 2003, because that also happened to be the day of the prestigious Whitney Handicap, named after the socialite's

6 Birdstone		B. c. 3 (May)	Life	3	2	0	0	$339,000	99	D.Fst	2	1	0	0	$312,000	94
Own: Marylou Whitney Stables		Sire: Grindstone (Unbridled) $5,000	2003	3	2	0	0	$339,000	99	Wet(333)	1	1	0	0	$27,000	99
Black Eton Blue, Brown Belt, Brown Cap		Dam: Dear Birdie (Storm Bird)								Turf(195)	0	0	0	0	$0	–
		Br: Marylou Whitney Stables (Ky)	**L 118**	2002	0	M	0	0	$0	–							
BAILEY J D (70 12 13 13 .17) 2003: (776 206 .27)		Tr: Zito Nicholas P(42 5 6 6 .12) 2003:(507 77 .15)	GP	0	0	0	0	$0	–	Dst(337)	1	1	0	0	$300,000	94

4Oct03–7Bel fst 1⅛ :234 :481 1:1331:44	Champgn–G1	94 3 4³ 3¹ 2½ 1ʰᵈ 12½ Bailey J D	L122	2.25	80– 26 Birdstone122² ChpelRoyl1226½ DshbordDrummer122² 3 wide, going away 7
30Aug03–8Sar fst 7f :222 :452 1:1021:232	Hopeful–G1	78 6 1 6¹½ 5¹½ 3¹ 46½ Prado E S	L122	2.30	83– 11 SilverWgon122⁴ ChpelRoyl122¹½ NotoriousRogu122¹ Hit gate start, 5 wide 7
2Aug03–4Sar my 6f :214 :454 :58 1:101	Md Sp Wt 45k	99 4 5 32½ 1³ 18 112½ Prado E S	L119	3.85	91– 12 Birdstone11912½ Bold Love1192½ Hornshope1197½ When ready, drew off 9
WORKS: Feb10 PmM 4f fst :50 B 24/47 Feb3 PmM 6f fst 1:152 B 6/7 Jan24 PmM 6f fst 1:482 B 15/29 Jan17 PmM 5f fst 1:022 B 15/38 ● Jan10 PmM 4f fst :482 B 1/31 Dec30 PmM 3f fst :372 B 1/3
TRAINER: 61–180Days(66 .09 $0.54) Dirt(518 .15 $1.98) Routes(322 .14 $1.55) Alw(187 .12 $1.22)

5 Boot Strap		B. f. 2 (Feb)	Life	0	M	0	0	$0	–	D.Fst	0	0	0	0	$0	–
Own: Marylou Whitney Stable		Sire: Storm Boot (Storm Cat) $15,000	2003	0	M	0	0	$0	–	Wet(330)	0	0	0	0	$0	–
Green Eton Blue Brown Hoop Blue Sleeves		Dam: Broad Legacy(Broad Brush)								Turf(300)	0	0	0	0	$0	–
		Br: Marylou Whitney Stables (Ky)	**118**	2002	0	M	0	0	$0	–							
CASTELLANO J J (18 2 3 2 .11) 2003:(707 101 .14)		Tr: Zito Nicholas P(14 2 2 2 .14) 2003:(299 39 .13)	Sar	0	0	0	0	$0	–	Dst(355)	0	0	0	0	$0	–

| WORKS: Jly26 Sar 5f fst 1:012 Bg26/74 Jly7 Sar tr.t 4f fst :501 B 13/35 Jun27 Sar tr.t 4f fst :51 B 12/22 Jun13 Sar tr.t 4f fst :513 Bg 12/31 Jun5 Sar tr.t 3f fst :372 B 8/14 |
| TRAINER: 1stStart(86 .03 $1.23) 2YO(146 .13 $1.34) Dirt(754 .16 $1.67) Sprint(334 .12 $1.70) MdnSpWt(307 .13 $1.63) |

late husband, Cornelius Vanderbilt Whitney. A lot of people guessed right, because the colt was fairly well-backed at just under 4–1.

Birdstone's 12½-length victory notwithstanding, Zito's 85 *other* first-time starters in 2004–05 had produced only two other winners. The vast majority of them performed like Boot Strap, a Marylou Whitney homebred *not* unveiled on Whitney Day, who finished eighth by 14¾ lengths while rightly dismissed at 31–1 for her bow later at the same Saratoga meet.

This was part and parcel of Zito's longstanding profile: Let the youngsters get their sea legs in a sprint or two, then stretch them out in the fall and start to get serious. The program worked: Zito won three straight renewals of the Grade 1 Champagne Stakes with The Groom Is Red (1998), Greenwood Lake (1999), and A P Valentine (2000); and coming off a predictable bounce in the Hopeful, Birdstone was a very logical bounce-rebound candidate when he became Zito's fourth Champagne winner in 2003.

Despite his long and well-known patterns with juveniles, Zito at Saratoga in 2006 was a leopard who had changed his spots: When Irish Ace won his debut by open lengths August 5, and C P West did the same thing the following week, Zito's long-term pattern necessarily took a backseat to the short-term pattern that

Irish Ace
Own: Farmer Tracy

B. c. 2 (Mar)
Sire: Grand Slam (Gone West) $50,000
Dam: Heartful Lady (Irish River*Fr)
Br: Tracy Farmer (Ky)
Tr: Zito Nicholas P(0 0 0 0 .00) 2006:(422 71 .17)

Life	2	1	0	0	$35,700	88	D.Fst	2	1	0	0	$35,700 88
2006	2	1	0	0	$35,700	88	Wet(353)	0	0	0	0	$0 -
2005	0	M	0	0	$0	-	Synth	0	0	0	0	$0 -
							Turf(336)	0	0	0	0	$0 -
Sar	2	1	0	0	$35,700	88	Dst(352)	0	0	0	0	$0 -

4Sep06-4Sar fst 7f :221 :444 1:10 1:23 Hopeful-G1 57 2 2 2½ 2hd 54¼ 517¾ Coa E M L120 8.40 71-15 CircularQuay1204¼ *SctDddy*1201 UnbridledExpress1203½ Vied inside, tired 5
5Aug06-2Sar fst 6½f :224 :462 1:104 1:172 Md Sp Wt 47k 88 3 4 1½ 1½ 14½ 14 Coa E M L119 6.80 87-11 Irish Ace1194 Flashstorm119nk Meritocracy1192 Set pace, drew away 8
WORKS: ●Aug27 Sar tr.t 4f fst :48 B *1/23* Aug17 Sar tr.t 4f fst :482 B *2/23* Jly31 Sar 4f fst :492 Hg *67/112* ●Jly21 Sar tr.t 4f fst :49 B *1/9* Jly7 Sar tr.t 4f fst :494 B *5/41* Jun21 Sar tr.t 3f fst :391 B *23/30*
TRAINER: +180Days(24 .21 $0.98) Dirt(542 .17 $1.80) Sprint(247 .17 $1.73) Stakes(132 .07 $0.39)

C P West
Own: LaPenta Robert V

Dk. b or b. c. 2 (Feb) KEESEP05 $425,000
Sire: Came Home (Gone West) $40,000
Dam: Queen's Legend (Dynaformer)
Br: Caldara Farm (Ky)
Tr: Zito Nicholas P(0 0 0 0 .00) 2006:(422 71 .17)

Life	1	1	0	0	$28,200	86	D.Fst	1	1	0	0	$28,200 86
2006	1	1	0	0	$28,200	86	Wet(338*)	0	0	0	0	$0 -
2005	0	M	0	0	$0	-	Synth	0	0	0	0	$0 -
							Turf(300*)	0	0	0	0	$0 -
Sar	1	1	0	0	$28,200	86	Dst(293)	1	1	0	0	$28,200 86

12Aug06-2Sar fst 6f :223 :462 :583 1:112 Md Sp Wt 47k 86 7 5 31 2hd 1½ 12¾ Bejarano R L119 3.10 83-18 C P West1192¾ Storm Breeze119nk Shipmate119nk Lugged in stretch 10
WORKS: Aug28 Sar tr.t 4f fst :494 B *12/20* Aug7 Sar tr.t 4f fst :474 H *4/30* Jly31 Sar 4f fst :492 Bg *69/112* Jly24 Sar 4f fst :48 B *4/44* Jly16 Sar tr.t 3f wf :384 B *2/3* Jly11 Sar 3f fst :36 B *1/3*
TRAINER: Route/Sprint(58 .21 $1.73) Dirt(542 .17 $1.80) Sprint(247 .17 $1.73) Stakes(132 .07 $0.39)

was beginning to percolate. Scarcely 24 hours after C P West had reported home, Ruby Crown edged clear late and kicked off the early pick four. Three days after Ruby Crown, those who backed Boogie Boggs were ready to rip up their tickets as he lagged well behind the leaders turning for home, but when the last sixteenth of a mile unfolded in a laborious seven seconds, the $650,000 yearling buy was able to get up in the final strides.

By this point at the meet, Zito-trained first-time starters had achieved must-use status, if not for win bets, at least for multirace pick-anythings. Debbie Got Even and Successful Ways gave the faithful some heart palpitations, but posted nose victories toward the end of August.

Debbie Got Even
Own: Hilbert Tomisue and Menard, John R

Ch. f. 2 (Apr)
Sire: Stephen Got Even (A.P. Indy) $25,000
Dam: Lady Esther (Seeking the Gold)
Br: Hilbert Thoroughbreds, Inc. (Ky)
Tr: Zito Nicholas P(0 0 0 0 .00) 2006:(422 71 .17)

Life	1	1	0	0	$28,200	66	D.Fst	1	1	0	0	$28,200 66
2006	1	1	0	0	$28,200	66	Wet(385)	0	0	0	0	$0 -
2005	0	M	0	0	$0	-	Synth	0	0	0	0	$0 -
							Turf(241)	0	0	0	0	$0 -
Sar	1	1	0	0	$28,200	66	Dst(368)	0	0	0	0	$0 -

20Aug06-7Sar fst 7f :223 :451 1:104 1:242 ⒻMd Sp Wt 47k 66 1 9 94½ 76¼ 41 1no Leparoux J R5 L113 5.90 82-09 *DebbieGotEven*113no TleoftheQueen118½ *Allude*1185¼ Stumbled badly start 9
WORKS: ●Sep1 Sar 4f fst :473 H *1/62* Aug7 Sar 4f gd :482 Bg *2/24* Jly31 Sar 4f fst :482 Hg *32/112* Jly25 Bel 5f fst 1:012 H *6/29* Jly16 Bel tr.t 5f fst 1:042 B *8/10* Jly9 Bel tr.t 4f fst :52 B *26/26*
TRAINER: 61-180Days(67 .15 $1.32) Dirt(542 .17 $1.80) Sprint(247 .17 $1.73) Stakes(132 .07 $0.39)

Successful Ways
Own: Kinsman Stable

Dk. b or b. c. 2 (Feb) OBSFEB06 $240,000
Sire: Successful Appeal (Valid Appeal) $25,000
Dam: Wicked Ways (Devil's Bag)
Br: Sort Holdings (Fla)
Tr: Zito Nicholas P(0 0 0 0 .00) 2006:(422 71 .17)

Life	1	1	0	0	$28,200	78	D.Fst	0	0	0	0	$0 -
2006	1	1	0	0	$28,200	78	Wet(427)	1	1	0	0	$28,200 78
2005	0	M	0	0	$0	-	Synth	0	0	0	0	$0 -
							Turf(321)	0	0	0	0	$0 -
Sar	1	1	0	0	$28,200	78	Dst(402)	0	0	0	0	$0 -

30Aug06-2Sar my 5½f :22 :461 :584 1:052 Md Sp Wt 47k 78 7 3 13 14½ 11 1no Jara F L119 b 5.40e 92-11 *SuccessfulWays*119no HometownBoy1194½ Reaffirm1194¾ Dug in along rail 8
WORKS: Aug21 Sar 4f fst :482 Hg *15/56* Jly31 Sar tr.t 4f fst :501 B *12/18* Jly16 Sar tr.t 4f wf :491 B *3/11* Jly8 Sar tr.t 3f fst :383 B *11/34* Jun30 Sar tr.t 3f fst :383 B *15/47* Jun22 Sar tr.t 3f fst :394 B *18/22*
TRAINER: +180Days(24 .21 $0.98) WonLastStart(91 .14 $0.96) Dirt(542 .17 $1.80) Sprint(247 .17 $1.73) Stakes(132 .07 $0.39)

Considering he was a $240,000 purchase out of the high-class OBSFEB sale, and that he carried an extremely high Tomlinson rating of 427, the victory by Successful Ways on a muddy track qualified him as a finalist for overlay of the meet, at least among the 2-year-old maiden races.

Workouts

It goes without saying that workouts can provide important clues about horses' form and their trainers' intentions. Thoroughbreds spend all but an hour or so of each day in their stalls, so what they accomplish during morning training hours is vital to their success in actual competition. In order to withstand the rigors and stress of racing—something they are less and less able to do, it seems—horses must have the proper conditioning foundation. Think of it this way: If you were going to compete in a 5K race, you wouldn't just pick yourself up off the couch and toe up at the starting line on race day; that would invite pulled muscles, ligament strains, and all manner of injuries. You'd give yourself enough time to gradually get into shape, stretching and toning your muscles, building your stamina through a series of long jogs, and sharpening your speed with wind sprints.

This is precisely what Thoroughbreds must do; if they are asked for too much exertion too soon without the proper preparation, they are much more susceptible to injury.

Horses can telegraph how they're doing via their morning workouts. One of the most notable examples concerned Holy Bull's dismal performance in the 1994 Kentucky Derby. His 12th-place finish at Churchill Downs might have been attributable to any number of factors, including a pedigree that was suspect at 1¼ miles, and a sloppy track that such greats as Easy Goer had disliked as well.

A week after Holy Bull's Derby fiasco, trainer Jimmy Croll announced that his colt would skip the Preakness and opt instead for the prestigious Metropolitan Mile against older horses. In the *Form*'s May 15 edition, Croll explained, "There is nothing seriously wrong with Holy Bull . . . but his blood tests indicated he was just a hair off. It's mostly the time element . . . this way he'll get a few more days of rest."

Holy Bull
Own: Croll Warren A Jr

NO RIDER (–)

Gr. c. 3 (Jan)
Sire: Great Above (Minnesota Mac)
Dam: Sharon Brown (Al Hattab)
Br: Pelican Stable (Fla)
Tr: Croll Warren A Jr (1 1 0 0 1.00)

116

Lifetime Record:	10	8	0	0	$1,290,760						
1994	6	4	0	0	$955,000	Turf	0	0	0	0	
1993	4	4	0	0	$335,760	Wet	2	1	0	0	$69,360
Bel	3	3	0	0	$386,160	Dist	0	0	0	0	

30May94-8Bel	fst	1	$:22^4$	:45	$1:09^2$	$1:33^4$	3↑ Metropltn H-G1	122	6	1	1^1	1½	$1^{2½}$	$1^{5¼}$	Smith M E	112	*1.00	94-09	Holy Bull$112^{5¼}$ Cherokee Run118^{no} Devil His Due122^2	Driving	10
7May94-8CD	sly	1¼	$:47^1$	$1:11^4$	$1:37^3$	$2:03^3$	Ky Derby-G1	85	4	6	$5^{3½}$	9^9	12^{12}	$12^{18¼}$	Smith M E	126	*2.20	76-06	Go For Gin126^2 Strodes Creek$126^{2½}$ Blumin Affair126¾		14
Off slow, in tight start, tired badly																					
16Apr94-9Kee	fst	1⅛	$:47^4$	$1:12^3$	$1:37^4$	1:50	Blue Grass-G2	113	1	1	1^3	1^2	$1^{1½}$	$1^{3½}$	Smith M E	121	*.60	84-26	Holy Bull$121^{3½}$ Valiant Nature121^5 Mahogany Hall$121^{2½}$	Sharp, ridden out	7
12Mar94-10GP	fst	1⅛	:46	1:10	$1:34^4$	$1:47^2$	Fla Derby-G1	115	6	1	$1^{2½}$	$1^{2½}$	1^5	$1^{5¾}$	Smith M E	122	2.70	100-06	Holy Bull$122^{5¾}$ Ride The Rails122^{no} Halo's Image122^1	Ridden out	14
19Feb94-9GP	gd	1 1/16	$:22^4$	$:45^3$	$1:10^2$	$1:44^3$	Ftn of YouthG2	57	4	1	1½	2^1	6^8	$6^{24¼}$	Smith M E	119	*1.30	63-19	Dehere119¾ Go For Gin$119^{1½}$ Ride The Rails$117^{3¾}$	Stopped badly	6
30Jan94-9GP	fst	7f	$:21^3$	:44	$1:08^1$	$1:21^1$	Hutcheson-G2	108	1	4	$1^{1½}$	$1^{1½}$	2½	1¾	Smith M E	122	*.50	97-11	Holy Bull122¾ Patton113^3 You And I119^3		5
Broke inward start, raced well off rail, ridden out																					
23Oct93-11Crc	fst	1 1/16	:23	$:46^2$	$1:11^3$	$1:46^1$	[R]FS In Rlty400k	93	9	1	$1^{1½}$	1^2	1^4	$1^{7½}$	Smith M E	120	*.50	88-12	Holy Bull$120^{7½}$ Rustic Light120^1 Forward To Lead$120^{1½}$	Ridden out	12
18Sep93-6Bel	sly	7f	$:22^2$	$:45^3$	$1:10^1$	$1:23^1$	Futurity-G1	103	2	1	1^1	1^1	$1^{2½}$	1½	Smith M E	122	3.10	87-14	Holy Bull122½ Dehere122^5 Prenup122^8	All out	6
2Sep93-7Bel	fst	6½f	:22	$:44^1$	$1:09^4$	1:17	Alw 28000N2x	91	3	1	1½	1^{hd}	$1^{2½}$	1^7	Smith M E	119	*.90	88-15	Holy Bull119^7 Goodbye Doeny117^3 End Sweep119½	Ridden out	6
14Aug93-7Mth	fst	5½f	$:21^3$	$:44^4$	$:57^1$	$1:03^4$	Md Sp Wt	101	1	3	1^1	$1^{1½}$	$1^{1½}$	$1^{2½}$	Rivera L Jr	118	*1.10	95-17	Holy Bull$118^{2½}$ Palance$118^{7½}$ Hold My Tongue118^9	Driving	9

WORKOUTS: May 28 Mth 4f fst $:46^4$ Bg 2/67 ●May 22 Mth 6f fst 1:11 H 1/4 ●May 16 Mth 4f gd $:46^4$ H 1/6 May 6 CD 3f fst $:36^3$ B 2/19 May 2 CD 6f fst $1:14^3$ H 3/6 Apr 24 Kee 5f fst $1:02^1$ B 3/13

Holy Bull took on some of the top older horses in training in the Met Mile, and won with complete authority, earning an extraordinary Beyer of 122 that would stand as his high-water mark. Just like that, Holy Bull was back, and he would not lose again in 1994 en route to winning the 3-year-old championship and Horse of the Year honors.

Alert handicappers who noted Holy Bull's lackluster workouts between the Blue Grass and the Kentucky Derby might have gotten a sense that all was not well with the colt, and that suspicion was confirmed in the paddock and during the post parade when his overall demeanor appeared lethargic and listless.

Indeed, it seemed as if Holy Bull had sleepwalked through his pre-Derby works, notably on May 2, when his six furlongs in 1:14⅗ was only third-best of six at the distance, and on May 6, when he blew out in 36⅗, galloping out another furlong for a crawling half-mile in 51 and change.

When Holy Bull was right, he worked fast—real fast. His drills leading up to the Met—a pair of handy bullets including a 1:11 on May 22, followed by a breeze from the gate six days later that was second-fastest of 67 at the distance, were strong indicators that Holy Bull had shaken off the effects of his pre-Derby malaise.

Horses routinely are afflicted with 24-hour bugs and minor physical ailments, and even react to the weather similarly to humans: They get the sniffles, spike fevers, suffer from aching feet, have stiff muscles, and endure the constant bumps, jostling, and bruises during the course of normal racing and training that human athletes are subjected to.

Since workouts are the principal medium through which trainers train, what happens in the morning—or doesn't happen—is frequently a harbinger of what happens in the afternoons.

When the 3-year-old filly November Snow was entered in the Grade 1 Test Stakes second time back from a layoff, her workout line made it perfectly clear that her 1 1/16-mile route against older fillies and mares had been designed strictly as a prep by legendary trainer Allen Jerkens. Tellingly, three of her last four workouts had been at the Test distance. She came from last to win going away, and paid $11.40.

At times, the absence of workouts casts doubt about the readiness of a short-priced contender.

The ninth race at Saratoga on August 27, 1993, was a $35,000 claimer on grass at 1 1/8 miles, and it appeared to be a two-horse contest between No Holme Keys and Madame Dahar, who were co-favorites at 2–1.

Since returning from a layoff of seven months, Madame Dahar had recorded Beyers of 69, 77, 81, and 77; another effort in the high 70s or low 80s would be good enough to defeat all her rivals in this field with the exception of No Holme Keys, whose figures in $35,000 grass routes the previous summer were all in the mid-to-upper 80s. It seemed she had recaptured that form in her second start back from a layoff, when she ran a figure of 86 for a convincing win. In fact, No Holme Keys showed six figures consistently superior to Madame Dahar's recent efforts, and she had won both her starts at Saratoga the previous year.

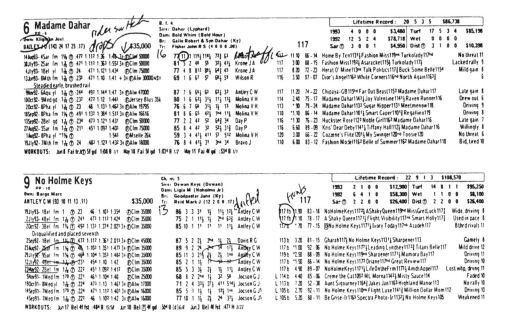

"Throw No Holme Keys out," was the advice to the audience from my friend Michael Kipness, a handicapper who makes selections under the nom de course of the Wizard, when we made our weekly appearance on Harvey Pack's paddock show that morning.

Whenever the Wizard summarily dismisses the chances of an obvious contender, it means he has seen something negative about the horse's record in his crystal ball that is not so obvious to most other handicappers. His reasoning was as follows: "Every time No Holme Keys has won, she's shown a workout. The absence of a workout raises serious concerns about her readiness for today's race."

Indeed, a subsequent check of the mare's past performances from four wins in 1992 revealed the following:

When No Holme Keys was brought back for a victory in her seasonal debut of May 23, 1992, her workout lines looked like this:

No Holme Keys
ANTLEY C W (56 10 2 7 $187,960)
Own.—Barge Marc

Ch. f. 4, by Dewan Keys—Ligia M, by Noholme Jr
$35,000 Br.—Mrs. Jane Goodpaster (Ky)
Tr.—Reid Mark J (8 2 0 2 $51,960)

117

Lifetime 14 4 0 3 $37,370

1991	14	4	0	3	$37,370
1990	0	M	0	0	
Turf	6	3	0	1	$24,050
Wet	1	1	0	0	$8,100

5Nov91- 1Med	fm	170	(T):461 1:104 1:40	(F)Clm 25000	68	8	2	2hd	1½	32	58	Jocson G J	Lb	114	4.40	85-06	Creme theCat1092MtMorna1142¾MistySauce114	Faded 10
19Oct91- 8Med	yl	1 1/16	(T):473 1:13 1:461	3↑(F)Alw 17000	71	2	4	33½	37½	412	514½	Jocson G J	Lb	113	7.20	52-38	AuntSigourney1166¾JksJn1165HighlndMnor113	No rally 10
14Sep91- 7Med	fm	170	(T):471 1:112 1:401	3↑(F)Alw 16000	85	5	1	1½	1½	12½	1nk	Jocson G J5	Lb	105	2.70	92-11	NoHolmKys110nkFlghtLx1141¾MllonDllrMm112	Driving 10
4Sep91- 7Med	fm	1 1/16	(T):46 1:102 1:42	3↑(F)Alw 16000	77	10	1	1½	2½	24	37½	Jocson G J5	Lb	105	5.20	80-11	BGrs-Ir1165SpctrPhoto-Ir1132¾NHlmKys105	Weakened 11
23Aug91- 6Atl	gd	*1	(T):491 1:151 1:423	(F)Clm 22500	79	7	2	2hd	11	15	14½	Jocson G J5	Lb	107	4.00	71-29	No Holme Keys1074½BlueJewel1114½CityCat112	Driving 12
20Jly91- 5Pha	fm	1 1/16	(T):483 1:142 1:473	(F)Clm 17000	64	2	5	42½	1hd	12½	1½	Molina V H	Lb	114	4.40	69-27	NoHolmKys114½MissMcCnn1102½TwoThrtyT112	Driving 10
29Jun91- 8Pha	fst	1	:47 1:122 1:40	(F)Alw 14000	60	6	4	43	52½	43½	45½	Jocson G J5	Lb	117	4.30	75-19	FrshSpry1161½ZnzritStorm116hdJckiP.116	Flattened out 8
12Jun91- 9Pha	fst	1 1/16	:464 1:113 1:46	(F)Clm 28000	58	2	2	3nk	1hd	22	31½	Castillo R E	Lb	112	3.80	77-10	Ddjol1161½MchllsFlly115noNHlmKys112	Came in, bmpd. 5
18May91-10Pha	fst	170	:48 1:132 1:46	(F)Alw 14000	63	4	4	41½	43	45	45½	Colton R E	L	122	8.60	60-35	Ginny Wolf1191½ Fresh Spray116no Damie'sSis116	Wide 8
6May91- 4Pha	sly	170	:472 1:131 1:45	(F)Md Sp Wt	57	8	5	54¾	32½	22½	11¾	Colton R E	L	122	3.40	71-21	NHlmKys1221¾OnPttQn122noFrFlsh122	Steadied,driving 9

Speed Index: Last Race: -9.0 3-Race Avg.: -5.3 6-Race Avg.: -4.8 Overall Avg.: -6.1

LATEST WORKOUTS May 19 Pha 5f sly 1:022 B May 13 Pha 4f fst :49 B May 5 Pha 5f fst :592 B Apr 28 Pha 4f fst :472 B

When she won her fourth straight race on August 23, 1992, her workout lines looked like this:

No Holme Keys
ANTLEY C W (118 26 18 15 .22)
Own.—Barge Marc

Ch. f. 4, by Dewan Keys—Ligia M, by Noholme Jr
$35,000 Br.—Goodpaster Jane (Ky)
Tr.—Reid Mark J (12 6 2 1 .50)

117

Lifetime 17 7 0 3 $76,970

1992	3	3	0	0	$39,600
1991	14	4	0	3	$37,370
Turf	9	6	0	1	$63,650
Wet	1	1	0	0	$8,100

29Jly92- 9Sar	fm	1 1/8	(T):464 1:104 1:482	3↑(F)Clm 35000	84	11	3	21½	2½	2½	1no	Antley C W	b	119	*2.50	88-09	NoHolmeKeys119noSharpener1171½MmorBy117	Driving 11
12Jly92- 4Bel	fm	1 1/16	(T):454 1:10 1:42	(F)Clm 35000	85	2	1	1½	11	12	12	Antley C W	b	117	*1.50	86-14	No Holme Keys1172Oriane117hdGreatReview117	Driving 10
23May92- 2Bel	fm	1 1/16	(T):451 1:092 1:412	(F)Clm 35000	85	5	3	3½	2½	1½	11¼	Antley C W	b	117	4.90	89-07	NHlKs1171¼LfOnthFr1173¼AdsAppl117	Lost whp, drvng 11
5Nov91- 1Med	fm	170	(T):461 1:104 1:40	(F)Clm 25000	68	8	2	2hd	1½	32	58	Jocson G J	Lb	114	4.40	85-06	Creme theCat1092MtMorna1142¾MistySauce114	Faded 10
19Oct91- 8Med	yl	1 1/16	(T):473 1:13 1:461	3↑(F)Alw 17000	71	2	4	33½	37½	412	514½	Jocson G J	Lb	113	7.20	52-38	AuntSigourney1166¾JksJn1165HighlndMnor113	No rally 10
14Sep91- 7Med	fm	170	(T):471 1:112 1:401	3↑(F)Alw 16000	85	5	1	1½	1½	12½	1nk	Jocson G J5	Lb	105	2.70	92-11	NoHolmKys110nkFlghtLx1141¾MllonDllrMm112	Driving 10
4Sep91- 7Med	fm	1 1/16	(T):46 1:102 1:42	3↑(F)Alw 16000	77	10	1	1½	2½	24	37½	Jocson G J5	Lb	105	5.20	80-11	BGrs-Ir1165SpctrPhoto-Ir1132¾NHlmKys105	Weakened 11
23Aug91- 6Atl	gd	*1	(T):491 1:151 1:423	(F)Clm 22500	79	7	2	2hd	11	15	14½	Jocson G J5	Lb	107	4.00	71-29	No Holme Keys1074½BlueJewel1114½CityCat112	Driving 12
20Jly91- 5Pha	fm	1 1/16	(T):483 1:142 1:473	(F)Clm 17000	64	2	5	42½	1hd	12½	1½	Molina V H	Lb	114	4.40	69-27	NoHolmKys114½MissMcCnn1102½TwoThrtyT112	Driving 10
29Jun91- 8Pha	fst	1	:47 1:122 1:40	(F)Alw 14000	60	6	4	43	52½	43½	45½	Jocson G J5	Lb	117	4.30	75-19	FrshSpry1161½ZnzritStorm116hdJckiP.116	Flattened out 8

LATEST WORKOUTS Aug 20 Sar 3f fst :382 B ●Aug 12 Sar 4f fst :472 H Jly 26 Bel 3f fst :351 H Jly 8 Bel 5f fst 1:011 H

Note the workouts preceding the wins: a work July 8 that was followed by a win July 12; a work July 26 that was followed by a win July 29; a work August 20 that was followed by a win August 23.

When she won again on October 2, 1992, her workout lines looked like this:

No Holme Keys — Ch. f. 4, by Dewan Keys—Ligia M, by Noholme Jr — Lifetime 19 8 1 3 $95,670
ANTLEY C W (57 14 4 7 .25) — $35,000 Br.—Goodpaster Jane (Ky) — 117
Own.—Barge Marc — Tr.—Reid Mark J (10 1 3 1 .10)

1992	5	4	1	0	$58,300
1991	14	4	0	3	$37,370
Turf	11	7	1	1	$82,350
Wet	1	1	0	0	$8,100

2Sep92-	1Bel	fm	1¼	Ⓣ:47^{2}	1:36^{1}	2:01^{3}	3↑ⒻClm 45000	87	5	2	2½	2hd	1½	2½	Davis R G	b	113	3.20	81–15	Gharah117½ No Holme Keys113^{1}½ Sharpener113	Gamely	8
23Aug92-	2Sar	fm	1⅛	Ⓣ:46	1:10^{3}	1:47^{3}	3↑ⒻClm 35000	89	9	2	2^{6}	2hd	1^{4}	1^{7}½	Antley C W	b	117	*1.00	92–06	NoHlmKys117^{7}½LdngLyndsy117^{2}¾TtnsBll117	Mild drive	12
29Jly92-	9Sar	fm	1⅛	Ⓣ:46^{4}	1:10^{4}	1:48^{2}	3↑ⒻClm 35000	85	11	3	2^{1}½	2½	2½	1no	Antley C W	b	119	*2.50	88–09	NoHolmeKeys119noSharpener117^{1}½MmorBy117	Driving	11
12Jly92-	4Bel	fm	1$\frac{1}{16}$	Ⓣ:45^{4}	1:10	1:42	ⒻClm 35000	85	2	1	1½	1^{1}	1^{2}	1^{2}	Antley C W	b	117	*1.50	86–14	No Holme Keys117^{2}Oriane117hdGreatReview117	Driving	10
23May92-	2Bel	fm	1$\frac{1}{16}$	Ⓣ:45^{1}	1:09^{2}	1:41^{2}	ⒻClm 35000	85	5	3	3½	2½	1½	1^{1}¼	Antley C W	b	117	4.90	89–07	NHlKs117^{1}¼LfOnthFr117^{3}¼AdsAppl117	Lost whp, drvng	11
9Nov91-	1Med	fm	170	Ⓣ:46^{1}	1:10^{4}	1:40	ⒻClm 25000	68	8	2	2hd	1½	3^{2}	5^{8}	Jocson G J	Lb	114	4.40	85–06	Creme theCat109^{2}Mt.Morna114^{2}½MistySauce114	Faded	10
19Oct91-	8Med	yl	1$\frac{1}{16}$	Ⓣ:47^{3}	1:13	1:46^{1}	3↑ⒻAlw 17000	71	2	4	3^{3}½	3^{7}½	4^{12}	5^{14}¾	Jocson G J	Lb	113	7.20	52–38	AuntSigourney116^{6}½JksJn116^{5}HighlndMnor113	No rally	10
14Sep91-	7Med	fm	170	Ⓣ:47^{1}	1:11^{2}	1:40^{1}	3↑ⒻAlw 16000	85	5	1	1½	1½	1^{2}½	1nk	Jocson G J^{5}	Lb	105	2.70	92–11	NoHolmKys110nkFlghtLx114^{1}¾MllonDllrMm112	Driving	10
4Sep91-	7Med	fm	1$\frac{1}{16}$	Ⓣ:46	1:10^{2}	1:42	3↑ⒻAlw 16000	77	10	1	1½	2½	2^{4}	3^{7}¼	Jocson G J^{5}	Lb	105	5.20	80–11	BGrs-Ir116^{5}SpctrPhoto-Ir113^{2}¼NHlmKys105	Weakened	11
23Aug91-	6Atl	gd	*1	Ⓣ:49^{1}	1:15^{1}	1:42^{3}	ⒻClm 22500	79	7	2	2hd	1^{1}	1^{5}	1^{4}½	Jocson G J^{5}	Lb	107	4.00	71–29	No Holme Keys107^{4}½BlueJewel111^{4}½CityCat112	Driving	12

LATEST WORKOUTS Sep 14 Bel 4f fst :47^{3} H Aug 20 Sar 3f fst :38^{2} B ●Aug 12 Sar 4f fst :47^{2} H

Note the workout in 47⅗ seconds on September 14.

It is true that Noholme Keys did not have a workout leading up to her half-length defeat on September 2, which was a sharp effort, but only a few days had elapsed between starts. Likewise, she had not worked before her first win of 1993, but only about two weeks had elapsed between starts.

For this race, however, No Holme Keys had been on the sidelines for nearly six weeks, and showed not a single workout. She had won off a layoff in the past, but always with at least two workouts as part of her training regimen. As corroborating evidence that No Holme Keys was probably not ready to race to her fullest potential, the Wizard noticed that she had worn front bandages in her two return starts in July, and referred to the comment line in the chart footnote for her win of July 19: " . . . took the lead while drifting out on the turn."

The lack of a recent workout, the addition of front bandages, and the drifting-out comment were indicators, taken together, that No Holme Keys was not in the kind of consistently good form she had been in the previous summer.

NINTH RACE **1⅛ MILES. (Inner Turf) (1.46^1) CLAIMING. Purse $21,500**
Saratoga
AUGUST 27, 1993

Value of Race: $21,500 Winner $12,900; second $4,730; third $2,580; fourth $1,290. Mutuel Pool $33,219,778.00 Exacta Pool $440,454.00

Last Raced	Horse	M/Eqt.	A.	Wt	PP	St	¼	½	¾	Str	Fin	Jockey	Cl'g Pr	Odds $1
14Aug93 ^{4}Sar^6	Madame Dahar		4	117	5	7	8^1	7½	6^{hd}	1½	1^{1½}	Bailey J D	35000	2.30
18Aug93 ^{5}Sar^8	Galloping Proudly		4	117	7	9	9^1	9½	9½	6^1	2no	Bisono C V	35000	69.50
18Aug93 ^{5}Sar^2	Ivory Today	b	5	117	6	8	7^{hd}	8^2	8½	7½	3^{nk}	Krone J A	35000	5.60
19Jly93 ^{1}Bel^2	A Shaky Queen	b	5	117	9	6	5½	5^1	5^2	3^{hd}	4^{1½}	Nelson D	35000	7.90
18Aug93 ^{5}Sar^5	Eskimo Song	b	4	117	3	5	6^1	6½	7^2	4½	5no	Smith M E	35000	14.30
4Aug93 ^{7}Sar^7	Miss Angel Too		4	117	1	4	4^{hd}	4^2	3½	5^{hd}	6^5	Nicol P A Jr	35000	7.50
18Aug93 ^{5}Sar^6	High Talent	b	4	117	4	3	2^{hd}	2^2	2^{1½}	2^{hd}	7^{3½}	Migliore R	35000	15.10
18Aug93 ^{5}Sar^4	Pretty Firm		4	117	10	10	10	10	10	9½	8^{1½}	Santos J A	35000	18.20
19Jly93 ^{1}Bel^1	No Holme Keys	bf	5	117	8	1	1^1	1^{1½}	1^{1½}	8^2	9^7	Davis R G	35000	2.20
14Aug93 ^{10}Sar^7	Take a Powder	b	5	117	2	2	3^1	3^{1½}	4^1	10	10	Chavez J F	35000	31.40

OFF AT 5:27 Start Good For All But. Won . Course firm.

TIME :23, :46^3, 1:11, 1:36^3, 1:49^4 (:23.06, :46.74, 1:11.02, 1:36.63, 1:49.90)

$2 Mutuel Prices:				
	6 – MADAME DAHAR	6.60	4.20	2.80
	8 – GALLOPING PROUDLY		33.00	11.20
	1a – IVORY TODAY			4.00
	$2 EXACTA 6–8 PAID $514.80			

B. f, (Apr), by Dahar – Bold Whim , by Bold Hour . Trainer Fisher John R S. Bred by Robert Gallo & Dahar Syndicate (Ky).

Owners– 1, Joel Kligman; 2, Four B Mice Stable; 3, Mitchell Zimmerman; 4, Jujugen Stable; 5, Our Junco Stable; 6, Virginia Kraft Payson; 7, Peter E Mariano; 8, Winbound Farms; 9, Marc Barge; 10, Jeff Odintz

Trainers– 1, Fisher John R S; 2, Bailie Sally A; 3, DiMauro Stephen L; 4, Carroll Henry L; 5, Monaci David; 6, Bond Harold James; 7, Belfiore Thomas; 8, Contessa Gary C; 9, Reid Mark J; 10, Odintz Jeff

Madame Dahar ran as expected, winning the race and paying $6.60. No Holme Keys, the slight favorite, also ran as the Wizard had expected, setting the early pace and tiring abruptly in the stretch to wind up next to last.

The significance of workouts may have to do with the type of horse under consideration. A habitual front-runner has done nothing of note when it blows out three furlongs swiftly, but a front-runner such as Appreciate It deserves extra credit for stamina-building workouts:

Appreciate It — B. g. 3(May), by Cannon Shell—My Appreciation, by Exclusive Native
Br.—Seymour John (NY)
Own.—Cohn Seymour
Tr.—Hushion Michael E (—)

Lifetime						
9 2 1 2	1992	9	2	1	2	$41,760
$41,760	1991	0	M	0	0	
	Turf	2	0	0	0	
	Wet	1	1	0	0	$16,200

21Oct92- 6Aqu	fst	6f	:22^1	:45^2	1:11^1	Clm 35000	—	5	1	2^1	3^{1½}	3^2	4^{3¼}	Madrid A Jr	b	117	7.50	82-18	ClvrKnv115^{nk}StrtFight117^{3}EstblishdLi115	Lacked rally	9
26Sep92- 9Bel	sly	6f	:22^1	:45	1:10^1	3↑ⓈAlw 27000	86	3	1	1^2	1^{3½}	1^2	1^3	Madrid A Jr	b	113	*2.60	89-14	ApprctIt113^{3}Drmnthdywy117^{2¾}EbonyBlu117	Ridden out	8
4Sep92- 7Bel	yl	1$\frac{1}{16}$ [T]	:48^2	1:12^3	1:44^1	3↑ⓈAlw 29000	61	2	1	1^{1½}	1^{hd}	4^5	8^{15½}	Migliore R		113	14.30	61-20	ShomrmScty117^{2¼}ClvrCty117^{1¼}EbnyBl117	Used in pace	10
23Aug92- 9Sar	fst	6f	:22	:45	1:10^1	3↑ⓈAlw 27000	73	6	4	1^1	1^{hd}	1½	3^{2¼}	Migliore R		119	9.80	91-07	PrincConsort117^{1¾}EbonyBlu117½ApprctIt119	Weakened	12
30Jly92- 9Sar	fst	6f	:22^2	:46	1:11	3↑ⓈMd Sp Wt	78	6	2	1^{1½}	1^2	1^5	1^9	Migliore R		116	*1.30	89-06	AppreciateIt116^{9}Bordagaray116^{nk}Concur116	Mild drive	12
20Jly92- 5Bel	fm	1$\frac{1}{16}$ (T)	:46^3	1:11^1	1:42^4	3↑ⓈAlw 29000	58	2	1	1^{1½}	1½	7^{3¼}	9^{11¼}	Migliore R		113	15.90	71-15	Imprgnbl117^{hd}Ptrt'sThndr111^{2½}TddyC.111	Used in pace	10
15Jly92- 9Bel	fst	6f	:21^4	:45^1	1:11^2	3↑Md 35000	69	12	1	1^1	1^3	1^2	3^{3½}	Migliore R		116	5.50	79-14	SgrHos116^{3}ToknofPowr112½ApprctIt116	Speed,faltered	13
18Jun92- 2Bel	fst	6f	:22	:45^4	1:11^3	3↑ⓈMd Sp Wt	54	10	4	1^1	1½	2½	5^4	Brocklebank G V		114	*1.00	78-13	Dark Palette113¾ Cap112^{1½} Jen's Shot104	Speed,tired	12
22May92- 9Bel	fst	6½f	:22^1	:45^2	1:17^3	3↑ⓈMd Sp Wt	64	4	2	2½	1^{hd}	1^{1½}	2^{3½}	Brocklebank G V		115	5.10	81-11	Mr. Lee115^{3½}AppreciateIt115^{1¾}OntheDocket115	Gamely	14

LATEST WORKOUTS Sep 22 Bel 7f fst 1:30 B Sep 18 Bel 1 fst 1:44^3 B

Appreciate It blew three clear leads in the first three starts of his career, so trainer Mike Hushion set him up for a maiden win July 30,1992, by legging him up in a turf route 10 days earlier.

After the gelding weakened as the pacesetter in his first allowance start, Hushion entered him in another turf route on September 4, breezed him a mile two weeks later, and breezed him seven furlongs shortly after that. Hushion was training Appreciate It with a purpose. There was no need to drill Appreciate It for speed in the mornings, because Hushion already knew the horse had good speed; what he needed was conditioning designed to improve his endurance, and that's what he got.

With the turf route and two stamina works under his belt, and blinkers on, Appreciate It took his usual position at the head of the field, but did not tire in the stretch on September 26, winning "ridden out" as a lukewarm favorite.

Similarly, a fast blowout can be significant when it appears out of character:

Mr. Baba	Ch. c. 3 (Mar)		Lifetime Record :	1 M 0 0	$0
Own: Paxson Mrs Henry O	Sire: Nepal (Raja Baba) Dam: Critical Miss (Reviewer) Br: Paxson Mrs Henry D (NY)		1994 1 M 0 0	Turf 1 0 0 0	
			1993 0 M 0 0	Wet 0 0 0 0	
KRONE J A (25 3 3 6 .12)	Tr: Dickinson Michael W (6 2 0 0 .33)	114	Bel⊕ 0 0 0 0	Dist⊕ 0 0 0 0	
2Apr94- 1Cam fm ¹ ①	1:43¹ 3↑ Md Sp Wt	— 3 10 9⁵½ 10¹⁶ 10¹⁵10¹4½ Simpson A 140	- — — Grenade 150¹ Island Skater 144½ Paddock Dancer 147¹½		Away slowly 12

WORKOUTS: May 24 Fai 3f fst :39 B ¹/¹ May 12 Fai 3f fst :35 Bg ¹/² May 7 Fai 6f fst 1:14³ B 2⁵ May 2 Fai 6f fst 1:15¹ B ³/³

Mr. Baba made his career debut at a hunt meet, of all places, and received the comment "Away slowly" for his distant 10th-place finish in a nonbetting event at Camden.

Brought to Belmont Park two months later, Mr. Baba was 8–1 against a field of New York-breds going 1¹⁄₁₆ miles on turf. The workout of May 12—35 seconds breezing from the gate—begged attention. Such a work strongly suggested Mr. Baba's slowness from the gate first out had been due to racing luck and/or inexperience, and was not a true measure of his actual ability.

While a :35Bg work might not have swayed a bettor in and of itself, it was a tipoff to look for other positive factors. The first came by looking back at trainer Michael Dickinson's previous winner at the meet, Matchless Dancer:

Matchless Dancer
Own: Prestonwood Farm
BAILEY J D (66 17 7 14 .26)

Gr. c. 4
Sire: Nijinsky II (Northern Dancer)
Dam: Matching (What Luck)
Br: Prestonwood Farms (Ky)
Tr: Dickinson Michael W (5 1 0 0 .20)

124

Lifetime Record:	7	2	2	0	$41,490						
1994	1	1	0	0	$18,000	Turf	7	2	2	0	$41,490
1993	6	1	2	0	$23,490	Wet	0	0	0	0	
Bel ⓣ	3	1	1	0	$25,320	Dist ⓣ	2	1	0	0	$19,710

11May94-6Bel	fm	1¼ ⓣ	:49	1:123	1:37	2:013	3↑ Alw 30000N1X	96	1	5	41½	11½	16	18¾	Bailey J D	119	3.70	82-21	Matchless Dancer1198¾ Musical Storm119nk Moscow Magic1124	Driving	9
13Aug93-4Sar	fm	1½ ⓣ	:501	1:143	2:052	2:293	3↑ Alw 28500N1X	85	6	9	816	44½	22	21½	Smith M E	113	4.00	80-15	GroomedToWin1121½ MatchlessDancer1133 Glenbarra1125½	Rallied inside	9
31Jly93-4Sar	fm	1⅜ ⓣ	:492	1:151	1:401	2:172	3↑ Alw 28500N1X	78	8	2	2½	21	43	63	Smith M E	113	*2.40	76-15	Noble Sheba111½ No Sneaker113nk Groomed To Win112hd	Tired	10
12Jly93-7Bel	fm	1¼ ⓣ	:493	1:134	1:374	2:02	3↑ Alw 28500N1X	86	4	5	31½	32	53	41	Smith M E	116	5.50	79-12	Dover Coast117¾ Shoaly Water117hd Jodi's The Best113nk	Mild rally	9
1Jly93-9Lrl	fm	1½ ⓣ	:48	1:134	2:081	2:321	3↑ Md Sp Wt	80	3	7	67	43	13	17½	Pino M G	114 f	*.40	89-13	Matchless Dancer1147½ FlashGorgeous1142½ GoForTheMagic1081½	Driving	9
14Jun93-5Bel	fm	1⅜ ⓣ	:493	1:134	1:382	2:142	3↑ Md Sp Wt	80	6	5	42½	31	2½	2nk	Smith M E	114	5.40	79-11	Noble Sheba114nk Matchless Dancer1144½ Off The Cuff1225	Gamely	9
30May93-3Pim	fm	1⅜ ⓣ	:491	1:171	1:423	2:204	3↑ Md Sp Wt	73	3	6	712	55	58	55½	Delgado A	113	5.60	— —	Gold Quoit1142½ Heroisbreezin'112nk Class First1141	Sluggish start	8

WORKOUTS: May 7 Fai 4f fst :53 B 3/8 May 2 Fai 5f fst 1:052 B 6/8

Matchless Dancer had provided Dickinson with back-to-back wins in 1¼-mile turf races when returned from a nine-month layoff, winning a first-level allowance with authority on May 11, and coming back to repeat against second-level allowance rivals, paying $6.20 on May 29. Matchless Dancer had been plenty fit enough, despite showing only a pair of breezing works at Fair Hill. This effectively squashed any concerns about the readiness of Mr. Baba, who showed substantially more activity at Fair Hill, with a couple of six-furlong works preceding the fast blowout.

The second positive sign came on race day, when track announcer Tom Durkin noted in his rundown of the scratches and late changes that Mr. Baba had been gelded—the ultimate equipment change.

A few hours later, Mr. Baba broke alertly and took up a forward position, challenged for command entering the stretch, and drew off to win, paying $18.40.

NINTH RACE 1$\frac{1}{16}$ MILES. (Turf) (1.38²) MAIDEN SPECIAL WEIGHT . Purse $27,000

Belmont

JUNE 4, 1994

Value of Race: $27,000 Winner $16,200; second $5,940; third $3,240; fourth $1,620. Mutuel Pool $233,215.00 Exacta Pool $345,986.00

Last Raced	Horse	M/Eqt.	A. Wt	PP	St	¼	½	¾	Str	Fin	Jockey	Odds $1
2Apr94 ¹Cam¹⁰	Mr. Baba		3 114	7	3	5¹½	3hd	4²	1¹	1³	Krone J A	8.20
27May94 ⁵Bel²	Watrals Sea Trip		3 114	8	9	8½	8½	8¹⁰	4¹	2¹	Graell A	3.60
22Nov93 ³Aqu³	Silver Safari	b	3 114	9	1	1hd	1¹	1¹	2¹	3³	Luzzi M J	2.10
6May94 ⁵Bel³	Wolf Shadow		4 122	6	2	4hd	5½	3hd	3²	4¾	Samyn J L	4.60
10May94 ⁵Bel⁵	Rogersdividends	bf	3 114	3	6	6¹	6²	5²	5½	5⁵½	Alvarado F T	10.30
28May94 ¹¹GS³	Joyful Bundle	b	3 114	10	4	2¹	2¹	2hd	6³	6⁷½	Bailey J D	4.60
17May94 ³Bel⁶	Grave Dancer	b	3 114	2	5	3¹	4¹	6hd	7¹¹½	7¹	Velazquez J R	46.60
24May94 ⁵Bel⁵	Buck Mulligan	b	5 122	4	8	7⁷	7⁹	7³½	8¹²	8³⁰	Migliore R	14.70
21Jly93 ⁵Bel⁹	Ricamisa		3 114	1	7	10	10	10	10	9	Leon F	48.60
27May94 ³Bel⁵	Pickwick Punch		4 122	5	10	9hd	9³	9⁴	9⁴	—	Lovato F Jr	79.10

OFF AT 5:33 Start Good For All But. Won . Course firm.

TIME :22³, :45², 1:10, 1:35⁴, 1:42² (:22.69, :45.55, 1:10.18, 1:35.94, 1:42.46)

$2 Mutuel Prices:	7 – MR. BABA.........................	18.40	8.20	5.20
	8 – WATRALS SEA TRIP................		5.40	3.20
	9 – SILVER SAFARI....................			3.00

$2 EXACTA 7–8 PAID $147.40

Ch. g, (Mar), by Nepal – Critical Miss , by Reviewer . Trainer Dickinson Michael W. Bred by Mrs Henry D Paxson (NY).

Owners– 1, Mrs Henry D Paxson; 2, Michael Watral; 3, Very Un Stable; 4, Boto Stable; 5, Mrs Thomas M Walsh; 6, Robert Perez; 7, David E Ahearn; 8, Nuesch Felix J; 9, Laurence P Miller; 10, William Drakos

Trainers– 1, Dickinson Michael W; 2, Brida Dennis J; 3, O'Connell Richard; 4, Turner William H Jr; 5, Walsh Thomas M; 6, Callejas Alfredo; 7, Trimmer Richard K; 8, Destasio Richard A; 9, Campo John P; 10, Beattie Richard L Jr

Sometimes, a fast workout is a negative sign, as was the case when Funny Cide was going for the Triple Crown in the 2003 Belmont Stakes, and Empire Maker stood in his way:

Empire Maker had handled Funny Cide by a well-measured half-length in the Wood Memorial, but came up with a minor foot injury the week before the Kentucky Derby that curtailed his training just enough to leave him a short horse in deep stretch.

Bobby Frankel regrouped, and shrewdly opted to skip the Preakness with Empire Maker, who healed and rested while Funny Cide ran away with the Preakness with a lifetime-best 114 Beyer figure—his third consecutive "effort" in five weeks.

The key to getting 1½ miles is for a horse to relax, so when Funny Cide tugged and dragged exercise rider Robin Smullen through five furlongs in a blistering 57⅘ seconds in his final work for the Belmont, it was apparent he was too keyed up to relax sufficiently in the early stages of such a long and grueling race.

Because mass hysteria somehow grips bettors when a 3-year-old is going for the Triple Crown in the Belmont Stakes, Funny Cide was pounded down to even money, and Empire Maker was a low-priced overlay as the 2–1 second choice:

ELEVENTH RACE
Belmont
JUNE 7, 2003

$1\frac{1}{2}$ MILES. (2.24) BELMONT S. Grade I. Purse $1,000,000 (Up To $72,000 NYSBFOA) FOR THREE YEAR OLDS. By subscription of $600 each to accompany the nomination if made on or before January 18, 2003, or $6,000 if made on or before March 29 2003, $10,000 to pass the entry box and $10,000 additional to start. At any time prior to the closing time of entries, horses may be nominated to The Belmont Stakes upon payment of a supplementary fee of $100,000 to The New York Racing Association Inc. The Purse to be divided 60% to the winner, 20% to second, 11% to third, 6% to fourth and 3% to fifth. Colts and Geldings, 126 lbs.; Fillies, 121 lbs. Starters to be named at the closing time of entries. The Belmont field will be limited to sixteen (16) starters.

Value of Race: $1,000,000 Winner $600,000; second $200,000; third $110,000; fourth $60,000; fifth $30,000. Mutuel Pool $21,283,153.00 Exacta Pool $11,308,960.00 Trifecta Pool $12,485,369.00

Last Raced	Horse	M/Eqt.	A.	Wt	PP	¼	½	1	1¼	Str	Fin	Jockey	Odds $1
3May03 $^{10}CD^{2}$	Empire Maker	L b	3	126	1	3^{2}	2^{1}	$2^{1\frac{1}{2}}$	1^{1}	$1^{1\frac{1}{2}}$	$1^{\frac{3}{4}}$	Bailey J D	2.00
3May03 $^{10}CD^{9}$	Ten Most Wanted	L f	3	126	6	$4^{\frac{1}{2}}$	5^{5}	4^{hd}	3^{4}	$2^{1\frac{1}{2}}$	$2^{4\frac{1}{4}}$	Day P	9.70
17May03 $^{12}Pim^{1}$	Funny Cide	L	3	126	4	1^{1}	1^{1}	1^{hd}	2^{1}	3^{5}	$3^{5\frac{1}{4}}$	Santos J A	1.00
10May03 $^{8}LS^{1}$	Dynever	L	3	126	5	5^{4}	4^{hd}	5^{7}	4^{3}	4^{10}	$4^{15\frac{1}{4}}$	Prado E S	8.50
24May03 $^{8}Bel^{3}$	Supervisor	L b	3	126	2	6	6	6	6	5^{1}	$5^{4\frac{1}{2}}$	Velazquez J R	14.80
17May03 $^{12}Pim^{3}$	Scrimshaw	L b	3	126	3	$2^{1\frac{1}{2}}$	3^{1}	3^{hd}	5^{4}	6	6	Stevens G L	11.00

OFF AT 6:40 Start Good. Won driving. Track sloppy.

TIME :23^{4}, :48^{3}, 1:13^{2}, 1:38, 2:02^{3}, 2:28^{1} (:23.85, :48.70, 1:13.51, 1:38.05, 2:02.62, 2:28.26)

$2 Mutuel Prices:

1 – EMPIRE MAKER	6.00	3.70	2.80
6 – TEN MOST WANTED		5.80	3.20
4 – FUNNY CIDE			2.70

$2 EXACTA 1-6 PAID $44.00 $2 TRIFECTA 1-6-4 PAID $67.50

Dk. b or br. c, (Apr), by Unbridled – Toussaud, by El Gran Senor. Trainer Frankel Robert. Bred by Juddmonte Farms Inc (Ky).

EMPIRE MAKER was taken to the outside approaching the first turn, stalked the pace while four wide along the backstretch, edged closer on the far turn, drew along side FUNNY CIDE to challenge at the three-eighths pole, surged to the front midway on the turn, shook off FUNNY CIDE to gain a clear advantage leaving the quarter pole, dug in when threatened in upper stretch, drifted out when struck left handed with the whip nearing the eighth pole then turned back TEN MOST WANTED through the final sixteenth of a mile. TEN MOST WANTED brushed with DYNEVER at the start, was strung out five wide on the first turn, continued wide while just behind the leaders along the backstretch, closed the gap a bit on the turn, launched a rally five wide entering the stretch, made a run outside the winner to threaten in deep stretch, but could not get up. FUNNY CIDE broke outward slightly at the start, rushed up to gain the early advantage on the first turn, set the pace well off the rail while in hand along the backstretch, led to the far turn, relinquished the lead to the winner at the three-sixteenths pole, battled along the inside to the top of the stretch then weakened from his early efforts. DYNEVER brushed with TEN MOST WANTED at the start, settled just off the pace while between horses for a mile, raced within striking distance to the turn then came up empty in the stretch. SUPERVISOR never reached contention after breaking a step slowly while racing wide throughout. SCRIMSHAW moved up along the rail to contest the early pace, raced close up along the inside for a mile, dropped back on the turn, drifted very wide at the quarter pole then gave way.

Owners– 1, Juddmonte Farms Inc; 2, Chisholm James Horizon Stable and Jarvis Michael et al; 3, Sackatoga Stable; 4, Wills Catherine and Karches Peter; 5, Lundock Rodney G; 6, Lewis Robert B and Beverly J

Trainers– 1, Frankel Robert; 2, Dollase Wallace; 3, Tagg Barclay; 4, Clement Christophe; 5, Rice Linda; 6, Lukas D Wayne

---

$2 Daily Double (7–1(ACORN/BELMONT)) Paid $20.20 ; Daily Double Pool $569,982 .
$2 Daily Double (10–1) Paid $16.00 ; Daily Double Pool $513,341 .
$2 Pick Three (5–10–1) Paid $84.00 ; Pick Three Pool $496,621 .
$2 Pick Four (2–5–10–1) Paid $271.00 ; Pick Four Pool $1,205,886 .
$2 Pick Six (5–6–2–5–10–1) 6 Correct Paid $900.00 ; Pick Six Pool $1,298,118 .
$2 Pick Six (5–6–2–5–10–1) 5 Correct Paid $24.20 .

Funny Cide rushed up to get the lead, held on well to the top of the stretch, and predictably weakened from his early energy expenditure. The fresher and more relaxed Empire Maker ranged alongside to challenge on the far turn, put Funny Cide away turning for home, and outfinished Ten Most Wanted, a 9–1 shot who was the only other entrant to have put up a big Beyer figure (110 for winning the Illinois Derby), and who was also withheld from the Preakness after bouncing in the Kentucky Derby.

·

CHAPTER 3

Playing the Game Today

"It is unwise to be too sure of one's own wisdom."
—Mahatma Gandhi

IN THE SPRING OF 2007, the National Thoroughbred Racing Association's advertising campaign consisted largely of a TV commercial in which the question "Who do you like today?" was posed by celebrities such as D. Wayne Lukas, Angel Cordero Jr., Kid Rock, Michael Imperioli, and *Jeopardy!* host Alex Trebek.

As if "who you like" has any relevance whatsoever. The definition of handicapping is not fixating on one horse to the exclusion of all others, but assessing and quantifying the fair odds of the contenders—and there are usually several with a realistic chance. You like the 5 horse? Exactly how much do you like him? What's the minimum price you will take? Is there an alternative if you don't get your price on the top choice?

The primary goal is not picking winners, as counterintuitive as that seems. The primary goal is to make M-O-N-E-Y, and the means to that end has only a little to do with picking winners and a lot more to do with betting acumen, sensible money management, and diligent record-keeping.

As Bill Parcells is fond of saying when one of his high-salaried football teams is struggling, "You are what your record says you are."

The bottom line is all that matters.

Laying the foundation for getting out of the red and into the black is what the remainder of this book is about. But just as we were off to see the Wizard of Odds, a slight detour materialized on the yellow-brick road.

They Paved Paradise and Put Up a Polytrack

As this was written in the spring of 2007, Thoroughbred racing was in the early stages of a seismic shift due to the emergence of all-weather racing surfaces.

Polytrack, Cushion Track, Tapeta Footings, and Pro-Ride are a combination of conventional and synthetic materials.

Polytrack and Cushion Track originated in England. The first Polytrack was installed in the late 1980s for English trainer Richard Hannon, and first came into use during actual racing at Lingfield Park in 2001, followed three years later by Wolverhampton and Kempton Park. In 2005, Turfway Park became the first U.S. racetrack with a Polytrack surface.

Trainer Michael Dickinson patented and installed the Tapeta surface, which is in use at his Tapeta Farm training center in Maryland.

The Pro-Ride surface, a mix of sand and polymeric binder, is currently in use only at several training centers in Australia.

The top layer of Polytrack is a seven-inch-thick mixture of polypropylene fibers, recycled rubber, and silica sand, all blended with a wax coating; in colder climates, chopped recycled telecommunications cable—or "jelly cable"—has been added to the mix. Next is a 2½-inch layer of porous asphalt, followed by a third layer of dust-free stones, and a fourth layer of dense crushed stone that slopes toward the drains. Below it all are perforated pipes set in trenches that carry water away from the track. It is an effective design where water flows vertically through the materials to the drainage system, as opposed to conventional dirt tracks that drain horizontally down toward the rail and are susceptible to washouts; indeed, Polytrack's drainage system is so effective that the surface is always considered to be "fast" regardless of weather conditions.

Whereas a dirt track must be harrowed and watered repeatedly during the course of morning workouts and before every race, Polytrack needs to be evened out only two or three times a day.

"One of the best things I can tell you about Polytrack is they don't touch it from 6:00 a.m. to 10:00 a.m. during training hours, and in those four hours you can't find one divot," said jockey Kent Desormeaux. "What that means is no twisted ankles."

Because of the decreased costs of maintenance, and an ability to withstand harsh weather conditions that means fewer canceled programs, all-weather surfaces are considerably more cost-efficient than dirt tracks. But their first and foremost selling point is a less-concussive surface that has (a) vastly improved safety statistics for horses and riders, (b) sharply decreased veterinary expenses, and (c) led to larger average-field size and increased betting handle.

After fatal breakdowns rose by more than 33 percent in California in 2005, all-weather surfaces were mandated for every track in the state. As was the case at Turfway Park during its first season of synthetic racing, injuries were dramatically reduced.

Turfway had 24 fatal breakdowns during its final season (2004–05) on conventional dirt; during the inaugural Polytrack season of 2005–06, there were only three.

An alarming total of 154 horses were euthanized in California in 2005. During the first four months of training and racing on Hollywood Park's newly installed Cushion Track, there were just two.

As of May 2007, the following tracks and training centers had installed or were in the process of installing all-weather surfaces:

Polytrack:
Arlington Park
Del Mar
Keeneland
Turfway Park
Woodbine

Cushion Track:
Hollywood Park
Santa Anita

Tapeta Footings:
Al Quoz Training Center (Dubai)
Fair Hill Training Center (Maryland)
Golden Gate Fields
Presque Isle Downs
Tapeta Farm (Maryland)

Pro Ride:
Skylight Training Center (Kentucky)

As the all-weather surfaces have quite literally broken new ground, there have been some start-up maintenance issues.

- Seeking to reduce "kickback" and quicken up the surface a bit, Turfway replaced 4,200 tons of Polytrack material prior to its 2006 fall meet. During the winter when the temperature turned colder, the new mixture tended to "ball up" in horses' hooves, and some trainers resorted to using Pam cooking spray as a preventive measure.
- During its inaugural Polytrack meet, Woodbine had some cold-weather problems "similar to what Turfway had," said manager of racing surfaces Irwin Dreidger. "There's a little more kickback

here than what they had. There was something similar last year in England as well. It tightens up when it rains, which is better."

- An increased kickback at Hollywood prompted concerns from riders, and an adjusted maintenance program tightened up the surface. "We're working on it and we're learning about it," said track superintendent Dennis Moore. "The track is very weather-sensitive."

At this writing Keeneland had completed its fall 2006 meet and 2007 spring meet on Polytrack, and no one knew quite what to make of that particular Polytrack. On one hand, 4½-furlong dashes for juveniles were being run in world-record time; but on the other hand, graded-stakes routes were being run through absurdly slow fractions. As it became apparent that finishing ability was paramount, jockeys grabbed hold of their mounts early, and the fields walked through the early fractions before fanning out across the track for an all-out sprint to the wire.

After crawling through fractions of 26.12, 51.46, and 1:16.65 in the 2007 Blue Grass, the field blazed the last three furlongs in 34.68 seconds, with Dominican rallying from four lengths behind—running his last three furlongs in under 34 seconds—to prevail in a cavalry charge over Street Sense, Zanjero, and pacesetter Teuflesberg. Making things more confounding was that, one race earlier, the seven-furlong Commonwealth Stakes went in a sharp 1:21.26.

The Blue Grass improved Dominican's record on synthetic tracks to 3 for 3, but leading up to the Kentucky Derby, trainer

Darrin Miller was asked if he'd like to see Churchill Downs convert to a Polytrack surface.

"Yes and no," he said. "I can't imagine Churchill Downs as a Polytrack racetrack. It's just tradition. It doesn't seem like it would be right."

In spite of his perfect record, it's hard to say whether Dominican is a true horse for synthetic courses. Oddly enough, though his maiden win on Polytrack was surrounded by four losses as a 2-year-old, all four received faster figures than the win. Perhaps the comparatively low figure of 65 was a function of a slow pace; at this point, handicappers cannot be sure.

A few days after Dominican's Blue Grass, the gray mare Asi Siempre came from last and erased a 10½-length deficit to win the Grade 3 Doubledogdare Stakes at 1¹⁄₁₆ miles. Amazingly, she won "gathered up late" after overtaking fractions that were even slower than those of the Blue Grass.

"All I've got to say about Polytrack is, I like it, number one, and number two, I think we're on a three-year learning curve on how to run on it," said trainer Carl Nafzger, who used the Blue Grass as the second of two spring prep races for Kentucky Derby winner Street Sense. "And the third thing is, we're on a seven-year learning curve on how we have to refurbish it. Riders don't know quite how to ride it; trainers don't know quite what to expect; and management, quite frankly, doesn't quite yet know how to manage it."

He might also have included handicappers among the roster of the confused. For those of us who have spent a lifetime grappling with the effects of early and late speed on conventional dirt, route races on Keeneland's Polytrack, at least thus far, might be better understood had they been run on the moon. Management at Keeneland surely meant well when they replaced their old conveyor belt with Polytrack, but it seems like they went overboard in the opposite direction.

Remember the good old track at Keeneland, over which horses like Sinister Minister and Flying Falcon went to the front and improved their position?

Speed handicappers looked forward to the old Keeneland the way kids look forward to Christmas, because horses that got loose on the lead tended to run freakishly big races, and they weren't hard to spot. Sinister Minister, coming off a huge pace figure in the California Derby, was among the biggest stakes overlays of 2006 when he wired the Blue Grass with a 116 Beyer, but he could never come close to that level on a normal racetrack.

A couple days before Sinister Minister, the need-to-lead mare Flying Falcon won off by nearly a dozen lengths; her only other remotely comparable race had been a front-running win on the same surface the previous fall at 40–1.

Pace handicappers zeroed in on the probable pacesetters, and bet with both hands for a couple of glorious weeks every spring and every autumn. It was like an annuity, and losing the old Keeneland surface was like losing a loved one.

Races on Polytrack, particularly routes, tend to develop more like turf races: slow early and fast late. That may be one reason why turf runners such as Asi Siempre have transitioned so well to all-weather tracks: Finishing ability counts heavily. Additional reasons for the success of grass runners may be that (a) all-weather tracks don't break away from horses' hind hooves as much as dirt tracks do, and (b) kickback is comparatively minimal.

But at this early stage, there is considerable guesswork involved in predicting which horses will take to synthetic tracks and which will not.

Wait a While
Own: Arindel Farm

Gr/ro. f. 4 (Mar) OBSFEB05 $260,000
Sire: Maria's Mon (Wavering Monarch) $60,000
Dam: Flirtatious (A.P. Indy)
Br: W. S. Farish & W. Temple Webber Jr. (Ky)
Tr: Pletcher Todd A

Life	15	8	1	3	$1,389,917	109	
2007	2	1	0	0	$66,000	102	
2006	9	5	1	2	$1,226,637	109	
D.Fst	4	0	1	3	$198,917	90	
Wet(416)	4	3	0	0	$206,400	90	
Synth	1	0	0	0	$6,000	88	
Turf(303)	6	5	0	0	$978,600	109	

14Apr07-6Kee	fst	1 1/16 ⊗	:243 :50 1:143 1:431	4↑ⒻJenyWily-G2	**88**	2	67	64½	53	54	56¾	Gomez G K	L123	*.50	85-15	MyTyphoon119nk PrciousKittn1234¼ FntstcShrl1171¾	Hop start,no rally,5w	6
4Mar07-7GP	fm	1 1/16 Ⓣ	:234 :473 1:11 1:391	4↑ⒻHonyFoxH-G3	**102**	2	11½	1½	1½	12	11¼	Velazquez J R	L123	*.40	94-04	Wait a While1231¼ Precious Kitten1172 Chaibia1161½	Rail, held sway	7
4Nov06-5CD	fm	1 3/8 Ⓣ	:493 1:144 1:384 2:142	3↑ⒻBCFMTrf-G1	**100**	7	51½	51½	32	31½	44¼	Gomez G K	L119	2.30	94 -	Ouija Board1232¼ Film Maker123nk Honey Ryder1231¾	Tracked,4w,empty	10
30Sep06-4OSA	fm	1¼ Ⓣ	:481 1:124 1:362 1:592	3↑ⒻYlwRibbn-G1	**109**	8	2½	21	2hd	12½	14½	Gomez G K	LB120	*.70	92-12	Wait aWhile1204½ DancingEdie123nk ThreeDegrees1231¼	Strong handling	8
18Aug06-8Sar	fm	1⅛ [T]	:484 1:121 1:35 1:462	ⒻLakePlcd-G2	**106**	3	2½	21½	2½	15½	14¾	Gomez G K	L120	*1.05	102-07	WaitaWhile1204¾ LadyofVenice1201½ DancingBnd1162	Quick move, in hand	5
2Jly06-8Hol	fm	1¼ Ⓣ	:474 1:12 1:36 1:591	ⒻAmrcnOks-G1	**105**	7	42	41½	11	13½	14½	Gomez G K	LB121	2.90	99-07	Wait a While1214½ Asahi Rising121½ Arravale1216	3wd move,clear,rail	8
3Jun06-8Bel	slyS	1⅛ ⊗	:474 1:122 1:362 1:491	ⒻSandsPnt-G3	**90**	3	1½	11	11½	15	14½	Gomez G K	L115	*.50	85-18	WaitaWhile1154½ DiamondSpirit11514 Hostess1151¾	Drew off when asked	4
5May06-10CD	fst	1⅛	:462 1:112 1:37 1:50	ⒻKyOaks-G1	**86**	8	65½	56	52	41½	43¾	Gomez G K	L121	8.30	83-06	Lemons Forever1211½ Ermine1211¼ [D]Bushfire1211	Between,no late gain	14
Placed third through disqualification																		
8Apr06-9Kee	fst	1 1/16	:231 :462 1:104 1:45	ⒻAshland-G1	**80**	3	32	31½	22	23½	26½	Velazquez J R	L121	3.40	81-19	Bushfire1216½ Wait a While1214¼ Balance1212¾	Reluctant gate,2ndbest	8
5Mar06-8GP	fst	1⅛	:48 1:12 1:36 1:481	ⒻBonnieMs-G2	**90**	7	21	21	2½	23½	36	Velazquez J R	L120	*1.10	95-08	Teammate1166 WonderLdyAnneL120hd WitWhile1207¾	Stalked, gave way	7
4Feb06-6GP	slyS	1⅛	:453 1:092 1:361 1:501	ⒻDvonaDal-G2	**86**	5	31½	21	2½	16	114	Velazquez J R	L119	3.40	91-04	WaitaWhile11914 Temmte115hd WonderLdyAnneL119hd	Drew off, driving	7
26Nov05-6Aqu	fst	1⅛	:494 1:144 1:393 1:524	ⒻDemoisel-G2	**82**	1	13½	13	12½	31½	34¼	Bailey J D	L119	3.10	72-18	WonderLdyAnneL1162¾ CinderellsDrm1191½ WitWhil1195½	Set pace, tired	5

WORKS: May27 Bel[T] 4f fm :50 B(d) *10/17* May20 Bel[T] 4f gd :50 B(d) *6/15* ●May13 Bel[T] 4f gd :472 H(d) *1/20* ●Apr8 Kee ◈4f fst :46 H *1/32* Apr2 PmMⓉ 4f fm :514 B(d) *10/16* Mar26 PmMⓉ 4f fm :522 B(d) *2/30*

For example, when Wait a While, the champion 3-year-old filly of 2006, ran in the off-the-turf Jenny Wiley Stakes on Blue Grass Day, it seemed reasonable to expect she would handle Polytrack. But although she is an exceedingly talented and versatile runner who is a multiple stakes winner on turf, as well as on wet conventional dirt tracks, Wait a While never ran a lick at 1–2.

Latent Heat
Own: Juddmonte Farms Inc

B. c. 4 (Mar)
Sire: Maria's Mon (Wavering Monarch) $60,000
Dam: True Flare (Capote)
Br: Juddmonte Farms, Inc. (Ky)
Tr: Frankel Robert J(0 0 0 0 .00) 2007:(150 40 .27)

Life	11	6	2	1	$432,400	111	D.Fst	9	5	2	1	$405,400	111
2007	2	1	0	0	$105,000	107	Wet(393)	1	1	0	0	$27,000	97
							Synth	1	0	0	0	$0	72
2006	8	5	1	1	$318,600	111	Turf(282)	0	0	0	0	$0	-
Op	0	0	0	0	$0	-	Dst(336)	1	1	0	0	$30,000	101

7Apr07-9Aqu	fst	7f		:213	:441	1:09	1:212	3↑CarterH-G1	105	5	1	1hd	1½	1hd	42¾	Flores D R	L119	2.20	91-09	Silver Wagon1181¼ Diabolical117¾ Ah Day115¾	Between rivals, tired	6
17Feb07-9SA	fst	7f		:222	:442	1:08	1:21	4↑SnCrlosH-G2	107	3	5	2hd	1hd	2hd	1nk	Prado E S	LB118	*1.00	95-10	LtentHet118nk ProudTowerToo1201¾ Rmsgt1141½	Fought back rail,game	10
26Dec06-8SA	fst	7f		:221	:45	1:09	1:211	Malibu-G1	111	11	3	3½	31	2½	12	Prado E S	LB115	5.70	94-13	*LatentHeat*1152 SpringAtLast119hd MidnightLute1191	Re-bid 3wd,cleared	12
13Oct06-9Kee	fst	*7f	◈	:224	:451	1:09	1:241	Perryvll-G3	72	9	6	41	2hd	96¾	913	Prado E S	L117	4.10	- -	Midnight Lute1174¾ Lewis Michael1173 CourtFolly123hd	Tracked,5w,tired	11
8Sep06-8Bel	fst	1		:231	:454	1:094	1:351	3↑OC 75k/N3x-N	101	5	31	3nk	11½	14½	13¼	Prado E S	L118	*.50	85-20	Latent Heat1183¼ *Tinseltown*120no Bucharest1201½	3 wide move, clear	6
11Aug06-3Sar	fst	6½f		:214	:45	1:093	1:16	3↑Alw 50960N3L	107	4	1	2hd	1hd	12½	13¾	Bejarano R	L119	*.75	94-13	*LatentHeat*1193¾ Tuffertiger1232½ IslandWrrior1195¼	Bumped start, clear	5
15Jly06-9Mth	fst	1 1/16		:232	:462	1:11	1:452	LBrnchBC-G3	94	2	1hd	1hd	2hd	2hd	21¼	Cruz J	L117	*.50	77-27	PryingforCsh1171¼ *LtentHet*117nk VictoryLke117¾	2path,brush,outfinishd	5
24Jun06-3Bel	myS	7f		:221	:453	1:102	1:23	3↑OC 75k/N1x-N	97	5	2	1½	11½	110	19½	Desormeaux K J	L117	*.20	86-17	Latent Heat1179½ Tilden117¾ Big Chief Bubba12117	With authority, handy	5
4Mar06-5SA	fst	1 1/16		:231	:461	1:101	1:414	StCtlina-G2	94	3	1½	1hd	1hd	21	34½	Valenzuela P A	LB118	3.20	86-06	*BrotherDerek*1221¾ SacredLight1152¾ *LtentHet*1183¾	Dueled btwn,held 3rd	8
21Jan06-3SA	fst	7f		:221	:451	1:102	1:23	Md Sp Wt 46k	97	7	1	2hd	11	12	12¾	Valenzuela P A	LB121	*.30	85-16	Latent Heat1212¾ Indy Weekend1213½ Tug o'War1214	Inside,clear,driving	10
26Dec05-6SA	fst	6½f		:214	:443	1:091	1:152	Md Sp Wt 47k	97	9	2	3½	31	1½	2½	Valenzuela P A	LB120	10.90	94-12	*Cindago*120½ *Latent Heat*1203 *Point Determined*1205	3deep, led, outgamed	13

WORKS: Apr1 Hol ◈5f fst 1:002 H *11/49* Mar26 Hol ◈6f fst 1:121 H *2/17* Mar20 Hol ◈5f fst 1:003 H *10/45* Mar14 Hol ◈4f fst :492 B *18/30* Feb10 Hol ◈6f fst 1:124 H *3/29* Feb4 Hol ◈6f fst 1:134 H *10/15*

TRAINER: 2Off45-180(115 .26 $1.65) Sprint/Route(89 .26 $1.77) Dirt(291 .29 $2.00) Routes(491 .24 $1.72) Stakes(197 .19 $1.53)

Latent Heat has been a gem of consistency throughout his career on conventional dirt, with five 100-plus Beyer figures on four different tracks on both coasts. Yet, as much as he apparently gets out of his training on Hollywood's Cushion Track, he ran an abysmal race on Polytrack, one that was totally out of character, in Keeneland's Perryville Stakes

"You learn little by little," said Rene Douglas, who won four riding titles on Arlington Park's old dirt track, and like everyone else was undergoing on-the-job training at that track's inaugural Polytrack meet in 2007. "You can't pick up everything right away. The key is to come from behind if you are able to relax your horse. When it rains, the track is kind of packed, making it a little faster, and horses last longer. Every time it rains, you have to be a little closer."

The Renaissance of the Track Profile

It was widely expected that synthetic surfaces would mark the beginning of the end as far as track and post-position biases were concerned, but by now handicappers have seen enough to realize nothing could be further from the truth. Consider that:

- Keeneland's old dirt track was extremely biased toward early speed, so much so that at the final meet on that track, spring

2006, no fewer than 48 percent of two-turn routes were won by the horse that got the early lead. At the 2007 spring meet on Polytrack, only 3 of 53 route races were won on the lead—less than 3 percent!

- Stretch-runners appeared to have an edge at Turfway through the first three weeks in March 2007, but on Lane's End Day the track suddenly and mysteriously changed so that virtually no one made up any significant ground in the stretch.
- Through the early stages of Hollywood Park's 2007 spring/summer session, inside posts were dominant in sprints. At six furlongs, horses from posts 1 through 4 won 10 of the first 20 races, and horses from posts 9 through 14 were a combined 0 for 37. At 6½ furlongs, posts 1 through 4 won 13 of the first 16 races, while horses from post 5 outward were a combined 3 for 76.

These and other idiosyncrasies become readily apparent to handicappers willing to spend a few minutes a day compiling a track profile. The procedure was first outlined by Tom Brohamer back in 1991 in the original version of *Modern Pace Handicapping*, which remains the definitive treatment of that subject.

In addition to the necessary development of getting to know the demands of all the new synthetic tracks, track profiles can point out changes in conventional dirt tracks, most of which undergo major or minor renovations from time to time:

- After a complete overhaul in 2005, Gulfstream Park's one-mile dirt track and seven-furlong turf course were reconfigured to 1⅛ miles and one mile, respectively.
- In preparation for hosting the Breeders' Cup in 2007, Monmouth Park put in a new turf course in 2006, and installed a completely new cushion on the main track for 2007.

Things change, and when the inherent demands of a racing surface change at a given distance, keepers of track profiles are the first to know. The procedure is simple. For each winner at each distance on dirt and turf, extract the winner's individual running line, along with the following data:

Date	Name	(Field)	Post	Line	$	Splits	Notes
5-28	Dave L.	(11)	4	8_9 5_4 2_2 1_1	$6.40	22.01 45.33 1:23.41	Turf to dirt

That's it. On May 28, the mighty Dave L. broke from post 4 in a field of 11, and rallied from off the pace to get up inside the final furlong. The low win mutuel showed him to be a logical contender, and the array is completed by the race fractions and any pertinent comment.

When a day pops up with a bunch of high-paying winners sharing a similar running style, it's a sign that a bias may have been in play.

The profile can be particularly enlightening when something unusual occurs. For example, inside biases generally go hand-in-hand with early speed, and when closers have the edge they can usually be found rallying outside the tiring leaders. But during the early stages of Saratoga's 1999 meet, a strong outside-speed bias prevailed. The six-furlong Honorable Miss Handicap was run on the sixth day of the meet, at which point each of the first 16 winners at the distance had either led or been within a length of the early lead, and the horses breaking from the three inside posts were 1 for 48. The race was wired by Bourbon Belle, while the deep closer Furlough rallied along the rail into the teeth of the bias. When Furlough returned later at the meet for her main objective, the seven-furlong, Grade 1 Ballerina Handicap, the bias was gone, and she came from out of the clouds to nail Bourbon Belle by a nose at 7–1.

Turf-to-synthetic has been a productive switch on all-weather tracks, where stamina is a key ingredient, but it is really just the latest offshoot of the turf-to-dirt angle that has been getting good-priced winners for decades when conventional dirt tracks become tiring in nature.

It's an angle especially worth keeping in mind at Saratoga.

On August 8, 1990, at the Spa, the main track was drying out and muddy early in the day, and upgraded to good for the last four races; it was the kind of gummy and "holding" mud that had many horses gasping for breath by the far turn, and the day's races were dominated by horses that had last raced on turf. They included a shipper from Rockingham Park named Pic Iron in the opener, and a filly named Cosmic Belle, who came out of an eighth-place finish on turf four days earlier and paid $39 in the second half of the daily double. Valid Delta, coming off a last-place finish in a $35,000 turf route, beat $50,000 sprinters at $41. Seattle Colony, eighth on grass last out, won an allowance at $26.80 as the longest shot in the field. The last race went to turf-to-dirt Totem Zone, by eight lengths at $12.60.

The main track at Saratoga underwent a subtle renovation in 2006, a year after the arrival of John Passero as track superintendent, and the surface was exceptionally tiring in the long sprints out of the chute, and also in the two-turn routes; horses that expended too much energy in the early going paid a heavy price in the stretch

Note the difference between renewals of several major stakes:

2005 TEST — 22.42, 45.46, 1:09.98, 1:22.76
2006 TEST — 22.02, 44.67, 1:10.03, 1:24.13

2005 A.G. VANDERBILT — 21.66, 43.85, 1:08.69
2006 A.G. VANDERBILT — 21.90, 45.01, 1:10.21

2005 JIM DANDY — 23.86, 47.38, 1:11.54, 1:36.35, 1:49.50
2006 JIM DANDY — 23.89, 47.36, 1:11.33, 1:37.12, 1:50.50

2005 WHITNEY — 23.56, 46.41, 1:09.76, 1:34.81, 1:48.33
2006 WHITNEY — 23.07, 47.21, 1:11.38, 1:36.73, 1:49.06

- The last furlong of the Test went from 12.78 in 2005 to 14.10 in 2006.
- The quarter splits of the 2005 Vanderbilt were 21.66, 22.19, and 24.84. In 2006 they were 21.90, 23.11, 25.20; note the second-quarter turn time was nearly a full second slower.
- Flower Alley ran the last three-eighths of his Jim Dandy in 37.96. A year later, the supremely talented Bernardini required 39.17.
- Particularly noteworthy was the Whitney comparison, with the eventual Horse of the Year in each field. The races set up very differently, because Commentator went to the front through fast splits and dared Saint Liam to catch him, and the last three-eighths went in 38.57, including a last eighth in 13.52. The 2006 match-up unfolded through a slower early pace, but given the nature of the track and how it was affecting come-home times, it was nevertheless quite impressive that the corresponding fractions were 37.68 and 12.33. The race stamped Invasor as the genuine article, and Sun King ran the season's finest losing race to miss in a head-bob finish.

Passero explained that loose cushion depth on the top layer of the surface was at 4½ to 4¾ inches in 2006. "That's probably a little more than last year, and quite a bit more than the year before," he said. "I'm not a handicapper, but if you're trying to run 21 and 44 you're going to get tired. Guys here are trying to zing 'em a little bit, and it catches up with you."

It caught up to the leaders in the Adirondack Stakes for 2-year-old fillies, in which the Todd Pletcher-trained Octave wore down favored Magical Ride through a last sixteenth of a mile in a laborious 7.13 seconds.

"It's a tiring track," noted Pletcher. "From the eighth pole to the wire, you have to be a very fit horse to get there."

When the New York-bred filly Samsincharge cut back from a turf route to win the seven-furlong Rogues Walk Stakes at better than 11–1 on opening day, track profilers got a sneak preview of the turf-to-dirt parade that was to follow in mid-August, when four more turf-to-dirt types won seven-furlong races on the tiring main track in quick succession, and lit up the tote board at odds ranging from 6–1 to 32–1:

Samsincharge									

Past performance chart for Samsincharge

Like Samsincharge, Knox, D Money, and Rocky Blue were turning back from routes:

Knox									

Past performance chart for Knox

D Money
Own: Monosson Daniel

B. c. 3 (Mar) SARAUG04 $40,000
Sire: Phone Trick (Clever Trick) $15,000
Dam: Naskra's de Light (Star de Naskra)
Br: Daniel Monosson (NY)
Tr: Carroll D W II(26 3 1 5 .12) 2006:(171 13 .08)

Life	9	2	0	1	$53,250	82	D.Fst	5	1	0	1	$27,494	82
2006	7	2	0	1	$51,810	82	Wet(374)	1	0	0	0	$210	49
							Synth	0	0	0	0	$0	-
2005	2	M	0	0	$1,440	49	Turf(229)	3	1	0	0	$25,546	61
Sar	1	1	0	0	$19,800	82	Dst(354)	1	1	0	0	$19,800	82

13Aug06- 1Sar fst 7f :23 :461 1:111 1:242 Clm 25000(25-20) 82 1 6 610 610 22½ 1nk Hill C L120 32.50 82- 22 *D Money*120nk *Low Creek*120¾ Unleaded Bridel1201¾ Along in time outside 7
26May06- 9Bel fm 1⅛ Ⓣ :491 1:132 1:37 1:484 3↑ Ⓢ Alw 44000N1x 18 5 98¾ 96¼ 98 927 930 Migliore R L118 9.90 51- 20 Dormeletto1184¾ *New Testament*1161½ Just Jack n' Water116½ Outrun 9
20May06- 5Bel yl 1 Ⓣ :234 :482 1:14 1:391 3↑ Ⓢ Alw 44000N1x 61 4 97 94¾ 116 105¼ 79¼ Fragoso P L118 28.00 55- 35 PrimeDimond1163½ *MeetMyBuddy*1221 Decourcey122¾ Inside, no response 12
28Apr06- 6Aqu fm 1 Ⓣ :251 :503 1:16 1:404 3↑ Ⓢ Md Sp Wt 42k 60 2 67½ 67¾ 54½ 31½ 13½ Hill C L118 *1.20e 70- 21 D Money1183½ *Big Boo Boo*118½ Makweti1181 Came wide, drew clear 8
12Apr06- 6Aqu fst 1 :231 :46 1:114 1:39 3↑ Ⓢ Md Sp Wt 42k 53 8 97¼ 76 62¾ 44 36 Migliore R L118 13.50 66- 24 Raff and Tumble118nk Dot'sbrush1185¾ *D Money*1181 Mild rally inside 10
8Mar06- 7Aqu fst 170 ⊡ :241 :483 1:14 1:444 3↑ Ⓢ Md Sp Wt 42k 56 8 810 87¾ 811 67¾ 46 Hill C L116 26.00 70- 23 Colors of Art1161¼ *Raff and Tumble*1161¼ *Ice Chief*1233½ Mild rally outside 10
16Feb06- 4Aqu fst 6f ⊡ :223 :461 :584 1:113 Ⓢ Md Sp Wt 41k 49 8 4 915 815 818 611½ Kaenel K5 L115 26.75 69- 16 *SaratogaJet*1201½ *PreciseAction*1205½ BckDoorDel113¾ Came wide, no rally 10
10Dec05- 4Aqu gd 170 ⊡ :234 :482 1:133 1:44 Ⓢ Md Sp Wt 42k 49 9 85¼ 84¼ 79 77½ 78¼ Fragoso P L120 b 8.70 70- 14 Share the World120¾ River Squire1202 Herbert T1202¼ No response 10
18Nov05- 4Aqu fst 5½f :222 :462 :583 1:051 Ⓢ Md Sp Wt 41k 42 1 10 1017 810 513 58½ Hill C5 L115 b 12.20 - - Everblzing1151¼ MidtownSouth1202¼ *HoustonRequest*1202¼ Greenly inside 11

WORKS: Aug8 Sar tr.t 4f fst :52 B *21/22* Jly31 Sar tr.t 3f fst :363 B *3/9* Jly21 Bel tr.t 5f fst 1:031 B *11/15* Jly16 Bel tr.t 4f fst :483 B *5/40* Jly10 Bel tr.t 4f fst :503 B *8/12* Jun13 Bel tr.t 4f fst :482 B *7/28*
TRAINER: 1-7Days(9 .00 $0.00) Dirt(178 .07 $1.42) Sprint(101 .05 $1.78) Stakes(8 .12 $1.08)

Rocky Blue
Own: Fox Hill Farms Inc

B. c. 3 (Feb) EASSEP04 $30,000
Sire: Citidancer (Dixieland Band) $7,500
Dam: Bald Beauty (Baldski)
Br: Huckleberry Farm LLC (Md)
Tr: Klesaris Steve(6 2 0 2 .33) 2006:(393 121 .31)

Life	11	3	2	2	$87,962	84	D.Fst	7	2	1	0	$48,282	84
2006	7	2	1	2	$54,302	84	Wet(372)	2	1	0	1	$27,580	74
							Synth	0	0	0	0	$0	-
2005	4	1	1	0	$33,660	73	Turf(277)	2	0	1	1	$12,100	81
Sar	1	1	0	0	$23,400	84	Dst(365)	1	1	0	0	$23,400	84

16Aug06- 1Sar fst 7f :23 :461 1:11 1:242 Clm 35000 84 3 4 1½ 1hd 13 15¾ Jara F L118 b 6.40 82- 16 Rocky Blue1185¾ Coach Kent118¾ Mr. Mugs1132¼ Drew clear when roused 8
27Jly06- 7Sar fm 1 1/16 Ⓣ :244 :501 1:133 1:43 Clm 40000(40-35) 81 3 41½ 13 12 3nk 31¾ Coa E M L120 b 8.10 82- 14 *Mascot*120nk Solewisher1201½ *Rocky Blue*1201¼ Steadied stretch 10
22Jun06- 9Bel fm 1 Ⓣ :24 :48 1:113 1:35 Clm 50000(50-40) 78 7 31 3½ 31½ 32½ 21 Coa E M L120 b 5.60 84- 14 *Mascot*1191 Rocky Blue1201 *Eye for Style*120½ 3 wide trip, gamely 7
Previously trained by Servis John C 2006(as of 5/13): (115 16 16 20 0.14)
13May06-10Pha fst 170 :23 :47 1:12 1:434 Alw 21577N1x 73 5 43¼ 42 1hd 12½ 11¾ Molina V H L116 b *1.60 82- 20 Rocky Blue1161¾ *Most Bossest*1163 Jurista116¾ Rated wide, drew away 9

WORKS: Aug9 Bel tr.t 3f fst :363 B *4/13* Jly15 Bel 4f fst :502 B *50/74* Jly8 Bel 3f fst :37 B *3/17* Jun18 Bel 3f fst :372 B *12/18*
TRAINER: Turf/Dirt(23 .39 $2.90) Route/Sprint(47 .32 $1.74) Dirt(488 .33 $2.14) Sprint(349 .34 $2.16) Stakes(67 .18 $1.56)

Heathrow was the exception, coming off a turf sprint at the same distance. Even so, his last win more than a year earlier was also the result of a turf-to-dirt switch, which certainly opened him up for consideration in any kind of a meaningful "spread" play in multirace exotics:

Heathrow
Own: Winning Move Stable Celebrity Group S

Ch. g. 5 (Feb)
Sire: A. P Jet (Fappiano) $5,000
Dam: Bonnie Thames (Bonnie Tim)
Br: Kathleen M. O'Connell (NY)
Tr: Contessa Gary C(105 8 17 15 .08) 2006:(945 167 .18)

Life	26	3	4	5	$168,516	79	D.Fst	19	3	3	4	$150,061	79
2006	9	1	2	3	$65,179	78	Wet(324)	5	0	1	1	$18,150	73
							Synth	0	0	0	0	$0	-
2005	8	1	1	1	$47,060	78	Turf(215)	2	0	0	0	$305	72
Sar	4	1	1	1	$53,700	78	Dst(303)	5	1	0	0	$35,297	78

11Aug06- 4Sar fst 7f :23 :463 1:121 1:244 3↑ Ⓢ OC 25k/N2x -N 78 1 5 42 41 1½ 13¼ Leparoux J R5 L116 b 15.30 80- 13 Hthrow1163¼ ThTripContinus117nk TrdingPro117nk Got through open rail 8
1Jly06- 7Bel fm 7f Ⓣ :222 :444 1:092 1:214 3↑ Ⓢ OC 30k/N2x -N 64 5 7 64 77¼ 96 89¼ Desormeaux K J L121 20.50 83- 08 Metro Meteor118¾ Drinkwater1211¾ Buff Naked1211 Inside, no response 12
8Jun06- 9Bel sly5 7f ⊗ :222 :453 1:101 1:234 3↑ Ⓢ OC 35k/N2x -N 51 6 7 51¾ 42½ 713 815¼ Prado E S L121 f 4.70 67- 17 NoAllegince1214¼ JustinFun1214¾ Mikethemoondog1211 4 wide trip, tired 9
13May06- 1Bel fst 1 :224 :453 1:102 1:37 3↑ Ⓢ OC 25k/N2x -N 78 5 32½ 2½ 21½ 25 34¾ Prado E S L122 6.70 71- 18 TouchdownKd1244¼ SkngthMony122½ Hthrow1221¼ Outfinished for place 6
8Apr06- 6Aqu sly5 1 :232 :471 1:13 1:391 3↑ Ⓢ OC 25k/N2x -N 66 9 51½ 31 2hd 3nk 53 Coa E M L122 f 4.90 68- 23 FreddytheCap122nk PyAttention1221¼ DH Nrgnsett122 4 wide move, faded 9
22Mar06- 7Aqu fst 1 ⊡ :234 :474 1:131 1:374 3↑ Ⓢ OC 25k/N2x -N 73 1 44 41 51¼ 31½ 32½ Coa E M L122 f 6.70 91- 16 TouchdownKd1221¾ PltnumCoupl116¾ Hthrow12212¼ Good finish outside 7
16Feb06- 9Aqu fst 170 ⊡ :242 :484 1:14 1:434 4↑ Ⓢ OC 25k/N2x -N 76 3 53¾ 41 41¾ 31½ 21¾ Coa E M L118 6.70 79- 18 Interior Designer1181¾ Heathrow118¾ Drizzly118hd Split rivals, gamely 9
25Jan06- 8Aqu fst 1 1/16 ⊡ :224 :47 1:124 1:463 4↑ Ⓢ OC 25k/N2x -N 76 3 79½ 310 2½ 2hd 21½ Coa E M L118 5.00 75- 22 Wellgiven1181½ Heathrow1181 *Dynergy*114¾ Bumped 1/2 mile pole 11
7Jan06- 7Aqu fst 170 ⊡ :24 :474 1:123 1:421 4↑ Ⓢ OC 25k/N2x -N 75 7 32 31½ 2hd 2hd 31½ Coa E M L118 12.20 87- 05 Step It Up118nk Drizzly1231¼ Heathrow118nk Shuffled back late 9
17Dec05-10Aqu fst 1 1/16 ⊡ :234 :48 1:122 1:434 3↑ Ⓢ OC 30k/N2x -N 75 7 2½ 2½ 3½ 23½ 56 Hill C5 L115 23.40 85- 13 Mr. Malaprop1184¼ Drizzly1171 Dynergy114¾ Pressed pace, weakened 12
27Nov05- 6Aqu fst 1 :23 :461 1:112 1:372 3↑ Ⓢ Alw 46000N2x 46 2 61¾ 1hd 74¾ 810 921¾ Gryder A T L120 19.50 56- 26 MetallicMoon1204¼ RpidRickey120nk *BoldDecision*118nk Vied inside, tired 11
21Oct05- 5Bel fst 1 :224 :453 1:102 1:363 3↑ Ⓢ Alw 46000N2x 78 1 58½ 510 53 44 45½ Santos J A L120 5.20 72- 22 Meniscus117½ Step It Up1192¾ Rapid Rickey1242¼ 4 wide move, tired 6
24Sep05-10Bel fst 7f :224 :454 1:103 1:234 3↑ Ⓢ Alw 45000N2x 64 6 4 61¾ 52¼ 47½ 411¼ Migliore R L121 4.80 70- 20 PreciseMotion1183¾ Calculator1214¼ FertheCpe1243¼ Bumped after start 9
21Aug05- 3Sar gd 1⅛ :483 1:133 1:393 1:533 3↑ Ⓢ Alw 50000N2x 73 4 43 42½ 32 25 25¼ Migliore R L120 3.30 62- 29 SesideSlute1235¼ Hethrow1206¼ Goldfingrstouch115½ 3 wide, second best 7
5Aug05- 7Sar fst 1⅛ :492 1:133 1:391 1:53 3↑ Ⓢ Alw 50000N2x 77 3 42½ 41½ 42 31½ 31¾ Migliore R L122 8.60 68- 30 YankeeMagic119nk *SeasideSalute*1241½ Heathrow1224 Good finish outside 7
4Jly05- 1Bel fst 7½f :23 :461 1:112 1:303 3↑ Ⓢ Alw 43000N1x 77 5 3 41 51½ 13 17½ Migliore R L122 2.55 84- 13 Heathrow1227½ Flight Ready117½ GeyserRoad117¾ Drew away under drive 8
15Jun05- 6Bel fm 1 Ⓣ :233 :463 1:103 1:354 3↑ Ⓢ Alw 44000N1x 72 10 72¼ 72¾ 42 66 67 Migliore R L122 35.75 75- 18 Dave122hd *Sicilian Boy*122½ LegendarySquire1223½ Wide throughout, tired 10

WORKS: Aug6 Bel 4f fst :49 B *11/42* Jly25 Bel 4f fst :51 B *41/53* May28 Bel 4f fst :49 B *29/63*
TRAINER: 1-7Days(41 .12 $0.77) Dirt(1238 .18 $1.64) Sprint(720 .15 $1.37) Stakes(134 .16 $2.17)

Bankroll Allocation and Strategy

In writing the record-keeping chapter for the 2001 DRF Press book *Bet with the Best,* I explained in the section on betting logs that I was primarily a win bettor. Repeated experience, along with a penchant for recording every aspect of my wagers that was borderline obsessive-compulsive, had convinced me this was the arena where I fared best. Consequently, the extent of my involvement with exotic wagers was little more than hedging win bets in protective exactas and trifectas.

In a most fortuitous development, however, the pick four (discussed shortly) was instituted in New York that year, and that bet now accounts for anywhere from 60 to 75 percent of my play.

Before the pick four, my money-management plan was to use what I referred to as, for want of a better term, the 6-4-2 method. The numbers reflected the percentage of bankroll to be risked, depending on the situation.

Horses deemed mortal locks with at least a 50 percent chance of winning rated an investment of 6 percent when offered at 2–1 or better. Getting such a bargain, obviously, is a situation that comes along only slightly more often than Halley's Comet.

More common were the bread-and-butter propositions that rated an exposure of 4 percent, i.e., horses in the odds range of 3–1 to 6–1 regarded as overlays.

To stay involved and attentive with the other races, which were the vast majority, I allowed myself up to three "action" bets a day at the level of 2 percent. These were the longshots at 8–1 and up that were somewhat intriguing for whatever reason, and would be a thorn in my side if they won without me. If I had already lost a 6-percent wager, or two 4-percent wagers, my action-bet privileges for that day were revoked.

Like system-peddling charlatans and phony phone-service touts, I'd love to tell you the track was my personal ATM for making sizable and regular withdrawals, but that was hardly the case. It was a sound and conservative approach, and I was always in action, but I just wasn't making that much money.

The reality is, even the finest handicappers in the world will have a hard time quitting their day jobs if they are betting mostly to win.

For the sake of illustration, assume that a 10 percent edge on an average of three prime bets daily (about 900 bets in a year) has been achieved:

A $20 bettor would invest $18,000 annually, for a profit of approximately $1,800.

A $200 bettor would invest $180,000 annually, for a profit of approximately $18,000.

A $400 bettor would invest $360,000 annually, for a profit of approximately $36,000.

None of these totals includes expenses; nor do the larger amounts factor in the psychological stress that goes along with daily cash outlays in the thousands of dollars, especially when the inevitable losing streaks occur.

And 36 grand a year isn't exactly going to pimp your ride.

But the kicker is that *even the very best* players have a much smaller edge than 10 percent. Ernie Dahlman, a renowned big bettor featured in a 2001 *New York Times Magazine* article, reportedly had an edge of only 3 to 4 percent. The catch is that he churned as much as $18 million through the windows during the course of a year!

Nowadays, most successful bettors are not steely-nerved grinders like Dahlman; they are exotic bettors whose annual bottom-line profits can be traced to a handful of big scores.

For seriously profit-motivated players with $5,000 in start-up capital, a recommended strategy divides it 40/60 into two separate bankrolls: $2,000 for overlays in the win pool, and $3,000 for exotic wagers.

For win bets, I now try to keep the vast majority of wagers at 2 percent of bankroll or less. This is my comfort zone where there is no hesitation forsaking the top choice in favor of the second or third choice, if that is what the odds dictate.

Whenever the bank grows in excess of $2,500, consider "paying yourself" and starting back at $2,000. For example, if the bank is hovering around $2,400 and a nice hit brings it up to $2,750, skim $750 off the top and start back at $2,000. Bringing about these paydays a handful of times during the year is a reasonable goal, and it then becomes an individual decision whether to increase the stakes, or take the money and spend it outside the realm of racing.

For exotic bets—in my case an occasional pick three or pick six, but usually the pick four—I tend to be more adventurous, and will risk as much as 6 percent of bankroll if a situation looks ripe for a score.

Unless you have significantly more than $3,000 to devote to exotic wagering, limit pick-6 wagers to the following situations:

- Take a percentage as a partner in a betting syndicate. It's far more realistic to have a 10 percent stake in a group play of $640 than to put in a $64 ticket on your own.
- If the sequence truly looks like it could be a parade of chalk, *and* there is a large carryover pool, consider putting in a small ticket. There was a two-day carryover of $262,675 into the May 31, 2007, card at Belmont Park, for example, and nearly $1.2 million was bet into it. When a string of logical winners came in, only one as high as 4–1, the payoff was $2,463 (a 20 percent bonus over the win parlay) to each of 311 winners.
- On the last day of a race meet, when the entire pool must be distributed regardless of whether there are any tickets with all six winners.

Value Pays the Rent

I know some excellent bettors who make an odds-line for every horse in every race, and others who don't formalize written odds-lines but nevertheless have a clear idea of what price they will accept on a horse.

Either way, it is something win bettors need to do. No one is saying you have to figure out exactly what the fair odds are, because no human can do that and neither can the world's most powerful computer. But you do need to develop some kind of a routine whereby you (a) designate the contenders and (b) assess their chances to the best of your ability. This is the essence of handicapping. Success or failure depends on your line-making skill and sound money management.

The vast majority of bettors spend most of their time looking into every nook and cranny of the past performances in search of hidden minutia that leads to the "right" horse. There is no such animal. Once handicappers have the contenders, they are much better served spending an equal amount of time and thought making a line.

In *Blink: The Power of Thinking Without Thinking,* author Malcolm Gladwell recounted a famous study in which a group of psychologists were given the case of a 29-year-old war veteran. In the first stage of the experiment, the psychologists received only the most basic information; in the second stage, they received a page-and-a-half summary of his childhood; in the third stage, they received two more pages of background on the veteran's high-school and college years; finally, they were given a detailed account of the veteran's time in the army and his later activities. After each stage, the psychologists were asked to answer a 25-item multiple-choice test about the veteran. The researcher found that as he gave the psychologists more and more information, their confidence in the accuracy of their diagnoses increased dramatically, but in reality they weren't getting more accurate.

"As they received more information," the researcher concluded, "their certainty about their own decisions became entirely out of proportion to the actual correctness of those decisions."

Steve Fierro, linemaker extraordinaire, put that same idea in a nutshell in his excellent book *The Four Quarters of Horse Investing* when he wrote, "If you don't have a contender selection process that gets to your contenders in any race within five to seven minutes, on average, you better get another one."

To construct a betting line, you will need to refer to the following odds-percentage table:

ODDS TO PERCENT CONVERSION TABLE

Odds	Percent	Odds	Percent
1-10	90.91	4-1	20.00
1-5	83.33	9-2	18.19
2-5	71.42	5-1	16.67
1-2	66.67	6-1	14.29
3-5	62.50	7-1	12.50
4-5	55.56	8-1	11.11
1-1	50.00	9-1	10.00
6-5	45.45	10-1	9.09
7-5	41.67	11-1	8.33
3-2	40.00	12-1	7.69
8-5	38.46	15-1	6.25
9-5	35.71	20-1	4.76
2-1	33.33	25-1	3.85
5-2	28.57	30-1	3.25
3-1	25.00	50-1	1.96
7-2	22.22	99-1	1.00

The betting line always adds up to 100 percent (the chance that someone will win the race), and it is different from the morning line in newspapers and track programs, which typically adds up to 120–125 percent to reflect takeout and breakage.

Morning lines are merely an estimate of how the crowd will bet the race, and their quality varies greatly from circuit to circuit. Moreover, morning-line makers are usually instructed to inflate the odds on prohibitive-looking favorites in an attempt to make them more enticing, so that a horse everyone knows will be odds-on may be listed at 6–5 in the track program.

Don't worry about the decimals; rounding off is fine. With a little practice, you won't even need to refer to the chart.

Depending on a race's level of difficulty (one of the things making a line forces you to consider), I designate a certain percentage of points to my noncontenders as a way of recognizing that chaos happens. In a five-horse field, that percentage may be nothing at all, or perhaps 5 to 10 points; in a 20-horse Kentucky Derby stampede, it might be as much as 30 to 35 points.

Usually it averages out to about 20 points, with the remaining 80 points divided up by the contenders.

A typical race contains a handful of contenders with some kind of a chance; the task is figuring what those chances are, and betting the horse(s) perceived to offer a bonus above and beyond fair odds, if any.

Importantly, this does not necessarily mean betting a high-odds horse just because of its price. Consider the following scenario in a five-horse field:

Horse	Your line	Actual odds
A	9–5	6–5
B	3–1	2–1
C	5–1	4–1
D	6–1	8–1
E	10–1	8–1

With just five horses to consider, we've assigned odds to all of them, so the betting line adds up to about 100 points: (9–5 = 35; 3–1 = 25; 5–1 = 16; 6–1 = 14; 10–1 = 9).

In this situation, the D horse is the only apparent overlay, because he has been pegged at 6–1, and he is going off at 8–1.

Everyone else's odds are lower than the betting line, so they are underlays, and cannot be bet.

A lot of bettors consider D to be an overlay, but in this situation that is not the case.

To begin with, odds of 8–1 really aren't much of a bonus over fair odds of 6–1, considering 6–1 is 14 percentage points and 8–1 is 11 percentage points, a negligible three-point difference. (Though it doesn't seem like it, getting 5–2 on a 2–1 shot is actually a bigger overlay when looked at in terms of percentages.)

But the most important thing is that D would not be a bet at 6–1 or 8–1, or even 10–1 or 12–1. This horse is exactly the kind of proposition that gets bettors into trouble, because he is already deemed to have less than a random chance of winning the race. If everything were absolutely equal about each member of the field, the random chance for any of them winning would be 1 in 5. Therefore, setting the odds at 6–1 for Horse D effectively means we believe he has less than a random chance of winning.

Horses like this are constantly espoused as offering "value" by public handicappers on television and in print, but they are usually fool's gold and a sure-fire way to get a losing streak snowballing down the hill. If this type of horse is sitting up there on the board at 15–1 or 20–1 and you cannot bear the thought of it winning without you, go ahead and make a small "action" bet, but nothing more. Win bettors will find they can make a small fortune with this type of overlay, but only if they start with a large fortune.

If you are considering the race as a "spread" for multirace exotic wagers such as the pick four, such horses may be thrown into the mix if they have any redeeming aspects in their records, but they should carry far less weight in the play than horses judged to be far more likely win candidates.

Let's go through some example races:

7 Belmont Park 1 1/16 MILES (1:392) OC 75k/N1X Purse $46,000 (UP TO $8,740 NYSBFOA)

For Three Year Olds And Upward Which Have Never Won A Race Other Than Maiden, Claiming, Starter, Or Restricted Or Which Have Never Won Two Races Or Optional Claiming Price Of $75,000 For Three Year Olds. Three Year Olds, 119 lbs.;Older, 123 lbs. Non-winners of $19,200 at a mile or over since April 9 Allowed 2 lbs.

Coupled – Meniscus and Organizer

---

2 Zinzan
Own: Derrick Smith Michael Tabor
White — Purple, White Seams, White Stripes On
VELAZQUEZ J R (3 2 0 0 .67) 2006: (365 106 .29)

B. c. 3 (Mar) KEESEP04 $1,300,000
Sire: Grand Slam (Gone West) $50,000
Dam: Sheza Honey (Honey Jay)
Br: Justice Farm Inc Greg Justice & Steve Justice (Ky)
Tr: Pletcher Todd A(37 11 12 3 .30) 2006:(502 153 .30)

L 117

Life	3	1	1	0	$38,265	81	D.Fst	2	1	1	0	$37,945	81
2006	3	1	1	0	$38,265	81	Wet(348)	1	0	0	0	$320	56
2005	0	M	0	0	$0	-	Turf(318)	0	0	0	0	$0	-
Bel	0	0	0	0	$0	-	Dst(336)	0	0	0	0	$0	-

28Apr06-10Kee fst 7f :223 :454 1:111 1:242 Md Sp Wt 50k 81 8 1 3½ 3½ 1½ 16½ Gomez G K L120 *1.50 86- 15 Zinzan1206½ AGiantValentine1203¾ ProphetJohn1201 Forced pace,driving 9
25Mar06-4GP fst 6½f :231 :463 1:112 1:172 Md Sp Wt 32k 72 5 3 2½ 2½ 21 25½ Bejarano R L122 3.00 79- 17 Goods1225½ Zinzan1221 Mutate122nk No match, held 2nd 8
4Feb06-3GP slys 6f :214 :45 :572 1:094 Md Sp Wt 32k 56 6 5 66½ 65 58½ 511¾ Velazquez J R L122 3.50 83- 04 Protagonus1221¾ Steel the Glory1228½ Crafty Chip122nk Failed to menace 7

WORKS: Jun5 Sar tr.t 4f my :522 B 2/2 May28 Sar tr.t 4f fst :512 B 16/17 ●May21 Sar tr.t 4f fst :494 B 1/8 May14 Sar tr.t 4f fst :503 B 14/22 Apr22 Kee tr.t ◇4f fst :52 B 7/9 ●Apr15 Kee 5f fst 1:00 B 1/14
TRAINER: Sprint/Route(172 .31 $2.25) 31-60Days(527 .31 $2.17) WonLastStart(354 .31 $2.09) Dirt(1049 .29 $1.96) Routes(972 .27 $2.06) Alw(437 .29 $2.11) J/T 2005-06 BEL(144 .26 $1.84) J/T 2005-06(622 .30 $1.98)

---

1 Meniscus
Own: Majesty Stud
Red — Royal Blue And Magenta Pink Diamonds
VELASQUEZ C (131 19 21 19 .15) 2006: (737 119 .16)

B. g. 4 (May)
Sire: Raffie's Majesty (Cormorant) $3,000
Dam: Imaginary (Rahy)
Br: Majesty Stud Inc (NY)
Tr: Galluscio Dominic G(31 1 6 7 .03) 2006:(130 22 .17)

L 121

Life	7	3	1	0	$98,975	92	D.Fst	6	3	1	0	$91,475	92
2005	7	3	1	0	$98,975	92	Wet(361)	1	0	0	0	$7,500	59
2004	0	M	0	0	$0	-	Turf(184)	0	0	0	0	$0	-
Bel	4	3	1	0	$87,800	92	Dst(379)	4	1	1	0	$39,275	91

Entered 8Jun06- 8 BEL
4Dec05-7Aqu fst 170 ⊡ :233 :473 1:132 1:424 3↑ OC 75k/N1x-N 77 2 44½ 67 64½ 68½ 68 Garcia Alan L122 fb 4.80 76- 19 BroadAcres1111¼ EmBAye1143¼ DancingJim1182¾ Lost whip deep stretch 8
21Oct05-5Bel fst 1 :224 :453 1:102 1:363 3↑ ⓈAlw 46000N2x 88 2 25 44½ 42½ 3½ 1½ Velasquez C L117 b *1.25 78- 22 Meniscus117½ Step It Up1192¾ Rapid Rickey1242¼ 3 wide move, prevailed 6
3Aug05-8Sar slys 1⅛ :463 1:113 1:384 1:53 ⓇNYStallion250k 59 1 33½ 34 48¼ 415 521¾ Velasquez C L119 b 4.30e 48- 35 GoldndRoss1236¾ GllopngGrcr1214¾ WstrnGlxy1159¾ Chased inside, tired 7
16Jly05-8FL fst 1 1/16 :24 :472 1:12 1:433 ⓈNYDerby168k 63 7 97¼ 96 75½ 611 517¾ Davila M A Jr L117 b 10.40 86- 12 Accountforthgold1213 GoldndRoss1246½ NughtyNwYorkr1216¾ No solid bid 10
29Jun05-5Bel fst 1 1/16 :231 :463 1:104 1:414 3↑ ⓈAlw 46000N2x 89 1 1½ 1½ 11½ 2hd 2nk Velasquez C L119 b *.45 91- 12 Tergesti117nk Meniscus1195 Rosie's Big Boy122no Dug in gamely on rail 8
2Jun05-2Bel fst 1 1/16 :233 :47 1:113 1:431 3↑ ⓈAlw 43120N1x 91 1 1hd 1½ 13½ 110 110¼ Velasquez C L117 b *.60 84- 18 Meniscus11710¼ SignoreWillim1221¾ EdgRod1195¾ When asked, ridden out 5
8May05-9Bel fst 7½f :23 :46 1:102 1:292 3↑ ⓈMd Sp Wt 41k 92 6 8 34½ 22½ 2hd 1½ Velasquez C L118 b 13.40 90- 15 Meniscus118½ Soulshine11819½ Keep 'Em Up There1241¼ Bumped stretch 9

WORKS: May28 Bel 5f fst 1:00 H 3/29 May21 Bel 5f fst 1:03 B 48/73 May14 Bel 5f fst 1:03 B 51/63
TRAINER: +180Days(15 .07 $0.39) Dirt(434 .16 $1.46) Routes(246 .16 $1.50) Alw(100 .12 $1.18) J/T 2005-06 BEL(25 .20 $2.32) J/T 2005-06(41 .22 $2.06)

1a Organizer
Own: Majesty Stud
Red — Royal Blue And Magenta Pink Diamonds
COA E M (165 29 23 23 .18) 2006: (688 145 .21)

Dk. b or br c. 4 (Mar)
Sire: Raffie's Majesty (Cormorant) $3,000
Dam: Treasure Always (Summer Squall)
Br: Majesty Stud LLC (NY)
Tr: Galluscio Dominic G(31 1 6 7 .03) 2006:(130 22 .17)

L 121

Life	10	3	5	0	$179,600	94	D.Fst	4	1	2	0	$43,500	83
2005	8	3	3	0	$163,000	94	Wet(355)	6	2	3	0	$136,100	94
2004	2	M	2	0	$16,600	77	Turf(160)	0	0	0	0	$0	-
Bel	5	2	3	0	$119,200	94	Dst(375)	3	1	2	0	$44,800	86

Entered 8Jun06- 8 BEL
12Nov05-7Aqu fst 1⅛ :482 1:124 1:38 1:51 3↑ OC 75k/N1x-N 83 6 34 45 33 33½ 45½ Coa E M L122 f 3.45 79- 19 MsterCommnd1221½ ApprovdbyDyln1132¼ Gorbsh1131¾ 3 wide move, faded 9
22Oct05-10Bel slys 1⅛ :453 1:10 1:363 1:504 3↑ ⓈEmpirClscH250k 94 5 32 34 31½ 1½ 21 Dominguez R A L115 f 13.30 76- 30 Spite the Devil1191 Organizer1151¼ Carminooch113nk Led late, caught 10
17Sep05-4Bel gd 1 1/16 ⊗ :232 :47 1:121 1:441 3↑ ⓈAlw 46000N2x 86 7 34 32½ 2hd 11½ 13¾ Coa E M L117 f *1.10 79- 21 Organizer1173¾ Emotrin121hd Sideways Glance1175½ 3 wide move, clear 9
20Aug05-8Sar mys 1⅛ :471 1:124 1:392 1:533 3↑ ⓈAlw 48000N1x 82 2 22 23½ 21 1hd 12½ Dominguez R A L117 f 5.40 67- 35 Orgnzr1172½ Nhssltdcstl1173¼ MdnghtSmmt1222½ When ready, drew clear 7
3Aug05-8Sar slys 1⅛ :463 1:113 1:384 1:53 ⓇNYStallion250k 60 7 48½ 56 513 517 421¼ Coa E M L115 f 4.30e 49- 35 GoldndRoss1236¾ GllopngGrocr1214¾ WstrnGlxy1159¾ 4 wide, no response 7
13Jly05-2Bel mys 1 1/16 :23 :463 1:121 1:454 3↑ ⓈAlw 43120N1x 65 1 46 43½ 2½ 25½ 27½ Coa E M L116 *.60e 63- 38 YankeeMagic1187½ Organizer1163 ChnceuxVous11119¼ 3 wide, second best 5
25Jun05-4Bel fst 7f :221 :451 1:102 1:233 3↑ ⓈMd Sp Wt 41k 77 9 2 2hd 2hd 12½ 17½ Coa E M L118 f *1.65 82- 15 Orgnizr1187½ FirstExprssion1181¾ OutforJustic118¾ Widened under drive 10
7Jan05-4Aqu gd 1⅛ ⊡ :473 1:133 1:402 1:534 ⓈMd Sp Wt 42k 62 11 2½ 2½ 22½ 27 28¾ Gryder A T L120 *1.05 66- 20 Liquid Romance1208¾ Organizer1207 Breeze On1204½ Second best 12
15Dec04-1Aqu fst 170 ⊡ :23 :48 1:142 1:434 ⓈMd Sp Wt 42k 77 3 11½ 11½ 11 11 21¼ Gryder A T L120 2.75 78- 23 StormThf1201¼ Orgnzr1202½ Twooutsnthnnth12013 Bumped st, outfinished 9
10Oct04-2Bel fst 6f :223 :461 :584 1:113 ⓈMd Sp Wt 41k 63 2 1 88¼ 65¼ 48 23 Gryder A T L119 21.50 78- 16 Summerland1193 Organizer119¾ Just in Fun1191¾ Altered course stretch 13

WORKS: Jun5 Bel 4f my :47 H 3/15 May29 Bel 5f fst 1:012 B 6/25 May22 Bel 5f fst 1:014 B 10/26 May15 Bel 3f fst :39 B 15/16
TRAINER: +180Days(15 .07 $0.39) Dirt(434 .16 $1.46) Routes(246 .16 $1.50) Alw(100 .12 $1.18) J/T 2005-06 BEL(40 .18 $1.60) J/T 2005-06(106 .27 $1.79)

---

3 Forest Phantom
Own: Moss Maggi
Blue — Royal Blue, Lime Green Sash, Lime Cuffs
SMITH M E (89 10 18 6 .11) 2006: (324 24 .07)

Dk. b or br g. 3 (Feb)
Sire: Running Stag (Cozzene) $5,000
Dam: Luck Abounds (Technology)
Br: Adena Springs (Fla)
Tr: Contessa Gary C(86 8 18 15 .09) 2006:(407 77 .19)

L 117

Life	5	1	3	0	$39,310	94	D.Fst	4	1	2	0	$30,510	94
2006	5	1	3	0	$39,310	94	Wet(324)	1	0	1	0	$8,800	76
2005	0	M	0	0	$0	-	Turf(196)	0	0	0	0	$0	-
Bel	2	0	2	0	$18,000	94	Dst(304)	1	0	1	0	$8,800	76

19May06-2Bel mys 1 1/16 :242 :48 1:13 1:45 3↑ Alw 50000s 76 2 41 43 41¾ 34 25¾ Desormeaux K J L116 *1.15 69- 26 SenzAglio1215¾ ForestPhntom1161¼ BetterGtBusy1216¼ Rallied for place 5
4May06-5Bel fst 1 :232 :463 1:104 1:344 3↑ Alw 46000N1x 94 5 41 41½ 35 37 28 Desormeaux K J L116 12.80 82- 13 HighFinnce1165 ForestPhntom1163½ MtllicMoon121hd Bump start, rallied 6
7Apr06-9Aqu fst 1 :223 :452 1:11 1:372 Md 50000(50-40) 85 8 58 67½ 42 1½ 11 Desormeaux K J L120 2.50 80- 22 ForstPhntom1201 HonrdNtn120nk OnStrryNt12010¾ 4 wide move, gamely 9
22Mar06-6Aqu fst 1 ⊡ :234 :474 1:131 1:384 3↑ Md 50000(50-40) 73 1 11 1hd 2½ 25½ 27 Dominguez R A L118 3.40 82- 16 CriticalDecision1187 ForestPhntom1187 BlueArdor118¾ Inside, second best 8
23Feb06-4Aqu fst 6f ⊡ :222 :454 :58 1:104 Md c-35000 51 7 6 75½ 68½ 612 511 Morales P5 L115 f 10.90 74- 16 SimpsonsLunch1205¼ Wildr1202½ NothingButKs1201¾ 3 wide trip, no rally 9
Claimed from Stronach Stables for $35,000, Nixon Justin Trainer 2005: (109 35 18 18 0.32)

WORKS: Jun1 Aqu 5f fst 1:014 H 6/6 ●May15 Aqu 4f fst :48 B 1/6 Apr28 Aqu 5f fst 1:02 B 4/7 ●Apr21 Aqu 5f fst 1:002 B 1/13 Mar15 Aqu⊡ 5f fst 1:013 H 5/6 Mar10 Aqu⊡ 1 fst 1:45 H 1/2
TRAINER: Dirt(881 .18 $1.84) Routes(468 .17 $1.58) Alw(233 .16 $2.02) J/T 2005-06 BEL(3 .00 $0.00) J/T 2005-06(5 .00 $0.00)

---

4 Scanlon's Song
Own: Paraneck Stable
Yellow — Black, Cherry Ball, Black 'P,' Cherry
ROJAS R I (4 0 0 0 .00) 2006: (4 0 .00)

Dk. b or br g. 3 (Apr) EASMAY05 $110,000
Sire: Partner's Hero (Danzig) $3,500
Dam: Pauline's Prospect (Allen's Prospect)
Br: Gretchen B Mobberley (Md)
Tr: Klanfer Alan(22 2 1 3 .09) 2006:(93 7 .08)

L 117

Life	7	1	0	1	$76,760	87	D.Fst	4	1	0	1	$33,380	87
2006	7	1	0	1	$76,760	87	Wet(365)	2	0	0	0	$42,000	86
2005	0	M	0	0	$0	-	Turf(264)	1	0	0	0	$1,380	65
Bel	1	0	0	0	$1,000	56	Dst(344)	2	1	0	0	$27,780	87

20May06-8Bel fst 1⅛ :48 1:123 1:371 1:491 PeterPan-G2 56 1 66¼ 52¾ 63½ 921 927¾ Fragoso P L116 fb 85.00 57- 30 Sunriver116nk LewisMichl1163¼ StrongContndr1162½ Finished after a half 9
30Apr06-4Aqu fm 1 1/16 Ⓣ :233 :484 1:134 1:424 Alw 46000N1x 65 5 88¾ 88¼ 710 614 510¼ Jara F L118 b 9.10 83- 11 Carnera1223¼ Church Service118no Galantas1186½ Inside trip, no rally 8
22Apr06-9Pim slys 1⅛ :471 1:12 1:373 1:504 FdrcoTesio124k 77 4 66½ 66 67 411 515¾ Kaenel K L116 fb 3.40 71- 25 AhDay1165½ VegasPly1206½ Putonyerdncinshuz1161 In close start,5wd 1/4 10
8Apr06-8Aqu slys 1⅛ :461 1:11 1:372 1:512 WoodMem-G1 86 9 914 819 613 411 48 Dominguez R A L123 f 38.25 70- 23 Bob and John1231½ Jazil123½ Keyed Entry1236 4 wide run second turn 9
Previously trained by Amonte Frank Jr 2005: (4 0 0 0 0.00)
19Mar06-8Aqu fst 1⅛ ⊡ :484 1:142 1:393 1:514 OC 100k/N1x-N 78 8 75½ 76 75½ 55¼ 35½ Dominguez R A L122 f *2.10 80- 22 MarcosTle1222¾ RobemBlind1182¾ ScnlonsSong1221½ Good finish outside 8
Previously trained by Pedersen Jennifer 2005: (368 31 40 36 0.08)
25Feb06-3Aqu fst 1 1/16 ⊡ :233 :474 1:122 1:441 OC 75k/N1x-N 72 7 75¼ 62¼ 63 59 59¾ Dominguez R A L122 f *.90 79- 10 GreeleysLegcy1225½ MensClub118½ RobemBlind1173¼ 3 wide trip, no rally 7
28Jan06-6Aqu fst 1 1/16 ⊡ :23 :464 1:12 1:453 Md Sp Wt 44k 87 2 1014 1012 98¾ 36½ 12¾ Rivera J L Jr L120 f 29.00 82- 21 ScanlonsSong1202¾ MarcosTale1205 Tasteyville1203¼ Rolled home outside 10

WORKS: ●Jun6 Aqu 4f fst :474 B 1/19 ●Jun1 Aqu 4f fst :463 B 1/7 May17 Aqu 5f my 1:00 H(d) 2/4 May10 Aqu 6f fst 1:142 H 2/2 Apr19 Aqu 5f fst 1:04 B 7/7 ●Mar29 Aqu 6f fst 1:13 H 1/4
TRAINER: Dirt(86 .08 $1.59) Routes(44 .07 $0.47) Alw(22 .05 $2.55) J/T 2005-06 BEL(2 .00 $0.00) J/T 2005-06(2 .00 $0.00)

The day before the 2006 Belmont Stakes, a field of seven (after scratches) contested a first-level allowance route at 1¹⁄₁₆ miles out of the chute.

The even-money favorite was Monsoon Rain, who had earned a Beyer of 96 in his first U.S. start, and first start on dirt. None of the others had matched that figure, but there were two caution flags: Monsoon Rain had run the big figure at six furlongs, and that had been his first start back from a very long layoff of well over 1½ years.

Meniscus and Regent Spirit looked like the logical alternatives, with top figures right around 90. Zinzan and Another Look were lightly raced and from top barns. I was a bit leery of Meniscus, a New York-bred meeting open company off a six-month layoff.

I liked the form/figure pattern of Regent Spirit, who was stretching out to a route after returning from a layoff with a pair of sprints. He had run his best race as a 2-year-old in his third start, winning a maiden race with an 85 Beyer, and was now making the third start of his initial 3-year-old form cycle after slightly exceeding that figure with an 89.

Zinzan and Another Look would need to improve, but there was a chance one or both might do so. Scanlon's Song and Wild Vicar looked like throw-outs.

Monsoon Rain was probably the one to beat, but he was susceptible to a bounce. The betting line vs. actual odds scenario looked like this:

	Betting line	Actual odds
Monsoon Rain	5–2	1–1
Regent Spirit	3–1	5–1
Meniscus	5–1	9–1
Zinzan	6–1	3–1
Another Look	8–1	9–1

The New York crowd loves their chalk, and they predictably pounded Monsoon Rain. But they also went way overboard on Zinzan, presumably because of his trainer, perennial Eclipse winner Todd Pletcher, and the colt's $1.3 million sticker price.

My line in this instance added up to 94 points, which reflected my thinking that if this race were run 100 times, either Scanlon's Song or Wild Vicar might jump up and surprise once in a blue moon, but probably no more often than that.

The choice was between Regent Spirit and Meniscus, who were both overlays. Just looking at the tote board made it seem like Meniscus was the bigger overlay, but if you're playing the percentages, and you should be, it was Regent Spirit who offered the greater value. Real odds of 9–1 compared to assigned odds of 5–1 for Meniscus equals 10 points vs. 16 points, which is a six-point differential. But Regent Spirit at real odds of 5–1 compared to assigned odds of 3–1 equals 16 points vs. 25 points, a nine-point differential.

When there is more than one overlay in a race, my approach is generally to give preference to the lower-odds overlay; they are usually better bargains in terms of the percentages anyway, and they win more often. But in this case, I wouldn't have argued with anyone who considered "dutching" the two overlays. And though exactas aren't my strong suit, I'm sure there were some who bet that way and scored out on this race:

SEVENTH RACE
Belmont
JUNE 9, 2006

1$\frac{1}{16}$ MILES. (1.39²) ALLOWANCE OPTIONAL CLAIMING . Purse $46,000 (UP TO $8,740 NYSBFOA) FOR THREE YEAR OLDS AND UPWARD WHICH HAVE NEVER WON A RACE OTHER THAN MAIDEN, CLAIMING, STARTER, OR RESTRICTED OR WHICH HAVE NEVER WON TWO RACES OR OPTIONAL CLAIMING PRICE OF $75,000 FOR THREE YEAR OLDS. Three Year Olds, 119 lbs.; Older, 123 lbs. Non–winners of $19,200 at a mile or over since April 9 Allowed 2 lbs. (Races where entered for $50,000 or less not considered in allowances).

Value of Race: $46,000 Winner $27,600; second $9,200; third $4,600; fourth $2,300; fifth $1,380; sixth $460; seventh $460. Mutuel Pool $426,960.00 Exacta Pool $358,767.00 Trifecta Pool $273,335.00

Last Raced	Horse	M/Eqt.	A.	Wt	PP	St	$\frac{1}{4}$	$\frac{1}{2}$	$\frac{3}{4}$	Str	Fin	Jockey	Cl'g Pr	Odds $1
20May06 2Pim²	Regent Spirit	L	3	117	5	2	3½	3½	3½	2²	1no	Rose J		5.70
4Dec05 7Aqu⁶	Meniscus	L b	4	121	2	3	1hd	1hd	11	1½	2³	Velasquez C		9.40
13May06 3Bel³	Monsoon Rain	L	4	121	4	5	5½	43½	45½	34½	38½	Castellano J J		1.00
28Apr06 10Kee¹	Zinzan	L	3	117	1	4	2hd	2½	2hd	48	43½	Velazquez J R		3.10
6May06 6Bel¹	Another Look	L	3	117	6	6	66	62½	62½	5hd	53	Desormeaux K J		9.00
20May06 8Bel⁹	Scanlon's Song	L bf	3	117	3	7	7	7	5½	66	611	Rojas R I		20.70
25May06 3Bel³	Wild Vicar	L bf	4	121	7	1	4hd	51	7	7	7	Hill C		19.50

OFF AT 4:07 Start Good. Won driving. Track fast.

TIME :23², :46², 1:10³, 1:35², 1:42 (:23.49, :46.50, 1:10.66, 1:35.57, 1:42.11)

$2 Mutuel Prices:

7 – REGENT SPIRIT	13.40	6.20	3.70
1 – MENISCUS		7.90	4.50
6 – MONSOON RAIN			2.40

$2 EXACTA 7–1 PAID $88.00 $2 TRIFECTA 7–1–6 PAID $225.00

Gr/ro. c, (Mar), by Concerto – Honeytab , by Al Hattab . Trainer Zito Nicholas P. Bred by Kinsman Farm (Fla).

REGENT SPIRIT raced with the pace while three wide, dug in determinedly outside and prevailed after a stiff drive. MENISCUS contested the pace while between rivals and dug in gamely to the finish. MONSOON RAIN was bumped after the start, was hard held early, came wide into the stretch and lacked a rally. ZINZAN contested the pace along the inside and tired in the stretch. ANOTHER LOOK raced wide and had no response when roused. SCANLON'S SONG was bumped after the start, raced wide and tired. WILD VICAR was finished early.

Owners– 1, Kinsman Stable; 2, Majesty Stud; 3, Darley Stable; 4, Tabor Michael B and Smith Derrick; 5, Gainsborough Farm LLC; 6, Paraneck Stable; 7, Turningforhome Stable and Sportsmen Stable

Trainers– 1, Zito Nicholas P; 2, Galluscio Dominic G; 3, Harty Eoin; 4, Pletcher Todd A; 5, McLaughlin Kiaran P; 6, Klanfer Alan; 7, Disanto Glenn B

Scratched– Organizer (08Jun06 8Bel²) , Forest Phantom (19May06 2Bel²) , That's a Given (13May06 4Bel¹)

$2 Daily Double (3–7) Paid $30.20 ; Daily Double Pool $102,467 .
$2 Pick Three (4–3–7) Paid $58.50 ; Pick Three Pool $58,918 .

Let's look at one more race before we move on. The Troy Stakes was a $70,000 restricted stakes at 5½ furlongs on Saratoga's outer turf course:

8 | Saratoga *5½ Furlongs* (Turf). (1:01) ℝTroy70k 3rd Running of THE TROY. Purse $70,000

For Four Year Olds And Upward Which Have Not Won A Graded Sweepstake On The Turf In 2005–06. No nomination fee. A supplemental nomination fee of $200 may be made at time of entry. $500 to enter. Starters to receive a $250 rebate. The added money and all fees to be divided 60% to the owner of the winner, 20% to second, 10% to third, 5% to fourth , 3% to fifth and 2% divided equally among remaining finishers. 123 lbs. TURF: Non–winners of $40,000 on the turf in 2006 allowed 3 lbs.; A sweepstake on the turfin 2005–06 or four races on the turf, 5 lbs.; three races on the turf, 7 lbs. DIRT: Non–winners of a graded Sweepstake on the dirt in 2005–06 allowed 3 lbs.; A sweepstake on the dirt in 2005–06, 5 lbs.; four races, 7 lbs. A presentation will be made to the winning owner. Closed Thursday, August 10, 2006 with 18 Nominations.

1 Safsoof — B. c. 4 (Feb) OBSMAR04 $275,000 — Life 18 4 3 4 $130,863 97
Own: Godolphin Stable — Sire: Gilded Time (Timeless Moment) $12,500 — L 116
Royal Blue, White Chevrons On Sleeves
GOMEZ G K (80 15 13 16 .19) 2006: (747 141 .19)

2 Weigelia — B. h. 5 (Feb) — Life 30 10 5 8 $761,170 109
Own: Balsamo Joseph J — Sire: Safely's Mark (Danzig) $3,000 — L 118
Red, Yellow Dots, Yellow Sleeves, Red
VELAZQUEZ J R (81 13 12 .16) 2006: (555 142 .26)

3 Second in Command — Dk. b or br h. 6 (Feb) — Life 27 6 3 3 $225,122 100
Own: Dubb Michael — Sire: Silver Deputy (Deputy Minister) $30,000 — L 116
Blue, Pink Circle And Rose, Yellow
PRADO E S (90 16 11 14 .18) 2006: (845 161 .19)

4 Yes Yes Yes — B. c. 4 (Feb) FTKJUL03 $150,000 — Life 11 3 5 1 $131,702 103
Own: Team Valor Stables — Sire: Yes It's True (Is It True) $35,000 — L 116
Yellow, Forest Green, Crimson Triangular Panel
JARA F (60 7 3 4 .12) 2006: (462 48 .11)

5 Pisgah
Own: Dunlap Tavner
Green Red, Silver Star, Blue Sleeves, Blue
VELASQUEZ C (98 14 12 13 .14) 2006: (1028 168 .16)

Ch. g. 5 (Apr)
Sire: Good and Tough (Carson City) $3,000
Dam: Ripped (Grey Dawn II*Fr)
Br: Tavner B Dunlap (Ky)
Tr: Lake Scott A(16 1 2 1 .06) 2006:(1392 374 .27)

L 120

Life	28	7	9	4	$294,993	112		
2006	10	4	1	1	$137,791	112		
2005	11	2	5	2	$101,980	108		
Sar ⓣ	0	0	0	0	$0	-		
D.Fst	20	4	8	2	$185,963	112		
Wet(385)	3	0	1	1	$12,530	81		
Turf(338)	5	3	0	1	$96,500	102		
Dstⓣ(387)	5	3	0	1	$96,500	102		

3Aug06-2Pen	fm	5f	ⓣ	:22 :44 :552	3↑ PaGovCupH50k	78	3	7	74¾	810	65½	42¼	Alvarado R Jr	L121 fb	*1.60	95-07	Procret1151½ SouthrnMissil117nk WhosBluffing114½	Rail turn, closed well	9
8Jly06-8Del	yl	*5f	ⓣ	:22 :462 :593	3↑ MoBay55k	102	2	7	75¼	53	22	1½	Alvarado R Jr	L121 fb	*1.70	85-15	Pisgah121½ Max West1236¼ Shades of Sunny1191	Ran down leader	7
29May06-8Pha	fm	5f	ⓣ	:221 :443 :563	3↑ TrfMonstrH100k	94	2	5	62¼	53¾	32½	31¾	Alvarado R Jr	L121 fb	*.50	94-04	Max West1151¾ Yankee Wildcat117hd *Pisgah*1212	In tight turn inside	6
13May06-8Bel	fst	6f		:212 :44 :554 1:082	3↑ BoldRlrH-G3	94	2	5	36	32	34	56¼	Alvarado R Jr	L115 fb	3.65	90-10	Tiger1143½ DarkCheetah1151¾ BishopCourtHill119¾	Inside move turn, tire	5
25Apr06-7Del	fst	6f		:22 :434 :553 1:074	3↑ OC 75k/N$Y-N	112	3	4	12	14	16	16	Alvarado R Jr	L123 b	1.00	102-11	Pisgah1236 Tour of the Cat119¾ Indian Lotus1193½	Kept to his task	5
29Mar06-4GP	fm	5f	ⓣ	:22 :434 :552	4↑ Alw 46000NC	92	5	7	62½	53½	43½	1nk	Alvarado R Jr	L122 fb	*2.30	91-09	*Pisgh*122nk AllHilStormy124no SummerSrvic124nk	Stumbled st, ckd bkstr	7
16Mar06-8GP	fst	6f		:214 :441 :554 1:082	4↑ OC 150k/N$Y-N	101	1	5	12	1½	2½	22½	Alvarado R Jr	L120 fb	2.90	99-08	Kelly's Landing1182½ *Pisgah*1205½ Gregson1183	Step slow st, 2nd best	6
Previously trained by Beattie Ryan 2005: (124 23 17 17 0.19)																			
19Feb06-6GP	fm	5f	ⓣ	:222 :442 :553	4↑ OC 75k/N3x-N	89	3	7	74¼	63	3½	11¾	Rose J	L120 fb	7.20	90-10	Pisgh1201¾ AllHilStormy120nk GinRummyChmp1201¼	Clipped heels early	9
Previously trained by Lake Scott A 2005: (1796 417 328 239 0.23)																			
5Feb06-6GP	gd	6½f		:222 :451 1:104 1:172	4↑ OC 75k/N3x-N	70	4	5	11½	11½	51¼	69½	Alvarado R Jr	L120 fb	2.60	75-16	BlzingPurrsuit1201¼ MiddlErth124½ ByByCrfty1201¼	Awkward start, tired	7
7Jan06-9GP	fst	6f		:223 :45 :562 1:082	3↑ MrProspH-G3	74	8	8	42½	31	89	814	Alvarado R Jr	L116 fb	11.80	88-05	Gaff113nk War Front115¾ Friendly Island1165¾	Very poor st, rushed	8
29Aug05-8Del	fst	6f		:214 :441 :563 1:094	3↑ Hockessin57k	103	3	3	12½	12½	11½	2hd	Alvarado R Jr	L120 fb	*1.10	92-14	SayMiNme123hd Pisgh120nk FoundingChirmn1204¼	Not good enough late	5
26Jly05-7Del	fst	6f		:211 :431 :554 1:09	3↑ Alw 43900N2x	108	4	2	13½	17	111	16¾	Alvarado R Jr	L123 fb	*.90	96-14	Pisgah1236¾ Sir Elite1194¾ Flaminsun115no	Fast pace, held sway	8

WORKS: ●Jly1 Del 4f fst :462 B *1/55*
TRAINER: Turf(180 .18 $2.07) Sprint(2425 .27 $1.77) Stakes(122 .25 $1.40)
J/T 2005-06 SAR(1 1.00 $9.20) J/T 2005-06(8 .25 $2.00)

6 Bingobear
Own: Queen Jack M
Black Colors Unavailable
LEPAROUX J R (73 9 8 10 .12) 2006: (1129 284 .25)

B. g. 5 (Apr)
Sire: Polish Numbers (Danzig) $20,000
Dam: Hushlu (Tsunami Slew)
Br: Jack M Queen (Md)
Tr: Shuman Mark(—) 2006:(162 30 .19)

L 116

Life	34	6	5	4	$130,154	96
2006	4	2	1	0	$42,370	96
2005	15	2	1	3	$40,020	84
Sar ⓣ	0	0	0	0	$0	-
D.Fst	17	1	3	2	$35,490	72
Wet(350)	5	1	1	0	$15,930	62
Turf(325)	12	4	1	2	$78,734	96
Dstⓣ(333)	4	2	1	0	$42,370	96

Entered 12Aug06- 9 MTH

16Jly06-7Mth	fm	5f	ⓣ	:204 :43 :543	3↑ JMcSorley55k	96	1	4	32½	34	32	21¾	Lezcano J	L118	8.50	100 -	Terrific Challenge1201¾ Bingobear118¾ Max West122nk	Finished well rail	9
19Jun06-8Cnl	fm	5½f	ⓣ	:224 :452 :571 1:033	3↑ OC 40k/N3x-N	88	2	2	21	2hd	1hd	1½	Fogelsonger R	L124	*1.20	93-09	Bingobear124½ *Warrior Within*1152½ Scruples In1151¾	3w,dueled,driving	7
29May06-9Pim	fm	5f	ⓣ	:213 :441 :554	3↑ Alw 30000N2x	93	6	1	12	11½	11½	13½	Rodriguez E D	L120	8.40	100-07	*Bingobear*1203½ Pasketty120½ [DH]*Sandbagger Jones*117	Sent, rail, driving	10
18May06-9Pim	gd	5f	ⓣ	:223 :473 1:00	3↑ OC 25k/N2x-N	63	7	1	52	65½	53	85¾	Karamanos H A	L120	8.20	73-21	MrNotebook120nk ILCULter1201½ DngerousRidg1201¼	Checked, steadied	10
4Dec05-8Lrl	fst	1⅛	⊗	:474 1:142 1:41 1:55	3↑ OC 25k/N2x-N	22	5	2½	1hd	54	1019	936¾	Panell D	L122	13.90	30-37	*Little Thunder*123hd Strike a Bargain1192 Easy Red1192¼	Dueled, gave way	10
12Nov05-7Lrl	fm	1⅛	ⓣ	:451 1:092 1:344 1:463	3↑ Alw 30000N2x	47	5	2½	1hd	1hd	1115	1320¼	Kobiskie D5	L119	5.60	77 -	Tour Dance1245½ Easy Red118hd Strike a Bargain1181¼	Dueled, faltered	14
29Oct05-10Lrl	fm	1⅛	ⓣ	:472 1:11 1:361 1:49	3↑ [S]FindH50k	84	7	12	1½	13½	11½	31¾	Karamanos H A	L114	10.10	83-15	Private Scandal117½ Tam's Terms1171½ Bingobear114nk	Rail, pace, faded	8
15Oct05-10Lrl	gd	1⅛	ⓣ	:48 1:122 1:381 1:513	3↑ [R]MdMillTurf142k	78	2	12½	14	13	2½	53½	Castellano A Jr	L119	14.10	68-28	LReinesTerms121¾ DrDetroit121nk RubiEcho119nk	Rail,checked 1/8,angld	9
25Sep05-4Del	fm	*1 1/16	ⓣ	:241 :48 1:122 1:431	3↑ Alw 5000s	83	2	1hd	1½	11½	15	15¼	Alvarado R Jr	L119	2.30	101-09	Bingobear1195¼ Sir Aly1192½ Warrant1191	Drew off steady drive	10
Previously trained by Shuman Joseph 2005(as of 8/28): (179 24 29 28 0.13)																			
28Aug05-4Mnr	fm	1	ⓣ	:232 :464 1:103 1:362	3↑ Alw 29200N4L	78	6	13	1hd	2hd	32½	36½	Barria J	L115	5.60	78-21	Oblat115¾ Burchfield1155¾ *Bingobear*115¾	Stumbled, rushed	7
7Aug05-4Mnr	fm	1	ⓣ	:223 :453 1:093 1:351	3↑ Alw 26000N2x	74	5	21	21½	33	45	58	Barria J	L115	4.60	83-17	Hunforgun1152 SouthChristn1151¼ Burchfld1154¼	No breathers, wore out	8
24Jly05-2Mnr	fm	7½f	ⓣ	:232 :461 1:283	3↑ Clm 20000(30-20)N3L	84	2	1	1½	12	16	16¼	Barria J	L114	12.30	94-07	Bingober1146¼ StoneColdCt115hd QuitetheGuy1153½	Set pace, opened up	10

TRAINER: Turf(79 .22 $1.67) Sprint(569 .25 $2.12) Stakes(53 .17 $2.11)

The favorite was Weigelia, a hard-knocking veteran who last out had fought for the lead to deep stretch in the Smile Sprint Handicap, a Grade 2 with a $500,000 purse. In his most recent start on turf, he was a front-running winner at Belmont in the course-record time of 1:07 for six furlongs.

The co-second choices were Second in Command and Yes Yes Yes.

Yes Yes Yes had run well in two previous turf sprints, but they had taken place more than a year earlier, and they had not been as fast as his better dirt races.

I was more intrigued by Second in Command, who had been a lower price than Weigelia when they met at Belmont in June. The reasons were twofold: (1) He had relished 5½ furlongs on this course the previous summer, winning both starts decisively. (2) He had been claimed from his last start by Rick Dutrow Jr., and Trainer Form showed Dutrow to be winning at a 45 percent clip first off the claim in 2005–06—and from a representative 49-horse sample.

My line looked like this, with 83 points divided among the top four choices, and 17 points left over for noncontenders Safsoof and Bingobear:

	Betting line	Actual odds
Weigelia	5–2	1–1
Second in Command	3–1	5–1
Yes Yes Yes	5–1	5–1
Pisgah	6–1	6–1

This was an easy decision. Despite his strong affinity for the course, and a change to a trainer who was 22 for 45 with newly claimed horses, Second in Command wasn't getting nearly enough respect from the crowd.

EIGHTH RACE
Saratoga
AUGUST 14, 2006

5½ FURLONGS. (Turf) (1.01) 3RD RUNNING OF THE TROY. Purse $70,000 FOR FOUR YEAR OLDS AND UPWARD WHICH HAVE NOT WON A GRADED SWEEPSTAKE ON THE TURF IN 2005–06. No nomination fee. A supplemental nomination fee of $200 may be made at time of entry. $500 to enter. Starters to receive a $250 rebate. The added money and all fees to be divided 60% to the owner of the winner, 20% to second, 10% to third, 5% to fourth , 3% to fifth and 2% divided equally among remaining finishers. 123 lbs. TURF: Non–winners of $40,000 on the turf in 2006 allowed 3 lbs.; A sweepstake on the turf in 2005–06 or four races on the turf, 5 lbs.; three races on the turf, 7 lbs. DIRT: Non–winners of a graded Sweepstake on the dirt in 2005–06 allowed 3 lbs.; A sweepstake on the dirt in 2005–06, 5 lbs.; four races, 7 lbs. (Maiden, claiming, starter and reestricted allowance races not considered for dirt and turf). The New York Racing Association reserves the right to transfer this race to the Main Track. A presentation will be made to the winning owner. Closed Thursday, August 10, 2006 with 18 Nominations. (If the Stewards consider it inadvisable to run this race on the turf course, this race will be run at Five and One Half Furlongs on the main track.). (Rail at 12 feet).

Value of Race: $71,500 Winner $42,900; second $14,300; third $7,150; fourth $3,575; fifth $2,145; sixth $1,430. Mutuel Pool $418,430.00 Exacta Pool $352,140.00 Trifecta Pool $266,403.00 Grand Slam Pool $40,645.00

Last Raced	Horse	M/Eqt.	A.	Wt	PP	St	¼	⅜	Str	Fin	Jockey	Odds $1
12Jly06 1Bel³	Second inCommand	L b	6	116	3	2	5½	5½	1½	1²¼	Prado E S	5.10
16Jly06 7Mth²	Bingobear	L	5	116	6	1	2hd	3hd	5⁶	2½	Leparoux J R	12.20
15Jly06 11Crc³	Weigelia	L	5	118	2	3	1½	1hd	2hd	3no	Velazquez J R	0.80
9Jly06 8CD²	Yes Yes Yes	L	4	116	4	4	3¹	2²	3½	4²¼	Jara F	5.40
21Jly06 8Mth¹	Safsoof	L	4	116	1	6	4hd	4hd	4½	5⁴¼	Gomez G K	8.40
3Aug06 2Pen⁴	Pisgah	L bf	5	120	5	5	6	6	6	6	Velasquez C	6.80

OFF AT 4:47 Start Good. Won driving. Course firm.
TIME :21, :43², :55, 1:01 (:21.07, :43.49, :55.05, 1:01.11)

(New Course Record)

$2 Mutuel Prices:

3 – SECOND IN COMMAND..............	12.20	5.80	3.20
6 – BINGOBEAR......................		9.90	3.90
2 – WEIGELIA........................			2.30

$2 EXACTA 3–6 PAID $121.50 $2 TRIFECTA 3–6–2 PAID $261.50

Dk. b or br. h, (Feb), by Silver Deputy – Stormeor , by Lypheor–GB . Trainer Dutrow Richard E Jr. Bred by Richard L Golden (Md).

SECOND IN COMMAND raced up close early between horses, eased back a bit slowly the backstretch, settled in good position to the turn, angled four wide to launch his bid at the quarter pole then unleashed a strong late run to win going away. BINGOBEAR pressed the early pace in the two path, dropped back on the turn, angled four wide entering the stretch then came back again to narrowly gain the place. WEIGELIA dueled through brisk fractions along the inside to the top of the stretch, relinquished the lead in midstretch and weakened from his early efforts. YES YES YES pressed the early pace while three wide along the backstretch, made a run from outside to challenge at the quarter pole but couldn't sustain his bid. SAFSOOF broke a bit slowly, saved ground while just off the pace for a half and lacked a strong closing bid. PISGAH trailed early, checked briefly on the far turn, lodged a mild rally four wide on the turn, angled in at the top of the stretch and tired.

Owners– 1, Dubb Michael; 2, Queen Jack M; 3, Balsamo Joseph J; 4, Team Valor Stables LLC; 5, Godolphin Racing LLC; 6, Dunlap Tavner

Trainers– 1, Dutrow Richard E Jr; 2, Shuman Mark; 3, Trombetta Michael J; 4, Pletcher Todd A; 5, bin Suroor Saeed; 6, Lake Scott A

Scratched– The Student (ARG) (03Jul06 9Mnr³)

$2 Grand Slam (4/6/7–1/2/5–5/8/9–3) Paid $40.20 ; Grand Slam Pool $40,645 .

Weigelia was softened up dueling for the lead with Yes Yes Yes, which was a perfect turn of events for the stretch-running Second in Command. He swept by the spent pacesetters approaching midstretch and drew off while setting a course record.

Because Weigelia had beaten Second in Command at Belmont, the crowd assumed the same thing would happen again, even though two significant factors—turf course and trainer change—favored the latter.

California-based handicapping essayist Joe Colville had a good take on this situation when he wrote the following:

"Is it more important to know the horses we bet on, or to understand the horseplayers we bet against? My opinion is that each is as important as the other. Horseplayers we bet against have a fondness for horses who have beaten horses they are running against. If Horse A beat Horse B, the public often feels it has one less horse to handicap; it can forget about Horse B and see how Horse A stacks up against the rest of the field."

The Pick Four: Making Chaos Work for You

For win bettors, a steady diet of esoteric overlays is a surefire way to go from zero to 20 losers in today's fast-paced simulcast action. But those kinds of horses do win races, and they produce lucrative windfalls for pick-four bettors who have a sense of when to take a stand and when to spread.

The pick four was introduced to New York bettors on opening day of Belmont's 2001 spring meet, and I had the grave misfortune to hit the thing with a $3 \times 3 \times 2 \times 1$ ticket for $18. After Coast to Coast held on to win the last leg, my little $18 ticket was worth $864, half the $2 payoff of $1,728, and I was wondering where the pick four had been all my life.

I didn't fully realize it at the time, but my beginner's luck was probably the worst thing that could've happened. I put in small tickets for a long time afterward and seldom came away with anything except a tough-beat story. Eventually, I started to allocate a larger portion of my bankroll to the pick four, filling out multiple tickets as Steven Crist and Barry Meadow had shown me how to do, and my results started to improve.

For well-capitalized conservative win bettors, the pick four provides a potentially dynamic alternative when a solid-looking spot play is in a sequence with a couple of inscrutable heats. The parimutuel power of this method was driven home to me at Saratoga on August 11, 1992, when a weekend guest left for the track with two opinions: He liked lukewarm favorite Balto Star in the eighth race, and thought Orientate, who would eventually be crowned that year's champion sprinter, had to fall down to lose the A. G. Vanderbilt Handicap. Instead of wise-guying himself away from singling Orientate at 2–5, he built a pick four around the mortal lock and Balto Star with a $10 \times 1 \times 1 \times 9$ ticket for $90, wheeling the other two legs.

When Balto Star ($9.90) and Orientate ($2.90) book-ended Play It Out ($36.20) and Gayle's Glory ($15.80), the $90 ticket cashed for half of the $3,978 payoff, nearly twice the win parlay.

A $90 win bet on Balto Star would have returned $445. By merely conceding one leg of the pick four to a 2–5 shot, and hitting the "all" button in two contentious legs, my astute friend turbocharged his return to $1,989, an improvement of more than 400 percent on a win bet.

That is what often happens when at least two winners in the sequence fall "outside the box" of all the small-ticket players who go $3 \times 3 \times 2 \times 1$, as I did on opening day at Belmont in the spring of 2001.

In the win pool, what you get is what you get. What I mean by that is that 3–1 shots reward their backers exactly the same way no matter the circumstances, whether the horse is the lukewarm favorite in a 10-horse field, or the second choice behind a 3–5 shot in a short field of six. But in multirace exotics such as the pick four, the potential returns are very different: That same 3–1 lukewarm favorite will be on the majority of small tickets, but the 3–1 horse that beats a 3–5 shot has blown up a truckload of small tickets, and may pave the way to a huge score.

It's a common misconception that you need to throw out short-priced favorites to cash worthwhile tickets in the pick four. That is simply not the case, as the late pick four at Saratoga on July 31, 2005, proved, because two of them were in the mix. The first leg was not terribly difficult. Mayo Post was the top-figure horse by a wide margin, and was never seriously threatened at $3.70. The third leg, the Grade 1 Go for Wand Handicap, was a five-horse field dominated by the champion filly Ashado, at a whopping $4.30.

The two bust-out winners, Secret Forest ($43.20) and Square Dancing ($37.40), triggered a pick four that paid $5,560 for $2, substantially more than the $2 win parlay of $3,213.

Secret Forest was the kind of horse that should be included whenever handicappers cast a wide net in pick fours, because she was switching to the turf for the first time, and was top-rated (375) on the Tomlinson numbers for grass:

Secret Forest won a stretch-long duel with Asti, who was odds-on despite having not won a race in over a year.

Square Dancing was dropping into a claiming race for the first time in her career, and had the field's third-fastest Beyer on grass.

The key to successful play in the multirace exotics is to successfully determine which races to take a stand in, and which races to include anyone and everyone with a pulse.

Evaluating the Favorite

Based on what has been covered so far, it should be apparent that the following types of races are likely to produce good-priced winners:

- Maiden races containing second-time starters that might improve at a moment's notice, or route-bred horses stretching out off a couple of sprints that might also jump up suddenly.
- Turf races containing horses trying the surface for the first time with suitable pedigrees.

In addition to those two situations, a third potential spread scenario comes about whenever the favorite looks vulnerable. This can be due to a variety of reasons. For example, in the 2007 running of the $1 million Sunshine Millions Classic, a two-turn route at 1⅛ miles at Gulfstream Park, the 19–10 favorite, Sweetnorthernsaint, drew post 12 in a race that featured a very short run to the first turn, and was hung out to dry in the early going; meanwhile, the 3–1 second choice was Silver Wagon, a late-running sprinter who had never been past one mile. The situation was ripe for an upset, and McCann's Mojave ($69.80), who was coming off two straight route wins, obliged by holding off the 42–1 bomb Summer Book through the stretch.

Another volatile situation occurs when no one in the field has run to the Beyer par. Such was the case in the 2005 Breeders' Cup Distaff, where DRF's *American Racing Manual* showed the Beyer par to be just under 108:

(EMIRATES AIRLINE) BREEDERS' CUP DISTAFF (G1), 1 1/8 Miles, Fillies and Mares, 3-Year-Olds and Up, Belmont Park, 2005 Purse: $1,834,000

Year	Winner	Age	Jockey	Wt.	Second	Wt.	Third	Wt.	Win Value	Time	Beyer
1984	Princess Rooney	4	E. Delahoussaye	123	Life's Magic	119	Adored	123	450,000	2:02.40	
1985	Life's Magic	4	A. Cordero Jr	123	Lady's Secret	119	Dontstop Themusic	123	450,000	2:02.00	
1986	Lady's Secret	4	P. Day	123	Fran's Valentine	123	Outstandingly	123	450,000	2:01.20	
1987	Sacahuista	3	R.P. Romero	119	Clabber Girl	123	Oueee Bebe	119	450,000	2:02.80	
1988	Personal Ensign	4	R.P. Romero	123	Winning Colors	119	Goodbye Halo	119	450,000	1:52.00	
1989	Bayakoa	5	L. Pincay Jr	123	Gorgeous	119	Open Mind	119	450,000	1:47.40	
1990	Bayakoa	6	L. Pincay Jr	123	Colonial Waters	123	Valay Maid	119	450,000	1:49.20	113
1991	Dance Smartly	3	P. Day	120	Versailles Treaty	120	Brought to Mind	123	520,000	1:50.80	107
1992	Paseana	5	C.J. McCarron	123	Versailles Treaty	123	Magical Maiden	119	520,000	1:48.00	105
1993	Hollywood Wildcat	3	E. Delahoussaye	120	Paseana	123	Re Toss	123	520,000	1:48.20	108
1994	One Dreamer	6	G.L. Stevens	123	Heavenly Prize	120	Miss Dominique	123	520,000	1:50.60	105
1995	Inside Information	4	M.E. Smith	123	Heavenly Prize	123	Lakeway	123	520,000	1:46.00	119
1996	Jewel Princess	4	C.S. Nakatani	123	Serena's Song	123	Different	123	520,000	1:48.40	114
1997	Ajina	3	M.E. Smith	123	Sharp Cat	120	Escena	123	520,000	1:47.20	108
1998	Escena	5	G.L. Stevens	123	Banshee Breeze	120	Keeper Hill	120	1,040,000	1:49.89	105
1999	Beautiful Pleasure	4	J.F. Chavez	123	Banshee Breeze	123	Heritage of Gold	123	1,040,000	1:47.56	109
2000	Spain	3	V. Espinoza	120	Surfside	120	Heritage of Gold	123	1,227,200	1:47.66	108
2001	Unbridled Elaine	3	P. Day	120	Spain	123	Two Item Limit	123	1,227,200	1:49.21	102
2002	Azeri	4	M. E. Smith	123	Farda Amiga	119	Imperial Gesture	119	1,040,000	1:48.64	111
2003	Adoration	4	P.A. Valenzuela	123	Elloluv	119	Got Koko	123	1,040,000	1:49.17	101
2004	Ashado	3	J.R. Velazquez	119	Storm Flag Flying	123	Stellar Jayne	119	1,040,000	1:48.26	102
2005	Pleasant Home	3	C. Velasquez	123	Society Selection	123	Ashado	123	1,040,000	1:48.34	107

Beyer Index: 107.75

Defending champion Ashado had come close on a couple of occasions in her career, but the fact remained that neither she nor anyone else in the field had ever run to the Beyer par, and that often lessens the predictive value of the figures.

8 Belmont Park 1⅛ MILES (1:45²) ℗ BCDistaf-G1 22nd Running of THE EMIRATES AIRLINE BREEDERS' CUP DISTAFF. Grade I. Purse $2,000,000 For Fillies And Mares, Three-year-olds And Upward. Northern Hemisphere three-year-olds, 120 lbs.; Older, 123 lbs.; Southern Hemisphere three-year-olds, 115 lbs.; Older, 123 lbs. $20,000 to pre-enter, $40,000 to enter, with guaranteed $2 million purse including nominator awards, of which 52% of all monies to the owner of the winner, 20% to second, 11% to third, 5.7% to fourth and 3% to fifth; plus stallion nominator awards of 2.6% of all monies to the winner, 1% to second and 0.55% to third and foal nominator awards of 2.6% of all monies to the winner, 1% to second and 0.55% to third. Closed with 14 pre-entries.

1 Society Selection

2 Stellar Jayne

[126]

3 Ashado
Own: Starlight St&Paul Saylor&Johns Martin
Royal Blue, Yellow Circled JI, Yellow
VELAZQUEZ J R (150 35 22 17 .23) 2005: (1016 216 .21)
Dk. b or br f. 4 (Feb) KEESEP02 $170,000
Sire: Saint Ballado (Halo) $125,000
Dam: Goulash (Mari's Book)
Br: Aaron U Jones & Marie D Jones (Ky)
Tr: Pletcher Todd A(90 19 14 13 .21) 2005:(949 199 .23)

L 123

Life 20 12 4 2 $3,711,440 106
2005 6 3 1 0 $841,000 105
2004 8 5 2 1 $2,259,640 106
Bel 6 4 1 1 $1,070,800 106

WORKS: Oct24 Bel 5f fst 1:00³ H 27/37 Sep26 Bel tr.t 5f fst 1:02⁴ B 27/37 ●Sep18 Bel tr.t 4f fst :47 B 1/42 Sep10 Bel 4f fst :49³ B 36/50 Aug22 Sar 5f fst 1:00³ B 11/65
TRAINER: WonLastStart(403 .26 $1.69) Dirt(1263 .25 $1.63) Routes(1099 .24 $1.73) GrdStk(316 .23 $1.90)

4 Nothing But Fun
Own: Barry K Schwartz
Black And White Halves, Black And White
SOLIS A (—) 2005: (640 136 .21)
Dk. b or br f. 3 (Mar) KEESEP03 $150,000
Sire: Dixie Union (Dixieland Band) $30,000
Dam: Zepa (Theatrical*Ire)
Br: Hudson Michael E (27 7 5 4 .26) 2005:(260 69 .27)

L 120

Life 4 4 0 0 $281,700 96
2005 4 4 0 0 $281,700 96
2004 0 0 0 0 $0 —
Bel 0 0 0 0 $0 —

WORKS: WonLastStart(119 .17 $1.39) Dirt(494 .24 $1.94) Routes(255 .15 $1.27) GrdStk(26 .08 $0.80)
TRAINER: WonLastStart(119 .17 $1.39) Dirt(494 .24 $1.94) Routes(255 .15 $1.27) GrdStk(26 .08 $0.80)

5 Yolanda B. Too
Own: West Point Stable
Gold, Blue Star, Gold Hoop On Black
COA E M (284 26 24 27 .13) 2005: (1179 177 .15)
Dk. b or br f. 3 (Apr) OBSMAR05 $70,000
Sire: Two Punch (Mr. Prospector) $25,000
Dam: Avie's Lady (Lord Avie)
Br: Dr & Mrs T Bowman & M Higgins III (Md)
Tr: Violette Richard A Jr(32 1 3 3 .03) 2005:(263 45 .17)

L 120

Life 5 2 2 1 $148,400 99
2005 4 1 2 1 $140,200 99
2004 1 1 0 0 $8,200 84
Bel 1 0 0 1 $25,000 95

WORKS: Oct24 Aqu 1 fst 1:45² B 1/1 Oct17 Aqu 6f fst :49⁴ B 13/23 Sep22 Sar 4f fst :49² B 18/45 Aug12 Sar 4f fst :49⁴ B 12/39
TRAINER: Dirt(375 .18 $2.02) Routes(299 .15 $1.88) GrdStk(44 .02 $0.14)

6 Healthy Addiction
Own: Pamela C Ziebarth
White Circle Z And Sash
GOMEZ E K (2 2 0 0 1.00) 2005: (1123 210 .19)
Dk. b or br f. 4 (Apr) KEESEP02 $100,000
Sire: Boston Harbor (Capote) $27,342
Dam: Lady Laika (Gone West)
Br: Diamond A Racing Corporation (Ky)
Tr: Sadler John W(—) 2005:(341 51 .15)

L 123

Life 14 6 5 0 $388,257 102
2005 8 4 2 0 $303,065 102
2004 5 2 3 0 $77,982 86
Bel 0 0 0 0 $0 84

WORKS: WonLastStart(112 .18 $1.31) Dirt(523 .15 $1.84) Routes(269 .21 $3.08) GrdStk(49 .10 $1.00)
TRAINER: WonLastStart(112 .18 $1.31) Dirt(523 .15 $1.84) Routes(269 .21 $3.08) GrdStk(49 .10 $1.00)

7 Happy Ticket
Own: Stewart M Madison
Red, Black Musical Note, Black Collar
ESPINOZA V (4 0 1 0 .00) 2005: (956 167 .17)
B. f. 4 (Feb)
Sire: Anet (Clever Trick) $5,000
Dam: Love and Happiness (Septieme Ciel)
Dam: Stewart Madison (La)
Tr: Leggio Andrew Jr(1 0 0 1 .00) 2005:(168 32 .19)

L 123

Life 12 10 2 0 $782,260 104
2005 4 4 0 0 $535,000 104
2004 7 7 0 0 $247,260 99
Bel 1 1 0 0 $150,000 102

WORKS: Oct26 Bel tr.t 5f fst 1:01² B 7/28 Oct22 Bel tr.t 5f fst 1:02⁴ B 25/5 Sep23 LaD 5f fst 1:01 B 2/24 ●Aug7 LaD 5f gd :59³ B 1/66
TRAINER: Dirt(180 .22 $2.84) Routes(121 .17 $2.06) GrdStk(7 .29 $1.94)

8 Island Fashion
Own: Jeffrey L Nielsen
Black, Red Mountain Emblem, Red Cap
BEJARANO R (76 9 12 10 .12) 2005: (1107 217 .20)
Gr/ro. m. 5 (Mar)
Sire: Petionville (Seeking the Gold) $15,000
Dam: Danzig Fashion (A Native Danzig)
Br: Everest Stables Inc (Ky)
Tr: Polanco Marcelo(—) 2005:(160 11 .07)

L 123

Life 25 6 5 1 $1,947,970 111
2005 4 1 0 0 $228,000 104
2004 5 2 1 0 $165,000 111
Bel 2 0 0 0 $135,000 102

WORKS: Oct22 SA 4f fst :48 H 10/19 Oct14 SA 4f fst :50⁴ B 27/34 ●Sep25 SA 5f fst 1:00 H 1/12 Sep21 SA 5f fst 1:01² B 1/29 Sep14 SA 4f fst :49³ H 4/25
TRAINER: Dirt(273 .10 $1.23) Routes(248 .09 $0.89) GrdStk(56 .04 $0.22)

9 Hollywood Story
Own: George Krikorian
Raspberry, Film Strip Emblem, Film Strip
VALENZUELA P A (3 0 0 2 .00) 2005: (802 161 .20)
Dk. b or br f. 4 (Mar) FTKJUL03 $130,000
Sire: Wild Rush (Wild Again) $40,923
Dam: Wife for Life (Dynaformer)
Br: Vinery (Ky)
Tr: Shirreffs John(—) 2005:(142 29 .20)

L 123

Life 18 3 5 4 $862,015 98
2005 6 1 2 2 $218,410 98
2004 7 1 1 1 $287,105 97
Bel 0 0 0 0 $0 —

WORKS: Oct22 Hol 6f fst 1:13⁴ H 10/12 Oct14 Hol 5f fst 1:01 H 4/15 Sep25 Hol 5f fst 1:00 H 3/50 ●Sep10 Hol 5f fst 1:00¹ H 1/11 Sep4 Hol 4f fst :49⁴ H 3/31
TRAINER: 2Off45-180(39 .15 $1.41) Dirt(187 .19 $2.37) Routes(181 .14 $1.92) GrdStk(49 .12 $3.31)

No one considered Pleasant Home a most likely winner, but this was not the fastest or most formidable field of distaffers ever assembled, and she did display a forging pattern after slightly exceeding her previous Beyer top; what's more, that new top of 95 had come in the Spinster, against the grain of the old speed-favoring surface at Keeneland, and her trainer, Shug McGaughey, had developed the likes of Distaff winners Personal Ensign and Inside Information.

Pleasant Home was improbable, but by no means impossible given the situation, and she turned out to be the missing link in a $17,303 pick four that included Horse of the Year Saint Liam

($6.80) in the Classic, and Artie Schiller ($13.20), the second choice in the Mile behind Leroidesanimaux—who was announced as wearing aluminum pads the morning of the race.

EIGHTH RACE
Belmont
OCTOBER 29, 2005

1⅛ MILES. (1.45^{2}) 22ND RUNNING OF THE EMIRATES AIRLINE BREEDERS' CUP DISTAFF. Grade I. Purse $2,000,000 FOR FILLIES AND MARES, THREE-YEAR-OLDS AND UPWARD. Northern Hemisphere three-year-olds, 120 lbs.; Older, 123 lbs.; Southern Hemisphere three-year-olds, 115 lbs.; Older, 123 lbs. $20,000 to pre-enter, $40,000 to enter, with guaranteed $2 million purse including nominator awards (plus Net Supplementary Fees, if any), of which 52% of all monies to the owner of the winner, 20% to second, 11% to third, 5.7% to fourth and 3% to fifth; plus stallion nominator awards of 2.6% of all monies to the winner, 1% to second and 0.55% to third and foal nominator awards of 2.6% of all monies to the winner, 1% to second and 0.55% to third. Closed with 14 pre-entries.

Value of Race: $1,834,000 Winner $1,040,000; second $400,000; third $220,000; fourth $114,000; fifth $60,000. Mutuel Pool $4,683,655.00 Exacta Pool $3,207,113.00 Trifecta Pool $2,778,062.00 Head2Head Pool $49,367.00 Superfecta Pool $941,048.00

Last Raced	Horse	M/Eqt.	A.	Wt	PP	St	¼	½	¾	Str	Fin	Jockey	Odds $1
9Oct05 ^{8}Kee^{2}	Pleasant Home	L	4	123	11	1	13	$12^{1\frac{1}{2}}$	11^{2}	1^{3}	$1^{9\frac{1}{4}}$	Velasquez C	30.75
1Oct05 ^{7}Bel^{3}	Society Selection	L	4	123	1	11	$10^{\frac{1}{2}}$	$9^{\frac{1}{2}}$	6^{hd}	$3^{1\frac{1}{2}}$	2^{nk}	Prado E S	11.80
1Oct05 ^{7}Bel^{1}	Ashado	L	4	123	3	7	6^{hd}	5^{hd}	$5^{\frac{1}{2}}$	$2^{\frac{1}{2}}$	$3^{2\frac{1}{4}}$	Velazquez J R	2.25
11Sep05 ^{9}Bel^{1}	Stellar Jayne	L b	4	123	2	8	2^{hd}	4^{hd}	2^{hd}	$5^{1\frac{1}{2}}$	$4^{2\frac{1}{4}}$	Dettori L	4.50
10Sep05 ^{7}Bel^{1}	In the Gold	L	3	120	10	13	11^{hd}	$11^{\frac{1}{2}}$	10^{hd}	6^{2}	5^{1}	Stevens G L	9.20
9Oct05 ^{8}Kee^{3}	Capeside Lady	L	4	123	13	2	1^{1}	$1^{\frac{1}{2}}$	$1^{1\frac{1}{2}}$	4^{2}	$6^{\frac{3}{4}}$	Decarlo C P	57.00
1Oct05 ^{9}Pha^{1}	Nothing But Fun	L f	3	120	4	12	12^{2}	$10^{2\frac{1}{2}}$	$8^{1\frac{1}{2}}$	$7^{2\frac{1}{2}}$	$7^{6\frac{1}{4}}$	Solis A	32.00
2Oct05 ^{7}OSA^{4}	Hollywood Story	L b	4	123	9	9	$7^{\frac{1}{2}}$	$7^{\frac{1}{2}}$	$12^{1\frac{1}{2}}$	10^{3}	$8^{3\frac{1}{4}}$	Valenzuela P A	30.25
1Oct05 ^{7}Bel^{4}	Sweet Symphony	L	3	120	12	10	9^{hd}	13	13	$9^{\frac{1}{2}}$	9^{4}	Bailey J D	7.70
2Oct05 ^{7}OSA^{3}	Island Fashion	L b	5	123	8	3	5^{1}	6^{hd}	$4^{\frac{1}{2}}$	$11^{2\frac{1}{2}}$	$10^{1\frac{1}{4}}$	Bejarano R	27.75
1Oct05 ^{7}Bel^{2}	Happy Ticket	L	4	123	7	5	$8^{1\frac{1}{2}}$	8^{1}	$3^{\frac{1}{2}}$	8^{1}	$11^{2\frac{1}{2}}$	Espinoza V	4.50
1Oct05 ^{9}Pha^{2}	Yolanda B. Too	L b	3	120	5	6	$3^{\frac{1}{2}}$	$2^{\frac{1}{2}}$	7^{hd}	12^{10}	$12^{24\frac{1}{4}}$	Coa E M	64.25
2Oct05 ^{7}OSA^{1}	Healthy Addiction	L b	4	123	6	4	4^{hd}	3^{1}	9^{hd}	13	13	Gomez G K	18.40

OFF AT 4:32 Start Good. Won driving. Track fast.

TIME :23^{1}, :46^{1}, 1:10^{3}, 1:35^{4}, 1:48^{1} (:23.33, :46.31, 1:10.74, 1:35.82, 1:48.34)

$2 Mutuel Prices:				
	11 – PLEASANT HOME	63.50	25.60	13.40
	1 – SOCIETY SELECTION		12.80	7.90
	3 – ASHADO			3.30

$2 EXACTA 11-1 PAID $692.00 $2 TRIFECTA 11-1-3 PAID $3,453.00
$2 HEAD2HEAD 6VS.12WINNER12 PAID $2.90
$2 SUPERFECTA 11-1-3-2 PAID $20,363.00

Dk. b or br. f, (May), by Seeking the Gold – Our Country Place , by Pleasant Colony . Trainer McGaughey III Claude R. Bred by Phipps Stable (Ky).

PLEASANT HOME trailed for a half, saved ground while rapidly making her move midway on the turn, swung out approaching the stretch, split horses while angling four wide at the quarter pole, quickly charged to the front in upper stretch, took command in midstretch and drew away with authority under steady right hand encouragement. SOCIETY SELECTION was unhurried for a half, worked her way forward along the rail midway on the turn, angled out for room at the quarter pole, exchanged bumps with ASHADO in upper stretch, battled inside the favorite through the lane and outfinished that one for the place. ASHADO checked in traffic along the backstretch, raced in the middle of the pack to the turn, launched a rally between horses entering the stretch, bumped with SOCIETY SELECTION while in tight at the three-sixteenths pole, fought into deep stretch and yielded second in the late stages. STELLAR JAYNE raced up close along the inside, saved ground for seven furlongs, dropped back on the turn and weakened in the drive. IN THE GOLD was outrun for a mile, circled five wide entering the stretch and passed only tiring horses. CAPESIDE LADY sprinted clear, set the pace under pressure to the top of the stretch and gave way in the drive. NOTHING BUT FUN never reached contention while five wide throughout. HOLLYWOOD STORY raced in the middle of the pack while six wide, steadied on the turn and lacked the needed response when called upon. SWEET SYMPHONY was never a factor. ISLAND FASHION showed speed for six furlongs and faltered. HAPPY TICKET raced in traffic along the backstretch, made a five wide middle move to threaten briefly on the turn and flattened out. YOLANDA B. TOO pressed the pace from outside to the far turn and gave way. HEALTHY ADDICTION was finished early while three wide.

Owners– 1, Phipps Stable; 2, Cowan Marge and Irving M; 3, Starlight Stable LLC Saylor Paul and Martin Johns; 4, Godolphin Racing LLC; 5, Live Oak Plantation; 6, So Madcapt Stable; 7, Schwartz Barry K; 8, Krikorian George; 9, Kinsman Stable; 10, Nielsen Jeffrey L; 11, Madison Stewart M; 12, West Point Stable; 13, Ziebarth Pamela C

Trainers– 1, McGaughey III Claude R; 2, Jerkens H Allen; 3, Pletcher Todd A; 4, bin Suroor Saeed; 5, Zito Nicholas P; 6, Pletcher Todd A; 7, Hushion Michael E; 8, Shirreffs John; 9, Mott William I; 10, Polanco Marcelo; 11, Leggio Andrew Jr; 12, Violette Richard A Jr; 13, Sadler John W

$2 Pick Three (3-2-11) Paid $8,668.00 ; Pick Three Pool $1,011,637 .

In an effort to crystallize exactly what kind of probabilities we're dealing with insofar as the post-time favorite is concerned, I asked Duane Burke of *Daily Racing Form*'s information-technology department to scour DRF's vast database, and he came up with some interesting data about favorites nationwide and on the New York circuit of Aqueduct, Belmont Park, and Saratoga.

The common perception is that favorites always have and always will win 33 percent of the time, but given a more sophisticated betting public and smaller average field size, favorites are actually winning more often than that in recent years. From 2000–2006, here are the results:

	Starts	Wins	Win Pct.	R.O.I.
FAVORITES @ ALL TRACKS:	491,327	168,474	34.3%	1.65
FAVORITES @ NY:	17,194	5,929	34.5%	1.67
ON DIRT @ ALL TRACKS:	453,121	156,395	34.5%	1.65
ON DIRT @ NY:	13,995	4,962	35.5%	1.68
DIRT SPRINT @ ALL TRACKS:	275,705	95,651	34.7%	1.66
DIRT SPRINT @ NY:	8,282	2,953	35.7%	1.71
DIRT ROUTE @ ALL TRACKS:	116,468	39,114	33.6%	1.64
DIRT ROUTE @ NY:	5,713	2,009	35.2%	1.65
ON TURF @ ALL TRACKS:	38,206	12,079	31.6%	1.62
ON TURF @ NY:	3,199	967	30.2%	1.63
TURF SPRINT @ ALL TRACKS:	9,745	3,175	32.6%	1.66
TURF SPRINT @ NY:	176	53	30.1%	1.61
TURF ROUTE @ ALL TRACKS:	28,460	8,903	31.3%	1.61
TURF ROUTE @ NY:	3,023	914	30.2%	1.63
GRADED STK @ ALL TRACKS:	5,503	1,916	34.8%	1.54
GRADED STK @ NY:	905	337	37.2%	1.63
2-YEAR-OLDS @ ALL TRACKS:	52,683	19,137	36.3%	1.66
2-YEAR-OLDS @ NY:	2,220	795	35.8%	1.69
MALES @ ALL TRACKS:	291,053	99,411	34.2%	1.66
MALES @ NY:	9,945	3,362	33.8%	1.66
FEMALE @ ALL TRACKS:	200,274	69,063	34.5	1.64
FEMALE @ NY:	7,249	2,567	35.4%	1.68
ALW @ ALL TRACKS:	67,563	24,299	36.0%	1.68
ALW @ NY:	4,758	1,738	36.5%	1.71
MSW @ ALL TRACKS:	46,958	17,337	36.9%	1.72
MSW @ NY	4,426	1,601	36.2	1.76

	Starts	Wins	Win Pct.	R.O.I.
MDCLM @ ALL TRACKS:	77,031	26,865	34.9%	1.67
MDCLM @ NY:	1,352	458	33.9%	1.62
3YO CLM @ ALL TRACKS:	42,259	13,606	32.2%	1.60
3YO CLM @ NY:	1,381	392	28.4%	1.48
OLDER CLM @ ALL TRACKS:	220,143	70,634	32.1%	1.62
OLDER CLM @ NY:	4,412	1,303	29.5%	1.56

Observations:

- Through nearly a half-million races in a seven-year period, favorites won at better than 34 percent overall.
- If you're considering any kind of a system that revolves around favorites and depends on frequency of winners, or looking for a single in multirace exotics, your best long-range prospects are graded stakes in New York, which are won by the favorite more than 37 percent of the time.
- Other exceptionally reliable favorites are dirt sprinters in New York (35.7 percent); 2-year-olds anywhere (around 36 percent); allowance horses anywhere (36 percent overall, a bit higher in New York); and maidens at all tracks (nearly 37 percent).
- Favorites win on turf considerably less often than on dirt, most likely due to larger average field size. In New York, the difference on dirt vs. turf is 35.5 percent vs. 30.2 percent, a sizable difference of 5.3 percent.
- Maiden-claiming favorites are surprisingly solid; they win at nearly 35 percent at all tracks.
- The least-reliable favorites are 3-year-old claimers in New York (28.4 percent), followed closely by older claimers in New York (29.5 percent). Out of 16 categories, they are the only ones that win at less than 30 percent, and they were considerably less reliable than their counterparts at all other tracks.

CHAPTER 4

·

The Handicapper's Handbook

"The races discussed in these pages were deliberately chosen to illustrate specific subtleties of handicapping. They were *not* chosen to show what a whiz-bang I am ... I may occasionally dispense a bit more theory than some of you want or need. It won't kill you."

—Tom Ainslie, from the introduction to *The Handicapper's Handbook* (1969)

WHEN I WAS JUST starting to get hooked on horse racing, most kids my age were reading literature such as J.R.R. Tolkien's *Lord of the Rings* trilogy, but my head was buried in *The Handicapper's Handbook*. Nearly four decades later, it is still my all-time favorite book on the subject, and one of my all-time favorite books, period.

It was an oversized hardcover of 197 pages, written in Tom Ainslie's inimitable style. On the front cover was a picture of a guy in a tweed sports jacket and tie who was standing next to the old paddock tote board at Belmont Park; he struck a thoughtful pose as his left hand held a fancy pen to his lip, and in his right hand was a neatly folded "Telly." Just above the picture, and below the title, potential readers were told, "The nation's foremost expert shows you exactly how he makes his own winning selections . . .

presented in workshop style—as informative as a private conference in his study, as exciting as an afternoon at the track!"

Wow!

Inside were large, easy-to-read reproductions of " . . . seven different allowance races, six specially selected maiden races, 16 typical claiming races, and two challenging days of racing at two big tracks."

I must've tested every system known to man on those races, and after a while I knew all the results by heart.

You can't buy a book like *that* for $7.50 anymore, let me tell you.

One of the two "challenging days" was the September 30, 1967, card at Aqueduct, highlighted by the 14th running of the weight-for-age Woodward, a showdown among titans that Damascus won decisively over Buckpasser and Dr. Fager. That tour de force performance was Damascus's 11th win from 14 starts as a 3-year-old, and wrapped up his Horse of the Year title. Imagine that, 14 starts in a season by a top-class 3-year-old.

Of course, Ainslie was all over Damascus, and collected the $5.60 win payoff.

The place pool was the only other avenue of wagering available on the Woodward, which was the seventh of eight races on the program. The exacta would not come into existence in New York until nearly three years later in June of 1970; the only "exotic" wager offered was the traditional daily double on the first two races. There was no late double, which was just as well, because not even Ainslie could come up with Beaustone, the 46–1 winner of the nightcap on Woodward Day, 1967.

"Such things happen," wrote Ainslie in an uncommonly succinct race recap. "You can't win them all."

More great handicapping books followed in coming years, such as Andrew Beyer's *Picking Winners* and William L. Quirin's *Winning at the Races: Computer Discoveries in Thoroughbred Handicapping,* and those books were terrific for learning the nuts and bolts of making figures, and memorizing the percentages for every conceivable situation. But *The Handicapper's Handbook* was different, because Ainslie took his readers by the hand through the entire process and showed them how he read between the lines to pick up on all sorts of things—things that never would have occurred to us.

Ainslie showed beyond a shadow of a doubt that the races really are the best teachers, and that is why this homage revisits two more "challenging" days of racing.

Big-Event Days—the Bettor's Best Bet

No one has to tell you there's a lot of bad racing out there on an everyday basis. On my home circuit, for example, the annual number of New York-bred races has risen steadily during the past several years, from 439 in 1998 to 770 in 2006. On a typical weekday during the winter at Aqueduct now, it's not uncommon for a card to consist of five maiden races, including three divisions of woeful maiden claimers for state-breds; a starter allowance restricted to maiden-claiming graduates; and a trio of cheap claiming races. For years, $10,000 was the basement claiming level, but races for $7,500 started popping up a few winters ago, and the Big A's 2006–07 winter meet ushered in the sub-basement era of the $5,000 claimer.

I confess to daydreaming some of those dreary afternoons away, envisioning opening day at Saratoga, or Belmont Stakes Day, or Breeders' Cup Day—any race day when there is a buzz of anticipation in the air. As Brad Free wrote in *Handicapping 101,* "Opening day at Santa Anita is the gift you open the day after Christmas."

On such memorable days, you never know when you may witness a truly astonishing performance: Damascus steamrolling Buckpasser and Dr. Fager; Secretariat moving like a tremendous machine; Personal Ensign lunging in the final stride to nail Winning Colors.

But beyond all the color and pageantry of big-race days, their real appeal to serious players is undoubtedly the fact that they offer prime opportunities to capitalize on exceptional value situations. The crowds are large, everyone's there to have a good time, and the payoffs for logical sequences of results are usually astounding.

And unlike Woodward Day of 1967, bettors today face no shortage of wagering options. In addition to the early daily double, we have a midday double, a late double, sometimes an instant double, exactas, quinellas, trifectas, superfectas, dime superfectas, rolling pick threes, pick fours, pick fives, pick sixes, the place pick all, and the grand slam (only in New York). If that is not enough, on Breeder's Cup Day, one can get down on a roster of head-to-head wagers.

Weekend warriors who desire to raise their game to the next level are advised to forego as much as possible the mundane processions of hapless horseflesh that run in anonymity during midweek, and concentrate on the big-event days and resort meets. Readers who are in the habit of putting in token pick-four tickets of $24 or $36 two or three times during the week are hereby admonished to cut out that foolishness and formulate more serious assaults on the "guaranteed" pick-anything pools advertised for the marquee weekend programs. Why hazard a guess as to who might be the least-slow horse in a mind-numbing weekday procession at Aqueduct, when you can bet on the cream of the crop on big-event days and take down some real bonanzas?

To give you an idea of the potential for value, consult the following roster of NTRA pick-three and pick-four payoffs dating back to 2003. Measured against a straight $2 win parlay, the payoffs are provocative, to say the least:

Races	Winners (Paid)	$2 Parlay	$2 Pick Three or Four
4/5/03			
Aventura	Dynever ($3.80)		
Illinois Derby	Ten Most Wanted ($6.60)		
SA Derby	Buddy Gil ($14.60)	$91	$115

Races	Winners (Paid)	$2 Parlay	$2 Pick Three or Four
4/12/03			
Wood Mem.	Empire Maker ($3.10)		
Blue Grass	Peace Rules ($3.20)		
Ark. Derby	Sir Cherokee ($113.20)	$280	$365
6/12/04			
Stephen Foster	Colonial Colony ($127.20)		
C. Whittingham	Sabiango ($28.80)		
Brooklyn	Seattle Fitz ($8.00)		
Fleur de Lis	Adoration ($7.00)	$25,643	$34,249
7/3/04			
Suburban	Peace Rules ($8.40)		
Firecracker BC	Quantum Merit ($13.40)		
U.N. 'Cap	Request for Parole ($11.40)		
American Oaks	Ticker Tape ($26.00)	$4,170	$7,879
9/9/04			
Atto Mile	Soaring Free ($6.30)		
Matron	Sense of Style ($2.70)		
Futurity	Park Avenue Ball ($23.60)		
Ruffian	Sightseek ($2.50)	$125	$178
4/9/05			
Carter	Forest Danger ($3.70)		
Wood Mem.	Bellamy Road ($7.10)		
Illinois Derby	Greeley's Galaxy ($5.60)	$36	$49
6/18/05			
Ogden Phipps	Ashado ($3.70)		
Fleur de Lis	Two Trail Sioux ($9.80)		
Stephen Foster	Saint Liam ($3.80)		
Californian	Lava Man ($19.40)	$334	$908
8/13/05			
Arlington Million	Powerscourt ($12.40)		
Sword Dancer	King's Drama ($6.70)		
Beverly D	Angara ($14.80)		
A.G. Vanderbilt	Pomeroy ($9.40)	$1,444	$2,603

Races	Winners (Paid)	$2 Parlay	$2 Pick Three or Four
10/1/05			
Joe Hirsch TC	Shakespeare ($3.80)		
Super Derby	The Daddy ($12.80)		
Jockey Club GC	Borrego ($10.60)		
Goodwood BC	Rock Hard Ten ($3.40)	$219	$416
4/14/06			
Instant Racing BC	Gasia ($10.00)		
Commonwealth BC	Sun King ($16.40)		
Blue Grass	Sinister Minister ($19.40)		
Arkansas Derby	Lawyer Ron ($3.00)	$1,193	$3,062
6/17/06			
Ogden Phipps	Take D'Tour ($8.70)		
Fleur de Lis	Happy Ticket ($5.00)		
Stephen Foster	Seek Gold ($185.40)		
Californian	Dixie Meister ($14.00)	$14,113	$22,147
8/12/06			
Arlington Million	The Tin Man ($13.00)		
Sword Dancer	Go Deputy ($15.40)		
Beverly D	Gorella ($4.60)		
A.G. Vanderbilt	War Front ($5.50)	$633	$1,297
9/30/06			
Kelso BC	Ashkal Way ($6.20)		
Ky. Cup Classic	Ball Four ($27.80)		
Yellow Ribbon	Wait a While ($3.40)		
C.L. Hirsch	The Tin Man ($3.00)	$219	$255
10/7/06			
Joe Hirsch TC	English Channel ($3.30)		
Shadwell Turf Mile	Aussie Rules ($11.80)		
Jockey Club GC	Bernardini ($2.30)		
Goodwood BC	Lava Man ($3.20)	$35	$44
10/14/06			
Frizette	Sutra ($27.00)		
First Lady	Gorella ($3.60)		
Champagne	Scat Daddy ($7.40)		
QE II Challenge Cup	Vacare ($15.60)	$1,402	$2.372

In 15 out of 15 instances for which I had complete data, the pick three or pick four paid more than the win parlay, sometimes two or three times as much.

Preakness Day, 2004

If you like the pick four, Pimlico offers two guaranteed pools of \$100,000 and \$250,000 on Friday of Preakness Weekend, and two more on Preakness Day, an early \$250,000 sequence, followed by the \$1 million pick four that ends with the Preakness.

There's no added value in guaranteed pools, because usually they attract much more than the minimum, so the track is not adding anything to the kitty; but they still attract a lot of what's known in the poker world as dead money. Have you ever seen what goes on in the infield at Pimlico on Preakness Day? Not a whole lot of serious handicapping, that's for sure.

Race 9: the Sir Barton Stakes—first leg of the \$1 million pick four

9 **Pimlico** **SirBarton100k** **$1\frac{1}{16}$ MILES** STARTA A FINISH

$1\frac{1}{16}$ MILES **($1:40^4$) 12th Running of THE SIR BARTON. Purse \$100,000 FOR THREE-YEAR-OLDS. By free subscription. \$500 to pass the entry box, \$500 additional to start, with \$100,000 Guaranteed, of which 60% to the winner, 20% to second, 11% to third, 6% to fourth and 3% to fifth. Supplemental nominations of \$1000 each will be accepted by the usual time of entry with all other fees due as noted. Weight 122 lbs. Non–winners of \$60,000 at one mile or over, allowed 3 lbs.; \$40,000 at one mile or over, 5 lbs.; \$30,000, 7 lbs. (Maiden and Claiming races not considered in estimating allowances). Preference to starters with highest career earnings. Horses may be placed on the also eligible list. Starters to be named through the entry box by the usual time of closing. Trophy to the owner of the winner. Supplemental nominee: Tap Dancer.**

1 Acclimate
Own: David I Miller
Red White, Violet Sash, Blue Bb, Violet &
VEGA H (1 0 0 0 .00) 2004: (273 46 .17)

Ch. c. 3 (Feb) FTFFEB03 \$110,000
Sire: Forestry (Storm Cat) \$50,000
Dam: Mended Heart (Le Fabuleux*Fr)
Br: Aaron U Jones & Marie D Jones (Ky)
Tr: Testerman Valora A(19 1 0 3 .05) 2004:(66 3 .05)

L 115

Life	10	2	2	2	\$67,044	86	D.Fst	8	2	2	1	\$58,970	86
2004	3	0	1	0	\$15,229	72	Wet(358)	2	0	0	1	\$8,074	62
2003	7	2	1	2	\$51,815	86	Turf(328*)	0	0	0	0	\$0	-
Pim	2	1	1	0	\$19,500	69	Dst(307)	7	2	2	0	\$55,549	86

Entered 15May04- 7 PIM

27Mar04- 8Lrl	fst	$1\frac{1}{16}$		$:25^2$	$:50^1$	$1:14^1$	$1:45^2$	PrivatTrms60k	**72**	3	2^2	$2^{1\frac12}$	$3^{2\frac12}$	$2^{4\frac12}$	$2^{3\frac34}$	Karamanos H A	L115 f	9.30	81- 20	*WaterCannon*$117^{3\frac34}$ Acclimate$115^{\frac12}$ MjorTnner$115^{4\frac14}$	2wd,steadied 3/8,game	6
28Feb04- 8Lrl	fst	$1\frac{1}{16}$		$:24$	$:47^4$	$1:12^3$	$1:45^1$	MiraclWood40k	**71**	5	$2^{2\frac12}$	1^{hd}	1^{hd}	1^{hd}	$4^{4\frac12}$	Karamanos H A	L115 f	7.70	81- 22	*Water Cannon*$115^{\frac12}$ Eastern Bay$115^{3\frac34}$ *Wanaka*115^{nk}	Bid btw,duel inside	7
7Feb04- 9Aqu	my	$1\frac{1}{16}$	⊡	$:22^4$	$:46^3$	$1:12$	$1:45^3$	Whirlaway82k	**45**	3	$1^{\frac12}$	1^{hd}	3^2	6^{14}	6^{22}	Bridgmohan S X	L118 f	11.50	61- 19	LittlMtthMn$118^{1\frac12}$ RskyTrck$116^{1\frac12}$ QuckActon$116^{13\frac14}$	Between rivals, tired	7
20Dec03- 6CT	gd	7f		$:23^4$	$:48^1$	$1:15^1$	$1:30$	StNick72k	**62**	10	8	3^1	3^{nk}	$1^{\frac12}$	3^3	Forrest C W	L119 f	2.90	68- 28	TakethePlunge119^2 Seeyouttheevent116^1 Acclimte119^{nk}	Weakened drive	10
15Nov03- 6Lrl	fst	$1\frac{1}{16}$		$:24$	$:48^1$	$1:12^4$	$1:43^4$	LrlFut-G3	**86**	2	1^{hd}	1^1	$2^{\frac12}$	$4^{2\frac12}$	$4^{6\frac34}$	Chavez J F	L122 f	26.10	83- 15	Tapit$122^{4\frac34}$ Polish Rifle$122^{\frac12}$ Ghost Mountain$122^{1\frac12}$	Rail,angled 1/8,willng	7
17Oct03- 6Lrl	fst	$1\frac{1}{16}$		$:24^2$	$:48^3$	$1:13^1$	$1:45$	OClm 50000(50-45)N	**74**	2	1^1	1^1	1^{hd}	$1^{\frac12}$	1^{nk}	Karamanos H A	L122 f	3.70	84- 19	Acclimate122^{nk} Venizia$119^{5\frac12}$ Potomac Chase$122^{\frac34}$	Rail,dueled,strong drv	6
20Sep03- 1Pim	fst	$1\frac{1}{16}$		$:24$	$:48^1$	$1:13^4$	$1:47$	Md Sp Wt 25k	**69**	5	$1^{1\frac12}$	$1^{1\frac12}$	1^1	$1^{3\frac12}$	$1^{6\frac12}$	Karamanos H A	L122 f	*1.40	72- 28	*Acclimate*$122^{6\frac12}$ Legend's Silver$122^{1\frac14}$ Mr. Smiley$122^{4\frac14}$	Pace, driving	8
5Sep03- 3Pim	fst	$1\frac{1}{16}$		$:24^2$	$:49^2$	$1:13^4$	$1:46^4$	Md Sp Wt 25k	**60**	1	2^1	$2^{\frac12}$	2^{hd}	2^{hd}	$2^{1\frac14}$	Cortez A C	L122 f	3.90	72- 24	Syoutthvnt$122^{1\frac14}$ *Acclimt*122^2 AfltCommnd$122^{1\frac14}$	Bobbled start,weakened	9
9Aug03- 5Lrl	fst	6f		$:22^1$	$:45^2$	$:58^3$	$1:11^4$	Md Sp Wt 25k	**53**	6	2	3^1	$2^{2\frac12}$	3^4	$3^{3\frac34}$	Cortez A C	L122 f	9.10	76- 16	King Carlos$122^{3\frac34}$ *Riviera*122^{hd} Acclimate$122^{5\frac12}$	3wd, faded	8
25Jly03- 5Lrl	fst	$5\frac12$f		$:22$	$:46$	$:58^1$	$1:04^3$	Md Sp Wt 25k	**46**	1	5	$4^{6\frac12}$	$4^{7\frac12}$	$4^{5\frac12}$	$4^{6\frac34}$	Cortez A C	L122 f	10.20	82- 15	*Hands On*$122^{1\frac34}$ Lord of the Cats122^2 *Venizia*122^3	Evenly	11

WORKS: May5 Pim ⓣ 5f fm $1:03^3$ B *1/2* **●Mar24 Pim 3f fst $:35^4$ H** *1/5*
TRAINER: 31-60Days(57 .11 \$1.80) Dirt(261 .08 \$1.08) Routes(78 .09 \$1.09) Stakes(12 .17 \$1.13)

2 Indian War Dance

White
Own: Sanford Goldfarb William Vidro & Ira
Black, Gold Yoke And Cgs, Gold
RODRIGUEZ R R (—) 2004: (1 1 0 .00)

B. c. 3 (Mar)
Sire: Cherokee Run (Runaway Groom) $40,000
Dam: Dancing Naturally (Fred Astaire)
Br: Jonabell Farm J Cornacchia E Swyer T McGinn & L (Ky)
Tr: Dutrow Richard E Jr(1 0 0 0 .00) 2004:(212 57 .27)

117

Life	8	2	0	1	$57,180	86	D.Fst	7	1	0	1	$30,780	85
2004	3	1	0	1	$41,400	86	Wet(377)	1	1	0	0	$26,400	86
2003	5	1	0	0	$15,780	73	Turf(253)	0	0	0	0	$0	-
Pim	0	0	0	0	$0	-	Dst(356)	2	1	0	0	$26,400	86

Entered 14May04- 8 BEL
10Apr04- 7Aqu fst 7f :221 :441 1:081 1:203 BayShore-G3 85 6 3 2hd 2½ 26 311 Coa E M L116 b 31.00 91- 04 ForestDnger1167½ Abbondnz1163½ IndinWrDnce1162½ Pressed pace, tired 8
7Mar04- 9FG fst 1$\frac{1}{16}$:222 :451 1:103 1:423 LaDerby-G2 50 8 1½ 11 1hd 1013 1029 Prado E S L122 b 17.40 68- 07 Wimbledon1222¼ Borrego122hd *Pollard's Vision*122¾ Set pace, stopped 11
5Feb04- 5Aqu gd 1$\frac{1}{16}$ ⊡ :233 :481 1:132 1:434 Alw 44000n1x 86 4 11½ 1½ 12½ 15½ 16½ Thornton T5 L112 b *2.55 92- 19 IndinWrDnce1126½ *RockinAgin*1171 RunthLight112nk Widened under drive 7
28Dec03- 4Aqu fst 6f ⊡ :23 :461 :584 1:121 Md c-(50-40) 73 1 7 2hd 2hd 1½ 13¾ Thornton T5 L115 b *1.85 83- 15 *IndinWrDnce*1153¾ *SnubtheDevil*1205½ FireHero1203¾ Dueled inside, driving 9
Claimed from Double C Stable for $50,000, Zito Nicholas P Trainer 2003(as of 12/28): (506 76 86 59 0.15)
1Nov03- 6Aqu fst 6f :214 :45 :572 1:104 Md Sp Wt 45k 57 4 7 52¾ 67¼ 69¼ 88¾ Gryder A T L120 b 13.50 77- 14 Swingforthefences1202¼ WarMarshall1202¼ Ginngo1201 Tired after a half 11
30Oct03- 2Bel fst 5½f :224 :464 :59 1:052 Md 75000(75-65) 66 4 3 51½ 52¾ 53¼ 44¾ Fragoso P5 L115 b 11.60 81- 22 MustWinSoon1202¼ *StormnGrk*116½ OnToughDud1202 Came wide, no rally 9
29Aug03- 6Sar fst 5½f :22 :452 :58 1:044 Md Sp Wt 45k 39 9 7 74¼ 79¼ 811 915¾ Coa E M L119 b 48.50 76- 10 *Smokume*1122¾ Malhoof1193 *Tales of Glory*1191¼ Stumbled start, steady 11
16Aug03- 5Sar fst 6f :22 :454 :583 1:121 Md Sp Wt 45k 6 5 7 76¾ 79¼ 723 728 Prado E S L119 9.10 53- 15 Actaeon1197 *Rainbow Rider*119hd *Redskin Warrior*1193 Off slowly, greenly 7
WORKS: May5 Aqu 5f fst 1:002 B *2/12* Apr29 Aqu 5f fst 1:02 B *3/13* Apr5 Aqu 4f fst :494 B *11/13* Mar29 Aqu 4f fst :493 B *5/6* Mar22 Aqu 5f fst 1:05 B *15/22* ●Mar5 FG 3f fst :354 B *1/12*
TRAINER: Sprint/Route(71 .28 $1.81) 31-60Days(303 .25 $1.65) Dirt(674 .26 $1.82) Routes(303 .24 $1.93) Stakes(77 .22 $2.22)

3 Humorously

Blue
Own: Oxbow Racing LLC
Red, Kelly Green Sash, Kelly Green
STEVENS G L (—) 2004: (122 24 .20)

Ch. c. 3 (Feb)
Sire: Distorted Humor (Forty Niner) $50,000
Dam: Taliesin (Talinum)
Br: L O R Stables Ltd (Ky)
Tr: White William P(—) 2004:(118 17 .14)

L 122

Life	6	2	1	0	$126,575	88	D.Fst	4	2	1	0	$125,360	88
2004	5	2	1	0	$125,700	88	Wet(416)	1	0	0	0	$875	51
2003	1	M	0	0	$875	51	Turf(273)	1	0	0	0	$340	23
Pim	0	0	0	0	$0	-	Dst(363)	4	2	1	0	$125,360	88

3Apr04-11GP fst 1$\frac{1}{16}$:234 :481 1:122 1:443 Aventura250k 88 8 21 2hd 22 22½ 24½ Bravo J L122 3.90 81- 15 Kaufy Mate1224½ Humorously122nk Baronage122½ No match, saved 2nd 8
15Mar04- 6OTC fst 1$\frac{1}{16}$:232 :471 1:121 1:441 ⓇOBSChamp100k 86 3 11½ 1½ 11 1½ 18½ Velasquez C L122 - 100- 01 Humorously1228½ ItsLucky122½ CheethSpeed1221½ Drew off when roused 7
Non-wagering event
29Feb04- 8GP fm *1⅛ Ⓣ :492 1:142 1:404 1:532 Alw 34000n1x 23 2 42¾ 32 53 911 1026¾ Velasquez C L118 14.50 48- 25 Big Booster1181½ Cervelo1201 My Lucky Mercury1181 Steadied 1st turn 10
12Feb04- 6GP fst 1$\frac{1}{16}$:24 :48 1:122 1:451 Md 62500(62.5-57.5) 80 6 21½ 22 21 12 15 Velasquez C L122 *2.90 83- 21 Humorously1225 Indian Prospector122½ Brickell1222 Drew off, driving 8
16Jan04- 2GP fst 1$\frac{1}{16}$:234 :483 1:14 1:46 Md 62500(62.5-57.5) 71 12 21 2hd 11 3nk 46¾ Velasquez C L122 9.70 72- 24 NorthernBallad122½ LordCrmen1223¼ GrretsGulch1223 Off rail, gave way 12
14Dec03- 9Crc sly 6f :221 :463 :591 1:122 Md 80000 51 5 9 77 74¾ 69 49 Bravo J 119 3.30 73- 20 Tenace1191½ *Private Promise*1195¼ Maniqui1142¼ Poor start 9
WORKS: May9 Crc 5f fst 1:022 B *11/23* May1 Crc 4f fst :48 H *2/55* ●Apr25 Crc 5f fst 1:014 H *1/9* ●Apr18 Crc 5f fst 1:002 H *1/21* ●Mar27 Crc 5f fst 1:002 H *1/37* ●Mar10 Crc 5f fst 1:001 H *1/20*
TRAINER: 31-60Days(92 .13 $0.85) Dirt(392 .20 $1.46) Routes(238 .13 $0.99) Stakes(54 .09 $0.43)

4 Tap Dancer

Yellow
Own: Gilbert G Campbell
Green, White Yoke, White 'Sf', White
ELLIOTT S (—) 2004: (460 105 .23)

Ch. c. 3 (Mar)
Sire: Sword Dance*Ire (Nijinsky II) $5,000
Dam: Heaven's Gate (Septieme Ciel)
Br: Gilbert G Campbell (Fla)
Tr: Allard Edward T(2 0 0 0 .00) 2004:(106 31 .29)

L 117

Life	9	2	2	1	$156,235	89	D.Fst	8	2	2	1	$153,235	89
2004	2	0	0	0	$7,500	89	Wet(309)	0	0	0	0	$0	-
2003	7	2	2	1	$148,735	85	Turf(298)	1	0	0	0	$3,000	83
Pim	0	0	0	0	$0	-	Dst(329)	4	0	1	0	$90,500	89

Previously trained by O'Connell Kathleen
3Apr04-11GP fst 1$\frac{1}{16}$:234 :481 1:122 1:443 Aventura250k 87 7 75 75¼ 65½ 67½ 55¼ Nunez E O L122 8.00 81- 15 Kaufy Mate1224½ **Humorously**122nk Baronage122½ 4 wd, no late response 8
14Mar04-11Tam fst 1$\frac{1}{16}$:233 :473 1:114 1:434 TampaDby-G3 89 4 64½ 83¼ 83¾ 74½ 76½ Houghton T D L116 23.70 92- 10 Limehouse118nk Mustanfr1161 Swingforthefences1161¾ Failed to menace 8
29Nov03-11Crc fm 1$\frac{1}{16}$ Ⓣ :221 :463 1:104 1:411 Mecke100k 83 4 77 94¼ 64 62¾ 52¾ Nunez E O L120 6.50 91- 08 Timo120½ Imperialism115¾ Cool Conductor1151¼ 4 wide, no late gain 12
11Oct03-11Crc fst 1$\frac{1}{16}$:234 :481 1:13 1:472 ⓇFSNReality400k 85 5 66½ 69½ 66¾ 65 22¼ Nunez E O L120 5.90 73- 22 *Sir Oscar*1202¼ Tap Dancer120nk Perpetual Peace1201¼ 3 wide, willingly 8
20Sep03-10Crc fst 170 :24 :483 1:141 1:45 FoolshPlsr100k 75 10 87 87 74 68 57¾ Nunez E O L116 2.50 92- 21 StolenTime116¾ *SecondofJune*1163¾ Imperilism1142¾ 3 wide, lacked a rally 10
30Aug03- 7Crc fst 1 :241 :481 1:132 1:421 Seacliff53k 78 2 74½ 65¾ 55 31 11¼ Nunez E O L115 4.10 70- 35 TpDncer1151¼ ChrmingJim1131¾ Hopefortheross1152¼ Stdy early, up late 10
16Aug03- 8Crc fst 1 :244 :50 1:154 1:413 Md Sp Wt 28k 78 1 2½ 2½ 1hd 12½ 110 Nunez E O L118 *.80 73- 30 *Tap Dancer*11810 Abroad1181¼ Sky Missile118¾ Rail trip, drew off 9
[illegible]ug03-10Crc fst 1 :234 :481 1:144 1:42 Md Sp Wt 28k 66 3 77½ 69 54½ 43¼ 21¼ Nunez E O L118 *2.10 70- 30 Hopefortheroses1181¼ *TapDncer*1182¾ SkyMissile1182¾ Stdy early, gaining 9
[illegible]ly03-13Crc fst 7f :231 :471 1:13 1:262 Md 25000(25-22.5) 58 1 7 85½ 63¾ 42 31¾ Nunez E O L118 9.50 80- 14 *Imperilism*1181½ FightingForum118nk TpDncer1183 Bmpd hard start & str 8
WORKS: May8 Pha 4f fst :482 B *4/54* Mar28 Crc 5f fst 1:04 B *9/16* ●Mar5 Crc 6f fst 1:153 H *1/4* Feb25 Crc 7f fst 1:323 Hg *1/1* Feb16 Crc 6f fst 1:172 B *4/4*
TRAINER: 1stW/Trn(18 .06 $0.76) 31-60Days(73 .25 $1.97) Dirt(458 .21 $1.71) Routes(200 .22 $1.59) Stakes(21 .05 $0.45)

5 P. Kerney

Green
Own: Robert S Evans
Dark Blue, Red Triangle, Blue & Red
PRADO E S (—) 2004: (552 103 .19)

B. c. 3 (Mar)
Sire: Pleasant Tap (Pleasant Colony) $15,000
Dam: Substantial (Stalwart)
Br: R S Evans (Md)
Tr: Motion H Graham(10 3 0 2 .30) 2004:(125 24 .19)

L 115

Life	3	2	0	0	$42,600	91	D.Fst	3	2	0	0	$42,600	91
2004	1	1	0	0	$21,000	91	Wet(370)	0	0	0	0	$0	-
2003	2	1	0	0	$21,600	75	Turf(287)	0	0	0	0	$0	-
Pim	0	0	0	0	$0	-	Dst(357)	0	0	0	0	$0	-

25Apr04- 8Del fst 6f :221 :46 :584 1:112 3↑ Alw 36500n1x 91 7 2 32 41 32 11¼ Dominguez R A L114 *2.80 84- 26 P. Kerney1141¼ *Bold Trick*1171¾ Salty Punch1153¼ Swung 4 wide, handily 10
31Jly03- 6Sar fst 5½f :22 :451 :571 1:034 Alw 47000n1x 41 8 8 42½ 42½ 69 717 Prado E S 120 17.20 80- 04 Hasslefree1204¾ Best to Be King1201 Rubi Echo1202¼ Chased 3 wide, tired 9
6Jly03- 6Del fst 6f :22 :453 :582 1:111 Md Sp Wt 36k 75 7 1 11½ 11½ 11½ 11 Madrigal R Jr 118 41.80 88- 10 P. Kerney1181 *Capejinsky*1184½ *Musical Vision*1181¾ Steady handling 8
WORKS: ●May10 Del 5f gd 1:021 B *1/4* Apr23 Del 4f fst :502 B *12/19* Apr16 Fai 5f fst 1:02 B *1/3* Apr6 Fai 4f fst :50 B(d) *1/2* ●Mar29 Fai 5f fst 1:023 B(d)g *1/5* ●Mar21 Fai 5f fst 1:023 B(d) *1/5*
TRAINER: 2OffOver180(17 .18 $1.12) Sprint/Route(51 .18 $1.85) Dirt(273 .14 $1.54) Routes(302 .19 $2.07) Stakes(78 .15 $2.92)

6 Irish Laddie

Black
Own: R Larry Johnson
Black & White Halves, Red Belt, Red Band
KARAMANOS H A (138 16 21 24 .12) 2004: (309 37 .12)

B. g. 3 (Mar) FTSAUG02 $75,000
Sire: Lil's Lad (Pine Bluff) $10,000
Dam: Galway Song (Irish Tower)
Br: Independence Enterprises (Ky)
Tr: Trombetta Michael J(16 4 1 3 .25) 2004:(62 12 .19)

L 115

Life	14	2	2	5	$62,030	87	D.Fst	12	2	1	5	$52,850	87
2004	5	2	0	2	$39,130	87	Wet(346)	1	0	1	0	$7,200	41
2003	9	M	2	3	$22,900	70	Turf(252*)	1	0	0	0	$1,980	46
Pim	1	0	0	1	$11,000	87	Dst(297)	8	2	1	4	$40,860	75

17Apr04- 9Pim fst 1⅛ :473 1:112 1:363 1:502 FdrcoTesio100k 87 3 32 44½ 33 37 3¾ Karamanos H A L115 b 32.00 91- 08 WaterCnnon119nk PwynePrincess114½ IrishLddie1152 Closed gap,outside 7
19Mar04- 8Lrl fst 1$\frac{1}{16}$:25 :494 1:144 1:46 Alw 25000n1x 75 5 108¼ 107¾ 84¾ 21 1hd Dominguez R A L117 b 3.00 82- 18 Irish Laddie117hd *Amerifly*1225¼ Quotidian1172¼ 6wd 3/16,drifted in,up 10
4Mar04- 7Lrl fst 1$\frac{1}{16}$:251 :50 1:143 1:45 Alw 25000n1x 72 5 58½ 53½ 55 46 35½ Dominguez R A L117 b 2.90 81- 20 ChequeMarqe117nk HrborWorker1175½ *IrishLddie*117nk Mild rally outside 7
8Feb04- 4Lrl fst 1$\frac{1}{16}$:25 :492 1:143 1:462 Md 40000(40-35) 67 7 76 42 1½ 13 12½ Dominguez R A L122 b 1.80 80- 21 Irish Laddie1222½ Honour Star118hd *Abroad*1225 Rail run,angld 3w,drvg 7
24Jan04- 6Lrl fst 1$\frac{1}{16}$:25 :491 1:153 1:481 Md Sp Wt 24k 54 4 53 21 21½ 34 47 Garcia Luis5 L117 b *1.50 64- 28 Local Yokel1224¾ Isbon122½ Magazine1221¾ Bumped early,3w,faded 8
28Dec03- 5Lrl fst 1$\frac{1}{16}$:241 :472 1:131 1:464 Md Sp Wt 25k 69 5 59½ 411 37 34 22½ Garcia Luis5 L117 b 7.40 72- 25 *Water Cannon*1222½ Irish Laddie1177¾ Wry Humor1223½ Rail, rallied 8
7Dec03- 2Lrl fst 1$\frac{1}{16}$:241 :473 1:121 1:452 Md Sp Wt 25k 70 2 43 44 44½ 37 31¾ Garcia Luis5 L117 b 6.10 80- 15 Wanaka122hd *Water Cannon*1221¾ Irish Laddie117no Urged inside,willingly 7
Previously trained by Motion H Graham
22Nov03- 1Lrl fst 1$\frac{1}{16}$:242 :482 1:131 1:452 Md 40000(40-35) 67 1 35 33½ 35½ 36 33½ Dominguez R A L122 b 2.10 78- 18 *Eastern Bay*1221¼ Worry Free1172½ Irish Laddie122½ Rail, evenly 6
26Oct03- 5Del gd 1 Ⓣ :234 :482 1:124 1:38 Md Sp Wt 33k 46 10 55 42 41½ 48½ 413¾ Umana J L L120 b 11.70 69- 17 *Seattle Borders*1204¼ Air Brush1209½ Tisawink120hd Stalked pace, no rally 10
31Aug03- 7Del fst 1 :234 :471 1:122 1:382 Md Sp Wt 33k 50 8 86¾ 65 65¼ 65¼ 58¾ Dominguez R A L119 b 6.80 83- 10 *Paddington*1192 Wanaka1192½ Unodatsrite1192¾ Failed to menace 8
WORKS: May5 Lrl 5f fst 1:01 H *2/13* ●Apr14 Lrl 3f gd :353 H *1/4* Apr7 Lrl 4f fst :482 H *6/26* Feb28 Lrl 4f fst :481 H *2/26* Feb21 Lrl 4f fst :483 H *4/19*
TRAINER: Dirt(161 .20 $1.54) Routes(57 .16 $1.01) Stakes(25 .20 $1.20)

7 Dashboard Drummer

Orange
Own: Double S Stable Preferred Pals Stable
Red, Purple Belt, Purple Cap
DOMINGUEZ R A (67 15 16 13 .22) 2004: (451 116 .26)

Dk. b or br g. 3 (Apr)
Sire: Alamocitos (Private Account) $2,000
Dam: Groovin Moment (Magic Moment II*Fr)
Br: Bob Pogue & Paulette Pogue (Okla)
Tr: Iwinski Allen(—) 2004:(191 43 .23)

L 117

Life	6	3	0	2	$183,850	87	D.Fst	5	2	0	2	$123,850	87
2004	2	0	0	1	$26,250	87	Wet(317*)	1	1	0	0	$60,000	85
2003	4	3	0	1	$157,600	85	Turf(254*)	0	0	0	0	$0	-
Pim	0	0	0	0	$0	-	Dst(329*)	2	0	0	1	$64,750	80

17Apr04- 9Kee fst 1$\frac{1}{16}$:231 :471 1:12 1:434 Lexingtn-G2 80 8 11½ 11 2hd 58 512½ Dominguez R A L116 23.00 80- 11 QuintonsGoldRush1162¾ *FrSlm*116nk SongofthSword1162 Pace, weakened 14
13Mar04-10GP fst 7f :22 :443 1:092 1:224 Swale-G3 87 4 1 44 44 44½ 34¼ Dominguez R A L120 14.30 84- 13 WynnDotComm120hd Eroslvr1204¼ DshbrdDrmmr1201 No gain, up for 3rd 5
4Oct03- 7Bel fst 1$\frac{1}{16}$:234 :481 1:133 1:44 Champagn-G1 78 5 31 41½ 42½ 38 39¼ Espinoza J L L122 15.20 71- 26 *Birdstone*1222½ ChpelRoyl1226¾ DshbordDrummr1222 Came wide, no rally 7
9Aug03-10Mth sly 6f :211 :434 :563 1:104 Sapling-G3 85 1 6 57½ 45½ 34 12½ Ferrer J C L120 4.40 85- 15 DshbordDrmmr1202½ DptyStrm120½ ChrmngJm1202 Drifted out,clear late 7
Previously trained by Pogue William R
27Jun03- 8PrM fst 5f :213 :451 :571 PrGldJuv55k 85 4 1 31 31 1½ 15 Quinonez L S B116 9.40 95- 14 *DshbordDrummer*1165 WlksLiknAngl1161 Chrnivsky1134 Drew off, driving 6
9May03- 1PrM fst 2f :221 Md Sp Wt 21k – 2 2 1½ 1¾ Quinonez L S B117 2.30 - - *Dashboard Drummer*117¾ Irish de Slew117¾ Soriano Cat1174 Driving 6
WORKS: May7 Del 6f fst 1:15 B *1/1* Apr10 GP 3f fst :361 B *5/19* Mar31 GP 1 fst 1:41 H *1/3* Mar6 GP 5f fst 1:02 B *14/22* ●Feb25 GP 6f fst 1:141 B *1/4* ●Feb16 GP 5f fst :593 Hg *1/17*
TRAINER: Dirt(712 .26 $1.92) Routes(348 .23 $1.69) Stakes(52 .19 $1.71)

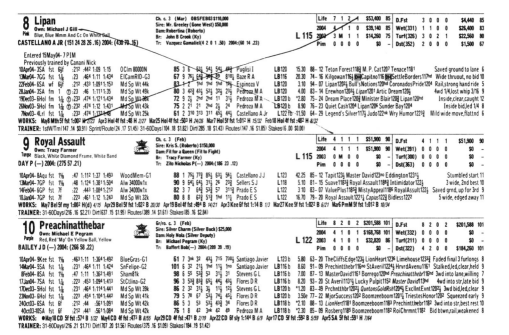

The Sir Barton's first three betting choices looked like the logical contenders, but I'm always distrustful of odds-on favorites like Preachinatthebar that are coming off an abysmal race—especially when they are drawn on the far outside with a short run to the first turn, and giving weight to most of the field. Preachinatthebar was originally being considered for the Kentucky Derby, but was withdrawn after failing to impress his connections in the mornings.

Second choice Royal Assault didn't fare much better at the draw, but deep closers like this aren't hindered as much by outside posts as horses like Preachinatthebar that typically press the pace. I also liked that he had moved up a few lengths on the figures when stretched out.

If you drew a line through Humorously's failed experiment on turf, he had never taken a backward step on the Beyer figures.

The plan: With Smarty Jones looming a short price on the back end of the pick-four sequence, it didn't make much sense to stand alone with a shaky 4–5 shot like Preachinatthebar. I probably should have tossed him out altogether, but used all three.

The running of the race: Jerry Bailey was one of the best position riders I've ever seen, but not this time. Preachinatthebar was hung out four-wide around the first turn, challenged for the lead turning for home, and weakened late. Royal Assault was deftly angled to the rail before reaching the first turn, trailed while within striking range down the backstretch, angled out entering the stretch, and edged away late.

RACE 9 Pim–15May04 $1\frac{1}{16}$ Miles (1.40^{4}), 3 yo SirBarton

Value of Race: \$100,000. 1st \$60,000 ; 2nd \$20,000 ; 3rd \$11,000 ; 4th \$6,000 ; 5th \$3,000 .
Mutuel Pools: \$1,168,298 Pick-3 \$115,914, DD \$53,316, Ex \$926,266, Super \$193,503 Tri \$720,523

Last Raced	Horse	M/Eq	A	Wt	PP	St	¼	½	¾	Str	Fin	Odds$1
10Apr04 ^{8}Aqu^{5}	Royal Assault	L	3	115	7	8	$7^{\frac{1}{2}}$	8	8	2^{1}	$1^{1\frac{3}{4}}$	3.80
17Apr04 ^{9}Kee^{5}	Dashboard Drummer	L	3	117	6	2	5^{1}	$4^{\frac{1}{2}}$	$3^{\frac{1}{2}}$	1^{hd}	$2^{\frac{1}{2}}$	8.50
3Apr04 ^{11}GP^{2}	Humorously	L	3	122	2	5	4^{hd}	$5^{\frac{1}{2}}$	7^{hd}	$4^{\frac{1}{2}}$	$3^{\frac{3}{4}}$	5.20
3Apr04 ^{11}GP^{5}	Tap Dancer	L	3	117	3	6	8	7^{2}	6^{1}	6^{2}	4^{hd}	15.00
10Apr04 ^{9}Kee^{7}	Preachinatthebar	Lb	3	122	8	7	2^{1}	2^{1}	$2^{1\frac{1}{2}}$	3^{2}	$5^{\frac{1}{2}}$	0.90
17Apr04 ^{9}Pim^{3}	Irish Laddie	Lb	3	115	5	3	$6^{1\frac{1}{2}}$	6^{hd}	$5^{1\frac{1}{2}}$	$5^{\frac{1}{2}}$	$6^{1\frac{1}{4}}$	18.90
25Apr04 ^{8}Del^{1}	P. Kerney	L	3	115	4	1	3^{1}	$3^{\frac{1}{2}}$	4^{hd}	$7^{1\frac{1}{2}}$	$7^{8\frac{3}{4}}$	8.20
27Mar04 ^{8}Lrl^{2}	Acclimate	Lf	3	115	1	4	$1^{1\frac{1}{2}}$	$1^{1\frac{1}{2}}$	1^{hd}	8	8	48.20

OFF 3:39 Start Good . Won driving. Track fast.

TIME :24^{2}, :48^{2}, 1:13, 1:39, 1:45^{3} (:24.45, :48.56, 1:13.01, 1:39.01, 1:45.63)

9 - ROYAL ASSAULT	**9.60**	**4.40**	**3.20**
7 - DASHBOARD DRUMMER		**7.60**	**4.80**
3 - HUMOROUSLY			**3.80**

\$2 Pick-3 (8-4/5/8-9) 85.20 \$2 DD (5-9) 26.80 \$2 Ex (9-7) 61.40
\$1 Super (9-7-3-4) 752.20 \$2 Tri (9-7-3) 254.20

Ch. c, (Feb), by Kris S. – Fit for a Queen , by Fit to Fight . Trainer Zito Nicholas P. Bred by Tracy Farmer (Ky).

ROYAL ASSAULT , taken to the rail early, saved ground around the first turn, eased out on the backstretch, swung four wide entering the stretch, bid for the lead in midstretch then drew clear under pressure. DASHBOARD DRUMMER , three wide both turns, gained the lead in upper stretch, dueled with the winner and weakened. HUMOROUSLY , shuffled back along the rail leaving the backstretch, raced three wide entering the stretch and rallied. TAP DANCER , wide the far turn, was fanned five wide entering the stretch and rallied mildly. PREACHINATTHEBAR , four wide the first turn, advanced two wide on the far turn, bid for the lead entering the stretch and gave way the final furlong. IRISH LADDIE , two wide between horses the far turn, weakened. P. KERNEY saved ground and lacked room in midstretch. ACCLIMATE , sent to the front, set the pace along the rail and gave way entering the stretch.

Jockeys– 1, Day P; 2, Dominguez R A; 3, Stevens G L; 4, Elliott S; 5, Bailey J D; 6, Karamanos H A; 7, Prado E S; 8, Vega H

Trainers– 1, Zito Nicholas P; 2, Iwinski Allen; 3, White William P; 4, Allard Edward T; 5, Baffert Bob; 6, Trombetta Michael J; 7, Motion H Graham; 8, Testerman Valora A

Owners– 1, Farmer Tracy; 2, Double S Stable Preferred Pals Stables & Edwin Wachtel; 3, Oxbow Racing LLC; 4, Campbell Gilbert G; 5, Pegram Michael E; 6, Johnson Larry R; 7, Evans Robert S; 8, Miller David I

Scratched– Indian War Dance (14May04 ^{8}Bel^{1}) , Lipan (10Apr04 ^{3}SA ^{4})

Race 10: the Dixie Handicap—second leg of the $1 million pick four

---

10 **Pimlico**

Dixie–G2

1⅛ MILES (Turf). (1:47) 103th Running of THE ARGENT DIXIE. Grade II. Purse $200,000 FOR THREE–YEAR–OLDS AND UPWARD. By subscription of $100. $950 to pass the entry box, $950 additional to start, with $200,000 Guaranteed, of which 60% to the winner, 20% to second, 11% to third, 6% to fourth and 3% to fifth. Supplemental nominations of $2000 each will be accepted by the usual time of entry with all other fees due as noted. Weights: Three–Year–olds, 116 lbs.; Older 124 lbs.; Non–winners of $100,000 at one mile or over in 2004, allowed 3 lbs.; $60,000 at one mile or over in 2004, allowed, 5 lbs. (Maiden and claiming races not considered in estimating allowances). Preference to starters with highest earnings in 2003–04. Horses may be placed on the also eligible list. Starters to be named through the entry box by the usual time of closing. Trophy to the owner of the winner. (If deemed inadvisable by management to run this race on the Turf course, it will be run on the main track at One Mile and One Eighth.) Supplemental nominee: My Lord.

Coupled – Wudantunoit and My Lord and White Buck

---

2 Warleigh

Own: Rosendo G Parra
White · Hunter Green, Gold Sunburst In Green
SELLERS S J (—) 2004: (439 100 .23)

Ch. h. 6 (Feb)
Sire: Lord At War*Arg (General*Fr)
Dam: Must Ask (Naskra)
Br: Wimborne Farm Inc (Ky)
Tr: Asmussen Steven M(—) 2004:(737 193 .26)

L 124

	Life	22	9	6	1	$481,512	108
	2004	3	1	1	0	$145,200	102
	2003	8	5	1	0	$217,545	108
	Pim	0	0	0	0	$0	—

D.Fst 2 0 1 0 $10,080 71
Wet(361) 1 1 0 0 $29,700 95
Turf(374) 19 8 5 1 $441,732 108
Dst(397) 9 5 2 0 $280,861 102

WORKS: May11 CD ④4f fm :51³ B(d) 6/6 May4 CD ⑦7f gd 1:35² B(d) 2/2 Apr27 CD ⑦6f fm 1:14³ B(d) 1/1 Mar28 FG ⑦7f fst 1:26 B 1/1 ●Mar22 FG ⑥f fst 1:13 B 1/6 Mar16 FG 5f fst 1:02 B 9/17
TRAINER: 2Off45–180(308 .25 $1.56) 31–60Days(842 .24 $1.57) Turf(436 .16 $0.99) Routes(1053 .24 $1.60) GrdStk(78 .17 $1.54)

---

3 Senor Swinger

Own: Robert B & Beverly J Lewis
Blue · Green, Yellow Hoops & Sleeves, Green Cap
DAY P (—) 2004: (267 52 .19)

Gr/ro. c. 4 (Apr)
Sire: El Prado*Ire (Sadler's Wells) $75,000
Dam: Smooth Swinger (Kris S.)
Br: Bob Ackerman (Ky)
Tr: Baffert Bob(—) 2004:(208 39 .19)

L 119

	Life	15	5	0	2	$417,155	103
	2004	3	1	0	0	$40,265	99
	2003	11	3	0	2	$361,290	103
	Pim	0	0	0	0	$0	—

D.Fst 4 2 0 0 $59,640 93
Wet(403) 2 0 0 0 $22,500 96
Turf(351) 30 3 0 2 $335,015 103
Dst(368) 3 2 0 0 $195,037 103

WORKS: May9 CD 4f fst :46⁴ B 4/46 Apr24 CD 6f gd 1:15⁴ B 2/3 ●Apr18 CD 5f fst :57⁴ B 1/43 Apr12 SA 1 fst 1:37³ H 1/2 Apr2 SA 5f fst :59 H 2/43 ●Mar28 SA ④4f fm :49 H(d) 1/9
TRAINER: 2Off45–180(187 .23 $1.46) Turf(175 .14 $1.57) Routes(374 .16 $1.95) GrdStk(174 .19 $2.60)

---

1 Wudantunoit

Own: Michael J Gill
Red · Blue, Blue Mmm And Cc On White Ball
KARAMANOS H A (131 16 20 24 .12) 2004: (302 37 .12)

Ch. g. 6 (Mar)
Sire: Dumaani (Danzig) $4,000
Dam: Cozzenette (Cozzene)
Br: Dr William A Reed & Stonecrest Farm (Ky)
Tr: Vazquez Gamaliel(4 2 0 1 .50) 2004:(59 14 .24)

L 119

	Life	37	8	4	5	$204,962	104
	2004	2	1	1	0	$17,000	94
	2003	11	3	1	3	$87,157	104
	Pim	0	0	0	0	$0	—

D.Fst 7 1 1 0 $9,888 89
Wet(330) 0 0 0 0 $0 —
Turf(351) 30 7 3 5 $195,074 104
Dst(339) 2 0 0 0 $0 85

WORKS: May8 Mth 5f fst 1:02 H 2/23 Apr16 Lrl 4f fst :47³ H 2/36 Mar22 FG 4f fst :47³ B 2/32
TRAINER: 1stClaim(109 .17 $1.12) 61–180Days(45 .18 $1.31) Sprint/Route(24 .17 $1.45) Turf(57 .14 $2.00) Routes(147 .16 $1.85) GrdStk(1.00 $0.00)

1a My Lord

Own: Michael J Gill
Red · Blue, Blue Mmm And Cc On White Ball
KARAMANOS H A (131 16 20 24 .12) 2004: (302 37 .12)

Ch. s. 5 (Apr)
Sire: Lord Carson (Carson City) $6,000
Dam: Love of Our Life (Vice Regent)
Br: Patricia Youngman (Cal)
Tr: Vazquez Gamaliel(4 2 0 1 .50) 2004:(59 14 .24)

L 119

	Life	25	5	5	5	$126,440	92
	2004	3	1	0	0	$21,000	93
	2003	12	1	3	2	$43,500	92
	Pim	0	0	0	0	$0	—

D.Fst 13 2 1 2 $42,280 92
Wet(383) 5 1 1 1 $22,700 89
Turf(301) 7 3 2 0 $61,460 92
Dst(327) 0 0 0 0 $0 —

WORKS: May8 Mth 5f fst 1:02 B 22/23 Apr16 Lrl 4f fst :47³ H 2/36 Mar22 FG 4f fst :47³ B 2/32
TRAINER: Sprint/Route(24 .17 $1.45) 61–180Days(103 .18 $1.94) Turf(57 .14 $2.00) Routes(147 .16 $1.85) GrdStk(1.00 $0.00)

---

4 Silver Tree
Own: Vegso Racing Stable
Yellow White, Red Chevrons, Red Bars On Sleeves
BAILEY J D (—) 2004: (262 56 .21)

Ch. c. 4 (Feb)
Sire: Hennessy (Storm Cat) $35,000
Dam: Blue Begum (With Approval)
Br: Vegso Racing Stable (Fla)
Tr: Mott William I(—) 2004:(217 42 .19)

L 119

Life	8	4	0	1	$413,460	98	D.Fst	1	0	0	0	$340 52
2004	2	1	0	0	$22,800	98	Wet(343)	0	0	0	0	$0 –
2003	6	3	0	1	$390,660	96	Turf(329)	7	4	0	1	$413,120 98
Pim(T)	0	0	0	0	$0	–	Dst(T)(346)	1	0	0	0	$0 96

21Mar04-8FG fm *1⅛ (T):49 1:122 1:361 1:481 4↑MMunzJrH-G2 96 1 21 1hd 31 22½ 84 Bailey J D L118 *2.30 99-05 Mystery Giver120¾ Herculated116½ Skate Away1171 Faltered mid stretch 10
21Feb04-9GP fm 1 (T):231 :461 1:092 1:331 4↑Alw 38000N3x 98 9 53½ 43½ 21½ 21 12¼ Bailey J D L118 *.70 100-06 Silver Tree1182¼ Tacirring1181¾ Fast Decision1181¾ Vigorous hand ride 10
30Nov03-9Hol fm 1¼ (T):51 1:172 1:41 2:041 HolDerby-G1 96 3 31½ 41½ 42 21½ 41 Prado E S B122 5.70 70-17 *SweetReturn*122½ FirlyRnsom122½ KickenKris122hd Pulld,stalked,outkickd 13
12Jly03-10Cnl fm 1¼ (T):474 1:114 1:361 2:01 VrgniaDrby500k 96 7 11 11 11½ 14½ 11½ Prado E S 115 5.50 105-03 Silver Tree1151½ *Kicken Kris*1151¾ King's Drama1152 Pace 2wd, driving 8
22Jun03-4WO fm 1 (T):224 :451 1:10 1:331 CBarley112k 90 12 73¾ 53½ 31½ 31½ 33½ Landry R C 118 *1.25 93-09 Moonshine Hall1181½ Strizzi1182 *Silver Tree*1184 4w,bid 3w, held pos 12
23Apr03-9GP fm *1 1/16 (T):223 :454 1:10 1:411 Alw 34000N1x 93 6 56 513 36 1hd 13¾ Boulanger G 122 *1.30 98-13 SilverTr1223¾ CommndingCrk1184¾ *NtivGnius*1182 Bmpd early, drew clear 10
27Mar03-6GP fm *1 1/16 (T):242 :511 1:153 1:46 Md Sp Wt 36k 90 3 21½ 32 31 22½ 11¼ Velasquez C 122 4.80 74-24 *SilverTree*1221¼ *SirLochinvar*1223 HonoraryMan122¾ Steadied bkstr & turn 10
22Feb03-6GP fst 7f :22 :442 1:10 1:232 Md Sp Wt 34k 52 9 5 54 57½ 57 512 Bailey J D 122 10.60 79-07 Bishop CourtHill1227½ *SaintLiam*1222¼ Reprimand1221 4 wide, no response 11

WORKS: May10 Bel 4f fst :494 B *16/29* May4 CD (T) 6f gd 1:172 B(d) *2/2* Apr27 CD (T) 5f fm 1:031 B(d) *5/9* Apr16 Pay 4f fst :503 B *2/17* Apr8 Pay 4f fst :512 B *13/20* Mar31 Pay 4f fst :513 B *4/8*
TRAINER: 31-60Days(308 .20 $1.68) Turf(452 .20 $1.85) Routes(676 .20 $1.62) GrdStk(86 .13 $1.28)

5 Millennium Dragon (GB)
Own: Darley Stable
Green Maroon, White Sleeves, White Cap
MIGLIORE R (—) 2004: (308 63 .20)

B. h. 5 (Jan)
Sire: Mark of Esteem*Ire (Darshaan*GB) $21,403
Dam: Feather Bride*Ire (Groom Dancer)
Br: Elsdon Farms (GB)
Tr: McLaughlin Kiaran P(—) 2004:(164 35 .21)

L 121

Life	22	6	4	2	$299,985	108	D.Fst	0	0	0	0	$0 –
2004	3	1	1	0	$110,000	108	Wet(293)	2	0	1	1	$25,390 100
2003	8	2	1	2	$112,990	103	Turf(285)	20	6	3	1	$274,595 108
Pim(T)	0	0	0	0	$0	–	Dst(T)(281)	2	0	1	1	$36,500 100

9Apr04-9Kee fm 1 (T):23 :451 1:09 1:332 4↑MakrsMrk-G2 100 4 65½ 65½ 62½ 66½ 62¼ Migliore R L116 7.50 103 - Perfect Soul116½ Burning Roma116hd RoyalSpy1161 Between,no late gain 10
31Jan04-8GP sly 1 1/16 ⊗:233 :471 1:114 1:444 3↑CanTurfH-G3 100 6 2hd 1½ 1½ 11 2nk Migliore R L118 *2.00 85-29 *Nwfondlnd*115nk MllnnmDrgn1188¾ EvrythngtGn1135¼ Drifted out stretch 6
4Jan04-9GP fm 1 (T):24 :49 1:114 1:342 3↑AppletnH-G3 108 7 11 11 1½ 11½ 11¼ Migliore R L116 4.10 94-07 MllnnumDrgon1161¼ PoltclAttck1184 *ProdMn*116nk Pace,held well driving 12
6Dec03-11Crc fm 1⅛ (T):451 1:09 1:34 1:454 3↑TropTrfH-G3 100 2 22½ 24 22 2hd 21¼ Cruz M R L116 3.30 100 - PoliticlAttck1161¼ *MillnniumDrgon*116no Sforz115nk Led far turn, saved 2d 12
1Nov03-8Aqu gd 1⅛ (T):50 1:14 1:381 1:502 3↑KnkrbkrH-G2 99 7 1½ 11½ 12 1½ 3¾ Migliore R L115 10.80 87-12 **BettrTlkNow**116½ DlMrShow116nk MillnniumDrgon1152¾ Set pace, gamely 12
4Oct03-8Bel fm 1 (T):24 :471 1:103 1:343 3↑KelsoBCH-G2 100 2 51¾ 42 51¼ 6½ 52¼ Velazquez J R L113 4.40 85-15 Freefourinternet113no ProudMn1141 Rouvrs1151¼ 4 wide move, weakened 10
17Sep03-8Bel fm 7f (T):231 :452 1:081 1:201 4↑Alw 56000c 103 1 4 2hd 1hd 1hd 12 Migliore R L116 2.85 98-02 MillenniumDrgon1162 *JoesSonJoy*1231 *MusicsStorm*1201 Vied inside, clear 8
16Aug03-8WO yl 7f (T):23 :462 1:102 1:232 3↑PlayKngH-G3 92 4 6 64 51¾ 67 65¾ Landry R C L116 6.50 79-15 SoaringFree1211½ JebsWild1141½ FrnksSelection1131 Stalk 4w, no factor 6
4Jly03-7Bel fm 1 (T):232 :461 1:10 1:34 3↑Alw 50000N3x 99 1 11½ 1½ 1hd 11½ 1½ Migliore R L120 3.80 90-17 MillenniumDrgon120½ ThfullCircl120¾ ClticSky1171½ Pace, dug in, held on 10
7Jun03-12Bel sly 7f ⊗:22 :443 1:091 1:222 4↑Alw 49000N3x 96 1 5 32 22½ 3½ 33¾ Migliore R L116 7.50 84-10 Clergy1162 TstyCberneigh1161¾ *MillnniumDrgon*1168 Chased inside, no bid 5

WORKS: ●May7 Sar tr.t 4f fst :483 B *1/14* ●Apr28 Kee 4f fst :472 H *1/36* Apr4 Kee 4f fst :50 B *19/43* Mar28 PmM 5f fst 1:002 H *8/26* Mar22 PmM 4f fst :474 H *3/19* Mar2 PmM 4f fst :483 B *5/29*
TRAINER: 2Off45-180(55 .25 $2.56) 31-60Days(102 .22 $1.79) Turf(119 .30 $3.00) Routes(238 .25 $2.24) GrdStk(69 .23 $2.69)

1x White Buck
Own: Michael J Gill
Red Blue, Blue Mmm And Gc On White Ball
CASTELLANO A JR (146 23 25 26 .16) 2004: (425 69 .16)

Gr/ro. g. 4 (Apr)
Sire: Thats Our Buck (Buckaroo) $1,000
Dam: Stephies Jig (Jig Time)
Br: Dr & Mrs Cornelius A Link (Fla)
Tr: Shuman Mark(28 8 1 5 .29) 2004:(302 58 .19)

L 119

Life	26	3	4	4	$163,083	98	D.Fst	17	1	4	2	$84,369 97
2004	4	0	0	0	$0	91	Wet(324)	2	1	0	0	$28,500 86
2003	14	2	1	3	$129,923	98	Turf(174)	7	1	0	2	$50,214 98
Pim(T)	0	0	0	0	$0	–	Dst(T)(273)	0	0	0	0	$0 –

Entered 15May04- 8 PIM
29Apr04-4Hol fm 1¼ (T):494 1:142 1:382 2:013 4↑OClm c-80000 89 7 63½ 52 73¼ 73¾ 74¼ Court J K LB118 b 6.10 79-21 LeprechunKid118¾ AmricnSon118½ Ringskiddy118nk 3-4wd to lane, no bid 8
Claimed from Manoogian Jay for $80,000, Mitchell Mike Trainer 2004(as of 4/29): (128 32 24 16 0.25)
18Apr04-9SA fm *1¾ (T)1:134 1:391 2:281 2:454 4↑SnJnCpoH-G2 87 6 44 54¾ 53½ 75¼ 68 Court J K LB113 b 20.80 77-17 MeteorStorm1161½ *RhythmMd*1151 RunwyDncr1152½ Pulled,chased,no bid 9
20Mar04-9SA fm 1½ (T):471 1:12 2:02 2:26 4↑SanLsRyH-G2 91 4 67½ 86 97½ 76¼ 65¾ Nakatani C S LB117 b 16.10 85-08 *MeteorStorm*115nk Labirinto114¾ GenedeCampeo114¾ Rail, split, improved 10
24Jan04-6SA fst 1⅛ :453 1:092 1:342 1:473 4↑[R]SMClassic1000k 90 7 911 107¾ 66 76¾ 710 Smith M E LB120 b 34.10 86-07 *SouthrnImg*1203 ExcssSummr1205 ThJudgSzWho122½ 4wd 2nd turn,no bid 12
29Dec03-7SA fm 1¼ (T):48 1:121 1:371 2:013 3↑OClm 62500N 98 3 55½ 55½ 44½ 22½ 11½ Smith M E LB117 b 11.30 85-19 White Buck1171½ *All the Boys*119nk Urban King1171½ Rank early,rallied 10
21Nov03-7Hol fm 1 1/16 (T):243 :471 1:113 1:414 3↑Alw 46000N2x 90 6 75¾ 714 76¼ 54½ 32¼ Nakatani C S LB117 b 8.80 85-17 *Expresso Bay*119nk Gold Sphinx1212 *White Buck*1171 Floatd out 7/8,late 3d 7
11Nov03-7Hol fm 1 (T):242 :482 1:11 1:343 [R]BienBien72k 91 3 53½ 41½ 32 32¼ 31¼ Desormeaux K J LB119 b 10.10 89-11 Special Rate114no Royal Place1151½ White Buck1191½ Pulled,steadied 7/8 7
27Sep03-11Fpx fst *1⅛ :483 1:133 1:382 1:51 PomonaDrby100k 74 5 72¾ 84¼ 85 87½ 710¼ Berrio O A LB116 b 8.20 82-08 Excess Summer1225 Tribe1141 Six Numbers117nk Shifted out, four wide 8
5Sep03-7Dmr fst 1 :22 :451 1:101 1:352 [R]ElCajon92k 97 1 610 610 63¾ 32 33 Nakatani C S LB120 b 22.90 94-10 *ExcessSummer*1182½ *FlytotheWire*118½ WhiteBuck1206 Saved ground to 1/4 7
24Aug03-8Dmr fst 1 :221 :452 1:10 1:362 3↑OClm 62500N 72 9 78 77 45½ 66½ 710¼ Flores D R LB116 b 4.10 82-02 McDab119no *Boss Ego*1191 Commander's Flag1194 3wd move,no late bid 9

WORKS: Apr12 Hol 6f fst 1:143 H *6/12* Apr5 Hol 6f fst 1:143 H *6/13* Mar29 Hol 4f fst :483 H *6/16* Mar13 Hol 7f fst 1:264 H *3/5* Mar8 Hol 6f fst 1:124 H *2/9* Mar1 Hol 6f fst 1:124 H *3/20*
TRAINER: 1stClaim(214 .27 $2.09) Turf(107 .06 $0.35) Routes(561 .17 $1.17) GrdStk(30 .03 $0.69)

6 Megantic
Own: Runnin Horse Farm Inc
Black Forest Green, Forest Green 'Rhf' On
BRAVO J (—) 2004: (448 74 .17)

B. h. 6 (Jan)
Sire: Theatrical*Ire (Nureyev) $75,000
Dam: Jade Flush (Jade Hunter)
Br: Allen E Paulson (Ky)
Tr: Pointer Norman R(—) 2004:(61 9 .15)

L 119

Life	20	6	2	5	$199,740	97	D.Fst	0	0	0	0	$0 –
2004	2	1	0	1	$32,140	97	Wet(338)	1	0	0	0	$6,000 70
2003	6	1	0	2	$30,960	94	Turf(337)	19	6	2	5	$193,740 97
Pim(T)	0	0	0	0	$0	–	Dst(T)(374)	3	2	0	0	$26,760 94

20Mar04-6GP fm 1½ (T):50 1:153 2:262 3↑PanAmerH-G2 97 1 74 63 31 23 32¼ Bravo J L112 20.90 84-14 QuestStar114½ RequestforParole1151¾ Megntic1122½ Steadied twice early 7
6Mar04-10GP fm *1⅛ (T):49 1:121 1:372 1:492 4↑Clm 50000(50-40) 94 2 99¼ 912 78½ 62¾ 11 ↓Guidry M L120 6.80 95-04 [DH]Megantic120 [DH]Mutmyyz1201 NoMoreChds120¾ Blocked, checked str 10
29Jun03-7Mth fm 1 1/16 (T):24 :474 1:112 1:41 +3↑Clm 50000(50-40) 74 7 73¼ 54 63 89¼ 810 Clemente A V L116 3.70 86-05 RoylAffrmd1142½ BrodwySnwmn1161¼ ThndrChf119nk Outside, weakened 8
7Jun03-10Pha sly 1½ :473 1:122 2:052 2:313 3↑GrenwodCpH100k 70 4 812 710 614 521 427½ Clemente A V L114 17.00 83-14 GoldenTicket11410¼ *AsongforBilly*113½ *YnkeDoodlBoy*11416¾ Wide, brushed 10
19Apr03-8GP fm 1 1/16 (T):242 :491 1:124 1:413 4↑OClm 80000 94 6 43½ 43 31½ 43 31½ Velez J A Jr L118 6.20 85-15 Glick1181¼ *Boastful*118nk Megantic1181¼ 3 wide, gained 3rd 7
27Mar03-9GP fm *1 1/16 (T):231 :482 1:124 1:452 4↑Clm c-(62.5-57.5) 93 4 1013 910 96 43½ 31¼ ↓Bailey J D L120 2.50 76-24 Thunder Chief1221 Jeeves118nk [DH]Hitchin' Post120 Lunged st, up for 3rd 10
Claimed from Brushwood Stable for $62,500, Mott William I Trainer 2002: (164 31 26 21 0.19)
13Feb03-9GP fm *1⅛ (T):492 1:134 1:394 1:513 4↑OClm 100000 93 4 917 716 69¾ 56 51½ Bailey J D L118 *2.70 81-23 Mr. Pleasentfar118nk Wertz118¾ ***Better Talk Now***122½ 4 wide, some gain 9
16Jan03-8GP fm *1⅛ (T):483 1:124 1:383 1:504 4↑Clm 50000(50-45) 94 1 912 913 87½ 33 11½ Bailey J D L120 *1.30 87-21 Megantic1201½ Port Henry120¾ Viva Pentelicus1201¾ 4 wide, up late 10
1Nov02-4CD gd 1 1/16 (T):233 :473 1:12 1:433 3↑OClm 80000N 82 6 54¼ 43 64 73½ 66½ Guidry M L117 3.20 79-17 Gretchen's Star117½ Grifter1171¾ Tubrok1172 4w,tired 7
25Oct02-7AP yl 1 3/16 (T):511 1:161 1:412 1:594 3↑JohnHenryH100k 86 6 56½ 42 2½ 43 65¼ Bailey J D L115 2.90 73-24 [D]*TpthAdmrl*114½ Rddlsdown1162 NtnlAnthm1152 In motion-hopped start 7

WORKS: Mar3 GP 4f fst :50 B *19/23* Feb24 GP 5f fst 1:02 B *6/16*
TRAINER: 31-60Days(55 .24 $4.92) Turf(77 .19 $4.13) Routes(171 .17 $2.31) GrdStk(4 .00 $0.00)

7 Mr O'Brien (Ire)
Own: Skeedattle II
Orange Green, Gold Band, Gold Band On Sleeves
DOMINGUEZ R A (67 15 16 13 .22) 2004: (446 115 .26)

Ch. g. 5 (Apr)
Sire: Mukaddamah (Storm Bird)
Dam: Laurel Delight*GB (Presidium*GB)
Br: Jack Ronan & Des Vere Hunt Farm Co (Ire)
Tr: Graham Robin L(6 1 1 0 .17) 2004:(18 1 .06)

L 119

Life	15	6	3	1	$190,290	100	D.Fst	7	1	3	1	$48,990 98
2004	2	1	0	0	$31,050	100	Wet(300)	1	1	0	0	$25,800 98
2003	7	2	3	1	$73,740	98	Turf(266)	7	4	0	0	$115,500 100
Pim(T)	2	2	0	0	$75,000	100	Dst(T)(238)	0	0	0	0	$0 –

1May04-9Pim fm 1 (T):24 :473 1:113 1:354 3↑HenryClark50k 100 2 32 31½ 12½ 18 19 Wilson R L119 8.50 90-11 Mr O'Brien1199 Spruce Run1192½ Tam's Terms1193¾ Brisk whipping 8
8Jan04-8Lrl fst 6f :221 :452 :582 1:111 4↑OClm 75000(75-65)N 81 4 1 45 43 44 56¼ Caraballo J C L117 7.00 80-20 TacticlSide1121 InsRocket1164¼ InnerHrbour117½ Chased,angld in,empty 6
30Nov03-8Lrl fst 1 1/16 :243 :483 1:13 1:434 3↑OClm 75000(75-65)N 89 1 32½ 33 32½ 22 33 Wilson R L119 2.70 87-22 Lyracist1191¾ Exclusive Run1141½ Mr O'Brien1191 Failed to sustain bid 7
15Nov03-7Lrl fst 1 1/16 :233 :462 1:111 1:424 3↑HailEmpror50k 93 4 37 38 33 34 57¾ Wilson R L119 5.20 87-15 Last Intention119no Toccet1237½ Quiet Gratitude119nk Gave way 8
Previously trained by Dutrow Anthony W
2Oct03-7Pim fst 1 1/16 :242 :483 1:131 1:431 3↑OClm 50000(50-45)N 96 5 11½ 11 11½ 1½ 2hd Pino M G L121 *1.50 91-24 MyKindofTown119hd MrOBrien12112½ CowboyMgic1164¾ Rail,grudgingly 6
22Aug03-8Lrl fst 1 1/16 :244 :491 1:13 1:433 3↑OClm 40000(40-35)N 98 2 22 21½ 2½ 14 1nk Pino M G L119 *1.00 91-15 Mr O'Brien119nk Hunter B.1191¾ Invent1191 Rated,2wd bid,driving 5
21Jly03-7Del fst 1 1/16 :232 :471 1:112 1:44 3↑OClm 100000N 98 2 11 1hd 1hd 1hd 24¾ Dominguez R A L119 *.70 83-20 CountryBeGold1174¾ *MrOBrin*1196¾ CityShrpstr11913 Lost whip, no match 5
21Jun03-6Del sly 1 :233 :47 1:113 1:37 3↑OClm 50000N 98 6 11½ 11 1hd 14½ 17 Black A S L117 *1.30 99-09 MrOBrien1177 SlyGrin1224¾ ForeignSecretry1171½ Quick pace, ridden out 6
11May03-8Pim fst 1 1/16 ⊗:231 :471 1:111 1:434 3↑OClm 30000(30-25)N 92 6 13 11 1½ 21½ 22 Pino M G L117 4.80 86-12 Doc Wild1172 *Mr O'Brien*1172½ *Thunder Chief*1196¾ Pace off rail, gamely 7
Previously trained by Dickinson Michael W
1Jly02-7Del fm 1 1/16 (T):232 :462 1:102 1:412 NShukMem75k 76 1 43 44 53½ 59 410¾ Vega H L122 2.70 89-09 Patrol1173½ Coco's Madness1172 Coahoma1195¼ Rank early, no factor 5

WORKS: ●Apr22 Lrl (T) 5f fm 1:03 B(d) *1/4* Apr15 Lrl 4f fst :49 B *4/15* Apr8 Lrl 5f fst 1:024 B *4/8* Mar31 Lrl 4f gd :503 B *9/18* Mar25 Lrl 3f gd :373 B *4/6* Mar20 Lrl 3f fst :373 B *5/11*
TRAINER: 2Off45-180(6 .00 $0.00) Turf(4 .25 $4.75) Routes(23 .17 $1.50)

8 Herculated

Own: Oak Crest Farm
Pink · Blue, Blue 'Oc' On Silver Ball, Silver
LOVATO F JR (—) 2004: (293 25 .09)

B. g. 4 (Mar)
Sire: Louis Quatorze (Sovereign Dancer) $10,000
Dam: Theriot's Treasure (Mac Diarmida)
Br: Oak Crest Farm (Ky)
Tr: Stidham Michael(—) 2004:(147 38 .26)

Life 8 5 1 1 $200,014 104
2004 3 2 1 0 $143,200 104
2003 5 3 0 1 $56,814 95
Pim 0 0 0 0 $0 —

D.Fst 1 1 0 0 $15,600 92
Wet(342) 1 0 0 1 $5,214 83
Turf(232) 6 4 1 0 $179,200 104
Dst(285) 1 0 1 0 $100,000 103

9 Better Talk Now

Own: Bushwood Stables
Tampa · Grape, Lime Green Collar & Sash, Grape
PRADO E S (—) 2004: (549 103 .19)

B. g. 5 (Feb)
Sire: Talkin Man (With Approval) $1,568
Dam: Bendita (Baldski)
Br: Wimborne Farm Inc (Ky)
Tr: Motion H Graham(10 3 0 2 .30) 2004:(124 23 .19)

Life 18 6 3 2 $337,437 101
2004 1 0 0 0 $0 88
2003 4 2 2 2 $240,152 101
Pim 0 0 0 0 $0 —

D.Fst 4 0 2 0 $16,360 90
Wet(297) 0 0 0 0 $0 —
Turf(376) 14 6 1 2 $321,077 101
Dst(309) 6 4 0 1 $186,060 101

10 Wando

Own: Gustav Schickedanz
Purple · Black And Red Stripes, White Sleeves
HUSBANDS P (—) 2004: (80 10 .12)

Ch. c. 4 (Feb)
Sire: Langfuhr (Danzig) $25,000
Dam: Kathie's Colleen (Woodman)
Br: Gustav Schickedanz (Ont-C)
Tr: Keogh Michael(—) 2004:(14 2 .14)

Life 14 9 2 1 $2,413,800 111
2004 1 0 0 0 $34,100 95
2003 8 5 1 1 $2,017,323 111
Pim 0 0 0 0 $0 —

D.Fst 9 6 1 1 $1,161,450 111
Wet(327) 1 1 0 0 $300,000 99
Turf(298) 4 2 1 0 $952,350 101
Dst(337) 0 0 0 0 $0 —

The Dixie was a wide-open betting race, with four horses in the range of 7–2 to 5–1, and several others with solid credentials as well. Wando and Herculated were co-favored, but neither inspired great confidence. The former was a pace-presser marooned out in post 11, and the latter had never won outside the Fair Grounds.

A case could be made for Warleigh, Millennium Dragon, and Mr O'Brien, all of whom had recorded triple-digit Beyer figures in their last starts. The latter was stepping up in class, to be sure, but was 2 for 2 over the Pimlico turf course, including a power-house performance two weeks earlier; he might bounce, but turf horses are less likely to do so than dirt horses, particularly when they come back on the same footing.

The plan: If there was a race to spread out in this pick four, the Dixie was the one. It's been my experience that in skull-busting races such as this, it's best to cast as wide a net as finances allow. I used the five aforementioned horses, and also threw in Senor Swinger, even though he seemed to prefer the Churchill Downs turf course.

The running of the race: In *Thoroughbred Form Cycles,* Mark Cramer wrote about how 5-year-old geldings can really come into their own. Mr O'Brien must have read that book too, because he ran right back to his big race in the Henry Clark and drew away in course-record time. Four horses were separated by heads and necks behind him for the minor awards.

RACE 10 Pim–15May04 1⅛ Miles Ⓣ (1.46¹), 3↑ DixieG2

Value of Race: $200,000. 1st $120,000 ; 2nd $40,000 ; 3rd $22,000 ; 4th $12,000 ; 5th $6,000 .
Mutuel Pools: $1,376,983 Pick–3 $134,441, DD $79,284, Ex $1,029,023, Super $197,885 Tri $792,779

Last Raced	Horse	M/Eq	A	Wt	PP	St	¼	½	¾	Str	Fin	Odds$1
1May04 9Pim¹	Mr O'Brien-Ire	L	5	119	8	8	7¹	7¹½	5hd	2½	1²	11.40
9Apr04 9Kee⁶	MillnniumDrgon-GB	L	5	121	6	4	3²	3½	3½	4²	2hd	7.00
10Apr04 7Hou¹	Warleigh	L	6	124	1	2	6²½	5½	6²½	5³	3nk	8.90
20Mar04 6GP³	Megantic	L	6	119	7	11	11	11	11	8²	4nk	32.50
29Apr04 6CD¹	Senor Swinger	L	4	119	2	6	8¹	9½	9¹	7¹½	5¹	4.80
12Mar04 9FG²	Wudantunoit	L b	6	119	3	1	1hd	1½	1¹½	1¹	6½	a-36.10
18Apr04 6Kee¹	Wando	L	4	119	11	7	2²	2²	2hd	3hd	7¹	3.60
21Mar04 8FG⁸	Silver Tree	L	4	119	5	3	4½	4²	4¹	6hd	8¾	5.00
10Apr04 7Hou⁸	Better Talk Now	L bf	5	119	10	10	10hd	10¹	10½	10¹	9³	10.70
21Mar04 8FG²	Herculated	L	4	119	9	9	9²½	8hd	8½	9hd	10¹¼	3.50
27Mar04 8FG¹	My Lord	L b	5	119	4	5	5hd	6¹	7¹	11	11	a-36.10

a–Coupled: Wudantunoit and My Lord.

OFF 4:26 Start Good . Won driving. Course firm.

TIME :23⁴, :46⁴, 1:10, 1:33⁴, 1:46¹ (:23.89, :46.80, 1:10.03, 1:33.93, 1:46.34)

(New Course Record)

7 – MR O'BRIEN–IRE	24.80	12.60	7.40
5 – MILLENNIUMDRGON–GB		8.20	5.80
2 – WARLEIGH			6.00

$2 Pick–3 (4/5/8–9–7) 357.60 $2 DD (9–7) 149.20 $2 Ex (7–5) 201.80
$1 Super (7-5-2-6) 6,678.60 $2 Tri (7-5-2) 1,334.60

Ch. g, (Apr), by Mukaddamah – Laurel Delight-GB , by Presidium-GB . Trainer Graham Robin L. Bred by Jack Ronan & Des Vere Hunt Farm Co (Ire).

MR O'BRIEN (IRE) settled off the rail, steadily advanced four wide nearing the lane, surged to command nearing the sixteenth marker, kicked clear racing on his left lead then held sway under a drive. MILLENNIUM DRAGON (GB) , forwardly placed along the inside, was put to urging nearing the quarter pole, was brushed and forced in by WANDO when attempting to get out for room in upper stretch, continued to lack room to the sixteenth marker then finished sharply once clear. WARLEIGH saved ground while never far back, moved closer nearing the lane, angled out leaving the three sixteenths marker and closed willingly. MEGANTIC hopped at the break then was angled in to settle along the rail, continued inside into the stretch, altered course to the outside in mid stretch then finished gamely. SENOR SWINGER saved ground while unhurried early, angled out in upper stretch then closed belatedly between rivals. WUDANTUNOIT broke alertly, set the pace along the inside, was collared leaving the furlong marker then weakened a bit. WANDO , sent up outside to prompt the pace, was put to urging leaving the three furlong marker, remained a presence to the eighth pole then faded. SILVER TREE , three wide most of the trip, stalked the pace to the head of the lane then gave way gradually. BETTER TALK NOW , unhurried early, came four wide for the drive and failed to respond. HERCULATED lost ground four wide, was urged along into the far turn and came up empty. MY LORD , rated between rivals early, dropped back after six and a half furlongs.

Jockeys– 1, Dominguez R A; 2, Migliore R; 3, Sellers S J; 4, Bravo J; 5, Day P; 6, Karamanos H A; 7, Husbands P; 8, Bailey J D; 9, Prado E S; 10, Lovato F Jr; 11, Castellano A Jr

Trainers– 1, Graham Robin L; 2, McLaughlin Kiaran P; 3, Asmussen Steven M; 4, Pointer Norman R; 5, Baffert Bob; 6, Vazquez Gamaliel; 7, Keogh Michael; 8, Mott William I; 9, Motion H Graham; 10, Stidham Michael; 11, Vazquez Gamaliel

Owners– 1, Skeedattle II; 2, Darley Stable; 3, Parra Rosendo G; 4, Runnin Horse Farm Inc; 5, Lewis Robert B and Beverly J; 6, Gill Michael J; 7, Schickedanz Gustav; 8, Vegso Racing Stable; 9, Bushwood Stables; 10, Oak Crest Farm; 11, Gill Michael J

Scratched– White Buck (29Apr04 4Hol⁷)

Race 11: the Maryland Breeders' Cup Handicap—third leg of the $1 million pick four

11

Pimlico

6 Furlongs (1:09) 18th Running of THE MARYLAND BREEDERS' CUP HANDICAP. Grade III. Purse $200,000 (plus $100,000 BC – Breeders' Cup) FOR THREE–YEAR–OLDS AND UPWARD. By subscription of $100 each, which should accompany the nomination, $700 to pass the entry box, $700 additional to start, with $100,000 Guaranteed and an additional $100,000 from the Breeders' Cup Fund for Cup nominees only. The Host Association's guaranteed monies to be divided, 60% of all monies to the owner of the winner, 20% to second, 11% to third, 6% to fourth and 3% to fifth. Supplemental nominations of $1000 each will be accepted by Saturday, May 8, 2004 with all other fees due as noted. Weights Sunday, May 9, 2004. Breeders' Cup Fund monies, also correspondingly divided providing a Breeders' Cup Nominee has finished in an awarded position. Any Breeders' Cup fund monies not awarded will revert back to the fund. This race will not be divided. Preference to Breeders' Cup nominees only of equal racing quality or weight assignment (respective of sex and weight for age). Starters to be named through the entry box by the usual time of closing. Trophy to the winning owner given by Breeders' Cup Ltd. Supplemental nominee: Iron Halo.

MdBCH–G3

Coupled – Highway Prospector and Native Heir

---

2 Mt. Carson
Own: David P Reynolds
White Purple, White Belt, White Sleeves
BAILEY J D (—) 2004: (266 58 .22)

Ch. c. 4 (Mar)
Sire: Lord Carson (Carson City) $6,000
Dam: Mt. Gibson Gold (Cox's Ridge)
Br: David P Reynolds (Ky)
Tr: Jenkins Rodney(1 0 0 0 .00) 2004: (76 12 .16)

L 113

Life 11 4 3 1 $212,180 105
2004 1 0 0 0 $1,230 82
2003 4 2 1 1 $109,500 105
Pim 1 1 0 0 $60,000 98

D.Fst 8 2 3 1 $92,180 105
Wet(378) 3 2 0 0 $120,000 98
Turf(277) 0 0 0 0 $0 —
Dst(394) 8 3 2 1 $146,930 105

---

3 Iron Halo (Arg)
Own: S M Mitchell Ranch LLC
Blue Red, White Circled Mr, Red and Blue
ESPINOZA V (—) 2004: (560 91 .16)

Dk. b or br. h. 5 (Oct)
Sire: Halo Sunshine (Halo)
Dam: Iliad*Arg (Equalize)
Br: Abolengo (Arg)
Tr: Kruljac J Eric(—) 2004: (131 27 .21)

L 112

Life 12 3 3 2 $110,245 107
2004 3 2 1 0 $101,000 107
2003 2 0 0 0 $1,160 84
Pim 0 0 0 0 $0 —

D.Fst 6 2 2 0 $101,979 107
Wet(353) 1 1 0 0 $2,720 —
Turf(258) 5 0 1 2 $5,546 84
Dst(355) 2 2 0 0 $91,200 107

Previously trained by Nelson Gonzalez Altez

---

4 Gators N Bears
Own: Leo S Nechamkin II
Yellow Kelly Green, Gold Diamonds, Gold
LOPEZ C C (—) 2004: (295 38 .13)

B. c. 4 (Feb)
Sire: Storm Atlantic (Storm Cat) $12,500
Dam: I'm Me Along (Notebook)
Br: Robert W Camac (NJ)
Tr: Nechamkin Leo S II(4 0 0 1 .00) 2004:(20 4 .20)

L 117

Life 20 8 5 5 $376,280 108
2004 3 1 1 1 $74,440 106
2003 13 5 3 4 $257,270 108
Pim 0 0 0 0 $0 —

D.Fst 16 7 4 5 $341,460 108
Wet(407) 4 1 1 0 $34,820 92
Turf(279) 0 0 0 0 $0 —
Dst(355) 15 7 4 3 $304,590 108

---

1 Highway Prospector
Own: Michael J Gill
Red Blue, Blue Mmm And Cc On White Ball
DOMINGUEZ R A (67 15 16 13.22) 2004: (451 116 .26)

Dk. b or br. g. 7 (Apr)
Sire: Crafty Prospector (Mr. Prospector) $20,000
Dam: Highway Queen (Wavering Monarch)
Br: James H Ibelin & Marvin Little Jr (Ky)
Tr: Shuman Mark(29 8 2 5 .28) 2004:(307 58 .19)

L 114

Life 45 12 3 12 $443,217 107
2003 13 5 1 4 $290,397 107
2002 10 2 2 2 $52,456 103
Pim 3 1 0 1 $17,000 97

D.Fst 36 11 1 9 $345,777 106
Wet(379) 8 1 2 3 $97,250 107
Turf(250) 1 0 0 0 $190 64
Dst(386) 15 4 3 2 $161,340 107

[148]

5 Gracious Humor
Own: Manorwood Stables S Goldfarb & I Davi
Grns Black, Gold Yoke And Cgs, Gold
PRADO E S (—) 2004: (552 103 .19)

B. g. 4 (Mar)
Sire: Distorted Humor (Forty Niner) $50,000
Dam: Gracious Granny (Lost Code)
Br: Charles Nuckols Jr & Sons (Ky)
Tr: Dutrow Richard E Jr(1 0 0 0 .00) 2004:(212 57 .27)

L 113

	Life	8	5	2	1	$113,300	103	D.Fst	7	4	2	1	$91,500	103
	2004	2	1	1	0	$30,800	103	Wet(410)	1	1	0	0	$21,600	82
	2003	6	4	1	1	$82,500	93	Turf(307)	0	0	0	0	$0	—
	Pim	0	0	0	0	$0	—	Dst(417)	6	4	2	0	$89,600	103

6 Fine Stormy
Own: Maggi Moss
Black Royal Blue, Lime Green Sash, Lime Green
DESORMEAUX K J (—) 2004: (259 49 .19)

Ch. g. 5 (Mar)
Sire: Rob's Freeze (It's Freezing)
Dam: Keyenergy (High Energy)
Br: Jack T Everett & Joey Foster (La)
Tr: Pino Michael V(1 0 1 .25) 2004:(144 33 .23)

L 113

	Life	22	8	5	4	$208,519	101	D.Fst	19	7	3	4	$175,419	101
	2004	3	2	1	0	$46,940	101	Wet(213)	2	0	2	0	$13,900	96
	2003	8	3	2	0	$74,739	96	Turf(215)	1	1	0	0	$19,200	68
	Pim	1	1	0	0	$18,240	100	Dst(240)	13	7	1	1	$152,979	101

7 Sassy Hound
Own: Toby Roth
Orange Orange, Black Cross Sashes, Black Bars
CASTELLANO A JR (151 24 20 26 .16) 2004: (430 70 .16)

Dk. b or br g. 7 (Apr)
Sire: Deerhound (Danzig) $5,000
Dam: Sassy Sue (Invincible Dooley)
Br: William R Harris (Md)
Tr: Feliciano Ben M Jr(23 7 6 2 .30) 2004:(78 20 .26)

L 115

	Life	43	16	8	9	$608,192	113	D.Fst	38	15	6	7	$516,392	113
	2004	3	1	0	1	$38,950	100	Wet(335)	5	1	2	2	$91,800	108
	2003	11	1	3	3	$89,420	102	Turf(230)	0	0	0	0	$0	—
	Pim	6	2	1	3	$90,980	101	Dst(301)	34	14	6	8	$499,869	113

9 Soaring Free
Own: Sam-Son Farms
Turqs Red, Gold Sleeves, Gold Cap
SELLERS S J (—) 2004: (439 100 .23)

Dk. b or br g. 5 (Jan)
Sire: Smart Strike (Mr. Prospector) $25,000
Dam: Dancing With Wings (Danzig)
Br: Sam-Son Farm (Ont-C)
Tr: Frostad Mark(—) 2004:(57 9 .16)

L 121

	Life	15	8	3	0	$875,044	109	D.Fst	6	3	2	0	$142,520	109
	2004	1	1	0	0	$71,362	101	Wet(448)	2	1	0	0	$51,062	109
	2003	8	5	1	0	$699,200	109	Turf(307)	7	4	1	0	$681,462	109
	Pim	0	0	0	0	$0	—	Dst(430)	2	1	0	0	$48,540	109

1a Native Heir
Own: Michael J Gill
Red Blue, Blue Mmm And Cc On White Ball
DOMINGUEZ R A (67 15 16 13 .22) 2004: (451 116 .26)

B. g. 6 (Apr)
Sire: Makin (Danzig) $2,800
Dam: Mary Had a Lot (Double Zeus)
Br: Spencer F Young (Va)
Tr: Shuman Mark(29 8 2 5 .28) 2004:(307 58 .19)

L 113

	Life	35	16	6	5	$560,711	109	D.Fst	24	8	5	5	$300,588	109
	2004	4	1	0	1	$26,275	89	Wet(382)	10	8	1	0	$257,723	105
	2003	10	4	3	1	$200,280	109	Turf(252)	1	0	0	0	$2,400	79
	Pim	2	2	0	0	$48,810	103	Dst(370)	17	9	5	1	$308,373	108

I narrowed this sprint down to the same four contenders as the crowd:—Gators N Bears, Soaring Free, Iron Halo, and Gracious Humor,—but it was somewhat surprising to see Soaring Free favored at 2–1, considering that his last seven races stretching back nearly a year had been on turf.

Gracious Humor had run impressively in his first start for Rick Dutrow Jr. at Aqueduct, but was stepping into a graded stakes for the first time.

Iron Halo's 107 Beyer was the best last-out figure in the race, but it was a considerable forward move off his two previous dirt starts in the U.S., and it had been a hard-fought effort to prevail in a second-level allowance against only three rivals; a bounce was likely.

Gators N Bears had been freshened since two credible races in graded stakes at seven furlongs, and was now cutting back to the distance at which he had notched seven of his eight lifetime victories. He had recorded a Beyer figure of 105 or better in seven of his last nine starts, a level that stamped him as the one to beat.

The plan: Few horses are more reliable than fast, consistent dirt sprinters—that's *conventional* dirt—who stalk the pace. They don't come any more consistent than Gators N Bears, who had never been out of the money in 16 prior starts on fast tracks. If you're going to stand alone in a multirace exotic like the pick four, Gators N Bears is the type of horse to hang your hat on.

The running of the race: Native Heir was hustled to the lead in an attempt to set things up for his late-running entrymate, Highway Prospector, and the rabbit did his job well. Gators N Bears attained his usual striking position, repelled Gracious Humor in midstretch, and held off Highway Prospector.

RACE 11 Pim-15May04 6 Furlcngs (1.09), 3↑ MdBCHG3

Value of Race: $186,000. 1st $120,000 ; 2nd $40,000 ; 3rd $11,000 ; 4th $12,000 ; 5th $3,000 .
Mutuel Pools: $1,399,970 DD $65,489, Ex $1,082,559, Super $202,281 Tri $838,535

Last Raced	Horse	M/Eq	A	Wt	PP	St	¼	½	Str	Fin	Odds$1
13Mar04 8Aqu2	Gators N Bears	L bf	4	117	3	4	$3\frac{1}{2}$	$4\frac{1}{2}$	$1\frac{1}{2}$	$11\frac{1}{4}$	2.50
15Nov03 10Lrl10	Highway Prospector	L b	7	114	4	8	9	9	$6\frac{1}{2}$	$21\frac{1}{4}$	a- 15.30
10Apr04 8Pim1	Sassy Hound	L b	7	115	7	6	$85\frac{1}{2}$	$6\frac{1}{2}$	41	$3\frac{1}{2}$	12.60
28Mar04 8Aqu2	Gracious Humor	L	4	114	5	5	$4\frac{1}{2}$	$3\frac{1}{2}$	2hd	42	6.30
15Apr04 6SA1	Iron Halo-Arg	L	5	112	2	9	$6\frac{1}{2}$	84	$5\frac{1}{2}$	5nk	5.50
18Apr04 8Pim1	Fine Stormy	L f	5	117	6	1	22	21	$31\frac{1}{2}$	6nk	14.70
1May04 7Del5	Mt. Carson	L	4	114	1	7	7hd	7hd	73	$73\frac{3}{4}$	7.60
10Apr04 7Kee1	Soaring Free	L	5	121	8	2	$5\frac{1}{2}$	$5\frac{1}{2}$	$8\frac{1}{2}$	$82\frac{1}{2}$	2.00
7Apr04 8CT3	Native Heir	L b	6	113	9	3	12	1hd	9	9	a- 15.30

a–Coupled: Highway Prospector and Native Heir.

OFF 5:11 Start Good . Won driving. Track fast.

TIME :223, :454, :581, 1:104 (:22.77, :45.99, :58.39, 1:10.84)

4 – GATORS N BEARS	7.00	4.00	3.00
1 – HGHWYPRSPCTR(a–entry)		11.60	5.80
7 – SASSY HOUND			5.20

$2 DD (7–4) 102.00 $2 Ex (4–1) 71.00 $1 Super (4–1–7–5) 1,262.10
$2 Tri (4–1–7) 444.80

B. c, (Feb), by Stormy Atlantic – I'll Be Along , by Notebook . Trainer Nechamkin Leo S II. Bred by Robert W Camac (NJ).

GATORS N BEARS raced along the rail stalking the pace, eased out two wide on the turn, brushed with NATIVE HEIR near the three sixteenths pole, accelerated to take command in midstretch and drove clear. HIGHWAY PROSPECTOR lacked speed, swung to the seven path entering the stretch and rallied under a hand ride. SASSY HOUND , five wide around the turn, failed to sustain his bid. GRACIOUS HUMOR chased the pace, raced three wide around the turn, bid for the lead in upper and gave way the final furlong. IRON HALO (ARG) lacked speed, was checked in tight quarters entering the turn, raced between horses and failed to rally. FINE STORMY prompted the pace two wide, gained a short lead in upper stretch, dueled to midstretch then gave way. MT. CARSON lacked speed, raced in the three path between horses entering the stretch and failed to rally. SOARING FREE , wide around the turn, gave way after a half mile. NATIVE HEIR , sent to the front, set the pace along the rail, brushed with the winner in upper stretch and faltered.

Jockeys– 1, Lopez C C; 2, Dominguez R A; 3, Castellano A Jr; 4, Prado E S; 5, Espinoza V; 6, Desormeaux K J; 7, Bailey J D; 8, Sellers S J; 9, Fogelsonger R

Trainers– 1, Nechamkin Leo S II; 2, Shuman Mark; 3, Feliciano Ben M Jr; 4, Dutrow Richard E Jr; 5, Kruljac J Eric; 6, Pino Michael V; 7, Jenkins Rodney; 8, Frostad Mark; 9, Shuman Mark

Owners– 1, Nechamkin Leo S II; 2, Gill Michael J; 3, Roth Toby; 4, Manorwood Stables S Goldfarb & I Davis; 5, S M Mitchell Ranch LLC; 6, Moss Maggi; 7, Reynolds David P; 8, Sam-Son Farms; 9, Gill Michael J

Scratched– Crossing Point (01May04 9Mnr2)

Race 12: the Preakness Stakes—final leg of the $1 million pick four

12 Pimlico

Prknss-G

1 3/16 MILES (1:522) 129th Running of THE PREAKNESS. Grade I. Purse $1,000,000 Guaranteed. 3-year-olds. Weight 126 lbs.

1 3/16 MILES — START / FINISH

---

1 Lion Heart
Red — Own: Tabor B. Michael — Colors Unavailable
SMITH M E (—) 2004: (316 52 .16)

Ch. c. 3 (Jan) FTFFEB03 $1,400,000
Sire: Tale of the Cat (Storm Cat) $16,518
Dam: Satin Sunrise (Mr. Leader)
Br: Sabine Stable (Ky)
Tr: Biancone Patrick L(—) 2004:(31 3 .10)

126

Life	6	3	3	0	$670,800	110	D.Fst	5 3 2 0	$500,800	110
2004	3	0	3	0	$360,000	110	Wet(331)	1 0 1 0	$170,000	103
2003	3	3	0	0	$310,800	103	Turf(303)	0 0 0 0	$0	-
Pim	0	0	0	0	$0	-	Dst(338)	1 0 1 0	$170,000	103

1May04-10CD	sly	1¼	:463 1:114 1:371 2:04	KyDerby-G1	103 3 12 11½ 1hd 2hd 22¾	Smith M E	126	5.40	76-21 **Smarty Jones**1262¾ Lion Heart1263¼ **Imperialism**1262	Bit off rail,2nd best 18
10Apr04-9Kee	fst	1⅛	:463 1:11 1:364 1:492	BlueGras-G1	110 5 2hd 11 12½ 11 2½	Smith M E	123	*.90	93-20 **The Cliff's Edge**123½ Lion Heart1236 Limehouse1233¾	3 wide early, gamely 8
6Mar04-7SA	fst	1	:223 :453 1:10 1:36	SnRafael-G2	104 7 3½ 1hd 1½ 11½ 2nk	Smith M E	B121	*1.00	91-11 **Imperialism**118nk Lion Heart1214½ Consecrate1151	4wd 7/8,clear,caught 10
20Dec03-4Hol	fst	1 1/16	:231 :462 1:103 1:424	HolFut-G1	99 4 12 12½ 11 11½ 13½	Smith M E	121	*.50	90-11 Lion Heart1213½ *St Averil*1211 That's an Outrage121½	Bit off rail,riddn out 5
15Nov03-7Hol	fst	7f	:221 :443 1:081 1:203	HolPrevu-G3	103 4 1 11½ 1½ 11½ 16	Smith M E	114	*.50	99-06 *Lion Heart*1146 Cooperation116no Voladero1134	Drifted bit,ridden out 5
24Oct03-6SA	fst	6f	:212 :44 :561 1:091	Md Sp Wt 42k	96 4 6 2½ 2hd 1hd 11	Stevens G L	118	2.40	92-13 *LionHeart*1181 Boomzeeboom1183 Preachintthebr1182	Dueled,led,gamely 10

WORKS: Apr26 CD 4f fst :474 B *7/55* ●Apr20 Kee 5f fst :582 H *1/9* ●Apr5 SA 5f fst :582 H *1/64* Mar29 SA 5f fst 1:012 H *36/42* Mar22 SA 1 fst 1:421 H *1/2* Mar17 SA 4f fst :483 B *11/20*
TRAINER: Dirt(106 .20 $1.35) Routes(102 .15 $1.21) GrdStk(35 .14 $0.79)

---

2 Borrego
White — Own: Kelly Jon Scott Brad Ralls and Foster — Colors Unavailable
ESPINOZA V (—) 2004: (555 91 .16)

Ch. c. 3 (May)
Sire: El Prado*Ire (Sadler's Wells) $75,000
Dam: Sweet as Honey (Strike the Gold)
Br: Jon S Kelly C Beau Greely Dr Sam Bradley & Brad S (Ky)
Tr: Greely C Beau(—) 2004:(56 2 .04)

126

Life	8	2	3	0	$399,580	105	D.Fst	3 1 2 0	$169,880	98
2004	4	0	3	0	$336,280	105	Wet(382)	2 0 1 0	$200,000	105
2003	4	2	0	0	$63,300	93	Turf(278)	3 1 0 0	$29,700	84
Pim	0	0	0	0	$0	-	Dst(355)	1 0 0 0	$0	83

1May04-10CD	sly	1¼	:463 1:114 1:371 2:04	KyDerby-G1	83 10 74¼ 94¾ 45 77¼ 1016¼	Espinoza V	L126 b	14.20	63-21 **Smarty Jones**1262¾ **Lion Heart**1263¼ **Imperialism**1262	Tight 1/2,no rally 18
10Apr04-9OP	my	1⅛	:464 1:113 1:364 1:492	ArkDerby-G2	105 1 42½ 52¼ 42¼ 23 21½	Espinoza V	L118 b	3.30	89-17 ***Smarty Jones***1221½ Borrego1181½ Pro Prado1223½	Slowly getting winner 11
7Mar04-9FG	fst	1 1/16	:222 :451 1:103 1:423	LaDerby-G2	97 1 1015 1014 98 43 22¼	Espinoza V	L122 b	5.50	95-07 Wimbledon1222¼ Borrego122hd *Pollard's Vision*122¾	8w, up for second 11
8Feb04-8SA	fst	1⅛	:47 1:11 1:362 1:491	Sham81k	98 1 32 32 31½ 1½ 21	Baze T C	LB120 b	7.90	87-13 MasterDavid1161 Borrego120hd *Preachinatthebr*116hd	3wd bid,led,held 2nd 7
27Dec03-5SA	fst	1 1/16	:23 :464 1:112 1:434	OClm 80000N	93 4 63½ 83½ 43½ 2½ 11½	Baze T C	LB120 b	9.00	85-15 Borrego1201½ Dwango1185½ Point Dume1188½	Squeezed start,3wd bid 8
29Nov03-5Hol	fm	1	Ⓣ :241 :473 1:112 1:352	Generous-G3	77 10 62¼ 75¼ 75¼ 75¾ 86¼	Valdivia J Jr	LB116 b	6.50	81-13 Castledale116no Dealer Choice1162 Lucky Pulpit1163	5wd,4wd,no rally 12
26Oct03-6SA	fm	1	Ⓣ :22 :46 1:102 1:352	Md Sp Wt 45k	84 6 57½ 56 32½ 32 1½	Espinoza V	LB117 b	4.80	85-18 Borrego117½ *Quiet Cash*1171½ Roi Charmant1173	Came out 1/8,gamely 10
3Oct03-3SA	fm	1	Ⓣ :234 :474 1:122 1:364	Md Sp Wt 53k	61 1 86¼ 87¾ 64¼ 63¾ 44½	Espinoza V	LB117	17.90	73-22 General Moody1171 Licari1172½ Cryptovinsky1171	Stdied early,3-wide 8

WORKS: ●May10 CD 4f fst :46 B *1/53* Apr25 CD 5f sly 1:033 B *23/27* Apr19 CD 3f fst :372 B *12/17* Apr5 OP 5f fst 1:011 H *6/11* Mar30 Hol 6f fst 1:152 H *4/5* Mar24 Hol 5f fst 1:023 H *15/24*
TRAINER: Dirt(90 .13 $2.01) Routes(143 .13 $2.85) GrdStk(35 .06 $2.25)

---

3 Little Matth Man
Blue — Own: Papandrea Vincent — Colors Unavailable
MIGLIORE R (—) 2004: (308 63 .20)

Dk. b or br c. 3 (May) OBSWIN02 $11,000
Sire: Matty G (Capote) $7,500
Dam: Lady's Legacy (Matchlite)
Br: Jill P Michaels & Edward Michaels (NY)
Tr: Ciresa Martin E(—) 2004:(47 2 .04)

126

Life	12	3	1	2	$185,355	89	D.Fst	10 1 1 2	$111,030	89
2004	4	1	1	1	$122,225	89	Wet(300)	2 2 0 0	$74,325	82
2003	8	2	0	1	$63,130	76	Turf(120)	0 0 0 0	$0	-
Pim	0	0	0	0	$0	-	Dst(304)	0 0 0 0	$0	-

10Apr04-8Aqu	fst	1⅛	:47 1:112 1:37 1:493	WoodMem-G1	80 7 98¼ 1110 98 89¾ 710¾	Fragoso P	L123 b	20.40	80-12 Tapit123½ Master David123no **Eddington**1231½	Came wide, no rally 11
20Mar04-8TP	fst	1⅛	:471 1:112 1:371 1:503	LanesEnd-G2	89 10 118¼ 1011 97¼ 46½ 32¼	Fragoso P	L121 b	10.80	81-17 Sinister G1211½ Tricky Taboo121¾ Little Matth Man1211	4w 1/4 pl, rallied 11
28Feb04-10TP	fst	1 1/16	:231 :464 1:111 1:443	JBttgliaMm100k	78 3 89½ 810 66½ 46½ 22¾	Uske S	L121 b	7.10	86-20 SilvrMnstr1212¾ LttlMtthMn1211 WhtMountnBoy1212¼	Swerved 6w 3/8 pl 11
7Feb04-9Aqu	my	1 1/16	⊡ :224 :463 1:12 1:453	Whirlaway82k	82 1 710 715 54½ 32 11½	Fragoso P	L118 b	9.70	83-19 LttlMtthMn1181½ RskyTrck1161½ QckActon11613¼	Came wide, along late 7
31Dec03-7Aqu	fst	170	⊡ :234 :482 1:141 1:434	Ⓢ Alw 44000N1x	76 2 63½ 63¼ 53½ 33 11	Fragoso P5	L113 b	13.20	75-25 *LittleMtthMn*1131 Eyeofthehunter1182¾ *GlicIssu*12221¼	Came wide, in time 7
Previously trained by Gyarmati Leah										
28Nov03-5Aqu	fst	6f	:222 :454 :582 1:121	Ⓢ Alw 43000N1x	60 8 47¼	Fragoso P5	L117 fb	60.50	72-20 *Scary Bob*122½ CostlyCastle1152¼ BondArbitrage1224½	3 wide, no rally, fog 10
13Oct03-5Bel	my	6f	:223 :463 :592 1:124	Ⓢ Md Sp Wt 41k	60 5 7 85¼ 56½ 45½ 11	Fragoso P5	L115 fb	32.00	75-19 LttlMtthMn1151 KrkormKpsk120½ CnfdntCt1203½	Altered course stretch 9
21Sep03-3Bel	fst	5½f	:224 :463 :59 1:052	Ⓢ Md Sp Wt 41k	42 2 1 52¼ 42¼ 58½ 79¼	Castillo H Jr	L119 fb	11.80	77-15 SltyChrcter1194¼ BubbSprks119no DylnsDestiny119nk	Chased inside, tired 10
26Jun03-4Bel	fst	5f	:221 :454 :58	Ⓢ Md Sp Wt 41k	37 5 4 3½ 3nk 36 39¼	Castillo H Jr	L118 f	12.70	84-12 KissnOptimist1186 SicilinBoy1183¼ LittleMtthMn1183½	Vied 3 wide, tired 7
11Jun03-4Bel	fst	5f	:22 :46 :582	Ⓢ Md Sp Wt 41k	40 6 4 2½ 2hd 45¼ 49¼	Castillo H Jr	L118 f	31.25	82-17 WorldClass1182¼ *SwingingGhost*1186¾ SicilinBoy118nk	Between foes, tired 8

WORKS: ●May10 Pha 4f fst :471 B *1/8*
TRAINER: 31-60Days(20 .30 $4.82) Dirt(157 .15 $1.40) Routes(87 .15 $1.63) GrdStk(4 .25 $4.00)

---

4 The Cliff's Edge
Yellow — Own: LaPenta V. Robert — Colors Unavailable
SELLERS S J (—) 2004: (439 100 .23)

Dk. b or br c. 3 (Apr) KEESEP02 $200,000
Sire: Gulch (Mr. Prospector) $50,000
Dam: Zigember (Danzig)
Br: Stonerside Stable (Ky)
Tr: Zito Nicholas P(—) 2004:(185 23 .12)

126

Life	9	4	2	1	$835,258	111	D.Fst	8 4 2 1	$835,258	111
2004	4	1	1	1	$580,000	111	Wet(399)	1 0 0 0	$0	89
2003	5	3	1	0	$255,258	101	Turf(337)	0 0 0 0	$0	-
Pim	0	0	0	0	$0	-	Dst(365)	1 0 0 0	$0	89

1May04-10CD	sly	1¼	:463 1:114 1:371 2:04	KyDerby-G1	89 9 1510 177¾ 86 55¾ 512½	Sellers S J	L126	8.20	66-21 **SmartyJones**1262¾ **LionHeart**1263¼ **Imperilism**1262	Wide,improved position 18
10Apr04-9Kee	fst	1⅛	:463 1:11 1:364 1:492	BlueGras-G1	111 2 710 713 67 21 1½	Sellers S J	L123	5.70	94-20 The Cliff'sEdge123½ **LionHeart**1236 Limehouse1233¾	Middle move, in time 8
13Mar04-9GP	fst	1⅛	:47 1:112 1:373 1:511	FlaDerby-G1	90 1 810 813 75 43¼ 31½	Sellers S J	L122	5.20	81-15 FriendsLake122¾ VluePlus122¾ *TheCliffsEdge*1222½	Fractious, bumped str 10
21Feb04-10Tam	fst	1 1/16	:232 :474 1:123 1:443	SamFDavis100k	88 11 1111 86½ [illegible] 4¾ 21¾	Sellers S J	L116	*.50	93-15 Kaufy Mate1161¾ The Cliff'sEdge1161½ Zakocity1182	Looped 5w,bid,wknd 11
29Nov03-11CD	fst	1 1/16	:241 :482 1:13 1:452	KyJC-G2	94 7 84¾ 31½ 1hd 11½ 1¾	Sellers S J	L122	*.90	81-24 TheCliffsEdg122¾ GrnProspct1161¾ ProprPrdo1183¾	4w, took over, lasted 8
2Nov03-9CD	fst	1	:222 :45 1:10 1:352	Iroquois-G3	101 2 86 53½ 3½ 14 17¾	Sellers S J	L117	*2.20	90-14 *TheCliffsEdge*1177¾ KorbynGold121½ GrndScore1171¼	Quick move, driving 9
4Oct03-6Kee	fst	1 1/16	:224 :462 1:102 1:432	BrdrsFut-G2	87 7 1019 1113 910 75½ 66¼	Sellers S J	L121	8.50	84-20 *Eurosilver*1214¾ Tiger Hunt121no *Limehouse*1211	Carried in start 11
13Sep03-10TP	fst	1 1/16	:231 :47 1:114 1:463	KyCupJuv-G3	83 7 79 66½ 3½ 22 31¼	Sellers S J	L114	3.50	78-17 Ⓓ Pomeroy116no Mr. Jester1181¼ The Cliff's Edge114¾	In air st, steadied 8
Placed second through disqualification										
24Aug03-2Sar	fst	6f	:222 :454 :581 1:104	Md Sp Wt 45k	82 1 5 1½ 12 12½ 14	Sellers S J	L119	4.10	88-12 ThCliffsEdg1194 ApplKrisp1195¼ HrborthGold1193½	Widened under drive 6

WORKS: May9 CD 4f fst :482 B *10/46* Apr26 CD 5f fst 1:01 B *4/25* Apr19 CD 5f fst :593 B *2/33* Apr3 Kee 6f fst 1:14 B *1/3* Mar27 Kee 5f fst 1:014 B *5/21* Mar8 PmM 5f fst 1:01 B *3/26*
TRAINER: Dirt(636 .15 $1.96) Routes(388 .14 $1.62) GrdStk(63 .19 $3.42)

---

5 Song of the Sword
Green — Own: Paraneck Stable — Colors Unavailable
ARROYO N JR (—) 2004: (257 28 .11)

B. c. 3 (Apr) OBSMAR03 $220,000
Sire: Unbridled's Song (Unbridled) $125,000
Dam: Appealing Ms Sword (Crusader Sword)
Br: Joe Carroll & Ernie Paragallo (Fla)
Tr: Pedersen Jennifer(—) 2004:(178 17 .10)

126

Life	6	3	1	1	$211,100	103	D.Fst	4 2 1 1	$186,500	103
2004	6	3	1	1	$211,100	103	Wet(334)	2 1 0 0	$24,600	82
2003	0	M	0	0	$0	-	Turf(305)	0 0 0 0	$0	-
Pim	0	0	0	0	$0	-	Dst(345)	1 0 0 0	$0	82

1May04-10CD	sly	1¼	:463 1:114 1:371 2:04	KyDerby-G1	82 2 138½ 74 1210 119½ 1117½	Arroyo N Jr	L126 b	55.90	61-21 **Smarty Jones**1262¾ **Lion Heart**1263¼ **Imperialism**1262	Checked 1st turn 18
17Apr04-9Kee	fst	1 1/16	:231 :471 1:12 1:434	Lexingtn-G2	97 2 85½ 64½ 41¼ 32½ 33	Arroyo N Jr	L116 fb	*4.00	90-11 QuntonsGoldRsh1162¾ *FrSlm*116nk SongofthSword1162	Bmp,in tight,start 14
3Apr04-7Haw	fst	1⅛	:474 1:123 1:374 1:504	IlnosDby-G2	103 5 62¾ 53¼ 21 22 22¾	Migliore R	L116 fb	3.40	100-21 PollardsVision1142¾ SongoftheSword1162¾ Suve1148½	Steadied first turn 11
5Mar04-8Aqu	fst	170	⊡ :243 :482 1:122 1:411	OClm 100000N	95 3 2hd 2hd 1no	Migliore R	L122 fb	*.50	92-17 Song of the Sword122no *Sinister G*1224¾ Delta Ghost11911	Long drive, fog 5
20Feb04-8Aqu	fst	170	⊡ :233 :473 1:123 1:413	Alw 44000N1x	92 4 54½ 54¾ 3nk 13½ 13	Migliore R	L117 fb	3.00	90-16 *SongoftheSword*1173 *Hornshope*1176½ StaciesBalldo117no	Came in 1/4 pole 7
4Feb04-4Aqu	my	6f	⊡ :231 :47 :59 1:113	Md Sp Wt 41k	71 2 8 1½ 11½ 16 13¾	Migliore R	L121 fb	3.00	81-14 *SongofthSword*1213¾ JckofClubs1164 Fision1212½	When roused, hand ride 8

WORKS: May12 Aqu 5f fst 1:014 B *5/6* Apr28 CD 4f fst :492 B *22/33* Apr15 Kee 4f fst :49 B *11/38* ●Mar30 Aqu 4f fst :462 H *1/11* Mar25 Aqu 6f fst 1:132 B *1/3* Mar16 Aqu 5f fst 1:012 H *3/8*
TRAINER: Dirt(467 .10 $1.34) Routes(197 .10 $1.55) GrdStk(23 .04 $1.37)

6 Sir Shackleton
Own: Farmer Tracy
Black Colors Unavailable
BEJARANO R (—) 2004: (655 176 .27)

Ch. c. 3 (Mar)
Sire: Miswaki (Mr. Prospector) $30,000
Dam: Naskra Colors (Star de Naskra)
Br: Tracy Farmer (Ky)
Tr: Zito Nicholas P(—) 2004:(185 23 .12)

126

Life	4	3	1	0	$127,427	97	D.Fst	4	3	1	0	$127,427	97
2004	4	3	1	0	$127,427	97	Wet(352)	0	0	0	0	$0	-
2003	0	M	0	0	$0	-	Turf(292)	0	0	0	0	$0	-
Pim	0	0	0	0	$0	-	Dst(339)	0	0	0	0	$0	-

24Apr04-9CD fst 1 :224 :461 1:1131:373 DerbyTrl-G3 93 2 3nk 2½ 2hd 11 11¾ Bejarano R L116 *1.20 82-22 SirShcklton1161¾ CourgousAct1168½ BwnChrl1225¼ Between,gamely,drvg 5
9Apr04-6Kee fst 7f :22 :451 1:1021:231 Alw 51575N1x 97 7 5 53 33 1hd 11¼ Bejarano R L120 *2.10 91-09 *Sir Shackleton*1201¼ Misty Appeal11713½ Mr.Trieste120hd 4-5w,steady drive 8
13Mar04-3GP fst 7f :221 :452 1:1041:23 Md Sp Wt 32k 93 5 3 3½ 1hd 12 11½ Castellano J J L122 2.40 87-13 *SrShcklton*1221½ WllyothVlly1227¾ SlthTroops1222½ Drifted str, prevailed 11
14Feb04-12GP fst 6f :22 :45 :5721:10 Md Sp Wt 32k 87 2 5 3nk 1hd 11½ 21½ Castellano J J 122 15.80 90-07 *Forest Danger*1221½ *Sir Shackleton*1224½ *Gold Gunner*122¾ Vied, outfinished 11
WORKS: ●May9 CD 5f fst :59 B *1/17* May4 CD 4f fst :51 B *45/55* Apr19 CD 4f fst :491 B *7/42* Apr3 Kee 5f fst 1:013 B *3/29* Mar27 Kee 5f fst 1:03 B *11/21* Mar6 PmM 5f fst 1:02 B *22/34*
TRAINER: Dirt(636 .15 $1.96) Routes(388 .14 $1.62) GrdStk(63 .19 $3.42)

7 Smarty Jones
Own: Someday Farm
Orange Red White And Blue
ELLIOTT S (—) 2004: (455 104 .23)

Ch. c. 3 (Feb)
Sire: Elusive Quality (Gone West) $41,294
Dam: I'll Get Along (Smile)
Br: Someday Farm (Pa)
Tr: Servis John C(4 0 1 0 .00) 2004:(92 22 .24)

126

Life	7	7	0	0	$6,763,155	108	D.Fst	5	5	0	0	$278,355	108
2004	5	5	0	0	$6,713,535	108	Wet(317)	2	2	0	0	$6,484,800	107
2003	2	2	0	0	$49,620	105	Turf(298)	0	0	0	0	$0	-
Pim	0	0	0	0	$0	-	Dst(325)	1	1	0	0	$5,884,800	107

1May04-10CD sly 1¼ :463 1:114 1:3712:04 KyDerby-G1 107 13 42½ 21½ 2hd 1hd 12¾ Elliott S L126 f *4.10 79-21 Smarty Jones1262¾ **Lion Heart**1263¼ **Imperialism**1262 Stalked,bid,clear 18
10Apr04-9OP my 1⅛ :464 1:113 1:364 1:492 ArkDerby-G2 107 11 2½ 2½ 1hd 13 11½ Elliott S 122 f *1.00 91-17 *Smarty Jones*1221½ **Borrego**1181½ Pro Prado1223½ Cleared at will,drivng 11
20Mar04-10OP fst 1 1/16 :232 :473 1:12 1:42 Rebel200k 108 7 21 21 2½ 11 13¼ Elliott S 122 f 3.50 100-16 *Smarty Jones*1223¼ Purge1173¾ Pro Prado1173¾ Kicked strongly clear 9
28Feb04-9OP fst 1 :224 :454 1:1111:372 Southwest100k 95 6 21½ 22½ 2hd 12 1¾ Elliott S 122 f *.50 97-18 *SmrtyJons*122¾ *TwoDownAtomtc*112½ ProPrd1177½ Chased,took over,drvng 9
3Jan04-8Aqu fst 170 ⊡ :231 :47 1:1131:412 CountFleet81k 97 7 31 31 2hd 1½ 15 Elliott S 116 f *.40 91-21 *Smarty Jones*1165 Risky Trick1166 Mr. Spock116½ Stumbled start, 3 wide 7
22Nov03-9Pha fst 7f :214 :441 1:0831:214 Ⓢ PennaNurse56k 105 1 10 12 12½ 18 115 Elliott S 117 f *.70 98-17 *SmartyJones*11715 SaltyPunch1172¼ IsleofMirth1171½ Off slow, dominated 11
9Nov03-6Pha fst 6f :221 :451 :5741:11 Md Sp Wt 23k 84 8 4 2hd 15 16 17¾ Elliott S 118 f *1.10 84-22 *Smarty Jones*1187¾ *Deputy Rummy*1132¾ Speedwell Beau1186 Handy score 10
WORKS: ●Apr24 CD 5f gd :58 B *1/34* ●Apr3 OP 5f fst :583 H *1/21* ●Mar13 OP 5f fst :583 H *1/35* ●Feb18 OP 6f fst 1:13 H *1/8*
TRAINER: Dirt(400 .21 $1.63) Routes(166 .20 $1.63) GrdStk(12 .25 $1.68)

8 Imperialism
Own: Taub Steve
Pink Colors Unavailable
DESORMEAUX K J (—) 2004: (259 49 .19)

Gr/ro. c. 3 (Apr)
Sire: Langfuhr (Danzig) $25,000
Dam: Bodhavista (Pass the Tab)
Br: Farnsworth Farms (Ky)
Tr: Mulhall Kristin(—) 2004:(48 12 .25)

126

Life	16	5	4	2	$522,605	104	D.Fst	8	3	2	1	$384,605	104
2004	5	2	1	1	$448,000	104	Wet(311)	5	2	0	1	$110,500	98
2003	11	3	3	1	$74,605	90	Turf(262)	3	0	2	0	$27,500	88
Pim	0	0	0	0	$0	-	Dst(335)	1	0	0	1	$85,000	98

1May04-10CD sly 1¼ :463 1:114 1:3712:04 KyDerby-G1 98 8 1710 136 108½ 66¾ 36 Desormeaux K J L126 b 10.90 73-21 **Smarty Jones**1262¾ **Lion Heart**1263¼ Imperialism1262 Stdied 7/8,6wd lane 18
3Apr04-8SA fst 1⅛ :464 1:11 1:362 1:491 SADerby-G1 100 1 76 77¾ 74¾ 41¼ 32 Espinoza V LB122 b 4.70 86-09 Castledale122hd ⒹRockHardTen1222 Imperilism1221 Rail bid,steadied 1/16 7
Placed second through disqualification
6Mar04-7SA fst 1 :223 :453 1:10 1:36 SnRafael-G2 104 3 107½ 109¾ 75½ 43 1nk Espinoza V LB118 b 7.40 91-11 Imperialism118nk **Lion Heart**1214½ Consecrate1151 5wd into lane,rallied 10
7Feb04-3SA fst 7f :222 :443 1:0911:221 SnVicnte-G2 101 1 6 610 67½ 42½ 11¼ Espinoza V LB116 b 14.10 94-11 *Imperialism*1161¼ Hosco120hd Consecrate1161 4wd rally,lugged in 6
Previously trained by Salinas Angel
1Jan04-9Crc fm 1⅛ Ⓣ :471 1:112 1:351 1:464 + TrpPkDby-G3 78 8 118 97 72¾ 53¼ 55¾ Velazquez J R L115 b 4.90 89-08 *KittensJoy*1194½ BrodwyViw112nk SovrignHonor117hd Even finish outside 11
29Nov03-11Crc fm 1 1/16 Ⓣ :221 :463 1:1041:411 Mecke100k 88 11 108½ 72¾ 52 41¼ 2½ Castro E L115 b 13.80 93-08 Timo120½ Imperialism115¾ Cool Conductor1151¼ Slow st, 4 wide, edged 12
8Nov03-9Crc sly 1 1/16 ⊗ :231 :474 1:14 1:48 Alw 20000N1x 90 8 64¾ 42½ 2hd 1½ 12 Castro E5 L112 b 3.60 72-37 Imperialism1122 Zakocity1179½ Rizzi Lee1173 Edged away late 9
16Oct03-5Crc fm 1 1/16 Ⓣ :233 :50 1:1421:442 Alw 30000N1x 71 4 74 53¼ 51¾ 54 2½ Cruz M R L117 b *2.00 77-22 GmblingNtive117½ *Imperilism*1171¼ MdowSoldir120¾ Checked str, gaining 10
20Sep03-10Crc fst 170 :24 :483 1:1411:45 FoolshPlsr100k 80 5 98 99¼ 105¾ 44 34¼ Homeister R B Jr L114 b 30.90 95-21 StolenTime116¾ *SecondofJune*1163¾ Imprilism1142¾ Bumped st, up for 3rd 10
30Aug03-7Crc fst 1 :241 :481 1:1321:421 Seacliff53k 69 3 96½ 98¼ 87¾ 75¾ 55¼ Karamanos H A L113 21.30 65-35 TpDncer1151¼ ChrmingJim1131¾ Hopefortheross1152¼ Improved position 10
WORKS: May10 Hol 3f fst :354 B *2/20* Apr22 CD 6f sly 1:172 B *8/9* Apr15 Hol 5f fst 1:011 H *4/12* ●Mar23 Hol 5f fst 1:004 H *1/16* Mar17 Hol 4f fst :473 H *4/19* Feb28 Hol 6f fst 1:162 H *26/30*
TRAINER: Dirt(47 .23 $2.22) Routes(114 .15 $1.99) GrdStk(37 .16 $3.15)

9 Eddington
Own: Willmott Stables Inc
Turqse Colors Unavailable
BAILEY J D (—) 2004: (262 56 .21)

Ch. c. 3 (Mar) KEEJUL02 $450,000
Sire: Unbridled (Fappiano) $200,000
Dam: Fashion Star (Chief's Crown)
Br: Carl Rosen Associates (Ky)
Tr: Hennig Mark(1 0 0 0 .00) 2004:(193 26 .13)

126

Life	6	2	2	2	$149,560	101	D.Fst	5	2	2	1	$129,560	101
2004	5	2	1	2	$140,360	101	Wet(405)	1	0	0	1	$20,000	90
2003	1	M	1	0	$9,200	75	Turf(285)	0	0	0	0	$0	-
Pim	0	0	0	0	$0	-	Dst(384)	0	0	0	0	$0	-

10Apr04-8Aqu fst 1⅛ :47 1:112 1:37 1:493 WoodMem-G1 97 8 52 42 3nk 2hd 3½ Bailey J D L123 b 3.20 90-12 Tapit123½ Master David123no Eddington1231½ 3 wide move, gamely 11
20Mar04-7Aqu gd 1 :214 :433 1:08 1:352 Gotham-G3 90 2 75¼ 74¼ 53 43½ 33 Prado E S L116 b *1.35 85-14 Saratoga County1162¼ Pomeroy116¾ Eddington1165¼ Bumped after start 8
28Feb04-1GP fst 1 1/16 :234 :474 1:1141:43 Alw 34000N1x 101 5 21 21 2hd 11 15½ Bailey J D L122 b *.30 94-14 Eddington1225½ *Tiger Heart*1186¾ Capias1225½ Greenly, drew off 6
7Feb04-6GP fst 1 1/16 :233 :473 1:1121:423 Md Sp Wt 32k 97 6 21 2½ 2hd 1½ 14¾ Bailey J D L122 b *1.20 96-09 *Eddington*1224¾ Forty Five1225¼ Shots122½ Drew away, driving 12
8Jan04-6GP fst 1 1/16 :241 :491 1:14 1:444 Md Sp Wt 32k 77 10 43½ 53¼ 42 33½ 26¾ Bailey J D L122 *2.10 78-18 Shaniko1226¾ *Eddington*1222½ Radiant Cat1221½ 3 wide, 2nd best 11
28Nov03-4Aqu fst 1 :232 :461 1:1131:39 Md Sp Wt 46k 75 4 2no Migliore R 120 7.10 70-29 OneToughDude120no Eddington12010½ *PesoPorBso*1201¾ Game on rail, fog 9
WORKS: May8 Bel 5f fst 1:00 B *4/39* May1 Bel 6f fst 1:123 B *1/3* Apr25 Bel 5f fst 1:00 B *3/27* ●Apr18 Bel 4f fst :463 H *1/52* Apr4 Bel tr.t 5f gd 1:034 B *7/17* ●Mar13 GP 5f fst :59 H *1/18*
TRAINER: 31-60Days(234 .10 $1.07) Dirt(578 .16 $1.87) Routes(424 .15 $1.50) GrdStk(62 .08 $0.50)

10 Rock Hard Ten
Own: Mercedes Stables LLC and Paulson
Purple Colors Unavailable
STEVENS G L (—) 2004: (122 24 .20)

Dk. b or br c. 3 (Apr)
Sire: Kris S. (Roberto) $150,000
Dam: Tersa (Mr. Prospector)
Br: Madeleine A Paulson (Ky)
Tr: Orman Jason(—) 2004:(19 4 .21)

126

Life	3	2	0	1	$147,600	103	D.Fst	3	2	0	1	$147,600	103
2004	3	2	0	1	$147,600	103	Wet(410)	0	0	0	0	$0	-
2003	0	M	0	0	$0	-	Turf(362)	0	0	0	0	$0	-
Pim	0	0	0	0	$0	-	Dst(378)	0	0	0	0	$0	-

3Apr04-8SA fst 1⅛ :464 1:11 1:362 1:491 SADerby-G1 103 6 33 32½ 4¾ 2hd 2hd Flores D R LB122 3.00 88-09 Castledale122hd ⒹRock Hard Ten1222 **Imperialism**1221 4wd bid,drifted in 7
Disqualified and placed third
3Mar04-2SA fst 1 :224 :454 1:1011:361 Alw 53872N1x 99 5 52¼ 41½ 42 21 11¾ Stevens G L LB118 *.60 90-18 RockHrdTn1181¾ TtonForst118½ JimmysInstnct1185 3 wide bid,ridden out 5
7Feb04-7SA fst 7f :223 :452 1:0941:221 Md Sp Wt 44k 101 5 5 32½ 31 21 11¼ Stevens G L LB120 6.40 94-11 *Rock Hard Ten*1201¼ StormPilot1204 *PointofFlight*1204 Moderate hand ride 8
WORKS: May10 CD 5f fst 1:00 B *6/32* May4 CD 7f fst 1:26 B *1/1* ●Apr26 CD 5f fst :592 B *1/25* Apr18 CD 7f fst 1:273 B *1/2* Apr13 CD 5f sly 1:014 B *3/8* Mar29 SA 5f fst :582 H *2/42*
TRAINER: 31-60Days(7 .14 $0.57) Dirt(16 .12 $1.12) Routes(11 .27 $2.53) GrdStk(1 .00 $0.00)

11 Water Cannon
Own: Nonsequitur Stable
Gray Colors Unavailable
FOGELSONGER R (145 28 28 28 .19) 2004: (316 51 .16)

Gr/ro. g. 3 (Feb) EASMAY03 $37,000
Sire: Waquoit (Relaunch) $5,000
Dam: Crying in the Rain (Baederwood)
Br: Mr & Mrs Charles McGinnes (Md)
Tr: Albert Linda L(13 3 2 0 .23) 2004:(49 13 .27)

126

Life	11	5	2	1	$166,750	88	D.Fst	11	5	2	1	$166,750	88
2004	4	4	0	0	$134,250	88	Wet(359)	0	0	0	0	$0	-
2003	7	1	2	1	$32,500	73	Turf(224)	0	0	0	0	$0	-
Pim	3	1	0	1	$64,250	88	Dst(349)	0	0	0	0	$0	-

17Apr04-9Pim fst 1⅛ :473 1:112 1:363 1:502 FdrcoTesio100k 88 7 11 22 21½ 23 1nk Fogelsonger R L119 b 2.80 92-08 WterCnnon119nk PwynePrincess114½ IrishLddi1152 Driving between foes 7
27Mar04-8Lrl fst 1 1/16 :252 :501 1:1411:452 PrivatTrms60k 78 2 57½ 31½ 1½ 14½ 13¾ Dominguez R A L117 b *.90 85-20 *WaterCannon*1173¾ Acclimate115½ MajorTnner1154¼ Brk slow,3wd,handily 6
28Feb04-8Lrl fst 1 1/16 :24 :474 1:1231:451 MiraclWood40k 79 6 12½ 3½ 41½ 51¼ 1½ Dominguez R A L115 b 3.50 86-22 *Water Cannon*115½ Eastern Bay1153¾ *Wanaka*115nk Waitd 3/16-1/4,hand rd 7
1Feb04-4Lrl fst 1 1/16 :253 :51 1:1531:451 Alw 24500N1x 80 2 11½ 12 11 17 16½ Rose J L122 b 4.20 86-24 *Water Cannon*1226½ Wanaka1193¼ *Cryptic Skier*1192½ Rail, strong hand ride 5
28Dec03-5Lrl fst 1 1/16 :241 :472 1:1311:464 Md Sp Wt 25k 73 1 21½ 24 23 13 12½ Rose J L122 b *.80 75-25 *Water Cannon*1222½ Irish Laddie1177¾ Wry Humor1223½ Driving 8
7Dec03-2Lrl fst 1 1/16 :241 :473 1:1211:452 Md Sp Wt 25k 73 1 12 1½ 1hd 21½ 2hd Rose J L122 *1.70 82-15 Wanaka122hd *WaterCannon*1221¾ IrishLaddie117no Rail,angled,came again 7
22Nov03-5Lrl fst 1 1/16 :234 :472 1:1231:442 Md Sp Wt 25k 63 5 41½ 31½ 52½ 35 211½ Rose J L122 7.90 75-18 CrypticSkier11711½ WaterCannon122½ *Wanak*12210½ Bumped start,4wd 1/4 8
23Oct03-6Lrl fst 1 1/16 :232 :471 1:1211:45 Md Sp Wt 25k 67 7 33½ 22 23 33 46½ Verge M E L122 *1.80 77-22 *WhtMountnBoy*122no *CryptcSkr*1173¾ WryHmor1222¾ Stalked, faded inside 8
11Oct03-5Lrl fst 7f :224 :461 1:1041:23 Ⓡ MdMilNrsry95k 65 7 7 87¼ 89¼ 68 612½ Verge M E L117 40.00 79-10 Polish Rifle1229 Musical Vision1221 Wanaka1171½ No factor 11
21Sep03-7Pim fst 6f :231 :462 :5841:113 Md Sp Wt 25k 54 11 4 42 45½ 46½ 38¼ Acosta J D 122 12.60 79-18 *Polish Rifle*1225 Mahican1223¼ Water Cannon122hd No threat 12
WORKS: ●May8 Bow 5f gd 1:004 B *1/19* May1 Bow 4f fst :493 B *9/18* ●Apr10 Bow 4f fst :472 B *1/27* Mar19 Bow 5f gd 1:03 B *4/8* Feb20 Bow 5f fst 1:013 B *2/14*
TRAINER: Dirt(241 .19 $2.10) Routes(126 .25 $2.75)

I could have saved myself some money and singled the 7-for-7 Smarty Jones, the first unbeaten Kentucky Derby winner since Seattle Slew, in the anchor leg. But at the time, I wasn't completely sure he was the lead-pipe cinch everyone seemed to think he was.

Lion Heart had held on well for second after setting the pace in the Kentucky Derby, and had posted the top figure in the field the last time he caught a fast track, in the Blue Grass. Speed figures earned on Keeneland's old dirt track did not always transfer reliably to other tracks, but Lion Heart had the rail, and figured to get loose on the lead once again. The main knock was that he had already blown three clear leads during the spring.

Rock Hard Ten was light on seasoning, with only three starts under his belt, but was obviously an up-and-coming talent.

I thought Eddington was on a nice "cycling" pattern: two big wins with blinkers added at Gulfstream, followed by a regression in a fast-paced renewal of the Gotham, and then a return to his better figures in the Wood Memorial.

The plan: If I had made it this far with my single, Gators N Bears, I certainly wanted to be alive with Smarty Jones, but I wanted the shot for a major score if Lion Heart, Rock Hard Ten, or Eddington managed to knock off the chalk.

The running of the race: Nothing makes you feel dumber than spreading with four horses and watching the odds-on favorite win by the length of the stretch.

I felt better, though, when the pick four came back at $1,506.40 for $2, which was well over twice the $2 win parlay of $708.20, and an exceptionally good value.

RACE 12 Pim–15May04 1$\frac{3}{16}$ Miles (1.52²), 3 yo Preaknes G1

Value of Race: $1,000,000. 1st $650,000 ; 2nd $200,000 ; 3rd $100,000 ; 4th $50,000 . Mutuel Pools: $21,823,303 Pick–3 $373,852, Pick–4 $1,248,189, DD $370,222, DD $475,094, Ex $12,034,370, Super $5,713,723 Tri $15,096,739

Last Raced	Horse	M/Eq	A	Wt	PP	St	¼	½	¾	Str	Fin	Odds$1
1May04 ¹⁰CD¹	Smarty Jones	L f	3	126	6	1	2½	2²	22½	1⁵	11¹½	0.70
3Apr04 ⁸SA³	Rock Hard Ten	L	3	126	9	4	7½	7ʰᵈ	6¹	2ʰᵈ	2²	6.90
10Apr04 ⁸Aqu³	Eddington	L b	3	126	8	8	6¹	6²	83½	7⁵	3ʰᵈ	13.20
1May04 ¹⁰CD²	Lion Heart		3	126	1	2	11½	12½	1¹	34½	4ʰᵈ	4.90
1May04 ¹⁰CD³	Imperialism	L b	3	126	7	3	3¹	4ʰᵈ	5½	4²	5¹	6.60
24Apr04 ⁹CD¹	Sir Shackleton	L	3	126	5	7	5½	5½	4ʰᵈ	5ʰᵈ	6¾	37.50
1May04 ¹⁰CD¹⁰	Borrego	L b	3	126	2	5	82½	8⁴	7ʰᵈ	6½	75½	12.80
10Apr04 ⁸Aqu⁷	Little Matth Man	L	3	126	3	10	10	10	10	82½	8²	45.00
1May04 ¹⁰CD¹¹	Song of the Sword	L b	3	126	4	6	4ʰᵈ	3ʰᵈ	3½	9²	93½	51.00
17Apr04 ⁹Pim¹	Water Cannon	L b	3	126	10	9	93½	9½	9½	10	10	39.50

OFF 6:25 Start Good For All But LITTLE MATTH MAN. Won driving. Track fast.

TIME :23³, :47¹, 1:11², 1:36², 1:55² (:23.65, :47.32, 1:11.53, 1:36.44, 1:55.59)

7 – SMARTY JONES		3.40	3.00	2.60
10 – ROCK HARD TEN			5.00	4.00
9 – EDDINGTON				5.20

$2 Pick–3 (7–4–4/7) 143.20 $2 Pick–4 (9–7–4–4/7) 1,506.40 $2 DD (4–7) 15.40
$2 DD ((SPECIAI/PREAKNESS) 4-7) 10.40
$2 Ex (7–10) 24.60 $1 Super (7–10–9–1) 230.70 $2 Tri (7–10–9) 177.20

Ch. c, (Feb), by Elusive Quality – I'll Get Along , by Smile . Trainer Servis John C. Bred by Someday Farm (Pa).

SMARTY JONES , away alertly, was taken in hand going past the wire the first time, tracked the leader while racing well off the rail into the backstretch, continued in hand to the far turn, launched his rally leaving the three eighths pole, angled to the inside of LION HEART mid way on the turn, drew on nearly even terms with that one approaching the quarter pole, took charge at the top of the stretch, quickly opened a commanding lead in mid stretch, extended his advantage when struck twice right handed leaving the furlong marker then drew off with authority under a vigorous hand ride. ROCK HARD TEN , fractious behind the gate delaying the start for several minutes, was strung out six wide around the first turn, raced in mid pack while continuing wide down the backstretch, made a sharp move from outside to reach contention leaving the three furlong marker, angled to the inside mid way on the turn, followed the winner into the stretch but was no match for that one while clearly besting the others. EDDINGTON , unhurried for a half while racing well off the rail, gradually gained five wide nearing the far turn, moved inside IMPERIALISM at the three eighths pole, circled five wide advancing into the stretch, altered course between rivals at the three sixteenths pole but failed to threaten while improving his position. LION HEART was guided well off the rail while sprinting clear soon after the start, set a moderate pace while four wide down the backstretch, continued on the front while remaining well out from the rail around the far turn, relinquished the lead to the winner entering the lane then tired from his early efforts. IMPERIALISM returned to the paddock prior to the post parade for a repair of his left front shoe, raced five wide around the first turn, continued wide in mid pack for six furlongs while lacked a late response when called upon. SIR SHACKLETON , between rivals the first turn, chased the pace in the two to three path down the backstretch, angled to the inside while racing within striking distance to the top of the stretch then steadily tired thereafter. BORREGO broke outward then steadied on heels soon after the start, saved ground to the quarter pole, angled out at the top of the stretch, raced between rivals past the eighth pole and came up empty. LITTLE MATTH MAN was bumped and pinched back at the start, trailed for a good part of the way then failed to mount a serious rally. SONG OF THE SWORD broke inward and bobbled at the start, raced close up for a half, made a run inside the winner to threaten nearing the far turn then gave way. WATER CANNON failed to threaten.

Jockeys– 1, Elliott S; 2, Stevens G L; 3, Bailey J D; 4, Smith M E; 5, Desormeaux K J; 6, Bejarano R; 7, Espinoza V; 8, Migliore R; 9, Chavez J F; 10, Fogelsonger R

Trainers– 1, Servis John C; 2, Orman Jason; 3, Hennig Mark; 4, Biancone Patrick L; 5, Mulhall Kristin; 6, Zito Nicholas P; 7, Greely C Beau; 8, Ciresa Martin E; 9, Pedersen Jennifer; 10, Albert Linda L

Owners– 1, Someday Farm; 2, Mercedes Stables LLC and Paulson; 3, Willmott Stables Inc; 4, Smith Derrick and Tabor Michael; 5, Taub Steve; 6, Farmer Tracy; 7, J & S Kelly R Ralls D Foster B Scott & B Greely; 8, Papandrea Vincent; 9, Paraneck Stable; 10, The Nonsequitur Stable LLC

Scratched– The Cliff's Edge

Belmont Stakes Day, 2006

Race 6: the True North Handicap

6 **Belmont Park** *6 Furlongs* (1:07³) **TruNrthH-G2** **28th Running of THE TRUE NORTH HANDICAP. Grade II. Purse $200,000 A Handicap For Three Year Olds And Upward. By subscription of $200 each, which should accompany the nomination; $1,000 to pass the entry box; $1,000 to start. The purse to be divided 60% to the winner, 20% to second, 10% to third, 5% to fourth, 3% to fifth and 2% divided equally among remaining finishers. Closed Saturday, May 27, 2006 with 20 Nominations.**

START / 6 FURLONGS / FINISH

Coupled – Tiger and Voodoo

2 Vicarage
Own: Dogwood Stable
White Green, Yellow Dots And Collar, Yellow
VELAZQUEZ J R (3 2 0 0 .67) 2006: (365 106 .29)
Dk. b or br c. 4 (Apr) FTKJUL03 $125,000
Sire: Vicar (Wild Again) $10,000
Dam: For Dixie (Dixieland Band)
Br: J D Squires (Ky)
Tr: Pletcher Todd A(37 11 12 3 .30) 2006:(502 153 .30)
L 116
Life 16 4 2 2 $415,085 105 | D.Fst 15 4 2 2 $414,765 105
2006 1 0 0 0 $0 84 | Wet(352) 0 0 0 0 $0 -
2005 11 3 2 2 $380,615 105 | Turf(208) 1 0 0 0 $320 58
Bel 3 2 0 0 $66,615 105 | Dst(377) 6 2 0 0 $72,365 105

15Apr06-8Kee fst 7f :214 :441 1:092 1:231 3↑CmwlthBC-G2 84 1 9 3¹½ 4¹½ 3⁴ 6⁶½ Velazquez J R L118 5.40 86-10 Sun King120²¾ Kazoo118no **Spanish Chestnut**118¹½ Inside, tired 12
30Oct05-9CD fst 7½f :221 :442 1:084 1:281 3↑AckAckH-G3 97 8 1 1hd 1hd 2hd 2¹¾ Bejarano R L117 *.90 97-12 StrightLine114¹¾ Vicrge117¹¾ LevlPlyingfild115²¾ Dueled,clear,no match 9
14Oct05-9Kee fst *7f :221 :444 1:092 1:26 Perryvll-G3 102 2 1 2¹ 1hd 1⁵ 1¹⁰ Velazquez J R L120 4.50 95-21 Vicarage120¹⁰ *StraightLine*123²½ SocialProbtion117¾ Inside,drew off,drvg 8
17Sep05-13TP fst 6f ◈ :22 :453 :573 1:093 KyCpSpnt-G3 89 6 2 3¹½ 3¹ 4⁴ 4⁵½ Bejarano R L116 *1.80 - - EstteCollction116¾ HumorAtLst116³½ GoingWild119¹½ 3 wide, tired drive 7
7Aug05-9Sar fst 6f :214 :45 :57 1:10 Amstrdam-G2 86 9 7 7²¾ 4¾ 5³¼ 6⁵½ Velazquez J R L117 3.70 84-15 SantanaStrings121¾ SocilProbtion116½ *SilverTrin*115¹ 4 wide, no response 9
15Jly05-8Bel fst 6f :223 :453 :571 1:093 ®SmkGlacken63k 105 1 1 3¹ 3½ 1¹½ 1⁴¼ Velazquez J R L118 1.60 91-18 Vicarge118⁴¼ BigAppleDddy120½ StormCreekRising118¹½ Drew away late 4
11Jun05-6Bel fst 6f :214 :442 :56 1:081 3↑TrNthBCH-G2 90 4 6 5³ 5³½ 5⁹ 7⁷¾ Velazquez J R L111 17.10 90-13 *Woke Up Dreamin*116² **Voodoo**113¾ Mass Media117¹ Chased outside, tired 10
30Apr05-11CD fst 1 :222 :45 1:102 1:36 DerbyTrial113k 83 3 3² 3² 1² 1²½ 3⁷¾ Albarado R J L116 *2.00 82-18 Don't Get Mad116⁷ Gallardo116¾ Vicarage116¹²¾ Drft start,faltered 7
2Apr05-12GP fst 1⅛ :454 1:094 1:36 1:492 FlaDerby-G1 74 5 4²½ 4³ 4³ 7¹⁰ 6¹⁷ Velazquez J R L122 7.20 - - High Fly122¹½ Noble Causeway122² B. B. Best122¹½ Hit gate, 4 wide 9
12Mar05-6FG fst 1 1/16 :232 :471 1:114 1:423 LaDerby-G2 98 8 2¹ 2¹ 2¹ 2² 2⁴ Velazquez J R L122 21.20 93-08 High Limit122⁴ Vicarage122³¾ Storm Surge122¾ No match, best of rest 9
5Feb05-5GP fst 7½f :23 :46 1:11 1:294 Hutchesn-G2 80 3 4 3¹ 4² 5²¾ 3⁶½ Decarlo C P L118 9.60 - - Proud Accolade120⁴½ Park Avenue Ball120² Vicarage118nk Off rail, tired 6
21Jan05-8GP fst 6f :222 :46 :582 1:104 Alw 33000N1x 90 8 2 7¹½ 6¹¾ 2hd 1²¾ Decarlo C P L118 9.30 - - Vicarage118²¾ Mr.ColdCall118⁴¾ RomanCandles118½ Bmpd st, 6 wide rally 11
WORKS: Jun5 Bel tr.t 4f gd :474 B *2/20* ●May28 Bel 5f fst :594 B *1/29* May21 Bel 5f fst 1:013 B *23/73* May14 Bel 4f fst :49 B *34/87* Apr29 CD 5f fst 1:004 B *18/49* Apr9 Kee 5f fst 1:02 B *7/10*
TRAINER: 31-60Days(527 .31 $2.17) Dirt(1049 .29 $1.96) Sprint(569 .25 $1.70) GrdStk(275 .21 $1.95) J/T 2005-06 BEL(144 .26 $1.84) J/T 2005-06(622 .30 $1.98)

3 Mach Speed
Own: Reeley Roland
Blue Purple, Turquoise Diamond, Purple 'R,'
LUZZI M J (118 18 17 13 .15) 2006: (559 97 .17)
Ch. g. 5 (Jan)
Sire: A.P. Indy (Seattle Slew) $300,000
Dam: Bay Harbor (Forty Niner)
Br: Overbrook Farm (Ky)
Tr: Testerman Valora A(1 1 0 0 1.00) 2006:(48 4 .08)
L 113
Life 26 6 4 2 $180,951 99 | D.Fst 17 4 2 1 $126,431 99
2006 7 2 1 0 $57,360 99 | Wet(427) 7 2 2 1 $54,520 93
2005 15 3 2 2 $79,470 93 | Turf(294) 2 0 0 0 $0 64
Bel 2 1 0 0 $31,900 98 | Dst(351) 1 0 0 0 $0 73

24May06-3Bel fst 7f :224 :453 1:093 1:221 4↑OC 75k/N3x 98 1 2 1½ 1½ 1½ 1nk Luzzi M J L118 b 19.40 90-12 Mach Speed118nk Tani Maru118nk Tenthirteen113½ Dug in gamely inside 5
4May06-9Pim fst 1 1/16 :231 :464 1:113 1:444 3↑OC 50k/N$Y-N 68 7 4⁵½ 5⁶ 9⁸¼ 9¹³ 9¹⁷¾ Rodriguez E D L120 b 19.40 69-13 RecklessWays117³¼ WaterCnnon120nk PlyBingo120²¾ 3wd turns, faltered 10
29Apr06-10Pim fm 1 Ⓣ :231 :461 1:11 1:352 3↑HenryClark69k 42 2 1½ 1hd 5²¼ 8¹⁸ 8²⁵¼ Santana J Z L118 b 12.80 69-15 SaintStephen120³½ FoufsWrrior118¹¼ RubiEcho118¾ Duel inside, faltered 8
18Mar06-10Lrl fst 7f :224 :453 1:101 1:23 3↑NrthrnWolf60k 77 8 1 5⁶ 5⁶½ 5⁸ 5¹¹¾ Karamanos H A L118 b 6.70 83-14 P. Kerney118⁵¼ Abbondanza120¹ **Celtic Innis**118½ Wide,gave way 8
1Mar06-8Lrl fst 1 :234 :47 1:114 1:384 4↑OC 40k/c-N 96 3 2¹½ 2³½ 2³ 2¹ 2nk Rodriguez E D L122 b *.90 89-21 Speed Whiz115nk Mach Speed122²¼ Skycrossing120¹ 3wd,bid,outfinished 4
9Feb06-8Lrl fst 1 :232 :46 1:111 1:373 4↑OC 32k/N3x-N 99 1 2³ 2⁴ 2³ 2¹½ 1½ Rodriguez E D L120 b *2.30 95-14 Mach Speed120½ Salary Cap120³¾ Timely Bid120½ Rail,angled,strng,drve 7
14Jan06-7Lrl myS 1 :233 :471 1:133 1:401 4↑NatvDancer65k 82 2 2hd 1hd 1hd 6⁸ 6⁹¼ Monterrey R L118 b 7.00 73-31 *Your Bluffing*120¹½ Aggadan118hd Marina Minister118nk Dueled, faltered 6
26Dec05-8Lrl gd 7f :214 :453 1:113 1:244 3↑OC 32k/N3x-N 93 12 1 6¹⁰ 6¹⁰ 2² 2¾ Monterrey R L122 b 23.00 85-24 CrftySchemer120¾ MchSpeed122³½ *CityWknd*121²¼ 4-5wd trip,steady gain 13
9Dec05-7Lrl slyS 1 :24 :473 1:13 1:383 3↑OC 32k/N3x 92 3 1hd 1hd 1hd 1² 1²¼ Monterrey R L120 b 22.30 - - MchSpeed120²¼ *CrftySchemer*120²¼ KnownBckHom120½ Drew off, driving 10
17Nov05-4Lrl fst 1 :231 :47 1:133 1:401 3↑Clm c-(25-20) 73 6 3³ 4³ 4⁴ 4¹⁰ 4⁸ Garcia Luis L122 fb 4.80 - - CrftySchmr120¾ Skiptomloumydrln118⁵¼ CtlkMov122² Angled 4wd, faded 7
Claimed from Overbrook Farm for $25,000, Foley Tom Trainer 2005(as of 11/17): (67 7 7 7 0.10)
9Nov05-8Lrl fst 7f :223 :453 1:103 1:243 3↑OC 40k/c-N 73 6 1 5³½ 5⁶ 6¹⁰ 6⁸¾ Garcia Luis L122 fb 11.00 78-21 *Wild Jam*120¾ P. Kerney120⁴¼ Auguri120¹ 3wd btw 1/4, faded 8
26Oct05-8Bel gd 1 :234 :47 1:11 1:362 3↑OC 75k/N3x-N 69 2 1¹ 1½ 4² 4⁹½ 4¹⁶¾ Fallon K L122 fb 15.70 62-27 Bailero120nk Ruler's Court122¹¼ Smokescreen117¹⁵¼ Set pace, tired 4
WORKS: Apr19 Pim Ⓣ 4f fm :512 B(d) *1/1* Apr15 Pim 4f fst :494 B *7/23*
TRAINER: WonLastStart(11 .09 $0.62) Dirt(183 .06 $1.14) Sprint(127 .06 $1.18) GrdStk(1 .00 $0.00) J/T 2005-06 BEL(1 1.00 $40.80) J/T 2005-06(2 .50 $20.40)

1 Tiger
Own: Susan and John Moore
Red White, Royal Blue Star, Blue Stars On
COA E M (165 29 23 23 .18) 2006: (688 145 .21)
Ch. g. 5 (Apr)
Sire: Storm Boot (Storm Cat) $15,000
Dam: Itstimetocelebrate (Timeless Native)
Br: William L S Landes III (Ky)
Tr: Jerkens James A(31 8 1 3 .26) 2006:(120 28 .23)
L 116
Life 8 4 1 0 $149,100 111 | D.Fst 7 3 1 0 $124,500 111
2006 4 3 1 0 $121,420 111 | Wet(345) 1 1 0 0 $24,600 96
2005 2 0 0 0 $2,760 65 | Turf(281) 0 0 0 0 $0 -
Bel 1 1 0 0 $64,020 110 | Dst(358) 7 4 1 0 $146,640 111

13May06-8Bel fst 6f :212 :44 :554 1:082 3↑BoldRlrH-G3 110 3 4 2³ 2½ 1½ 1³½ Coa E M L114 f *1.50 96-10 Tiger114³½ Dark Cheetah115¹¾ Bishop Court Hill119¾ Speed outside, clear 5
13Apr06-8Aqu fst 6f :22 :45 :563 1:082 4↑OC 35k/N2x-N 111 6 2 2hd 1² 1¹ 1⁷¼ Coa E M L120 f *.80 96-19 *Tiger*120⁷¼ Callmetony118¹¼ *Introspect*118⁴¼ Vigorous hand ride 6
26Mar06-8Aqu fst 6f ⊡ :222 :453 :573 1:104 4↑OC 35k/N2x-N 95 5 5 2½ 3nk 2½ 2½ Castellano J J L120 f *.80 84-18 **Anew**118½ *Tiger*120² Introspect118no Dug in gamely inside 8
16Feb06-9GP fst 6f :22 :441 :554 1:082 4↑Alw 33000N1x 100 1 4 1¹ 1½ 1¹ 1³½ Castellano J J L120 f 3.50 102-05 Tiger120³½ Southern Missile120⁴¾ *Kopper Kilgoar*120¾ Inside, repulsed bid 8
Previously trained by Dickinson Michael W 2005(as of 8/17): (102 22 10 21 0.22)
17Aug05-8Del fst 5½f :213 :452 :583 1:052 3↑Alw 41300N1x 65 6 5 4²¾ 3³ 4³ 4³½ Castellano A Jr L119 f 2.60 86-14 KipperVille123¹ *CrossInder*119hd HrleysRod119²½ Lacked needed response 6
17Jly05-7Del fst 6f :212 :433 :561 1:093 3↑Alw 42500N1x 48 5 6 8⁴ 6⁹ 8¹⁷ 9¹⁹¾ Dominguez R A L119 fb 2.30 73-12 *Pisgah*119⁴ Upscaled114⁵½ Cool Days114² No factor 10
Previously trained by Jerkens James A 2004(as of 4/3): (45 5 9 6 0.11)
3Apr04-6Aqu my 6f :214 :444 :57 1:094 3↑Md Sp Wt 41k 96 4 4 1½ 1¹½ 1⁴½ 1⁵½ Santos J A L116 fb 3.30 89-18 Tiger116⁵½ *John's Interview*116³ Gainango111⁷½ Set pace, drew away 7
6Mar04-9GP fst 6f :212 :441 :571 1:103 Md Sp Wt 32k 50 2 9 8⁸¾ 6⁸ 5⁷ 6¹²½ Santos J A 122 f 13.90 76-08 *Choose*122no *Stalwart Memory*122⁵½ *Caballero Negro*122³½ Off slowly, 3 wide 10
WORKS: Jun4 Bel tr.t 5f gd :59 H *1/3* May29 Bel tr.t 3f fst :37 B *3/6* ●May5 Bel 5f fst :594 B *1/22* Apr27 Bel tr.t 3f fst :383 B *6/9* Apr10 Bel tr.t 4f fst :481 B *8/42* Apr5 Bel tr.t 4f gd :502 B *3/4*
TRAINER: WonLastStart(77 .32 $2.47) Dirt(269 .25 $2.00) Sprint(157 .22 $1.79) GrdStk(37 .24 $1.46) J/T 2005-06 BEL(20 .30 $2.40) J/T 2005-06(40 .28 $1.84)

4 Celtic Innis
Own: E Allen Murray Jr
Yellow Colors Unavailable
VELASQUEZ C (131 19 21 19 .15) 2006: (737 119 .16)
Dk. b or br g. 4 (Feb)
Sire: Yarrow Brae (Deputy Minister) $3,000
Dam: Harp Innis (Phone Trick)
Br: Mr & Mrs E Allen Murray (Md)
Tr: Keefe Timothy L(—) 2006:(97 5 .05)
L 113
Life 15 5 3 4 $222,150 102 | D.Fst 14 5 3 4 $219,900 102
2006 5 0 1 2 $43,250 102 | Wet(321) 1 0 0 0 $2,250 94
2005 7 4 1 1 $158,310 102 | Turf(227) 0 0 0 0 $0 -
Bel 0 0 0 0 $0 - | Dst(349) 11 5 3 1 $209,430 102

20May06-9Pim fst 6f :231 :461 :574 1:094 3↑MdBCH-G3 102 5 1 4¹½ 4¹½ 3¹½ 2¾ Napravnik A R L111 24.80 97-06 Friendly Island116¾ Celtic Innis111hd Gaff116²¼ Circled, rallied wide 7
23Apr06-8Pim gd 6f :224 :452 :571 1:10 3↑Hoover75k 94 1 6 5⁴½ 6⁶½ 5⁹ 5²¾ Napravnik A R L118 11.40 94-09 *The Student*118¾ P. Kerney120¹¾ Gold Cluster118hd Inside trip, willingly 7
18Mar06-10Lrl fst 7f :224 :453 1:101 1:23 3↑NrthrnWolf60k 88 6 3 4⁴ 4⁵ 3⁵ 3⁶¼ Napravnik A R L118 11.40 89-14 P. Kerney118⁵¼ Abbondanza120¹ Celtic Innis118½ 3 wide, evenly 8
10Feb06-8Lrl fst 6f :222 :454 :581 1:111 4↑OC 75k/N$Y-N 74 2 5 3²½ 4⁵½ 3⁴½ 3⁸½ Fogelsonger R L120 4.60 77-24 Dale's Prospect120⁵½ Saay Mi Name120³ CelticInnis120²¼ Rail, in tight 1/8 5
16Jan06-8Lrl fst 6f :223 :462 :582 1:112 4↑FirePlug63k 84 7 6 7⁷½ 6³½ 6⁶¾ 6⁶½ Castellano A Jr L124 4.00 78-22 Abbondanz120¹¼ *CrftySchemer*118nk *DlesProspect*120¹¾ 4-5wd turn, empty 8
4Jly05-5Mth fst 6f :211 :434 :554 1:081 JerShrBC-G3 102 1 5 4³½ 4²½ 2½ 2¹¾ Turner T G L122 4.80 97-08 Joey P.117¹¾ Celtic Innis122²¾ Razor122¹ Btwn 1/8,willingly 5
11Jun05-9Mth fst 6f :213 :442 :564 1:093 CornadoQst60k 93 1 6 3¹ 3nk 1³ 1³½ Turner T G L123 6.20 92-12 CelticInnis123³½ MiracleMan120¾ DimondIsle116³¾ 3-wide bid,drew clear 6
21May05-4Pim fst 6f :23 :46 :581 1:104 3↑OC 32k/N3x-N 87 6 5 5⁵½ 4¾ 1² 1nk Hamilton S D L119 4.20 93-06 *Celtic Innis*119nk LastFrontier120½ Acclimate120½ Off duel,5wd sweep,gme 7
23Apr05-7Pim fst 6f :231 :46 :584 1:121 ®MdStallnSt97k 83 2 4 4⁵½ 3²½ 2¹½ 1¾ Hamilton S D L116 12.70 86-16 *Celtic Innis*116¾ Mojodajo116¹½ Monster Chaser122²¾ 3wd 1/4, driving 7
31Mar05-7Lrl fst 6f :224 :46 :58 1:103 Alw 24500N1x 75 2 2 2² 2½ 1¹½ 1²¼ Hamilton S D L118 2.40 89-16 *Celtic Innis*118²¼ Busy Prospect118⁴ Karbobway118³ 2wd turn, driving 5
2Mar05-6Lrl fst 5½f :221 :461 :59 1:054 Alw 24500N1x 61 4 5 4⁵ 3³½ 3⁵ 3⁶¼ Hamilton S D L120 5.90 77-24 *Mojodajo*113²½ *Hesa Big Star*118³¾ *Celtic Innis*120¹¾ No rally 5
29Jan05-6Lrl fst 7f :234 :482 1:124 1:251 Alw 25000N1x 72 4 4 2¹ 2¹ 4²½ 4³ Rocco J S Jr L122 8.70 81-18 Daddy Joe122no Draiman113nk *Timely Bid*122²¾ Bobbled,2wd,faded 8
WORKS: ●Jun6 Lrl 3f fst :36 B *1/8* May10 Lrl 4f fst :492 B *14/21* ●Apr15 Lrl 5f fst :593 H *1/19* ●Apr1 Lrl 5f fst :591 H *1/19* Mar11 Lrl 4f fst :50 B *27/43*
TRAINER: Dirt(187 .10 $0.92) Sprint(160 .09 $1.04) GrdStk(2 .00 $0.00)

5 Spanish Chestnut
Gr/ro
Own: Michael Tabor Derrick Smith
Royal Blue, Orange Ball, Orange Stripes
LEPAROUX J R (9 0 1 2 .00) 2006: (825 228 .28)

Ch. g. 4 (Mar) OBSFEB04 $500,000
Sire: Horse Chestnut*SAf (Fort Wood) $10,000
Dam: Baby Rabbit (No Sale George)
Br: Don Graham & Ocala Oaks (Fla)
Tr: Biancone Patrick L (2 0 0 0 .00) 2006:(123 33 .27)

117

Life	11	4	2	2	$271,990	100		D.Fst	8	2	2	2	$217,320	93
2006	2	1	0	1	$63,570	100		Wet(358)	3	2	0	0	$54,670	100
2005	5	1	0	1	$124,000	93		Turf(345)	0	0	0	0	$0	–
Bel	0	0	0	0	$0	–		Dst(360)	2	2	0	0	$44,670	100

WORKS: ●Jun6 Sar tr.t 4f fst :462 H 1/52 May30 Sar tr.t 5f fst 1:022 B 3/9 ●Apr11 Kee 4f fst :462 H 1/28 Apr4 Kee 5f fst 1:022 B 5/9 ●Mar27 SA 4f fst :461 H 1/34
TRAINER: 31-60Days(61 .23 $1.79) Dirt (228 .22 $1.50) Sprint(102 .28 $1.89) GrdStk(84 .17 $1.94)
J/T 2005-6 BEL (2 .00 $0.00) J/T 2005-06(104 .29 $1.90)

6 Uncle Camie
Black
Own: Telesca Carmine Guerrera John Guerrer
Lime Green, Dark Green Cross, Dark Green
MIGLIORE R (77 12 11 13 .16) 2006: (122 22 .18)

Dk. b or b. h. 6 (May)
Sire: Abagnone (Devil's Bag) $289
Dam: Final Style (Smart Style)
Br: Carmine Telesca (NY)
Tr: Hushion Michael E (20 4 3 2 .20) 2006:(122 22 .18)

L 115

Life	21	8	3	2	$320,110	109		D.Fst	17	8	3	1	$296,100	109
2004	8	2	3	0	$124,690	109		Wet(305)	3	0	0	1	$23,430	96
2005	7	1	1	1	$86,820	109		Turf(196)	1	0	0	0	$580	59
Bel	7	1	1	1	$86,820	109		Dst(303)	16	8	2	0	$282,000	109

WORKS: ●Jun6 Bel tr.t 4f fst :471 H 1/76 May31 Bel 5f fst 1:002 B 2/18 May24 Bel 5f fst :592 B 2/20 May11 Bel tr.t 4f fst :503 B 20/27 May6 Bel 4f fst :504 B 39/48 May1 Bel tr.t 4f fst :514 B 10/10
TRAINER: +180Days(23 .17 $1.63) Dirt (365 .26 $2.32) Sprint(243 .28 $2.68) GrdStk(22 .14 $1.34)

1a Voodoo
Red
Own: Susan and John Moore
White, Royal Blue Star, Blue Stars On
CASTELLANO J J (69 15 9 10 .22) 2006: (488 85 .17)

Ch. g. 8 (Feb)
Sire: Petionville (Seeking the Gold) $15,000
Dam: Slide Show (Slewacide)
Br: Everest Stables Inc (Ky)
Tr: Jerkens James A (31 8 1 3 .26) 2006:(120 28 .23)

L 114

Life	36	7	7	5	$680,030	111		D.Fst	31	7	6	4	$649,484	111
2005	8	0	3	1	$100,848	106		Wet(329)	4	0	1	1	$30,212	99
2004	6	0	2	0	$124,826	104		Turf(240)	1	0	0	0	$334	84
Bel	4	3	0	0	$330,168	111		Dst(357)	13	3	5	3	$319,910	108

WORKS: Jun6 Bel tr.t 3f gd 1:001 B 2/17 May27 Bel tr.t 5f fst 1:013 B 2/4 May10 Bel tr.t 5f fst 1:004 B 2/7 May10 Bel tr.t 3f :362 B 4/22 Mar30 Bel tr.t 3f fst :37 B 8/12
TRAINER: +180Days(16 .19 $1.58) Dirt (269 .25 $2.00) Sprint(157 .22 $1.79) GrdStk(37 .24 $1.46)
J/T 2005-06 BEL (25 .32 $2.64) J/T 2005-06(52 .31 $2.16)

7 Anew
Orange
Own: Chrome Cowboy Racing Stable Vitolo Ra
Yellow, Two Black Horseshoes, Black
GARCIA ALAN (40 5 5 5 .12) 2006: (410 60 .15)

Dk. b or br g. 5 (Feb)
Sire: Awesome Again (Deputy Minister) $125,000
Dam: Lucinda (Olympio)
Br: John R Mulholland & Martha Jane Mulholland (Ky)
Tr: Asmussen Steven M (4 7 1 1 .50) 2006:(915 196 .21)

L 113

Life	17	5	3	1	$139,096	108		D.Fst	12	4	3	0	$107,166	108
2006	5	2	0	0	$61,200	108		Wet(421)	3	1	0	0	$26,890	80
2005	14	2	3	1	$77,896	93		Turf(283)	2	0	0	1	$5,040	80
Bel	4	1	1	0	$31,290	108		Dst(346)	7	3	1	0	$70,095	108

WORKS: Jun5 Bel tr.t 5f my :52³ B 13/15 May28 Bel 5f fst 1:03⁴ B 28/29 May21 Bel 5f fst 1:02³ B 43/73 May14 Bel 4f fst :54 B 87/87 May3 Bel 4f fst :52² B 39/41 Apr17 Bel 5f fst 1:02⁴ B 9/10
TRAINER: 31-60Days(862 .22 $1.51) WonLastStart(601 .23 $1.43) Dirt (2656 .22 $1.51) Sprint(2043 .21 $1.44) GrdStk(100 .13 $1.16)
J/T 2005-06 BEL (1 1.00 $8.10) J/T 2005-06(3 1.00 $18.63)

One of the best things about making a betting line is you never have to rack your brain about which races to make a win bet on—they come to you.

Handicapping the True North beforehand, it didn't seem as if there would be much of an opportunity for a win bet, because the race was clearly between Tiger and Anew. To paraphrase Damon Runyon, the race isn't always to the swift, but that's the way to bet, and they were lengths faster than their rivals based on anything they had done in 2006.

Tiger had benefited from patient handling, as Jimmy Jerkens, the son of legendary Hall of Famer Allen Jerkens, gave him all the time he needed to get over some nagging injuries. The patience had paid off in the form of three wins from four starts at age 5, including the Bold Ruler Handicap in his first start over the Belmont strip.

Anew was headed to oblivion toward the end of 2005, but he had completely turned around since being gelded, winning all three of his starts—including a win over Tiger in the saltiest second-level allowance sprint on Aqueduct's inner track that winter.

The sticking point for both 5-year-old geldings was the possibility of a bounce. Tiger had essentially paired up 111–110 figures that represented a considerable forward move off his previous top; and Anew's 108 was also his fastest figure by a wide margin.

My betting line for this race was quite simple. Tiger and Anew split up 80 points (6–5 odds = 45; 9–5 odds = 35), and the rest of the field got the remaining 20:

	Line	Actual odds
Tiger	6–5	4–5
Anew	9–5	5–1

Even though Anew had beaten Tiger at Aqueduct, Tiger had a brutally tough trip that day, and I thought he deserved to be favored . . . but not by such a lopsided margin.

The plan: Bet Anew to win.

The running of the race: Anew broke like a shot and was quickly clear of Spanish Chestnut (who for some unfathomable reason was bet down to second choice at 7–2), put that rival away entering the stretch, and never faced a serious challenge from Tiger, who was along for second.

SIXTH RACE
Belmont
JUNE 10, 2006

6 FURLONGS. (1.07³) 28TH RUNNING OF THE TRUE NORTH HANDICAP. Grade II. Purse $200,000 A HANDICAP FOR THREE YEAR OLDS AND UPWARD. By subscription of $200 each, which should accompany the nomination; $1,000 to pass the entry box; $1,000 to start. The purse to be divided 60% to the winner, 20% to second, 10% to third, 5% to fourth, 3% to fifth and 2% divided equally among remaining finishers. A trophy will be presented to the winning owner. Closed Saturday, May 27, 2006 with 20 Nominations.

Value of Race: $200,000 Winner $120,000; second $40,000; third $20,000; fourth $10,000; fifth $6,000; sixth $1,334; seventh $1,334; eighth $1,332. Mutuel Pool $1,485,589.00 Exacta Pool $1,106,225.00 Trifecta Pool $886,242.00

Last Raced	Horse	M/Eqt. A. Wt	PP	St	¼	½	Str	Fin	Jockey	Odds $1
5May06 1Bel1	Anew	L 5 113	8	1	1¹	1½	1⁵	13½	Garcia Alan	5.20
13May06 8Bel1	Tiger	L f 5 116	3	3	3½	33½	33½	2¹½	Coa E M	a- 0.85
15Apr06 8Kee3	Spanish Chestnut	4 117	5	7	2½	22½	2hd	3½	Leparoux J R	3.80
24May06 3Bel1	Mach Speed	L b 5 114	2	5	8	6⁵	4½	4½	Luzzi M J	48.75
15Apr06 8Kee6	Vicarage	L 4 116	1	4	5½	5hd	5hd	52½	Velazquez J R	6.70
20May06 9Pim2	Celtic Innis	L 4 115	4	6	7¹	4hd	6⁶	67½	Velasquez C	15.40
24Nov05 8Aqu2	Voodoo	L b 8 114	7	8	6hd	7¹⁰	7	7	Castellano J J	a- 0.85
10ct05 6Bel10	Uncle Camie	L f 6 116	6	2	4¹	8	—	—	Migliore R	13.00

a–Coupled: Tiger and Voodoo.

OFF AT 3:10 Start Good. Won driving. Track fast.
TIME :22, :44², :55⁴, 1:08 (:22.12, :44.46, :55.82, 1:08.10)

$2 Mutuel Prices:

7 – ANEW	12.40	4.30	3.00
1 – TIGER(a-entry)		2.50	2.10
5 – SPANISH CHESTNUT			2.80

$2 EXACTA 7–1 PAID $21.80 $2 TRIFECTA 7–1–5 PAID $60.00

Dk. b or br. g, (Feb), by Awesome Again – Lucinda , by Olympio . Trainer Asmussen Steven M. Bred by John R Mulholland & Martha Jane Mulholland (Ky).

ANEW broke running, soon opened a clear lead, set the pace along the inside, turned back a bid from SPANISH CHESTNUT approaching the stretch, drew away when roused and remained well clear under a drive. TIGER raced close up early, angled out and came wide into the stretch, responded to steady pressure and finished well outside. SPANISH CHESTNUT was hustled from the gate, chased the pace, tried the winner turning for home, could not get by that rival and tired in the drive. MACH SPEED was outrun early, raced inside and finished well on the rail. VICARAGE raced inside and had no response when roused. CELTIC INNIS raced three wide throughout and tired in the stretch. VOODOO raced four wide and tired. UNCLE CAMIE tired badly and was eased in the stretch.

Owners– 1, Chrome Cowboy Racing Stable and Vitolo Raymond; 2, Moore Susan and John; 3, Tabor Michael B and Smith Derrick; 4, Reeley Roland; 5, Dogwood Stable; 6, Murray E Allen Jr; 7, Moore Susan and John; 8, Telesca Carmine and Guerrera John and Marilyn

Trainers– 1, Asmussen Steven M; 2, Jerkens James A; 3, Biancone Patrick L; 4, Testerman Valora A; 5, Pletcher Todd A; 6, Keefe Timothy L; 7, Jerkens James A; 8, Hushion Michael E

$2 Pick Three (8–3–7) Paid $87.50 ; Pick Three Pool $222,483 .

Race 8: the Woody Stephens Breeders' Cup—first leg of the $1 million pick four

8

Belmont Park *7 Furlongs* (1:20) **WStphnBC–G2** 22nd Running of THE WOODY STEPHENS BREEDERS' CUP. Grade II. Purse $250,000 (include $50,000 BC – Breeders' Cup) For Three Year Olds. By subscription of $200 each, which should accompany the nomination; $1,000 to pass the entry box; $1,000 to start. The NYRA purse to be divided 60% to the winner, 20% to second, 10% to third, 5% to fourth, 3% to fifth and 2% divided equally among remaining finishers. Breeders' Cup Fund monies also correspondingly divided. Any Breeders' Cup fund monies not awarded will revert back to the fund. If this race overfills, preference will be given to Breeders' Cup nominees only of equal weight assignment and or Condition Eligibility Ties Broken by gross lifetime earnings. 123 lbs. Non-winners of $60,000 other than restricted stake in 2006 or $45,000 twice in 2006 allowed 2 lbs.; $50,000 other than restricted stake, 4 lbs.; $35,000, or three races, 6 lbs.; two races, 8 lbs. Closed Saturday, May 27, 2006 with 27 Nominations.

1 Too Much Bling
Own: Stonerside Stable Blazing Meadows Fa
White, Dark Green Triangular Panel
GOMEZ G K (79 19 14 13 .24) 2006: (508 101 .20)

2 Likely
Own: Thomas F Van Meter II Miller Morris A
Green, Red Hoop, White Hoop On Sleeves
LEPAROUX J R (90 12 .00) 2006: (825 228 .28)

3 Noonmark
Own: Bolton George Corrigan Joan Beck Ant
Dark Blue and Yellow Stripes, White
BRIDGMOHAN S X (—) 2006: (501 62 .12)

4 Fabulous Strike
Own: Downey Walter
White And Camel Quarters, White Sleeves
VEGA H (5 1 0 0 .20) 2006: (428 101 .24)

5 Keyed Entry
Own: Starlight Stables Saylor Paul H Lucar
Blue, Yellow Circle And 'JL' Yellow
VELAZQUEZ J R (3 2 0 0 .67) 2006: (365 106 .29)

6 Doc Cheney
Own: My Meadowview Farms
Black Cap, Black Diagonal
HILL C (101 12 15 9 .12) 2006: (463 42 .09)

[160]

In a sloppy running of the Bay Shore Stakes at Aqueduct on Wood Memorial Day, Too Much Bling had turned in the most impressive performance of the season by a 3-year-old sprinter, when he shrugged off Songster and drew off by nine lengths, and recorded a Beyer of 113. The Bay Shore had been Too Much Bling's third straight win since blinkers had come back on, and he was leading off this marquee pick four as the shortest-priced horse in the sequence.

There was only one thing troubling about Too Much Bling's recent winning streak: He had broken from an outside post, and this had allowed his rider, Garrett Gomez, the option of either stalking the early pace or seizing command, depending on the break. Too Much Bling was a muscular, long-striding sprinter at his best when able to settle into a rhythm and gradually gather momentum, but that sort of trip is much more difficult to attain when a horse is drawn on the rail. Too Much Bling had won from the rail before, but that was against three maidens at Thistledown, and he had needed to run a first quarter in only 22.80 seconds to put that race in his pocket.

Songster, meanwhile, had also run exceptionally well in three starts when drawn toward the outside, but had been stuck inside Too

Much Bling in the Bay Shore. Songster had come back six weeks later to demolish his rivals in the Hirsch Jacobs Stakes on the Preakness undercard, and now it was he who was drawn on the outside.

The plan: Too Much Bling was formidable, but Songster had the positional speed to make good use of his outside draw, which was a major tactical advantage, especially in a long sprint. Using them both probably locked up the race.

The running of the race: Too Much Bling was outsprinted for the early lead by Fabulous Strike, and remained stuck down on the fence while shuffled back a bit inside the pacesetter around the turn. Songster broke on top and easily secured perfect position in the clear beneath Edgar Prado, and wrested command inside the eighth pole. Too Much Bling came again gamely, but was unable to reach Songster, a legitimately talented horse who enjoyed a perfect trip.

"That Vega, he must have been working for Prado," chirped Too Much Bling's trainer, Bob Baffert, afterward. "He rode my horse the whole way. I knew we were in trouble when we drew the one hole."

EIGHTH RACE
Belmont
JUNE 10, 2006

7 FURLONGS. (1.20) 22ND RUNNING OF THE WOODY STEPHENS BREEDERS' CUP. Grade II. Purse $250,000 (includes $50,000 BC – Breeders' Cup) FOR THREE YEAR OLDS. By subscription of $200 each, which should accompany the nomination; $1,000 to pass the entry box; $1,000 to start. The NYRA purse to be divided 60% to the winner, 20% to second, 10% to third, 5% to fourth, 3% to fifth and 2% dividedequally among remaining finishers. Breeders' Cup Fund monies also correspondingly divided. Any Breeders' Cup fund monies not awarded will revert back to the fund. If this race overfills, preference will be given to Breeders' Cup nominees only of equal weight assignment and or Condition Eligibility (respective of sex allowance). Ties Broken by gross lifetime earnings. 123 lbs. Non–winners of $60,000 other than restricted stake in 2006 or $45,000 twice in 2006 allowed 2 lbs.; $50,000 other than restrictedstake, 4 lbs.; $35,000, or three races, 6 lbs.; two races, 8 lbs. (Maiden, claiming, starter or restricted races not considered in allowances). Trophy to winning owner presented by Breeders' Cup Ltd. Closed Saturday, May 27, 2006 with 27 Nominations.

Value of Race: $250,000 Winner $150,000; second $50,000; third $25,000; fourth $12,500; fifth $7,500; sixth $2,500; seventh $2,500. Mutuel Pool $1,552,502.00 Exacta Pool $1,138,679.00 Trifecta Pool $876,690.00

Last Raced	Horse	M/Eqt.	A.	Wt	PP	St	¼	½	Str	Fin	Jockey	Odds $1
20May06 ^{6}Pim^{1}	Songster	L	3	123	7	1	$3^{3\frac{1}{2}}$	$2^{\frac{1}{2}}$	2^{hd}	1^{2}	Prado E S	2.85
8Apr06 ^{7}Aqu^{1}	Too Much Bling	L b	3	123	1	5	2^{hd}	3^{1}	$3^{2\frac{1}{2}}$	$2^{\frac{3}{4}}$	Gomez G K	1.25
29Apr06 ^{9}CD^{6}	Noonmark	L	3	115	3	4	$4^{1\frac{1}{2}}$	4^{2}	$4^{1\frac{1}{2}}$	3no	Bridgmohan S X	12.60
10May06 ^{3}Bel^{1}	Fabulous Strike	L f	3	119	4	3	$1^{1\frac{1}{2}}$	$1^{\frac{1}{2}}$	1^{hd}	$4^{\frac{3}{4}}$	Vega H	7.70
6May06 ^{11}CD^{2}	Likely	L	3	123	2	7	$6^{1\frac{1}{2}}$	$5^{1\frac{1}{2}}$	5^{6}	$5^{5\frac{1}{2}}$	Leparoux J R	5.00
29Apr06 ^{3}Aqu^{2}	Doc Cheney	L	3	115	5	6	7	6^{hd}	6^{6}	$6^{9\frac{1}{4}}$	Hill C	10.50
19May06 ^{3}Bel^{1}	Saint Daimon	f	3	119	6	2	5^{hd}	7	7	7	Samyn J L	22.20

OFF AT 4:31 Start Good. Won driving. Track fast.

TIME :22^{1}, :44^{4}, 1:08^{4}, 1:21^{2} (:22.31, :44.96, 1:08.88, 1:21.45)

$2 Mutuel Prices:

9 – SONGSTER	7.70	3.40	2.80
1 – TOO MUCH BLING		2.90	2.50
3 – NOONMARK			4.60

$2 EXACTA 9–1 PAID $15.80 $2 TRIFECTA 9–1–3 PAID $101.00

Blk. c, (Mar), by Songandaprayer – Peppy Lapeau , by French Deputy . Trainer Albertrani Thomas. Bred by Richard Giacopelli (Fla).

SONGSTER came away well, raced with the pace from the outside while in hand, was urged after the pacesetter approaching the stretch, dug in determinedly when roused in upper stretch and drew clear late, driving. TOO MUCH BLING showed good speed from the start, chased the pace along the inside and dug in stubbornly on the rail to earn the place award. NOONMARK was hustled along early, advanced three wide on the turn and finished gamely outside. FABULOUS STRIKE was hustled to the front, set the pace while between rivals and weakened while between foes in the final furlong. LIKELY was outrun early, came wide into the stretch and offered a mild rally outside. DOC CHENEY was outrun early, raced four wide on the turn and had no response when roused. SAINT DAIMON tired after a three wide trip.

Owners– 1, Darley Stable; 2, Stonerside Stable and Blazing Meadows Farm LLC; 3, Bolton George Corrigan Joan and Beck Antony; 4, Downey Walter; 5, Thomas F Van Meter II Miller Morris A; 6, My Meadowview Farm; 7, Hobeau Farm

Trainers– 1, Albertrani Thomas; 2, Baffert Bob; 3, Asmussen Steven M; 4, Beattie Todd M; 5, Biancone Patrick L; 6, Zito Nicholas P; 7, Jerkens H Allen

Scratched– Keyed Entry (06May06 ^{10}CD ^{20}) , Dontfearthereaper (10May06 ^{3}Bel^{2})

$2 Pick Three (7–2–9) Paid $69.00 ; Pick Three Pool $299,997 .

Race 9: the Acorn Stakes—second leg of the $1 million pick four

6 Miraculous Miss
Black — Own: Puglisi Stables Steve Klesaris
Black, Red Diamond Frame, White 'P,' Red
DESORMEAUX K J (65 9 8 12 .14) 2006: (280 53 .19)

Ch. f. 3 (May) EASMAY05 $350,000
Sire: Mr. Greeley (Gone West) $35,000
Dam: No Small Miracle (Silver Deputy)
Br: Dr Akijiro O'Hara (Ky)
Tr: Klesaris Steve(2 0 0 1 .00) 2006:(153 37 .24)

L 121

Life	6	5	0	0	$297,120	86	D.Fst	5	5	0	0	$294,120	86
2006	3	2	0	0	$183,000	85	Wet(359)	1	0	0	0	$3,000	73
2005	3	3	0	0	$114,120	86	Turf(285)	0	0	0	0	$0	-
Bel	0	0	0	0	$0	-	Dst(350)	1	1	0	0	$90,000	82

15Apr06-8Aqu	fst	1	:22^3	:45^3	1:10	1:36^3	ⒻComely-G2	82	2	5^10	4^4	4^6	3^4	1^1¼	Desormeaux K J	L122	*.80	84- 16	MrculousMss122^1¼ *RglEnggmnt*120^5 DytmProms120^hd	Came wide, in time	6
5Mar06-10GP	fst	7f	:22	:44^2	1:09^3	1:22^3	ⒻFrwrdGal-G2	85	2	8	10^9¼	10^9½	5^3½	1^1¾	Rose J	L120	18.30	95- 07	*Miraculous Miss*120^1¾ India116½ Misty Rosette120¾	Steadied turn, up late	10
4Feb06-4GP	sly^S	6½f	:21^3	:44	1:09^1	1:16	ⒻOldHat-G3	73	5	4	6^6	6^6½	5^6	5^7½	Dominguez R A	L119	2.60	84- 04	MistyRosette115^4 SwapFliproo119^1¾ SmrtNPretty115^hd	3 wide, no factor	6
20Nov05-8Aqu	fst	6f	:21^3	:44^4	:57^3	1:11	ⒻVllyStrm-G3	86	3	5	5^10	5^6¼	4^1¾	1^2	Dominguez R A	L118	9.60	83- 13	Miraculous Miss118^2 Diamond Spirit116^1½ *India*116½	Hit gate, ridden out	5
17Oct05-6Del	fst	5½f	:21^4	:46^3	:59^3	1:06^1	ⒻAlw 43000N1x	62	4	4	5^2¾	5^3¼	3^1½	1^1	Dominguez R A	L120	*1.40	86- 15	*MrculousMss*120^1 ScessflRomnc116^3 CsblncBb120^2½	Handily, edging away	5
19Sep05-4Del	fst	4½f	:22^2	:46^2		:52^4	ⒻMd Sp Wt 40k	60	6	6	7^8¼		5^4½	1^hd	Dominguez R A	L120	*1.00	98- 11	*MirculousMiss*120^hd TrueCountry120^2¾ *AfletLulu*120^1	Ran down leader late	7

WORKS: Jun4 Fai 6f fst (W) 1:14^1 B *1/1* May28 Fai 1 fst 1:45^3 B *1/1* ●May20 Fai 5f fst 1:00^1 B *1/6* May14 Fai 4f fst :49 B *2/2* May5 Fai 5f fst 1:01^4 B *2/6* ●Apr10 Fai 4f fst :48^3 B *1/5*
TRAINER: 31-60Days(158 .23 $1.64) WonLastStart(115 .23 $1.22) Dirt(485 .27 $1.78) Routes(201 .17 $1.08) GrdStk(19 .16 $3.34) J/T 2005-06(1 1.00 $3.60)

7 Teammate
Orange — Own: Allen Joseph
Green And White Blocks, Green Sleeves
VELASQUEZ C (131 19 21 19 .15) 2006: (737 119 .16)

Gr/ro. f. 3 (Mar)
Sire: A.P. Indy (Seattle Slew) $300,000
Dam: Starry Dreamer (Rubiano)
Br: Joseph Allen (Ky)
Tr: Jerkens H Allen(33 6 3 5 .18) 2006:(127 18 .14)

L 121

Life	7	2	3	1	$151,486	100	D.Fst	6	2	2	1	$121,486	100
2006	3	1	2	0	$126,600	100	Wet(412)	1	0	1	0	$30,000	63
2005	4	1	1	1	$24,886	78	Turf(308)	0	0	0	0	$0	-
Bel	2	0	1	1	$12,900	66	Dst(407)	1	0	1	0	$6,600	84

5Mar06-8GP	fst	1⅛	:48	1:12	1:36	1:48^1	ⒻBonnieMs-G2	100	2	1^1	1^1	1½	1^3½	1^6	Velasquez C	L116	5.20	101- 08	Teammate116^6 **WonderLadyAnneL**120^hd WaitWhile120^7¾	Strong hand ride	7
4Feb06-6GP	sly^S	1⅛	:45^3	1:09^2	1:36^1	1:50^1	ⒻDvonaDal-G2	63	2	2^1	3^2	4^2½	3^7½	2^14	Velasquez C	115	*1.90	77- 04	WaitaWhile119^14 *Teammate*115^hd **WonderLdyAnneL**119^hd	In tight 1st turn	7
13Jan06-9GP	fst	1	:23^2	:45^2	1:09^4	1:36^4	ⒻAlw 33000N1x	84	9	5^2¼	3^1	2^1	2^1½	2^hd	Velasquez C	119	6.90	87- 16	**Bushfire**119^hd Teammate119^3¼ Nancy Creek119^3½	Just missed	11
11Dec05-8Crc	fst	1 1/16 ⊗	:23^3	:49^4	1:16^2	1:48	ⒻMd Sp Wt 19k	78	6	2^3	2^3½	1^hd	1^4½	1^8¾	Velasquez C	118	*2.70	78- 21	Teammate118^8¾ Reigning Emerald118^3 Rosa Rose118^no	Drew off, handily	9
20Nov05-4Aqu	fst	5½f	:22^1	:45^4	:58^4	1:05^4	ⒻMd Sp Wt 43k	38	3	3	6^3	6^6¾	8^7¾	8^11¼	Santos J A	120	*1.85	- -	*Yachats*120¾ Endless Virtue115¾ Bella Lago115^1¼	Jumped shadows turn	8
24Jun05-2Bel	fst	5f	:22^1	:45^3		:58^2	ⒻMd Sp Wt 40k	61	4	2	2½	2½	2^1½	2^2½	Migliore R	118	*.90	89- 11	Truart118^2½ Teammate118^17¾ Colonial Promise118^7	Second best	4
3Jun05-2Bel	fst	5f	:21^3	:45^1		:57^4	ⒻMd Sp Wt 43k	66	2	4	5^11	5^9	4^4	3^4¼	Hill C^5	113	7.80	91- 10	Folklore118^4 *Truart*118^nk Teammate113^1¾	Pinched back start	6

WORKS: Jun5 Bel tr.t 7f gd 1:27 B *1/1* May31 Bel 6f fst 1:14^2 B *1/1* May27 Bel 5f fst 1:00^4 H *10/17* May23 Bel tr.t 4f fst :48^3 B *5/21* May17 Bel tr.t 3f fst :37^4 B *11/11* Apr8 Bel 6f fst 1:14^3 B *1/2*
TRAINER: 61-180Days(36 .17 $1.68) WonLastStart(80 .14 $1.09) Dirt(412 .17 $1.56) Routes(202 .17 $1.46) GrdStk(63 .10 $1.08) J/T 2005-06 BEL(1 1.00 $19.60) J/T 2005-06(17 .29 $2.88)

8 Hello Liberty
Pink — Own: Ferris John Riley Mike Gamble David J
White And Red Stripes, Blue And White
ARROYO N JR (53 6 2 9 .11) 2006: (323 54 .17)

B. f. 3 (Feb) KEESEP04 $75,000
Sire: Forest Camp (Deputy Minister) $25,000
Dam: Witness Post (Gone West)
Br: Brereton C Jones (Ky)
Tr: Jones J Larry(1 1 0 0 1.00) 2006:(113 24 .21)

L 121

Life	7	4	2	1	$233,314	97	D.Fst	6	3	2	1	$188,314	97
2006	4	2	2	0	$183,840	97	Wet(365)	1	1	0	0	$45,000	81
2005	3	2	0	1	$49,474	74	Turf(282*)	0	0	0	0	$0	-
Bel	1	1	0	0	$124,560	97	Dst(341)	0	0	0	0	$0	-

6May06-8Bel	fst	7f	:22^1	:44^3	1:09	1:22^3	ⒻNasauCBC-G2	97	4	4	2^1½	2^3	2^3	1^nk	Arroyo N Jr	L120 f	9.60	88- 15	HlloLibrty120^nk WnMcCool116^5¼ SwpFlproo119^2½	Determined, along late	6
22Apr06-8Del	sly^S	6f	:21^4	:45^3	:57^4	1:10^3	ⒻPeachBloss75k	81	4	1	3^3½	3^2½	1^1½	1^3½	Dominguez R A	116 f	2.60	88- 13	*HelloLiberty*116^3½ *Amandtude*116^nk LdyofSummer116^5	4p,clear 1/8,handily	5
23Mar06-9OP	fst	5½f	:22^4	:46^3	:58^3	1:04^4	ⒻOC 100k/N2x -N	83	6	5	1^hd	1^hd	2^hd	2^1½	Elliott S	L117 f	2.10	92- 20	WildctBettieB121^1½ *HelloLibrty*117½ NwHopSvn117^3	Briefly clear,held 2nd	6
1Mar06-2OP	fst	6f	:21^2	:44^3	:57^3	1:10^3	ⒻOC 75k/N2x -N	75	1	5	3^2	4^2¼	2^1½	2^3½	Thompson T J	L118 f	3.40	86- 14	JzzyOkie118^3½ HelloLiberty118^1½ Redyforcocktils120^5¾	Slit foes, 2nd best	6
28Oct05-8Kee	fst	7f	:22^4	:46^1	1:12^3	1:27	ⒻAlw 49660N2L	68	4	6	3^2	3^1½	2^hd	1^nk	Thompson T J	L116 f	3.40	72- 23	HelloLiberty116^nk GlmingElgnc118^nk BroknSmil116^3	Bmp start,4w,all out	7
3Jly05-8PrM	fst	5f	:22	:45^1		:57^4	PrGldJuv50k	74	5	6	2^hd	1^1	1^hd	3^1	Rini W	B113 f	3.40	95- 10	CounterfeitGold116¾ *DwnofWr*112^nk *HelloLiberty*113^3½	Dueled, outfinished	7
17Jun05-1PrM	fst	5f	:22^2	:45^4		:58^2	ⒻMd Sp Wt 20k	59	5	5	4^3½	1^1	1^3½	1^2½	Rini W	B118 f	1.70	93- 13	Hello Liberty118^2½ Cherokee Cat118^5¼ Town Scandal118^3¾	3 wide, handily	6

WORKS: Jun4 Del 5f fst 1:02^1 B *5/13* ●Apr14 Kee 5f fst 1:02 B *1/6*
TRAINER: Sprint/Route(34 .12 $1.12) 2Sprints/Route(1 .00 $0.00) 31-60Days(86 .15 $1.67) WonLastStart(77 .21 $1.64) Dirt(393 .21 $2.43) Routes(93 .15 $1.75) J/T 2005-06 BEL(1 1.00 $21.20) J/T 2005-06(5 .20 $4.24)

9 Ermine
Turqse — Own: Oxbow Racing
Red, Green Sash, Green Diamonds On Slvs
ALBARADO R J (—) 2006: (459 79 .17)

Ch. f. 3 (Jan) OBSAUG04 $45,000
Sire: Exchange Rate (Danzig) $10,000
Dam: Red Mischief (Thirty Six Red)
Br: Amy Bondon-Peltz (Fla)
Tr: Werner Ronny(—) 2006:(112 26 .23)

L 121

Life	6	2	3	0	$217,274	93	D.Fst	5	2	3	0	$217,274	93
2006	4	2	1	0	$201,774	93	Wet(404)	1	0	0	0	$0	-
2005	2	M	2	0	$15,500	81	Turf(360*)	0	0	0	0	$0	-
Bel	0	0	0	0	$0	-	Dst(315)	1	0	0	0	$0	-

5May06-10CD	fst	1⅛	:46^2	1:11^2	1:37	1:50	ⒻKyOaks-G1	90	12	11^10	12^10	9^3¾	3^1	2^1½	Albarado R J	L121	10.50	85- 06	Lemons Forever121^1½ Ermine121^1¼ **Bushfire**121^1	Steady 1st turn,3w bid	14
25Mar06-10OP	fst	1 1/16	:23	:46^4	1:12^1	1:44^2	ⒻHoneybee75k	93	2	2^3½	2^3½	2^1	1½	1^3	Borel C H	L116	5.90	84- 22	Ermine116^3 Brownie Points119^3½ Morner115^2	Chased, bid, held sway	6
16Feb06-2OP	fst	1 1/16	:23^3	:47^4	1:13^2	1:46^2	ⒻMd Sp Wt 32k	76	1	2½	2½	2^1	1^hd	1^3	Albarado R J	L121	*.70	74- 29	*Ermine*121^3 SkywrdExchnge121^1¼ AngelFlying121^4	Stalked,brisk handling	12
22Jan06-6OP	sly^S	1	:23^2	:47^4	1:14	1:42^1	ⒻMd Sp Wt 32k	–	11	2^1	2^hd	1^1	1^3	-	Torres F C	L121	2.60	- 31	ShytoeLfeet121^6 RunnrsHigh121^5¼ SouthrnSss121^2½	Ducked in,lost rider	12
31Dec05-6LaD	fst	7f	:22^2	:45^3	1:10^4	1:24^1	ⒻMd Sp Wt 39k	81	8	3	4^3	3^1½	2^1	2¾	Albarado R J	L119	*1.70	89- 11	Sweet Sugaree119¾ Ermine119^7¼ Triestes Song119^3¼	2nd best outside	10
5Nov05-5CD	fst	6f	:21^4	:45^1	:57^2	1:09^4	ⒻMd Sp Wt 39k	70	10	1	3^1	2^2	2^2	2^3½	Castanon J L	L120	10.20	88- 08	Triple It120^3½ Ermine120^2¾ Tattletale120^4½	5w,second best	12

WORKS: Jun4 CD 4f fst :48^3 B *17/66* May27 CD 5f fst :59^4 B *4/34* May19 CD 5f fst 1:01 B *7/26* Apr27 CD 5f fst 1:01^1 B *5/22* Apr18 CD 6f fst 1:13^2 B *2/5* Apr10 CD 5f fst 1:02^3 B *23/38*
TRAINER: 31-60Days(85 .21 $2.44) Dirt(226 .22 $2.12) Routes(93 .12 $1.02) GrdStk(10 .20 $3.02) J/T 2005-06(49 .27 $1.89)

The 76th running of the Acorn was an exceedingly treacherous race to handicap, because during the last 15 years, the Beyer par for the Acorn was 97, and none of the 3-year-old fillies in the race could be counted on to run to that level.

Adieu had run a 96 in the La Troienne, but that had been a significant forward move off her best figures as a 2-year-old, and it had been her first start in more than six months.

Based on their most recent races, Teammate (100) and Hello Liberty (97) also had what it historically took to win the Acorn, but in each case those figures were far better than anything else in their records. Moreover, Teammate had not raced in three months, and Hello Liberty was the only entrant who had never been past seven furlongs.

Ermine and Bushfire had run respectably in the Kentucky Oaks, but that race had gone well below par after the last three-eighths unfolded in a slow 38.60 seconds.

The plan: Use everybody under 10–1, which eliminated only Last Romance and She's Excellent.

The running of the race: Bushfire, who had rallied from off the pace and lugged in through the stretch of the Kentucky Oaks, reverted back to the running style of her four previous victories, and was aggressively hustled up on the rail to get the lead. Hello Liberty collared her approaching the quarter pole, and the two fillies battled shoulder to shoulder through the length of the stretch in a thrilling, albeit slow (26.46 seconds) final quarter.

NINTH RACE
Belmont
JUNE 10, 2006

1 MILE. (1.32¹) 76TH RUNNING OF THE ACORN. Grade I. Purse $250,000 FOR FILLIES THREE YEARS OLD. By subscription of $250 each, which should accompany the nomination; $1,250 to pass the entry box; $1,250 to start. The purse to be divided 60% to the winner, 20% to second, 10% to third, 5% to fourth, 3% to fifth and 2% divided equally among remaining finishers. 121 lbs. Trophies will be presented to the winning owner, trainer and jockey. A special permanent trophy will be presented to the owner of the winner if the same filly wins all legs of the Triple Tiara (The Acorn, The Mother Goose and The Coaching Club American Oaks). Closed Saturday, May 27, 2006 with 27 Nominations.

Value of Race: $250,000 Winner $150,000; second $50,000; third $25,000; fourth $12,500; fifth $7,500; sixth $2,500; seventh $2,500. Mutuel Pool $1,841,736.00 Exacta Pool $1,169,630.00 Trifecta Pool $781,221.00 Superfecta Pool $195,169.00

Last Raced	Horse	M/Eqt.	A.	Wt	PP	St	¼	½	¾	Str	Fin	Jockey	Odds $1
5May06 ¹⁰CD⁶	Bushfire	L	3	121	3	3	1½	1½	2¹½	2²	1ⁿᵏ	Solis A	4.60
6May06 ⁸Bel¹	Hello Liberty	L f	3	121	6	1	2²	22½	1½	1ʰᵈ	21¾	Arroyo N Jr	9.00
5May06 ¹⁰CD⁷	Last Romance	L	3	121	1	6	5⁷	5⁶	3¹½	33½	31¾	Prado E S	15.20
6May06 ⁶CD²	Adieu	L	3	121	2	4	4²	41½	4²	4½	4½	Gomez G K	1.80
5May06 ¹⁰CD²	Ermine	L	3	121	7	5	65½	6⁶	63½	5²	5¹	Albarado R J	3.10
14May06 ⁵Bel¹	She's Excellent	L b	3	121	4	7	7	7	7	6¹½	66¾	Jara F	34.75
5Mar06 ⁸GP¹	Teammate	L	3	121	5	2	3ʰᵈ	3ʰᵈ	5½	7	7	Velasquez C	3.70

OFF AT 5:20 Start Good. Won driving. Track fast.
TIME :22¹, :45, 1:09², 1:35⁴ (:22.28, :45.00, 1:09.43, 1:35.89)

$2 Mutuel Prices:

3 – BUSHFIRE	11.20	5.70	4.20
8 – HELLO LIBERTY		8.10	5.40
1 – LAST ROMANCE			7.30

$2 EXACTA 3–8 PAID $100.50 $2 TRIFECTA 3–8–1 PAID $877.00
$2 SUPERFECTA 3–8–1–2 PAID $3,363.00

B. f, (Mar), by Louis Quatorze – Traki Traki , by Mo Power . Trainer Kenneally Eddie. Bred by Moreau Bloodstock International and Mandolynn Hill Farm (Fla).

BUSHFIRE was hustled from the gate, set the pace along the inside, dug in when headed by HELLO LIBERTY turning for home, responded to steady pressure and came again on the rail to get the job done. HELLO LIBERTY pressed the pace from the outside, earned a short lead approaching the stretch, led from the outside past the eighth pole and dug in gamely but could handle the winner late. LAST ROMANCE was urged along early, rallied three wide nearing the stretch and finished well outside. ADIEU raced close up along the inside, was hustled along inside around the turn, came wide into the stretch and stayed on well outside. ERMINE was outrun early, put in a run from the outside nearing the stretch and was going well late. SHE'S EXCELLENT was outrun early, advanced inside on the turn, angled out in upper stretch and offered a mild rally outside. TEAMMATE raced close up outside, chased the pace while three wide and tired after the opening three quarters.

Owners– 1, Ronald Rashinski Rashinski Ricki; 2, Ferris John Riley Mike Gamble David and Jones J Larry; 3, Goldfarb S Dubb M Bunch of Characters Stable Bradley III P Zerolo M; 4, Michael Tabor Magnier Mrs John Derrick Smith; 5, Oxbow Racing LLC; 6, Perez Robert; 7, Allen Joseph

Trainers– 1, Kenneally Eddie; 2, Jones J Larry; 3, Dutrow Richard E Jr; 4, Pletcher Todd A; 5, Werner Ronny; 6, Ortiz Juan; 7, Jerkens H Allen

Scratched– Wonder Lady Anne L (05May06 ¹⁰CD⁴) , Miraculous Miss (15Apr06 ⁸Aqu¹)

$2 Daily Double (9–3) Paid $55.00 ; Daily Double Pool $179,018 .
$2 Pick Three (2–9–3) Paid $70.50 ; Pick Three Pool $378,767 .
$2 Consolation Pick 3 (2–9–5/6) Paid $10.20 .
$2 Consolation Daily Double (9–5/6) Paid $7.50 .

Race 10: the Manhattan Handicap—third leg of the $1 million pick four

10

Belmont Park *1¼ MILES* **(Inner Turf). (1:57 3) ManhttnH-G1 105th Running of THE MANHATTAN HANDICAP. Grade I. Purse $400,000 A Handicap For Three Year Olds And Upward. By subscription of $400 each, which should accompany the nomination; $2,000 to pass the entry box; $2,000 to start. The purse to be divided 60% to the winner, 20% to second, 10% to third, 5% to fourth, 3% to fifth and 2% divided equally among remaining finishers. In the event that this race istaken off the turf, it may be subject to downgrading upon review by the Graded Stakes Committee. Closed Saturday, May 27, 2006 with 28 Nominations.**

1 Good Reward

Red
Own: Phipps Stable
Black, Cherry Cap
CASTELLANO J J (69 15 9 10 .22) 2006: (488 85 .17)

B. h. 5 (Mar)
Sire: Storm Cat (Storm Bird) $500,000
Dam: Heavenly Prize (Seeking the Gold)
Br: Phipps Stable (Ky)
Tr: McGaughey III Claude R(18 3 1 10 .17) 2006:(72 7 .10)

L 118

Life	21	5	1	5	$817,902	106	D.Fst	5	1	0	0	$51,000	98
2006	3	0	0	1	$35,549	103	Wet(430)	1	0	0	0	$0	92
2005	6	1	0	2	$305,000	106	Turf(345)	15	4	1	5	$766,902	106
Bel (T)	3	1	1	0	$257,860	106	Dst(T)(305)	4	2	0	0	$545,410	106

6May06-9CD fm 1⅛ (T) :481 1:12 1:352 1:47 3↑ TurfClsc-G1 102 9 53 55½ 51¾ 64 72¾ Prado E S L126 b 19.30 95-04 **English Channel**122½ **Cacique**122¾ Milk It Mick126no 5-6w trip,empty 10
14Apr06-9Kee fm 1 (T) :24 :474 1:112 1:34 4↑ MakrsMrk-G2 103 3 46 42 2½ 2hd 32 Prado E S L117 b 7.30 95-03 MisqusApprovl117no ArtiSchllr1232 GoodRwrd1172½ Between,no late gain 6
11Mar06-9GP fm 1 1/16 (T) :234 :482 1:104 1:39 3↑ CanadaTrfH100k 99 5 52¾ 43 42½ 3½ 42¾ Prado E S L118 b 8.50 93-09 ***EnglishChannel***119¾ *MiesquesApprovl*116½ *SilverTree*1171½ Rail bid, gave way 9
24Sep05-7Haw slyS 1¼ :48 1:121 1:373 2:043 3↑ HawGldCp-G2 92 9 74½ 86½ 76 67½ 68¾ Bridgmohan S X L114 b 7.00 74-23 SuperFrolic118hd LordoftheGme1172½ DesertBoom1153½ 3 wide, no factor 10
13Aug05-9AP yl 1¼ (T) :482 1:124 1:384 2:031 3↑ ArlMilln-G1 89 3 48½ 55 104½ 1013 812 Bailey J D L126 b 11.40 70-20 Powerscourt1263 KittensJoy126no *FourtyNinersSon*126no Inside, gave way 10
11Jun05-10Bel fm 1¼ (T) :494 1:133 1:37 2:003 3↑ ManhttnH-G1 106 2 41 2hd 2hd 1½ 1½ Bailey J D L117 b 14.90 93-14 GoodRewrd117½ **RelxedGesture**116no *ArtieSchillr*122½ Dug in resolutely rail 11
21May05-9Pim gd 1⅛ (T) :514 1:164 1:404 1:523 3↑ Dixie-G2 93 5 53½ 53 52½ 33½ 32½ Bailey J D L118 b 3.70 66-25 Cool Conductor118no Artie Schiller1242½ *Good Reward*1182½ No rally 5
15Apr05-9Kee fm 1 (T) :233 :47 1:104 1:34 4↑ MakrsMrk-G2 99 1 63 63¾ 51½ 32½ 33 Velazquez J R L123 b 5.70 94-10 ArtiSchllr1212½ GulchApprovl117¾ GoodRwrd123nk Lack room 1/4p,5w bid 10
5Feb05-9SA fst 1⅛ :45 1:093 1:353 1:491 Strub-G2 98 2 88½ 88¾ 74¾ 54 46½ Nakatani C S LB123 b 10.70 81-16 *RockHrdTen*121no Imperilism1193½ *LoveofMoney*1233 Washy,3wd into lane 9
28Nov04-9Hol fm 1¼ (T) :471 1:121 1:37 2:012 HolDerby-G1 104 5 83¾ 82 74½ 41½ 1½ Bailey J D LB122 b 16.10 85-17 GoodReward122½ FastndFurious1221 Imperilism1222 Bumped lane,rallied 13
10Oct04-4Kee fm 1 (T) :233 :472 1:12 1:362 StormCat110k 98 6 77½ 75 54 43 1¾ Prado E S L117 b 2.70 90-12 *Good Reward*117¾ Fort Prado120nk Silver Ticket123½ Rallied 6-7w,driving 8
6Sep04-10Sar fm 1 3/16 (T) :482 1:123 1:362 1:534 SaranacH-G3 89 2 54½ 55 51½ 51¾ 43¾ Santos J A L115 b 4.10 92-09 *PrinceArch*123hd *Mustanfr*1212½ CtchtheGlory1151½ Bumped upper stretch 6

WORKS: Jun4 Bel 5f sly 1:01 B *1/1* May24 Bel 4f fst :503 B *29/38* Apr30 Kee 5f gd 1:012 B *1/2* Apr25 Kee 4f fst :50 B *18/27* Apr9 Kee 4f fst :49 B *18/49* Apr1 GP 5f fst 1:004 B *2/15*
TRAINER: 31-60Days(73 .07 $0.59) Turf(75 .15 $2.05) Routes(195 .21 $2.28) GrdStk(42 .21 $3.87)
J/T 2005-06 BEL(5 .20 $1.32) J/T 2005-06(7 .29 $9.49)

2 Relaxed Gesture (Ire)

White
Own: Moyglare Stud
Black, White Triangular Panel, White
DESORMEAUX K J (65 9 8 12 .14) 2006: (280 53 .19)

Ch. h. 5 (Mar)
Sire: Indian Ridge*Ire (Ahonoora*GB) $88,800
Dam: Token Gesture*Ire (Alzao)
Br: Moyglare Stud Farm Ltd (Ire)
Tr: Clement Christophe(25 6 6 5 .24) 2006:(162 31 .19)

L 119

Life	13	4	5	2	$1,403,219	109	D.Fst	1	0	0	0	$0	61
2006	1	0	0	0	$0	-	Wet(284)	0	0	0	0	$0	-
2005	7	3	3	1	$1,326,186	109	Turf(391)	12	4	5	2	$1,403,219	109
Bel (T)	4	1	2	1	$188,800	107	Dst(T)(261)	3	1	2	0	$139,091	105

25Mar06 Nad Al Sheba (UAE) gf *1½ (T) LH 2:314 4↑ Dubai Sheema Classic-G1 1227¾ Nakatani C S 123 - Heart's Cry1234¾ Collier Hill1231¼ Falstaff1233½ 14
Timeform rating: 75 Stk 5000000 *Tracked in 4th,close 2nd 5f out,4th 3f out,wknd.OuijaBoard4th*
23Oct05-8WO yl 1½ (T) :493 1:14 2:06 2:323 3↑ CanIntnl-G1 109 4 99¾ 88¼ 43½ 1½ 14½ Nakatani C S L126 11.20 66-30 RelxedGesture1264½ *MtorStorm*126nk (D)***GrySwllow***1261¼ Rallied 7w,driving 10
10Sep05-9Bel fm 1⅜ (T) :471 1:11 1:354 2:113 3↑ ManOWar-G1 107 10 28 28 2hd 1hd 3¾ Nakatani C S L126 3.30 104-06 BetterTlkNow126nk KingsDrm126½ *RelxedGstur*1264¼ Dug in gamely inside 11
13Aug05-8Sar gd 1½ (T) :483 1:14 2:032 2:271 3↑ SwrdDncr-G1 108 4 1hd 2½ 2hd 2½ 2¾ Santos J A L116 2.90 83-20 KingsDrama116¾ RelxedGesture1163¼ Vngelis118¾ Dug in gamely outside 8
16Jly05-8Bel fm 1⅜ (T) :514 1:17 1:404 2:152 3↑ BwlnGrnH-G2 105 7 31 31 41½ 2½ 2hd Blanc B L117 *1.05 83-17 CchtWells114hd RelxedGesture1172¾ **Drednught**117hd Game finish outside 7
11Jun05-10Bel fm 1¼ (T) :494 1:133 1:37 2:003 3↑ ManhttnH-G1 105 8 3½ 71½ 72 42 2½ Blanc B L116 13.80 92-14 **GoodRewrd**117½ RelxedGesture116no *ArtieSchillr*122½ Game finish outside 11
14May05-7Bel fm 1¼ (T) :501 1:133 1:371 2:004 3↑ Alw 48000N2x 98 6 43½ 41¾ 31 1hd 11¼ Blanc B L124 *.55 92-08 Relaxed Gesture1241¼ *Ershaad*122¾ *Brickell*122hd Lunged through gate 6
14Apr05-9Kee fm 1⅛ (T) :47 1:113 1:362 1:481 4↑ Alw 45755N1x 96 11 62 64 51¾ 11½ 16¾ Blanc B L118 4.50 94-05 *RelaxedGesture*1186¾ BritishBlue1183 Qusspug118nk Lunge start,hand urg 11
Previously trained by Weld Dermot
9May04 Leopardstwn (Ire) yl 1¼ (T) LH 2:101 Derrinstown Stud Derby Trial-G2 21½ Smullen P J 126 5.50 Yeats1261½ *Relaxed Gesture*1261 *Medicinal*1262½ 4
Timeform rating: 112+ Stk 154000 *Rated in last,2nd over 1f out,stayed on*
25Oct03-7SA fst 1 1/16 :221 :45 1:094 1:433 BCJuvnle-G1 61 11 97¾ 108¼ 129¾ 1014 818 Smullen P J LB122 20.00 68-07 Action This Day1222¼ Minister Eric1225 Chapel Royal122no No factor 12

WORKS: Jun5 Bel (T) 4f gd :52 B(d) *9/19* May28 Bel (T) 4f fm :483 B(d) *9/12* ●May21 Bel (T) 4f yl :48 B(d) *1/7* May14 Bel (T) 4f gd :493 B(d) *5/9* May4 Bel 4f fst :494 B *19/29* Apr22 Pay 4f fst :512 B *7/7*
TRAINER: 61-180Days(105 .24 $1.85) Turf(373 .23 $1.71) Routes(422 .20 $1.52) GrdStk(46 .24 $2.60)
J/T 2005-06(5 .60 $2.74)

3 Sabre d'Argent

Blue
Own: Darley Stable
Maroon, White Sleeves, Maroon Cap, White
COA E M (165 29 23 23 .18) 2006: (688 145 .21)

Dk. b or br h. 6 (Feb)
Sire: Kris S. (Roberto) $150,000
Dam: Sterling Pound (Seeking the Gold)
Br: Philip Freedman (Ky)
Tr: Albertrani Thomas(9 1 2 1 .11) 2006:(81 18 .22)

L 114

Life	9	5	0	2	$154,607	95	D.Fst	0	0	0	0	$0	-
2006	4	1	0	1	$40,720	95	Wet(406)	1	1	0	0	$10,320	93
2005	1	1	0	0	$15,311	-	Turf(341)	8	4	0	2	$144,287	95
Bel (T)	0	0	0	0	$0	-	Dst(T)(353)	4	4	0	0	$111,368	-

20May06-10Pim fm 1⅛ (T) :481 1:12 1:37 1:482 3↑ DixieG2-G 95 5 64¼ 67¼ 57½ 65 43½ Castellano J J L118 b 13.60 85-08 BetterTlkNow124hd **Drednught**118nk ArtieSchiller1243¼ Wide, no response 7
22Apr06-7Aqu fm 1 1/16 (T) :233 :49 1:133 1:424 3↑ FtMarcyH-G3 87 3 56 55 54 54¼ 34½ Prado E S L115 b *1.35 88-07 Foreverness1154½ Pa Pa Da114hd Sabred'Argent1151½ Checked after start 6
1Apr06-10GP fm 1½ (T) :482 1:131 2:012 2:241 3↑ PanAmerH-G3 84 6 42½ 31½ 31 45 55 Castellano J J L115 b 4.20 103 - **Silver Whistle**115nk Ramazutti1132 Go Deputy118hd 3 wide, tired 8
4Feb06-9Tam wf 1 1/16 (X) :231 :47 1:121 1:453 4↑ OC 60k/c -N 93 4 47 38 35 33½ 12 Lezcano J L118 b *1.40 91-22 SbredArgent1182 CherokPrinc1181¾ SiphonCity1181½ Hard to load,up late 5
Previously trained by Saeed bin Suroor
4Jun05 Doncaster (GB) gf 1¼ (T) LH 2:084 3↑ Carling Conditions Stks(1 1/4m,60y) 11¼ Queally T P 128 *1.85 *Sabre d'Argent*1281¼ Big Bad Bob1354 Persian Majesty1285 5
Timeform rating: 112+ Alw 26400 *Tracked in 3rd,2nd over 2f out,led 1f out,driving*
Previously trained by David Loder
9Aug03 Haydock (GB) gf 1 5/16 (T) LH 2:103 3↑ Rose of Lancaster Stakes-G3 1½ Ahern E 119 b 5.00 *Sabre d'Argent*119½ Far Lane1297 Izdiham1299 5
Timeform rating: 119+ Stk 96100 *Rank in 4th,2nd 1-1/2f out,led 150y out*
31May03 Newmarket (GB) gf 1¼ (T) Str 2:083 Fairway Stakes (Listed) 12 Dettori L 124 b 4.00 *Sabre d'Argent*1242 Rocket Force1241 Roskilde124½ 6
Timeform rating: 106+ Stk 52300 *Rated in 5th,led over 1f out,drifted right,ridden out*
3May03 Newmarket (GB) gd 1½ (T) RH 2:34 Ruinart Champagne Cndtns Stks 317 Dettori L 126 *.70 Westmoreland Road1267 Calibre12610 *Sabre d'Argent*1264 4
Timeform rating: 87+ Alw 22900 *Slowly away,rated in 3rd,weakened 2f out*
15Apr03 Newmarket (GB) gf 1¼ (T) Str 2:103 Museum Maiden Stakes 13½ Dettori L 126 *.80 Sabre d'Argent1263½ Financial Future126hd Lodger1263 6
Timeform rating: 101+ Maiden 13000 *Tracked in 3rd,led over 1f out,drifted right,driving*

WORKS: Jun1 Bel 5f fst 1:033 B *26/28* May11 Bel 5f fst 1:012 H *4/23* May5 Bel 5f fst 1:014 H *12/22* Apr18 Bel 5f fst 1:023 B *17/19* Mar24 Pay 4f fst :52 B *16/20* Mar18 Pay 5f fst 1:05 B *2/4*
TRAINER: Turf(51 .25 $4.57) Routes(145 .21 $2.98) GrdStk(20 .35 $5.70)
J/T 2005-06 BEL(9 .33 $1.86) J/T 2005-06(30 .27 $1.74)

4 Cacique (Ire)
Own: Juddmonte Farms
Yellow Green, Pink Sash, White Sleeves, Pink
PRADO E S (123 26 22 27 .21) 2006: (582 105 .18)
Dk. b or br h. 5 (May)
Sire: Danehill (Danzig) $39,277
Dam: Hasili*Ire (Kahyasi*Ire)
Br: Juddmonte Farms (Ire)
Tr: Frankel Robert(13 5 0 3 .38) 2006:(237 54 .23)
L 120

Life	13	5	3	1	$572,331	107	D.Fst	0	0	0	0	$0	-
2006	2	0	1	0	$104,432	107	Wet(372)	0	0	0	0	$0	-
2005	4	1	0	1	$79,576	-	Turf(416)	13	5	3	1	$572,331	107
Bel Ⓣ	0	0	0	0	$0	-	DstⓉ(328)	2	0	1	0	$181,010	-

6May06–9CD fm 1⅛ Ⓣ :481 1:12 1:352 1:47 3↑ TurfClsc-G1 **107** 3 42 44½ 41¾ 43½ 2½ Valenzuela P A L122 *2.00 97– 04 **English Channel**122½ Cacique122¾ Milk It Mick126no In tight start,5w bid 10
4Mar06–7SA gd 1 Ⓣ :224 :462 1:094 1:342 4↑ FKilroeH-G1 **107** 5 119½ 116¾ 105½ 94½ 4nk Valenzuela P A LB118 *1.40 91– 18 Milk ItMick116hd Aragorn119no ChineseDragon116hd 8wd into lane,rallied 13
Previously trained by Andre Fabre
4Sep05 Longchamp (Fr) gd *1 Ⓣ RH 1:36 3↑ Prix du Moulin de Longchamp-G1 Stk 376000 — 75¼ Hughes R 128 4.50 *Starcraft*1282½ Gorella120nk Majors Cast128½ 9
Timeform rating: 116 — *Trckd pacesetting winner,3rd 150y out,wknd.Whipper4th,Valixir5th*
12Jun05 Chantilly (Fr) gd *1 Ⓣ RH 1:371 4↑ Prix du Chemin de Fer du Nord-G3 Stk 90900 — 12½ Soumillon C 127 2.00 Cacique1272½ Special Kaldoun122no Tiganello124nk 6
Timeform rating: 122 — *Set slow pace,quickened clear 1-1/2f out.Whipper 4th*
22May05 Longchamp (Fr) gd *1⅛ Ⓣ RH 1:504 4↑ Prix d'Ispahan (1 1/8m,55y)-G1 Stk 251000 — 32¾ Peslier O 128 *1.80e *Valixir*1282 Elvstroem128¾ *Cacique*128½ 8
Timeform rating: 119+ — *Rated in 7th,gained 3rd 1f out.Touch of Land 4th*
1May05 Saint-Cloud (Fr) gd *1 Ⓣ LH 1:372 4↑ Prix du Muguet-G2 Stk 154400 — 53¼ Soumillon C 127 *2.00 Martillo1271½ Autumn Glory123no Whipper1301½ 9
Timeform rating: 113+ — *Rated in 5th or 6th,evenly late*
2Oct04 Longchamp (Fr) gd *1 Ⓣ RH 1:372 3↑ Prix Daniel Wildenstein-G2 Stk 136000 — 1½ Soumillon C 123 *1.00 Cacique123½ Hurricane Alan129hd Mister Sacha1231½ 11
Timeform rating: 117+ — *Rated towards rear,rallied to lead 1f out,held well*
17Aug04 York (GB) gd 1 5/16 Ⓣ LH 2:114 3↑ Juddmonte Intl Stks(1 1/4m,88y)-G1 Stk 840000 — 46½ Stevens G L 123 10.00 *Sulamani*131¾ Norse Dancer131¾ Bago1235 9
Timeform rating: 115 — *Rated in 6th,drifted left 2f out,evenly late.Tycoon9th*
29Jly04 Chantilly (Fr) gd *1⅛ Ⓣ RH 1:544 Prix Daphnis-G3 Stk 87800 — 11½ Stevens G L 121 *.30 Cacique1211½ Ershaad1211½ DH High Flash121 6
Timeform rating: 112+ — *Set slow pace,quickened clear 2f out,handily*
27Jun04 Longchamp (Fr) gd *1¼ Ⓣ RH 2:053 Grand Prix de Paris-G1 Stk 608000 — 2½ Stevens G L 128 3.50 Bago128½ *Cacique*1285 Alnitak128nk 4
Timeform rating: 117 — *Trckd ldr,led 2-1/2f out,met challenge,headed late*

WORKS: Jun7 Bel tr.t 4f gd :50 B *28/38* Jun1 Bel 5f fst 1:003 B *10/28* ●May26 Bel 5f fst 1:01 B *1/10* May3 CD 4f fst :511 B *53/60* Apr25 Kee Ⓣ 5f fm 1:023 B(d) *6/8* ●Apr18 Kee Ⓣ 6f fm 1:13 H(d) *1/4*
TRAINER: 2Off45-180(113 .27 $1.63) 31-60Days(251 .22 $1.60) Turf(467 .21 $1.37) Routes(549 .24 $1.53) GrdStk(180 .20 $1.45) J/T 2005-06 BEL(14 .21 $1.06) J/T 2005-06(52 .23 $1.19)

5 Grey Swallow (Ire)
Own: Vega FZE Weld Mrs Marguerite
Green Colors Unavailable
SOLIS A (—) 2006: (348 74 .21)
Gr/ro. h. 5 (Feb)
Sire: Daylami*Ire (Doyoun*Ire) $29,600
Dam: Style of Life (The Minstrel)
Br: Mrs C L Weld (Ire)
Tr: Weld Dermot K(—) 2006:(1 1 1.00)
L 122

Life	13	6	0	1	$1,580,786	101	D.Fst	0	0	0	0	$0	-
2006	1	1	0	0	$150,000	101	Wet(258*)	0	0	0	0	$0	-
2005	4	1	0	0	$306,861	100	Turf(304*)	13	6	0	1	$1,580,786	101
Bel Ⓣ	0	0	0	0	$0	-	DstⓉ(306)	2	0	0	0	$60,237	-

13May06–6Hol fm 1½ Ⓣ :512 1:17 2:041 2:271 3↑ JMrryMmH-G2 **101** 2 21 2hd 2½ 11 15 Solis A LB121 *.60 89– 09 GreySwllow1215 BreconBecon1181 RunwyDncer115nk Bid,led, drew clear 5
23Oct05–8WO yl 1½ Ⓣ :493 1:14 2:06 2:323 3↑ CanIntnl-G1 **100** 2 76¼ 64¾ 22½ 33½ 34¾ Smullen P J L126 6.70 61– 30 **RelxedGesture**1264½ *MetorStorm*126nk D *GrySwllow*1261¼ Bid 5-deep,bmp'd 10
Disqualified and placed 4th
10Sep05 Leopardstwn (Ire) yl 1¼ Ⓣ LH 2:034 3↑ Irish Champion Stakes-G1 Stk 1241000 — 66½ Smullen P J 130 5.00 Oratorio123½ Motivator123hd Alexander Goldrun1271 10
Timeform rating: 111 — *Rated in 5th,2nd 2f out,wknd 1f out.Ace4th,Azamour5th*
23Jly05 Newbury (GB) gf 1½ Ⓣ LH 2:281 3↑ King George VI & Queen Eliz Stks-G1 Stk 1222000 — 712 Smullen P J 133 3.30 Azamour1331¼ Norse Dancer133no Bago1335 12
Timeform rating: 105 — *Mid-pack throughout.Ace 5th,Phoenix Reach 10th*
22May05 Curragh (Ire) yl 1 5/16 Ⓣ RH 2:15 4↑ Tattersalls Gold Cup-G1 Stk 314000 — 1¾ Smullen P J 126 6.50 Grey Swallow126¾ Bago1261 Ace126nk 6
Timeform rating: 128 — *Tracked in 4th,3rd 3f out,led 1-1/2f out.Azamour 4th*
3Oct04 Longchamp (Fr) gd *1½ Ⓣ RH 2:25 3↑ Prix de l'Arc de Triomphe-G1 Stk 1986000 — 1819 Smullen P J 123 7.00 *Bago*123½ Cherry Mix1231 *Ouija Board*1202 19
Wide in 8th,weakened 2-1/2f out
11Sep04 Leopardstwn (Ire) gf 1¼ Ⓣ LH 2:014 3↑ Irish Champion Stakes-G1 Stk 1226000 — 41½ Smullen P J 123 4.50 Azamour123½ Norse Dancer130nk Powerscourt130¾ 8
Timeform rating: 122 — *Rated in 5th,3rd 1-1/2f out,outfinished.Doyen 7th*
27Jun04 Curragh (Ire) gf 1½ Ⓣ RH 2:283 Irish Derby-G1 Stk 1584000 — 1½ Smullen P J 126 10.00 Grey Swallow126½ North Light1261½ Tycoon126nk 10
Timeform rating: 127 — *Tracked in 5th,3rd 2f out,led 1f out.Rule Of Law 4th*
22May04 Curragh (Ire) gf 1 Ⓣ Str 1:40 Irish 2000 Guineas-G1 Stk 479000 — 31½ Smullen P J 126 2.00 Bachelor Duke1261 *Azamour*126½ *Grey Swallow*1261½ 8
Timeform rating: 116 — *Tracked in 4th,3rd 1-1/2f out,no late response*
1May04 Newmarket (GB) gd 1 Ⓣ Str 1:363 2000 Guineas Stakes-G1 Stk 533000 — 43¾ Smullen P J 126 10.00 Haafhd1261¾ Snow Ridge1261 Azamour1261 14
Timeform rating: 118 — *Slowly away,rated in 10th,up for 4th.Whipper 5th*

WORKS: Jun5 Bel T 7f gd 1:402 B(d) *1/1* May28 Bel T 7f fm 1:30 B(d) *1/2* May7 Hol Ⓣ 1 fm 1:391 H(d) *1/2*
TRAINER: WonLastStart(1 .00 $0.00) Turf(5 .20 $0.64) Routes(6 .17 $0.53) GrdStk(5 .20 $0.64) J/T 2005-06(2 .50 $1.60)

6 Interpatation
Own: Mavorah Elliot
Black White, Black Dots, White Cap, Black
TURNER T G (2 0 0 1 .00) 2006: (445 .11)
Dk. b or br g. 4 (Feb) KEENOV02 $31,000
Sire: Langfuhr (Danzig) $20,000
Dam: Idealistic Cause (Habitony*GB)
Br: Larry Cassaday & Jack O Thompson (Ky)
Tr: Barbara Robert(20 2 2 3 .10) 2006:(98 14 .14)
L 113

Life	16	3	2	3	$207,314	93	D.Fst	3	0	0	0	$2,099	73
2006	3	1	0	2	$38,500	93	Wet(365)	1	0	0	0	$2,300	53
2005	9	2	1	1	$155,435	89	Turf(262)	12	3	2	3	$202,815	93
Bel Ⓣ	3	1	1	1	$41,800	93	DstⓉ(330)	2	0	0	1	$55,000	83

24May06–6Bel fm 1 1/16 Ⓣ :234 :48 1:12 1:404 4↑ OC 75k/N3x -N **93** 4 64 52½ 52¼ 42 33 Turner T G L118 5.00 86– 15 FishyAdvice1181 SabreBaby1202 Interpatation118nk Between foes, rallied 9
25Feb06–9Tam fm 1 1/16 Ⓣ :231 :47 1:104 1:403 4↑ TampaBayBC95k **93** 8 63 85½ 62¾ 65½ 33 Turner T G L120 14.30 94– 12 *Fort Prado*1222 Icy Atlantic1161 Interpatation120¾ Some late gain 5 wide 12
28Jan06–5GP fm 1⅛ Ⓣ :464 1:102 1:343 1:462 4↑ Alw 35000N2x **90** 4 93¾ 95¾ 94½ 31 1nk Turner T G L120 9.70 91– 08 Interpatation120nk Forecourt120nk Bastille1201¼ 4 wd, up final strides 12
8Nov05–5Aqu fm 1 1/16 Ⓣ :23 :472 1:113 1:414 3↑ Alw 48000N2x **76** 3 97½ 97¼ 105 109½ 108 Velasquez C L118 7.70 90– 05 Settle Up120no Charlevoix122½ *No Theatrics*118¾ Inside, no response 11
8Aug05–8Sar fm 1⅛ T :471 1:111 1:354 1:48 HalOFame-G2 **67** 7 41½ 42 96½ 912 911¾ Coa E M L122 26.50 85– 08 *T.D.Vance*119no **SilverWhistle**1151¾ CrownPoint119½ Wide both turns, tired 9
16Jly05–9Cnl yl 1¼ Ⓣ :494 1:142 1:381 2:022 VaDby-G3 **77** 6 87 86½ 76¾ 711 712 Luzzi M J L118 27.30 81– 13 **EnglishChnnel**1203¼ ChtthoocheWr120¾ *RblRbl*116½ 3-4wd turns, no factor 9
25Jun05–10Cnl fm 1⅜ Ⓣ :51 1:142 1:392 1:561 CnlTurfCup500k **83** 2 41½ 41½ 41½ 66½ 34¼ Turner T G L118 16.90 106 - *EnglishChnnel*1183¼ ExcptionlRid116¾ Intrpttion1181 Std'd 3/16,angled,clsd 6
11May05–7Bel fm 1 1/16 Ⓣ :234 :47 1:103 1:403 Alw 46000N1x **89** 4 42½ 55 53½ 5¾ 1nk Prado E S L122 4.50 90– 07 Interpatation122nk All Trumps118½ Argento118¾ Along late outside 10
21Apr05–8Kee fm 1⅛ Ⓣ :471 1:112 1:354 1:482 Forerunner110k **81** 2 52½ 63¼ 73¾ 65¾ 45½ Turner T G L123 8.50 87– 10 Gun Salute1172½ *Mad Adam*117¾ Cosmic Kris1172½ 6w lane,minor gain 8
26Mar05–10GP fm 1⅛ Ⓣ :481 1:112 1:35 1:47 PalmBch-G3 **88** 5 41 53½ 74½ 64½ 1no Turner T G L116 38.60 - - Interpatation116no Tadreeb118½ *Fishy Advice*118nk Late rush, just up 8
5Mar05–4GP gd 1 Ⓣ :232 :463 1:102 1:342 Md Sp Wt 32k **79** 4 53½ 53¾ 43 32 21½ Velasquez C L122 *2.40 - - Fishy Advice1221½ *Interpatation*1221¾ Honest Trader1222¼ Mild response 12
19Feb05–7GP fst 1 :232 :462 1:114 1:372 Md Sp Wt 32k **73** 12 61 5¾ 41 44½ 58 Potts C L L122 23.30 - - *Flower Alley*122¾ Wall Street1225¾ Celestial Arc122½ 3 wide, gave way 12

WORKS: May6 Bel 5f fst 1:013 B *14/34* Mar26 GP 5f fst :591 H *2/12* Mar18 GP 4f fst :48 B *5/29*
TRAINER: 2Off45-180(32 .03 $0.10) Turf(102 .12 $2.85) Routes(182 .10 $2.26) GrdStk(17 .12 $5.80) J/T 2005-06 BEL(2 .00 $0.00) J/T 2005-06(14 .21 $8.50)

7 Silver Whistle
Own: Stronach Stables
Orange Black, Gold Ball, Red Emblem, Two Red
VELASQUEZ C (131 19 21 19 .15) 2006: (737 119 .16)
Gr/ro. c. 4 (Mar)
Sire: Alphabet Soup (Cozzene) $25,000
Dam: Polish Polka (Polish Numbers)
Br: Adena Springs (Ky)
Tr: Mott William I(22 4 1 1 .18) 2006:(246 49 .20)
L 116

Life	9	3	3	0	$250,330	97	D.Fst	0	0	0	0	$0	-
2006	2	1	1	0	$97,350	93	Wet(385)	1	0	0	0	$1,280	61
2005	7	2	2	0	$152,980	97	Turf(316)	8	3	3	0	$249,050	97
Bel Ⓣ	2	2	0	0	$54,000	87	DstⓉ(315)	4	2	1	0	$121,380	97

1Apr06–10GP fm 1½ Ⓣ :482 1:131 2:012 2:241 3↑ PanAmerH-G3 **93** 4 32½ 41½ 21 2½ 1nk Prado E S L115 2.60 108 - Silver Whistle115nk Ramazutti1132 Go Deputy118hd Up final strides 8
22Feb06–6GP fm 1⅜ Ⓣ :491 1:134 1:37 2:123 4↑ Alw 35000N2x **93** 1 63½ 63 73 51¾ 2hd Velasquez C L120 *1.40 94– 13 Dynntoni120hd *SilverWhistle*1201¼ MinistersJoy120nk Steadied repeatedly 7
4Sep05–10Sar fm 1⅜ Ⓣ :482 1:13 1:364 1:541 Saranac-G3 **97** 1 75¼ 62½ 63¼ 2hd 2no Bailey J D L115 *1.65 94– 09 Jambalaya121no SilverWhistle1152¼ WoodInder121hd 4 wide move, gamely 9
8Aug05–8Sar fm 1⅛ T :471 1:111 1:354 1:48 HalOFame-G2 **93** 3 73¾ 75¼ 86½ 52¾ 2no Dominguez R A L115 6.20 97– 08 *T. D. Vance*119no Silver Whistle1151¾ Crown Point119½ Traffic second turn 9
16Jly05–9Cnl yl 1¼ Ⓣ :494 1:142 1:381 2:022 VaDby-G3 **91** 6 76 76 66½ 55 44½ Dominguez R A L116 14.60 88– 13 **EnglishChannel**1203¼ ChtthoocheeWr120¾ *RebelRebel*116½ Swung wide 3/16 9
25Jun05–5Bel fm 1¼ T :49 1:122 1:36 2:001 3↑ Alw 46000N1x **87** 8 3½ 1hd 1hd 11 1¾ Bailey J D L119 3.35 95– 05 Silver Whistle119¾ Victory Circle122no *Angliana*112½ Pace, clear, driving 8
19May05–1Bel fm 1¼ T :493 1:152 1:39 2:023 3↑ Md Sp Wt 44k **81** 6 51¼ 73¾ 42½ 3nk 1hd Santos J A 118 3.50 83– 18 *Silver Whistle*118hd Bid118hd Tour de Force118¾ 4 wide run, prevailed 7
15Apr05–7GP fm 1 1/16 Ⓣ :23 :463 1:103 1:41 Md Sp Wt 32k **69** 10 77½ 610 78 87¼ 53½ Castro E 122 *1.50 - - Clevedale1221 Caesar's Bit1221¾ Double Tap Entry122½ Poor st, willingly 10
16Jan05–6GP gd 7f :223 :454 1:114 1:25 Md Sp Wt 32k **61** 4 6 97 810 45 410 Santos J A 122 13.60 - - MonrchLne1225¾ NorthrnGnt122½ SpnishMission1223¾ Passed tired rivals 12

WORKS: Jun5 Bel T 5f gd 1:041 B(d) *4/8* May28 Bel T 6f fm 1:132 B(d) *1/2* May21 Bel T 5f yl 1:031 B(d) *11/16* May14 Bel 5f fst 1:021 B *43/63* Apr29 Bel 4f fst :503 B *51/62* Mar27 Pay 4f fst :523 B *15/17*
TRAINER: 61-180Days(105 .22 $1.25) WonLastStart(173 .24 $1.54) Turf(580 .23 $1.95) Routes(699 .22 $1.84) GrdStk(125 .21 $1.62) J/T 2005-06 BEL(35 .20 $2.28) J/T 2005-06(191 .20 $2.03)

8 English Channel — Own: Scatuorchio James T — Pink — Peacock Blue, Beige Diamonds, Two Beige
VELAZQUEZ J R (3 2 0 0 .67) 2006: (365 106 .29)

Ch. c. 4 (Apr) KEESEP03 $50,000
Sire: Smart Strike (Mr. Prospector) $50,000
Dam: Belva (Theatrical*Ire)
Br: Keene Ridge Farm (Ky)
Tr: Pletcher Todd A(37 11 12 3 .30) 2006:(502 153 .30)

L 122

Life	11	7	2	0	$1,499,028	108	D.Fst	0	0	0	0	$0 -
2006	2	2	0	0	$327,937	108	Wet(408)	0	0	0	0	$0 -
2005	8	4	2	0	$1,143,491	106	Turf(373)	11	7	2	0	$1,499,028 108
Bel Ⓣ	2	0	1	0	$218,400	106	DstⓉ(362)	3	2	1	0	$830,000 104

6May06-9CD	fm	1⅛ Ⓣ	:481 1:12 1:352 1:47	3↑TurfClsc-G1	**108**	8	31½	33	3nk	21	1½	Gomez G K	L122	3.50	98-04	English Channel122½ **Cacique**122¾ Milk It Mick126no	4w,stiff drive	10
11Mar06-9GP	fm	1 1/16 Ⓣ	:234 :482 1:104 1:39	3↑CanadaTrfH100k	**105**	2	21½	21	2½	1hd	1¾	Velazquez J R	L119	*1.80	96-09	*English Channel*119¾ *Miesque's Approval*116½ *SilverTree*1171½	Fully extended	9
29Oct05-9Bel	gd	1½ Ⓣ	:474 1:131 2:05 2:291	3↑BCTurf-G1	**99**	10	48½	32½	2½	56½	58½	Velazquez J R	L121	11.40	80-15	*Shirocco*1261¾ Ace126nk Azamour126¾	Outside move, tired	13
1Oct05-8Bel	fm	1½ Ⓣ	:503 1:154 2:03 2:271	3↑TfClscIv-G1	**106**	2	32½	31	1hd	2hd	2hd	Velazquez J R	L121	5.10	99-04	Shakespeare126hd English Channel121¾ Ace1261	Gamely between rivals	7
13Aug05-11AP	yl	1¼ Ⓣ	:481 1:132 1:384 2:033	Secretar-G1	**104**	1	2hd	1hd	1½	2½	21¾	Velazquez J R	L126	*.90	78-20	*GunSlute*1231¾ EnglishChnnel1265 ChtthoochWr1214	Vied, inside, resisted	8
16Jly05-9Cnl	yl	1¼ Ⓣ	:494 1:142 1:381 2:022	VaDby-G3	**99**	3	21½	21½	22	1½	13¼	Velazquez J R	L120	*1.10	93-13	EnglishChnnel1203¼ ChtthoocheeWr120¾ *RebIRbl*116½	Bobbled 5/8,driving	9
25Jun05-10Cnl	fm	1⅜ Ⓣ	:51 1:142 1:392 1:561	CnlTurfCup500k	**92**	4	31	31	3½	11½	13¼	Velazquez J R	L118	*.40	110 -	*EnglishChnnl*1183¼ ExcptionlRid116¾ **Intrpttion**1181	3wd,roused 1/4,drw off	6
21May05-5Pim	gd	1 1/16 Ⓣ	:241 :493 1:143 1:452	Woodlawn100k	**90**	2	75	73¾	63¼	31	14	Velazquez J R	L118	*.50	75-25	*English Channel*1184 *United*1162½ Holy Ground1162¾	In traffic 5/16,drivng	8
13Apr05-9Kee	gd	1 1/16 Ⓣ	:234 :48 1:123 1:424	Alw 54000n1x	**93**	7	43½	2½	2hd	11½	15¾	Velazquez J R	L123	*2.80	93-12	*English Channel*1235¾ No Theatrics119¾ *Spring House*1175½	4w,steady drive	10
13Mar05-5GP	fm	1 Ⓣ	:232 1:112 1:334	Alw 33000n1x	**72**	5	93¾	93¾	73¼	76¾	44½	Velazquez J R	L118	*1.80	- -	*DrumMajor*1183¼ *ClassicCampaign*120nk Dynantoni1181	Swung out, greenly	10
6Aug04-4Sar	fm	1 1/16 Ⓣ	:241 :49 1:122 1:422	Md Sp Wt 46k	**73**	1	98	77¾	75¾	54¼	11	Velazquez J R	L118	3.10	83-17	English Channel1181 Zurich1181 *Apollo Jones*1181½	Off slowly, greenly	10

WORKS: Jun5 Bel 🅃 4f gd :524 B(d) *11/19* May28 Bel 🅃 4f fm :48 B(d) *4/12* May21 Bel 🅃 4f yl :492 B(d) *4/7* May2 CD 4f sly :514 B *9/15* Apr25 CD Ⓣ 5f fm 1:02 B(d) *8/16* Apr17 CD 4f gd :484 B *2/24*
TRAINER: 2Off45-180(205 .26 $1.88) 31-60Days(527 .31 $2.17) WonLastStart(354 .31 $2.09) Turf(492 .22 $1.87) Routes(972 .27 $2.06) GrdStk(275 .21 $1.95) J/T 2005-06 BEL(144 .26 $1.84) J/T 2005-06(622 .30 $1.98)

9 Dreadnaught — Own: Trillium Stable — Turqse — Dark Blue, Tan Cross Sashes, Tan Cuffs
GOMEZ G K (79 19 14 13 .24) 2006: (509 101 .20)

B. g. 6 (Feb)
Sire: Lac Ouimet (Pleasant Colony) $4,000
Dam: Wings of Dreams (Sovereign Dancer)
Br: David S Pennington (Ky)
Tr: Voss Thomas H(—) 2006:(55 4 .07)

Blinkers OFF **L 115**

Life	25	6	6	3	$485,744	103	D.Fst	1	0	0	0	$1,380 26
2006	2	0	1	0	$50,000	103	Wet(378)	0	0	0	0	$0 -
2005	8	1	1	3	$130,221	101	Turf(262)	21	6	4	3	$477,164 103
Bel Ⓣ	5	1	0	2	$55,167	100	DstⓉ(299)	3	0	1	0	$12,643 93

20May06-10Pim	fm	1⅛ Ⓣ	:481 1:12 1:37 1:482	3↑DixieG2-G	**103**	2	54	57	46	22	2hd	Solis A	L118 b	12.00	89-08	BttrTlkNow124hd Drdnught118nk ArtiSchillr1243¼	Btw 3-1/2,angld 4w,gme	7
28Apr06-9Kee	fm	1½ Ⓣ	:512 1:163 2:061 2:294	4↑Elkhorn-G3	**92**	7	75	106¼	84¾	94½	83½	Bejarano R	L118 b	5.30	86-09	Pellegrino118¾ Go Deputy118no *Silverfoot*1181	Offered no rally	11
17Dec05-11Crc	fm	1½ Ⓣ	:483 1:124 2:01 2:254	3↑WLMcKntH-G2	**101**	7	107¾	75¾	62	33½	41¾	Samyn J L	L116 b	11.90	93-09	Meteor Storm118nk *Revved Up*1171½ Scooter Roach114no	Late gain	12
19Nov05-9Lrl	fm	1⅛ Ⓣ	:464 1:101 1:344 1:472	3↑LrlTurfCup75k	**94**	9	914	813	79¾	31½	1hd	Bailey J D	L118 b	3.10	93-04	Dreadnaught118hd Major Rhythm1181 Patrol1181	Wide, driving	13
12Nov05-8Aqu	fm	1⅜ Ⓣ	:493 1:143 1:392 2:151	3↑RedSmthH-G2	**96**	1	43½	43	31	21	33½	Samyn J L	L117 b	7.70	103-02	KingsDrm1222½ RousngVctory1141 *Drdnught*1171¾	3 wide move, weakened	8
7Oct05-7Kee	fm	1½ Ⓣ	:504 1:163 2:074 2:341	3↑SycamrBC-G3	**94**	4	54	42½	41	4¾	23¾	Samyn J L	L122	6.80	64-31	Rochester1203¾ Dreadnaught122½ Vangelis1221¼	4w bid,no match	8
10Sep05-9Bel	fm	1⅜ Ⓣ	:471 1:11 1:354 2:113	3↑ManOWar-G1	**90**	9	815	711	84¼	810	610	Samyn J L	L126	15.00	95-06	BetterTlkNow126nk KingsDrm126½ ***RelxedGesture***1264¼	4 wide, no response	11
13Aug05-8Sar	gd	1½ 🅃	:483 1:14 2:032 2:271	3↑SwrdDncr-G1	**89**	8	33	3½	3½	65½	611	Samyn J L	L120	7.80	73-20	King's Drama116¾ **RelaxedGesture**1163¼ Vangelis118¾	Chased 3 wide, tired	8
16Jly05-8Bel	fm	1⅜ 🅃	:514 1:17 1:404 2:152	3↑BwlnGrnH-G2	**100**	1	41½	41½	63½	53½	32¾	Samyn J L	L117	6.10	80-17	CchtWells114hd **RelxedGesture**1172¾ Drdnught117hd	Steadied second turn	7
25Jun05-7Bel	fm	1⅜ 🅃	:494 1:14 1:37 2:13	4↑Hcp 60000	**95**	5	35½	36	36½	36½	32¾	Samyn J L	L121	2.15	92-05	Salic Law1172¼ Muqbil117½ Dreadnaught1214¼	Game finish outside	5
18Dec04-11Crc	fm	1½ Ⓣ	:491 1:134 2:03 2:263	3↑WLMcKntH-G2	**101**	4	75½	73¼	62¾	42¼	1nk	Samyn J L	L116	*3.10	91-10	Drednught116nk Demeteor112½ ScooterRoch115½	4w lane,responded well	12
20Nov04-8Aqu	gd	1⅜ Ⓣ	:514 1:174 1:431 2:184	3↑RedSmthH-G2	**101**	4	52½	51½	41½	1hd	1no	Samyn J L	L115	5.60	90-10	*Dreadnaught*115no Certifiably Crazy1123 Alost116nk	Rank gate, 4 wide run	10

WORKS: Jun5 AHT 4f fst :482 B *1/3* Apr26 AHT 3f fst :361 B *1/2* ●Apr15 Cnl Ⓣ TR1 1 1/4 fm 2:142 B *1/6* Apr10 AHT 5f fst 1:03 B *1/3* Mar18 AHT 4f fst :48 B *1/3*
TRAINER: BlinkOff(20 .25 $4.20) Turf(118 .08 $0.63) Routes(216 .14 $1.01) GrdStk(25 .08 $0.00)

On paper, not much separated the four contenders in the 105th Manhattan. In his U.S. debut, the regally bred Cacique had suffered through one of the widest trips in memory when fourth, beaten two heads and a nose, in the Kilroe Mile. Two months later, he had run his last three-eighths in under 35 seconds, but fell a half-length short of English Channel.

As their co-favoritism at 2–1 reflected, there wasn't much separating them.

Relaxed Gesture and Grey Swallow were also getting roughly the same amount of support, each hovering around the range of 7–2 to 4–1. Relaxed Gesture had narrowly missed in the Manhattan a year ago to a perfect-trip winner, and his U.S. form had been so consistent that his no-show in Dubai sans Lasix could easily be forgiven. What was not so easy to forgive was the fact that he had run in four Grade 1 or Grade 2 races in the U.S., and had lost all four by less than a length.

Grey Swallow's two Beyers in North America, 100 and 101, were not as high as the other three, but the Irish-bred horse had been classy enough to beat Arc de Triomphe winner Bago in a Group 1 stakes at equal weights the previous year. His first start of 2006, though a bit "light" on the Beyers, had been a clear-cut win in a Grade 2 stakes at 1½ miles, in which he had run the last quarter mile in 23 seconds. A multiple Grade 1 and Grade 2 winner that can kick home that strongly is never without a chance on turf, regardless of what sort of final-time figures are consulted.

The plan: Use all four, sit back, and enjoy the show.

The running of the race: In a change of tactics, Cacique broke running, secured his position on the hedge, and alternated for the lead with English Channel through measured early fractions. Relaxed Gesture and Grey Swallow brought up the rear, but rallied in tandem turning for home, and a four-horse cavalry charge ensued. Cacique somehow held on, and Relaxed Gesture came up just short yet again, after his rider lost the whip.

TENTH RACE
Belmont
JUNE 10, 2006

1¼ MILES. (Inner Turf) (1.57³) 105TH RUNNING OF THE MANHATTAN HANDICAP. Grade I. Purse $400,000 INNER TURF A HANDICAP FOR THREE YEAR OLDS AND UPWARD. By subscription of $400 each, which should accompany the nomination; $2,000 to pass the entry box; $2,000 to start. The purse to be divided 60% to the winner, 20% to second, 10% to third, 5% to fourth, 3% to fifth and 2% divided equally among remaining finishers. Trophies will be presented to the winning owner, trainer and jockey. The New York Racing Association reserves the right to transfer this race to the Main Track. In the event that this race istaken off the turf, it may be subject to downgrading upon review by the Graded Stakes Committee. Closed Saturday, May 27, 2006 with 28 Nominations.

Value of Race: $400,000 Winner $240,000; second $80,000; third $40,000; fourth $20,000; fifth $12,000; sixth $4,000; seventh $4,000. Mutuel Pool $2,028,828.00 Exacta Pool $1,294,072.00 Trifecta Pool $1,090,721.00

Last Raced	Horse	M/Eqt.	A.	Wt	PP	¼	½	¾	1	Str	Fin	Jockey	Odds $1
6May06 ⁹CD²	Cacique-Ire	L	5	120	3	1½	2¹½	1½	1ʰᵈ	1ʰᵈ	1ʰᵈ	Prado E S	2.20
25Mar06 ⁸NAS¹²	Relaxed Gesture-Ire	L	5	119	1	6ʰᵈ	7	7	5ʰᵈ	3½	2ⁿᵏ	Desormeaux K J	4.00
13May06 ⁶Hol¹	Grey Swallow-Ire	L	5	122	4	7	6ʰᵈ	6ʰᵈ	6³½	4½	3ʰᵈ	Solis A	3.80
6May06 ⁹CD¹	English Channel	L	4	122	6	2½	1ʰᵈ	2¹	2¹	2²½	4³¾	Velazquez J R	2.35
1Apr06 ¹⁰GP¹	Silver Whistle	L	4	116	5	4ʰᵈ	3ʰᵈ	4¹½	3¹½	5²	5⁶¼	Velasquez C	12.30
20May06 ¹⁰Pim⁴	Sabre d'Argent	L b	6	114	2	3ʰᵈ	5¹	3ʰᵈ	4¹½	66	6⁵¼	Coa E M	31.75
20May06 ¹⁰Pim²	Dreadnaught	L	6	115	7	5½	4ʰᵈ	5ʰᵈ	7	7	7	Gomez G K	14.80

OFF AT 5:55 Start Good. Won driving. Course yielding.
TIME :24³, :51¹, 1:16³, 1:40², 2:04 (:24.71, :51.30, 1:16.66, 1:40.45, 2:04.10)

$2 Mutuel Prices:

4 – CACIQUE–IRE	6.40	3.60	3.00
2 – RELAXED GESTURE–IRE		4.30	3.40
5 – GREY SWALLOW–IRE			4.00

$2 EXACTA 4–2 PAID $31.60 $2 TRIFECTA 4–2–5 PAID $103.00

Dk. b or br. h, (May), by Danehill – Hasili–Ire , by Kahyasi–Ire . Trainer Frankel Robert. Bred by Juddmonte Farms (Ire).

CACIQUE (IRE) came out running and positioned himself in front at the hedge, argued the pace from the inside, dug in resolutely when set down in upper stretch and got the nod after a long drive. RELAXED GESTURE (IRE) was rated along at the back of the field, saved ground on both turns, came wide into the stretch, dug in gamely while between rivals in the drive and just missed despite his rider having lost his whip above the sixteenth pole. GREY SWALLOW (IRE) was rated along early, raced between rivals. came wide into the stretch and finished gamely outside. ENGLISH CHANNEL argued the pace from the outside and stayed on stubbornly while between rivals in the drive. SILVER WHISTLE raced close up early while between rivals, put in a three wide run approaching the stretch and faded in the drive. SABRE D'ARGENT was rated along inside, saved ground throughout and had no response when roused. DREADNAUGHT was rated along outside, raced three wide on both turns and tired in the stretch.

Owners– 1, Juddmonte Farms Inc; 2, Moyglare Stud Farm Ltd; 3, Vega FZE Weld Mrs Marguerite; 4, Scatuorchio James T; 5, Stronach Stables; 6, Darley Stable; 7, Trillium Stable

Trainers– 1, Frankel Robert; 2, Clement Christophe; 3, Weld Dermot K; 4, Pletcher Todd A; 5, Mott William I; 6, Albertrani Thomas; 7. Voss Thomas H

Scratched– Good Reward (06May06 ⁹CD 7) , Interpatation (24May06 ⁶Bel3)

$2 Daily Double (3–4) Paid $45.40 ; Daily Double Pool $154,599 .

Race 11: the Belmont Stakes—fourth leg of the $1 million pick four

11

Belmont Park *1 ½ MILES* (2:24) **Belmont–G1** 138th Running of THE BELMONT.
Grade I. Purse $1,000,000 For Three Year Olds. By subscription of $600 each, to accompany the nomination, if made on or before January 21, 2006, or $6,000, if made on or before March 25, 2006. The purse to be divided 60% to the winner, 20% to second, 11% to third, 6% to fourth and 3% to fifth. Colts and Geldings, 126 lbs.; Fillies, 121 lbs. Starters to be named at the closing time of entries.

1½ MILES
START ▲ FINISH

---

1 Platinum Couple
Gr/ro. c. 3 (Apr)
Own: Team Tristar Stable
Red Black, Red Yoke, Red Stars On Sleeves
Sire: Tale of the Cat (Storm Cat) $50,000
Dam: Ingot's Dance Away (Gate Dancer)
Br: Tri Star Stables LLC (NY)
Tr: Lostritto Joseph A (15 1 1 0 .07) 2006:(64 4 .06)
ESPINOZA J L (64 14 3 .02) 2006: (265 16 .06)
Blinkers ON
L 126
Life 10 2 1 2 $125,457 82
2006 5 0 1 1 $42,734 82
2005 5 2 0 1 $82,723 73
Bel 3 0 0 1 $5,373 73
D.Fst 7 2 1 1 $98,634 78
Wet(392) 3 0 0 1 $26,823 82
Turf(266) 0 0 0 0 $0 –
Dst(254) 0 0 0 0 $0 –

Entered 9Jun06-10 BEL

WORKS: Jun6 Bel 3f fst :37⁴ B 12/22 May31 Bel 4f fst :51³ B 28/32 May15 Bel 4f fst :51¹ B 25/47 Apr29 Bel tr.t 5f fst 1:01¹ B 3/8 Apr3 Bel tr.t 4f fst :48² B 5/42 ▪
TRAINER: 1stBlink(6 .17 $4.00) BlinkOn(8 .12 $3.00) Dirt(150 .05 $1.37) Routes(98 .10 $1.59) GrdStk(2 .00 $0.00)
J/T 2005-06 BEL (9 .00 $0.00) J/T 2005-06(32 .09 $1.92)

---

2 Sunriver
Dk. b or br c. 3 (Mar)
Own: Aaron U and Marie D Jones
White White, Red Cross Sashes, Red Diamond
Sire: Saint Ballado (Halo) $125,000
Dam: Goulash (Mari's Book)
Br: Aaron U Jones & Marie D Jones (Ky)
Tr: Pletcher Todd A (37 11 12 3 .30) 2006:(502 153 .30)
BEJARANO R (11 2 3 2 .18) 2006: (731 140 .19)
L 126
Life 7 3 2 1 $281,400 102
2006 5 2 1 1 $246,400 102
2005 2 1 1 0 $35,000 82
Bel 2 1 1 0 $128,600 102
D.Fst 6 3 2 1 $281,400 102
Wet(373) 1 0 0 0 $0 80
Turf(316) 0 0 0 0 $0 –
Dst(257) 0 0 0 0 $0 –

WORKS: Jun5 Bel tr.t 5f pd 1:00¹ B 2/17 May14 Bel 5f fst 1:00 B 5/63 May7 CD 5f fst 1:12¹ B 2/4 Apr29 CD 6f fst 1:13³ B 5/11 ▪Apr23 CD 6f fst 1:14¹ B 1/4 Apr15 CD 5f fst 1:00¹ B 2/24
TRAINER: 2Off45-180(205 .26 $1.88) WonLastStart(354 .31 $2.08) Dirt(1049 .29 $1.96) Routes(972 .27 $2.06) GrdStk(275 .21 $1.95)
J/T 2005-06 BEL (8 .25 $1.19) J/T 2005-06(63 .38 $2.26)

---

3 Hemingway's Key
Ch. c. 3 (Jan) OBSFEB05 $210,000
Own: Kinsman Stable
Blue Blue, Green Sash, Brown Hoop On
Sire: Notebook (Well Decorated) $15,000
Dam: Whirl's Girl (Island Whirl)
Br: Ocala Stud Farm (Fla)
Tr: Zito Nicholas P(15 3 4 3 .20) 2006:(196 32 .16)
ROSE J (3 1 0 0 .33) 2006: (449 70 .16)
L 126
Life 7 2 0 1 $159,498 95
2006 5 0 0 1 $120,000 95
2005 2 2 0 0 $39,498 80
Bel 0 0 0 0 $0 –
D.Fst 6 2 0 1 $159,498 95
Wet(391) 1 0 0 0 $0 67
Turf(280) 0 0 0 0 $0 –
Dst(280) 0 0 0 0 $0 –

WORKS: Jun1 Sar tr.t 5f fst 1:01¹ B 3/9 May14 Sar tr.t 5f fst 1:00¹ B 2/8 Apr18 Kee 4f fst :50 B 14/33 ▪Apr13 Kee 5f fst 1:00² B 1/7 Apr6 Kee 5f fst 1:00³ B 3/15 Mar16 GP 5f fst :58⁴ H 2/18
TRAINER: Dirt(607 .19 $1.61) Routes(400 .19 $1.57) GrdStk(141 .11 $0.69)
J/T 2005-06 BEL (1 1.00 $4.50) J/T 2005-06(151 .18 $1.28)

---

4 Bob and John
Dk. b or br c. 3 (May)
Own: Stonerside Stable
Yellow White, Dark Green Triangular Panel
Sire: Seeking the Gold (Mr. Prospector) $125,000
Dam: Minister's Melody (Deputy Minister)
Br: Stonerside Stable (Ky)
Tr: Baffert Bob(—) 2006:(188 50 .27)
GOMEZ G K (79 19 14 13 .24) 2006: (509 101 .20)
L 126
Life 10 4 1 3 $680,070 102
2006 5 3 0 1 $572,700 102
2005 5 1 1 2 $107,370 93
Bel 0 0 0 0 $0 –
D.Fst 9 3 1 3 $230,070 102
Wet(408) 1 1 0 0 $450,000 99
Turf(277) 0 0 0 0 $0 –
Dst(250) 0 0 0 0 $0 –

Disqualified and placed third

WORKS: ▪Jun5 SA 6f fst 1:12¹ H 1/12 ▪May26 SA 7f fst 1:25³ H 1/5 ▪May20 SA 6f fst 1:10⁴ H 1/14 ▪Apr30 SA 6f fst 1:11² H 1/3 ▪Apr24 SA 7f fst 1:25 H 3/6
TRAINER: 31-60Days(152 .22 $1.84) Dirt(580 .23 $1.57) Routes(276 .21 $1.74) GrdStk(93 .23 $1.87)
J/T 2005-06(39 .38 $2.92)

---

5 High Finance
Own: West Point Stable
Green — Gold, Black Star, Black Sleeves, Gold
Ch. c. 3 (Mar) FTKJUL04 $120,000
Sire: Talk Is Money (Deputy Minister) $10,000
Dam: Margay (Conquistador Cielo)
Br: Dan Borislow (Ky)
Tr: Violette Richard A Jr(25 4 5 3 .16) 2006:(145 25 .17)

L 126

COA E M (165 29 23 23 .18) 2006: (688 145 .21)

Life 5 2 2 1 $75,145 103
2006 5 2 2 1 $75,145 103
2005 0 M 0 0 $0
Bel 1 1 0 0 $27,500 103

4May06–5Bel fst 1	103
15Apr06–2Kee fst 7f	91
4Mar06–1GP fst 1	75
11Feb06–11GP fst 6½f	82
14Jan06–3GP fst 7f	71

WORKS: Jun6 Aqu 6f fst 1:13³ B 1/3 May28 Bel 1 fst 1:38² B 1/1 May21 Aqu 4f fst :48³ B 9/24 Apr25 Kee 4f fst :50 B 18/27 Apr10 Kee 5f fst 1:00 H 1/11 Mar29 PmM 4f fst :49 B 3/19
TRAINER: 31-60Days(159 .20 $1.93) WonLastStart(82 .13 $1.29) Dirt(355 .20 $2.01) Routes(287 .15 $1.97) GrdStk(24 .00 $0.00)

6 Oh So Awesome
Own: Team Valor Stables
Black — Forest Green, Crimson Triangular Panel
B. c. 3 (Jan) KEESEP04 $90,000
Sire: Awesome Again (Deputy Minister) $125,000
Dam: Identify*Ire (Persian Bold*Ire)
Br: Highland Farms (Ky)
Tr: Jerkens James A(31 8 1 3 .26) 2006:(120 28 .23)

126

SMITH M E (89 10 18 6 .11) 2006: (324 24 .07)

Life 7 1 2 2 $33,262 91
2006 4 1 1 1 $26,794 91
2005 3 M 1 1 $6,468
Bel 1 0 0 1 $7,205 91

WORKS: Jun7 Bel tr.t 4f gd :48³ B 7/38 Jun1 Bel 7f fst 1:27⁴ B 1/3 May26 Bel tr.t 4f fst :50² B 10/13 May17 Bel tr.t 4f fst :48⁴ B 3/7 May10 Bel tr.t 4f fst :49⁴ B 13/21
TRAINER: 1stLasix(20 .25 $2.17) Dirt(269 .25 $2.00) Routes(191 .26 $2.42) GrdStk(37 .24 $1.46)

7 Deputy Glitters
Own: LaCombe Stables
Orange — Dark Blue, Tan Diamond, Tan Chevrons On
B. c. 3 (Apr)
Sire: Deputy Commander (Deputy Minister) $10,000
Dam: Glitters (Glitterman)
Br: Joseph LaCombe Stables Inc (Ky)
Tr: Albertrani Thomas(9 1 2 1 .11) 2006:(81 18 .22)

L 126

PRADO E S (123 26 22 27 .21) 2006: (582 105 .18)

Life 8 2 1 0 $205,548 102
2006 5 1 1 0 $174,080 102
2005 3 1 0 0 $31,468 92
Bel 1 0 0 0 $10,000 43

WORKS: Jun6 Bel 5f fst :59⁴ B 6/47 May25 Bel 5f fst 1:01⁴ B 14/25 May23 Bel 5f fst 1:01 B 4/14 May6 CD 5f fst 1:03¹ B 14/25 Apr26 Bel 5f fst 1:01² B 11/25 Apr1 Pay 5f fst 1:03³ B 2/9
TRAINER: 31-60Days(76 .24 $2.96) Dirt(161 .22 $2.04) Routes(145 .21 $2.98) GrdStk(203 .25 $5.70)

8 Jazil
Own: Shadwell Stable
Pink — Royal Blue, White Epaulets, Blue Cap
B. c. 3 (Feb) KEESEP04 $725,000
Sire: Seeking the Gold (Mr. Prospector) $125,000
Dam: Better Than Honour (Deputy Minister)
Br: Skara Glen Stables (Ky)
Tr: McLaughlin Kiaran P(23 4 8 3 .17) 2006:(185 35 .19)

L 126

JARA F (66 5 4 2 .08) 2006: (280 25 .09)

Life 7 1 3 0 $272,217 97
2006 4 0 2 0 $236,930 97
2005 3 1 1 0 $35,287 78
Bel 1 0 0 0 $287 53

WORKS: May27 Bel 5f fst :59³ H 4/17 May21 Bel 4f fst :49 B 22/31 Apr29 CD 5f fst 1:00² B 8/49 Apr21 Bel 4f fst :50³ B 27/37 Mar31 Bel tr.t 5f fst 1:00 H 9/44 Mar24 Bel tr.t 4f fst :48² B 28/55
TRAINER: 31-60Days(207 .17 $2.02) Dirt(446 .17 $2.32) Routes(356 .15 $1.66) GrdStk(59 .07 $2.07)

9 Bluegrass Cat
Own: WinStar Farm
Turqse — White, Green And Black Emblem, Green
B. c. 3 (Jan)
Sire: Storm Cat (Storm Bird) $500,000
Dam: She's a Winner (A.P. Indy)
Br: WinStar Farm LLC (Ky)
Tr: Pletcher Todd A(32 11 12 3 .30) 2006:(502 153 .30)

L 126

VELAZQUEZ J R (3 2 0 0 .67) 2006: (365 106 .29)

Life 8 4 2 0 $761,280 101
2006 4 3 0 0 $213,780 96
2005 4 1 2 0 $547,500 101
Bel 2 2 0 0 $93,780 96

WORKS: Jun3 Bel 5f fst :59³ B 1/13 ●May21 Bel 5f fst 1:00 H 1/19 ●May14 Bel 4f fst :47 B 1/54 Apr29 CD 5f fst :59⁴ B 2/25 ●Apr9 CD 5f fst 1:01² B 1/26 ●Apr2 PmM 5f fst :59 H 1/12
TRAINER: 31-60Days(527 .31 $2.17) Dirt(1049 .29 $1.94) Routes(972 .27 $2.06) GrdStk(275 .21 $1.95)

10 Double Galore
Own: Myung Kwon Cho
Purple — Colors Unavailable
B. c. 3 (Apr)
Sire: Grand Slam (Gone West) $50,000
Dam: Squall Linda (Summer Squall)
Br: Cho Myung Kwon (Ky)
Tr: Cho Myung Kwon(—) 2006:(5 2 .33)

L 126

LUZZI M J (118 18 17 13 .15) 2006: (559 97 .17)

Blinkers ON

Life 5 1 0 1 $38,720 90
2006 3 M 0 1 $38,320 90
2005 1 M 0 0 $400 45
Bel 0 0 0 0 $0

WORKS: Jun6 Hol 4f fst :48² H 1/21 May13 Hol 5f fst 1:00 H 8/45 Apr26 Hol 4f fst :48² H 9/25 Apr19 Hol 3f fst :35³ H 1/15 Apr6 Hol 3f fst :36 H 6/9 Mar20 Hol 5f fst 1:01 H 4/39
TRAINER: BlinkOn(1 1.00 $5.20) Dirt(15 .20 $6.39) Routes(5 .20 $2.16)

[171]

11 Steppenwolfer — Own: Robert E and Lawana L Low — Gray — Purple, Forest Green Ball, Purple
ALBARADO R J (—) 2006: (459 79 .17)

Gr/ro. c. 3 (Mar) OBSAPR05 $375,000
Sire: Aptitude (A.P. Indy) $20,000
Dam: Wolfer (Wolf Power*SAf)
Br: Nursery Place & Partners (Ky)
Tr: Peitz Daniel C(7 1 2 0 .14) 2006:(29 6 .21)

L 126

Life	9	3	2	3	$561,520	98	D.Fst	7	2	2	3	$539,830	98
2006	6	2	2	2	$529,920	98	Wet(381)	1	1	0	0	$20,400	93
2005	3	1	0	1	$31,600	84	Turf(294)	1	0	0	0	$1,290	68
Bel	0	0	0	0	$0	-	Dst(306*)	0	0	0	0	$0	-

6May06-10CD	fst	1¼	:46 1:104 1:37 2:011	KyDerby-G1	**98**	2	131011 6¼	65¼	56	38½	Albarado R J	L126	16.30	90- 04	Barbaro1266½ **BluegrassCt**1262 Steppenwolfer1261	Bmp start,forced in,6w	20		
15Apr06-9OP	fst	1⅛	:462 1:104 1:373 1:511	ArkDerby-G2	**94**	2	116¾	1110	86¼	34½	22¾	Albarado R J	L118	7.20	79- 22	LwyerRon1222¾ Steppenwolfr1181½ PrivtVow1227¼	Trafic 3/8,steady gain	13	
18Mar06-10OP	fst	1 1/16	:233 :473 1:124 1:44	Rebel-G3	**88**	10	89	97¼	51¾	22½	33¼	Albarado R J	L118	2.70	83- 18	*LwyerRon*1223 RedRymond117nk Steppenwolfer118nk	5-w, outfinished 2nd	10	
25Feb06-10OP	fst	1	:231 :48 1:133 1:40	Southwest250k	**94**	7	911	96½	54	21	2¾	Lanerie C J	L117	6.00	83- 25	*LwyerRon*122¾ Steppenwolfr1173¼ RdRymond1172½	Advanced,not enough	10	
3Feb06-2OP	gd	1	:233 :482 1:141 1:402	Alw 34000N2x	**93**	2	66	63	51¾	12	14½	Albarado R J	L121	*1.50	82- 28	Steppenwolfer1214½ RocktButy116no KingsChllng1215¼	Moved out, clear	6	
7Jan06-7LaD	fst	1 1/16	:24 :49 1:142 1:47	OC 50k/N1x-N	**78**	3	87½	84¼	73¾	33	1hd	Albarado R J	L119	*1.70	81- 14	*Steppenwolfer*119hd AnchorSteam1221 *KipDeville*1171¼	Traffic 5/16, in time	10	
17Dec05-8LaD	fst	1 1/16	:24 :483 1:134 1:452	OC 50k/N1x-N	**84**	7	76¼	77	76¾	63¾	35	Pettinger D R	L122	4.30	84- 20	MrkofSuccess1174¾ TommysTurn119nk *Stppnwolfr*1221	Mild rally outside	8	
12Nov05-4Aqu	fst	7f	:221 :452 1:104 1:242	Md Sp Wt 43k	**77**	11	1	55	41	1hd	1no	Santos J A	L120	6.90	79- 19	Steppenwolfer120no ***Jazil***1201 Don'tParkNow1201½	3 wide move, prevailed	11	
28Sep05-4Bel	gd	6f Ⓣ	:221 :451 :57 1:093	Md Sp Wt 43k	**68**	7	4	54	79¼	58½	55½	Santos J A	L118	22.70	91- 04	Pimm's O'Clock1182 Wrigley1183¼ *Racketeer*118hd	Going well late	10	

WORKS: Jun2 Bel tr.t 6f gd 1:101 B *1/1* ●May27 Bel 6f fst 1:13 B *1/8* May21 Bel tr.t 5f fst 1:001 B *5/21* Apr29 CD 6f fst 1:13 B *4/11* Apr8 OP 5f fst 1:003 H *2/24* Apr1 OP 5f fst 1:02 B *5/25*
TRAINER: 31-60Days(29 .17 $1.92) Dirt(56 .16 $2.21) Routes(76 .12 $1.15) GrdStk(4 .00 $0.00) J/T 2005-06(9 .33 $1.82)

12 Sacred Light — Own: Amerman Stables — Lime — Dark Blue, White Epaulets, White Hoops
ESPINOZA V (—) 2006: (512 106 .21)

Gr/ro. c. 3 (Apr)
Sire: Holy Bull (Great Above) $15,000
Dam: Summer Glimmer (Summer Squall)
Br: Amerman Racing LLC (Ky)
Tr: Hofmans David(—) 2006:(49 8 .16)

L 126

Life	7	1	2	2	$148,340	99	D.Fst	7	1	2	2	$148,340	99
2006	5	0	2	2	$114,340	99	Wet(363)	0	0	0	0	$0	-
2005	2	1	0	0	$34,000	78	Turf(252)	0	0	0	0	$0	-
Bel	0	0	0	0	$0	-	Dst(254)	0	0	0	0	$0	-

6May06-3CD	fst	1 1/16	:234 :471 1:114 1:432	3↑ Alw 54000N1x	**91**	5	65	66½	85¼	62¼	21¼	Bejarano R	L113 b	*1.70	92- 04	Nolan's Cat1201¼ Sacred Light113nk Casino Evil113nk	Inside trip,all out	10
8Apr06-6SA	fst	1⅛	:472 1:111 1:351 1:48	SADerby-G1	**76**	4	43½	44½	46	414	419	Gryder A T	LB122 b	8.70	77- 10	BrothrDrk1223½ PointDtrmind1221½ APWrror12214¼	Stumbled badly start	5
4Mar06-5SA	fst	1 1/16	:231 :461 1:101 1:414	StCtlina-G2	**99**	8	64¼	64¾	54¼	43½	21¾	Gryder A T	LB115 b	19.10	89- 06	*BrotherDerek*1221¾ ScredLight1152¾ LtentHet1183¾	Came out str,2nd best	8
4Feb06-3SA	fst	1⅛	:484 1:12 1:362 1:49	Sham-G3	**92**	4	42½	31½	33	34½	36	Gomez G K	LB118 b	3.20	85- 09	**Bob and John**1204½ Hawkinsville1181½ Sacred Light1186¾	Off rail,best rest	5
20Jan06-6SA	fst	1 1/16	:234 :482 1:13 1:444	Alw 52800N1x	**87**	2	76½	78¼	79¼	57½	33	Gomez G K	LB118 b	7.70	73- 26	***Bob and John***1183 The Five J's118no Sacred Light1183¾	3wd into lane,rallied	7
25Aug05-2Dmr	fst	1	:222 :461 1:113 1:373	Md Sp Wt 57k	**78**	3	31½	41¾	31	2½	2hd	Gomez G K	LB119 b	22.40	86- 14	DPrechinmndn119hd ScredLight1195 LongRidr1194½	Tight,stdied 3/16,rail	9
Placed first through disqualification																		
17Jly05-7Hol	fst	5½f	:213 :451 :573 1:034	Md Sp Wt 46k	**42**	5	7	913	919	917	914¼	Baze T C	LB120	21.20	75- 13	A. P. Warrior1204 Jitterbug Ball1203 Gold Maker1203	Off rail, no factor	9

WORKS: Jun6 Bel 6f fst 1:162 H *6/6* May28 Hol 7f fst 1:28 H *1/1* May21 Hol 6f fst 1:184 H *26/26* May3 CD 4f fst :50 B *29/60* Apr26 Hol 7f fst 1:28 H *1/1* Apr20 Hol 5f fst 1:013 H *7/21*
TRAINER: 31-60Days(35 .11 $2.19) Dirt(97 .18 $2.13) Routes(65 .09 $1.33) GrdStk(15 .20 $2.09) J/T 2005-06(17 .24 $2.91)

Without the Kentucky Derby or Preakness winner, the Belmont's 138th edition attracted a full field of 12, and confusion reigned. Three horses—Bob and John, Steppenwolfer, and Bluegrass Cat—were the "favorites" at 9–2. Not far behind in the wagering at 6–1 were Sunriver, the Peter Pan winner; and Jazil, who was still eligible for first-level allowance conditions.

About the only thing I was reasonably confident about was tossing the top-figure horse, High Finance, who had run the field's best Beyer of 103 five weeks earlier. Figures earned while in control of the pace at a mile against first-level allowance horses are unlikely to be reproduced at 1½ miles against far more seasoned competition.

The plan: Key around Bob and John and the two Pletcher horses, Bluegrass Cat and Sunriver. Use Steppenwolfer and Jazil on backup tickets.

The running of the race: Bob and John proved his up-the-track finish in the Kentucky Derby was no fluke, setting the pace and giving way readily on the far turn. Bluegrass Cat moved willingly to reach even terms for the lead approaching the stretch, but was immediately set upon by Jazil, who inched away in the final furlong.

Those who were smart enough to mix-and-match the contenders correctly in the four stakes received a $2 pick four payoff of $1,869, nearly twice as much as the win parlay.

In retrospect, I probably should've given more respect to Jazil's paired Beyers of 97, figures not normally associated with a Belmont Stakes winner, but which represented a forward-moving figure pattern in a softer-than-usual Belmont.

Such things happen. You can't win them all.

ELEVENTH RACE
Belmont
JUNE 10, 2006

1½ MILES. (2.24) 138TH RUNNING OF THE BELMONT. Grade I. Purse $1,000,000 FOR THREE YEAR OLDS. By subscription of $600 each, to accompany the nomination, if made on or before January 21, 2006, or $6,000, if made on or before March 25, 2006. The purse to be divided 60% to the winner, 20% to second, 11% to third, 6% to fourth and 3% to fifth. Colts and Geldings, 126 lbs.; Fillies, 121 lbs. Starters to be named at the closing time of entries. The winning owner will be presented with the August Belmont Memorial Cup to be retained for one year as well as a trophy for permanent possession and trophies to the winning trainer and jockey.

Value of Race: $1,000,000 Winner $600,000; second $200,000; third $110,000; fourth $60,000; fifth $30,000. Mutuel Pool $14,697,715.00 Exacta Pool $9,214,787.00 Trifecta Pool $12,198,978.00 Superfecta Pool $4,543,658.00

Last Raced	Horse	M/Eqt.	A.	Wt	PP	¼	½	1	1¼	Str	Fin	Jockey	Odds $1
6May06 10CD4	Jazil	L	3	126	8	12	12	7½	1hd	1½	11¼	Jara F	6.20
6May06 10CD2	Bluegrass Cat	L	3	126	9	5½	51½	3½	21½	21½	22¼	Velazquez J R	4.90
20May06 8Bel1	Sunriver	L	3	126	2	61½	6½	6hd	3½	3½	31¼	Bejarano R	6.00
6May06 10CD3	Steppenwolfer	L	3	126	11	8½	7½	11½	4hd	46	45	Albarado R J	4.80
19May06 7Bel3	Oh So Awesome	L b	3	126	6	11½	11½	12	7½	5hd	52	Smith M E	12.00
20May06 12Pim3	Hemingway's Key	L	3	126	3	104½	101	10½	85	71½	64½	Rose J	15.10
20May06 12Pim6	Platinum Couple	L bf	3	126	1	7hd	94½	5½	61	86	72½	Espinoza J L	38.00
6May06 10CD17	Bob and John	L b	3	126	4	1½	1½	1hd	51	6hd	84¼	Gomez G K	4.70
6May06 3CD2	Sacred Light	L b	3	126	12	92½	8hd	8½	9½	93½	96½	Espinoza V	26.50
4May06 5Bel1	High Finance	L	3	126	5	2hd	3½	2½	104	106	1011¼	Coa E M	10.40
6May06 10CD8	Deputy Glitters	L	3	126	7	31	2½	4½	118	11	11	Prado E S	12.20
19May06 1Hol1	Double Galore	L b	3	126	10	4hd	4½	9hd	12	—	—	Luzzi M J	45.75

OFF AT 6:35 Start Good. Won driving. Track fast.

TIME :23, :47^{1}, 1:12, 1:37^{2}, 2:02^{3}, 2:27^{4} (:23.02, :47.36, 1:12.14, 1:37.53, 2:02.69, 2:27.86)

$2 Mutuel Prices:				
	8 – JAZIL	14.40	6.70	4.70
	9 – BLUEGRASS CAT		6.40	4.70
	2 – SUNRIVER			6.10

$2 EXACTA 8–9 PAID $92.00 $2 TRIFECTA 8–9–2 PAID $436.00
$2 SUPERFECTA 8–9–2–11 PAID $1,085.00

B. c, (Feb), by Seeking the Gold – Better Than Honour, by Deputy Minister. Trainer McLaughlin Kiaran P. Bred by Skara Glen Stables (Ky).

JAZIL hit the side of the gate at the start, the rider quickly regained his iron and angled to the inside, saved ground on the first turn, began to move out midway down the backstretch, split horses to launch his rally on the far turn, swung six wide to challenge on the turn, surged to the front leaving the five-sixteenths pole, battled outside BLUEGRASS CAT entering the stretch, opened a clear advantage leaving the furlong marker then edged away under strong left hand urging. BLUEGRASS CAT was strung out five wide while contesting the pace on the first turn, stalked the leaders while continuing very wide along the backstretch, launched his bid on the far turn, drew on even terms with the leaders while six wide on the turn, fought gamely inside the winner into upper stretch, dug in gamely in midstretch then continued on well to clearly best the others. SUNRIVER was taken in hand early, was caught wide along the backstretch, moved between horses on the far turn, swung seven wide while gaining a bit nearing the quarter pole, raced just outside the winner into upper stretch and finished willingly to gain a share. STEPPENWOLFER raced well back for six furlongs, checked in traffic on the far turn, raced behind a wall of horses approaching the quarter pole, followed the winner while gaining at the top of the stretch and rallied mildly through the final eighth. OH SO AWESOME lunged in the air after hesitating at the start, was outrun for a mile, angled out leaving the backstretch, swung wide at the three-sixteenths pole, gained a bit to reach contention entering the stretch then flattened out late. HEMINGWAY'S KEY was unhurried, saved ground while racing far back for most of the trip then passed only tiring horses. PLATINUM COUPLE was rated along the inside, lodged a mild bid slightly off the rail on the far turn then lacked a further response. BOB AND JOHN rushed up to gain the early advantage, set the pace while well off the rail for six furlongs, relinquished the lead midway on the turn and steadily tired thereafter. SACRED LIGHT caught wide on the first turn, continued seven wide throughout and failed to mount a serious rally when asked for run on the turn. HIGH FINANCE moved up inside, slipped through along the rail to contest the pace along the backstretch, pressed the issue inside BOB AND JOHN for a mile then gave way on the turn. DEPUTY GLITTERS moved up quickly from outside in the early stages, pressed the pace six wide to the far turn then gave way abruptly on the turn. DOUBLE GALORE raced up close between horses while five wide along the backstretch, raced in good position in hand to the far turn and steadily tired thereafter then was eased through the final furlong.

Owners– 1, Shadwell Stable; 2, WinStar Farm LLC; 3, Jones Aaron U and Marie D; 4, Low Lawana L and Robert E; 5, Team Valor Stables LLC; 6, Kinsman Stable; 7, Team Tristar Stable; 8, Stonerside Stable; 9, Amerman Racing Stables LLC; 10, West Point Stable; 11, Joseph Lacombe Stable Inc; 12, Cho Myung K

Trainers– 1, McLaughlin Kiaran P; 2, Pletcher Todd A; 3, Pletcher Todd A; 4, Peitz Daniel C; 5, Jerkens James A; 6, Zito Nicholas P; 7, Lostritto Joseph A; 8, Baffert Bob; 9, Hofmans David; 10, Violette Richard A Jr; 11, Albertrani Thomas; 12, Cho Myung Kwon

---

$2 Daily Double (4–8) Paid $67.50 ; Daily Double Pool $543,766 .
$2 Pick Three (3–4–8) Paid $390.50 ; Pick Three Pool $511,790 .
$2 Pick Four (9–3–4–8) Paid $1,869.00 ; Pick Four Pool $1,983,864 .
$2 Pick Six (7–2–9–3–4–8) 6 Correct Paid $17,541.00 ; Pick Six Pool $1,411,084 .
$2 Pick Six (7–2–9–3–4–8) 5 Correct Paid $200.00 .